Tourism and Hospitality Marketing in Ireland

TOURISM AND HOSPITALITY MARKETING IN IRELAND

Alex Gibson and Monica Nielsen

GILL & MACMILLAN

Gill & Macmillan Ltd
Hume Avenue
Park West
Dublin 12
with associated companies throughout the world
www.gillmacmillan.ie

© Alex Gibson and Monica Nielsen 2000
0 7171 2971 3
Index compiled by John Loftus
Print origination by Carole Lynch

The paper used in this book is made from the wood pulp of managed forests.
For every tree felled, at least one tree is planted, thereby renewing natural resources.

A catalogue record is available for this book from the British Library.

To Mary and Luke (AG)

To Richard, Robert and Emily (MN)

Contents

Preface

Our respective experiences as lecturers prompted the writing of this book. In preparing lectures for our students there were no books which applied marketing theory to the Irish tourism and hospitality market. There was a shortage of Irish case study material that would enable students to bridge the gap between theory and practice. Our hope is that our experience as lecturers, coupled with our industry experience and contacts, has given us the insights necessary to write a book that is both educational and interesting.

Tourism and Hospitality in Ireland is at a crossroads today. A decade of unparalleled growth is being followed by a pause for reflection. Can the country continue to manage the growing numbers of tourists? How can we sustain the welcome visitors currently receive, and preserve the landscape they cherish so much? How can Ireland stand out from the increasingly professional marketing campaigns of competing destinations? At the centre of the debate concerning the above questions, marketing professionals will have an influential voice. The role of marketing is now acknowledged in the tourism and hospitality sectors as being of critical importance for survival and growth. Educational institutions are responding by enhancing the marketing content and curricula on existing courses, and by developing innovative programmes in tourism marketing. We hope that this book will be viewed as an important resource for these courses.

Finally, tourism marketing is constantly evolving. To try to reflect the dynamic nature of the tourism marketing environment, and to provide a resource for student, educator and practitioner, we are establishing a web site to act as a complement to the text. We hope that the site will contain more background to featured case studies, and provide links to relevant research sources. The site will also provide the reader with a simple means of offering comments and suggestions, which will be greatly appreciated. The site's address is www.dit.ie/tour/tourismmarketingbook.

Alex Gibson
Monica Nielsen

July 2000

Acknowledgments

This book would not have been possible without a huge amount of assistance from academic colleagues, and the Irish tourism and hospitality industry. Whilst these are too numerous to credit individually, we would like to thank those lecturers from a variety of third level institutions who have contributed exhibits to the text. We would particularly like to thank those in the tourism and hospitality sector for giving so freely of their time in helping us to ensure that the material contained as much 'real-life' material as possible. We also acknowledge the help of various publishers and organisations who permitted us to reprint extracts of their publications. A special thanks to Nessa Skehan of Bord Fáilte for furnishing us with up-to-date statistics. To Ailbhe O'Reilly of Gill & Macmillan, a special word of thanks for her constant support during the writing of this book.

We acknowledge the assistance that our respective employers have given in the writing of this book; Dublin Institute of Technology and Galway Mayo Institute of Technology. A particular word of thanks to the Internal Research Fund and the Research and Consultancy Unit of GMIT for their financial contribution.

Last, but certainly not least, we would like to thank our families for their patience and encouragement during the writing of this book.

CHAPTER 1

Introduction to Marketing in the Tourism and Hospitality Industry in Ireland

CHAPTER OBJECTIVES

After studying this chapter, you should be able to:

- Understand the basic philosophy of marketing as applied to the tourism and hospitality industry
- Differentiate between the product, production, sales, marketing and societal concepts
- Appreciate the need for marketing in the Irish tourism and hospitality industries and the importance of customer satisfaction
- Understand the nature of tourism and hospitality as a product, and be aware of issues affecting its marketing

THE TOURISM AND HOSPITALITY INDUSTRY IN IRELAND

The tourism and hospitality industry in Ireland has grown from strength to strength in recent years. The performance of Irish tourism is well ahead of European and world averages. In 1999, expenditure by tourists to Ireland (including receipts paid to Irish carriers by foreign residents) was estimated to be worth over £2.4 billion (Bord Fáilte, 2000). Overseas tourist visits to Ireland grew by seven per cent to 6 million (these are the estimated figures at time of print) — the eighth successive year of growth. In the last decade tourist visits have grown by 128 per cent. The World Tourism Organisation's estimates for Europe show an increase of three per cent in arrivals and 3·6 per cent in receipts, compared with estimates for world tourism which show an increase of 2·4 per cent in arrivals and two per cent in receipts. The growth in overseas tourism is phenomenal and this is added to £879 million domestic tourism.

The hospitality industry is a valuable contributor to the creation of this wealth. There are over 820 hotels in Ireland with almost 36,000 bedrooms and 440 guesthouses with 4,700 rooms (IHF, 1999). Other forms of accommodation include 4,267 farmhouses and town and country homes; 4,435 self-catering units; 13 university accommodation providers; 133 caravan and camping sites and 224 hostels (Bord

Fáilte, 1999). Bedroom capacity has increased by sixteen per cent over 1997 (*see* Exhibit 2.2 in Chapter 2 for a more detailed analysis of the excess capacity in hotels). The importance of good marketing is vital for an industry where rates of growth are so high. John Power, chief executive of the Irish Hotels Federation claims that 'The level of additional capacity available underlines the continuing need to focus on the effective marketing of Ireland overseas.' In particular, segments such as main holidaymakers, conference delegates, incentive recipients and language students need to be targeted in the future.

WHAT IS MARKETING?

The science of marketing has evolved from the practice of the private sector with its pursuit of profit and exchange of goods to current marketing emphasis on a range of activities in various sectors — including the marketing of services, people, places and ideas. Non-profit organisations such as museums, heritage sites and charities all rely on marketing for income generation and to build public awareness.

The term *marketing* is probably one of the most misunderstood terms in the business world today. Marketing is usually understood as the process of *making a sale*. Many people think of marketing only as advertising and selling, and it is frequently referred to as the process of encouraging people to buy goods that they do not want!

Therefore, you may be surprised to learn that selling and advertising are only the tip of the marketing iceberg. Although they are important, they are only two of the many marketing functions. In fact, Kotler (1996) claims that when a marketer does a good job of identifying customer needs, develops products and services that deliver superior value, distributes and promotes them effectively, these goods and services will sell very easily and thus the *selling* function will be superfluous. The aim is to know and understand the customer so well that the product or service fits their needs and sells itself (Drucker, 1973).

This does not mean that selling and advertising are unimportant. Instead they are simply viewed as tools that the marketer uses to achieve his or her goal, i.e. customer satisfaction. It is through customer satisfaction that business success and profitability is achieved. This makes perfect business sense. If a company seeks to produce a product or service that is needed in the market-place at a price that the consumer can afford, then it makes sense that the company will be profitable providing it has worked out its cost structure. The greater the need (demand) the greater the potential success of the business. Conversely, if customers have no need for a product, or a similar product already exists, then customers have no need to purchase. Marketers must give consumers as many reasons as possible to buy their product or service. In tourism and hospitality these reasons often include convenient location, cheaper price, better quality, unique experience, status, better product or a trendy image.

MARKETING DEFINED

Marketing has been defined in various ways. Marketing involves an exchange process and this is central to one of the simplest definitions of marketing, which is:

'Marketing is satisfying customers' needs at a profit.'

Or

'It is the process by which sellers are brought together with buyers to exchange their goods and services for something of value.'

As customers we expect to have a choice when we spend money. We can also choose not to spend any money at all by deciding not to buy a product. When we do decide to buy, an exchange takes place. Money is exchanged for the chosen product such as a holiday, a meal in a restaurant or a stay in a hotel. The outcome of the exchange is that both parties will feel happy with their side of the bargain, a *win-win* situation. The purchase of one product or service inevitably means the sacrifice of not being able to buy something else with the money spent — the opportunity cost of the purchase.

FIGURE 1.1 — THE EXCHANGE PROCESS

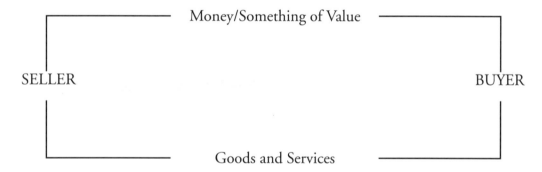

While the above definitions are easy to remember, they provide no indication of the potential relevance and scope of the subject. Kotler (1999) addresses this aspect better in the definition:

'Marketing is a social and managerial process by which individuals and groups obtain what they want and need through creating, offering, and exchanging products of value with others.'

This definition elaborates on the various activities that are carried out when marketing a product or service. These include market research, product development, pricing, promotion and distribution. Key words to note in this definition are the words *of value*. An important concept in marketing is the view that businesses will only exist if they bring something of value to the market-place. This may be a product, a service, an expertise or even ideas. Ultimately it is the market-place that will decide what is of value and what is obsolete.

Other definitions of marketing include:

- Marketing is the performance of business activities that direct the flow of goods and services from producer to consumer or user
- Marketing is selling goods that do not come back to people who do
- Marketing is a business philosophy guiding an organisation's overall activities
- Marketing is getting the right goods and services to the right people, at the right place, at the right time and at the right price
- Marketing is the creation and delivery of a standard of living
- Marketing is an overall term that includes market research, product development, pricing, promotion, distribution and selling
- Marketing is the process of planning and executing the conception, pricing, promotion and distribution of ideas, goods and services to create exchanges that satisfy individual and organisational objectives

You can see that all of these definitions are relevant in the context of the selection of everyday purchases such as shopping for clothes, foods, cars, places to eat, destinations to visit and places to stay. Some definitions focus on the process of marketing while others place more emphasis on the outcomes of the activity. The writings of well-known management theorists such as Drucker and Levitt have influenced the development of marketing. Levitt (1962) claimed that the purpose of a business is to create and maintain profitable customers, while Drucker (1973) declared that marketing is such an integral part of the organisation that 'it cannot be seen as a separate function'. These writers helped develop a market-oriented view in contrast to a production orientation, where the firm's activities are geared to existing technology, products or production. In contrast, a number of writers stress the supplier or management system rather than the consumer:

> 'Marketing consists of individual organisational activities that facilitate and expedite satisfying exchange relationships in the dynamic environment through the creation, distribution, promotion and pricing of goods, services and ideas.'

(Dibb et al, 1994)

As you can see there is no one single, universally agreed definition of marketing. There are definitions that emphasise marketing as a process, a concept or philosophy of business or an orientation.

THE EXCHANGE PROCESS

As in all specialist subjects, marketing has specific meanings to words that have general usage. The specialists' terminology includes words such as: needs and motives for purchase, wants, demands, products, value, cost and competition, exchange, transactions, relationship marketing as well as tourism and hospitality markets.

Needs and Motives for Purchase

The most basic concept underlying marketing is that of human need. A human need is a state of felt deprivation. Human beings have many complex needs and these are well illustrated by Maslow's *Hierarchy of Needs*. This model includes: basic physical needs for food and clothing, warmth and safety; social needs for belonging, affection, fun and relaxation; esteem needs for prestige, recognition and fame; and finally, individual needs for knowledge and self-expression. These needs are part of the human make-up, and Maslow claims that the lower physical and safety needs have to be satisfied before the higher levels are addressed. In tourism and hospitality the main focus is social, status and self-actualisation needs.

When a need is not satisfied a void exists. A dissatisfied person will do one of two things: look for an object that will satisfy that need or try to reduce the need. Thus the need can be satisfied by the purchase of a product or service. A busy executive is feeling tired and stressed and may decide to *purchase* a relaxing holiday to satisfy his or her needs. Some hotels and tourism destinations have built a business aimed at satisfying the esteem needs for prestige and recognition. The famous K Club (Kildare Hotel and Country Club) is one of the most famous five-star hotels in Ireland. Staying at the K Club is a sign that one is financially successful, and so the hotel addresses customers' needs for status and reward.

THE KILDARE HOTEL & COUNTRY CLUB

IRELAND'S ONLY 5 RED STAR HOTEL:
THE KILDARE HOTEL & COUNTRY CLUB IS A SUMPTUOUSLY
RESTORED GEORGIAN ESTATE SET IN 300 ACRES OF GARDENS,
WALKS AND LUSH IRISH COUNTRYSIDE.

Advertisement for the Kildare Hotel and Country Club communicates its five-star qualities.

FIGURE 1.2 — CORE MARKETING CONCEPTS

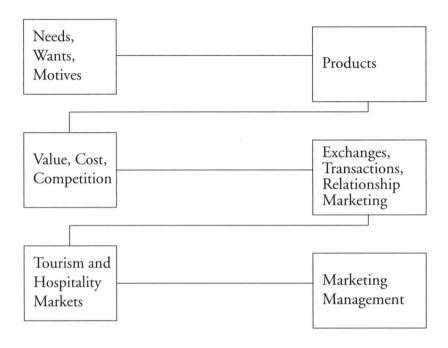

Wants

Human want is the form taken by human needs that are shaped by culture and individual personality. Wants are how people communicate their needs. Wants are described in terms of objects that will satisfy needs. As society evolves, the wants of its members expand. As people are exposed to more objects that arouse their interest and desire, producers try to produce more want-satisfying products and services. Restaurants in Ireland used to focus on the classic *meat, potato and vegetable* for dinner — today the restaurants include all the major European cuisines as well as American and Asian. Irish people want to try new foods.

Levitt (1962) introduced the term 'marketing myopia', referring to the shortsightedness of producers. Many sellers often confuse needs with wants. A hotel manager may think that the customer wants a drink in a bar but what the customer really needs is to socialise and meet new people. Producers can be so taken with their products that they only focus on existing wants and lose sight of the customer's underlying needs. They forget that a physical product is only a tool to solve a consumer problem. These sellers get into trouble if a new product comes along that serves the need better or cheaper. The customer will have the same need but want a new product.

Satisfying Demands with Products and Services

People have almost unlimited wants, but limited resources. They choose products that produce the most satisfaction for their money. When backed by buying power, wants become demands. Listing demands in a society at a given time is easy. During 1999, over six million foreigners chose to visit Ireland and spent a total of £2·4 billion. Consumers view products as bundles of benefits and choose those products and services that give them the best bundle for their money.

A *product* is anything that can be offered to a market for attention, acquisition, use or consumption that might satisfy a need or want. Suppose that a family feels the need to spend more time together. All the products that can satisfy this need are called the *product choice set*. They may include a family meal in a favourite restaurant, a weekend away in a hotel or going to a sporting event together. The closer the product matches the consumers' want, the more successful the producer will be. One of the reasons given for the success of Virgin Airlines was the belief by its owner Richard Branson that he was not just satisfying the needs of customers to be transported, instead he viewed the airline as being in the entertainment business. Ryanair, on the other hand, satisfies the need of price conscious travellers and offers low rates and no extras on its flights.

Value, Cost and Competition

Value is the consumer's estimate of the product's overall capacity to satisfy his or her needs. Costs not only involve money, but everything one gives up to gain the product. Costs can also include time, effort and the *hassle* involved in the purchase. Satisfaction with a product is determined by how well the product or service meets the customer's expectations. In the tourism and hospitality industry in the 1990s, competition has reached an extraordinarily intense level. So what makes customers choose one brand of hotel or tour operator over another? The extensive choice available now means that basic facilities and price are no longer the dominant deciding factor, but rather the quality and *added-on value* attributed to the service. To paraphrase Sir Colin Marshall, chairman of British Airways, anyone can fly aeroplanes — but few organisations can excel in serving people. Excellent service is a hard competence to develop; it is also hard for competitors to copy or match. Providing a quality service is of paramount importance if a business wants a sustainable competitive advantage. In a survey of business travellers conducted by Hotel and Motel Management in America (1997), the single biggest response of candidates (thirty-seven per cent) asked why they selected a particular chain of hotels as their favourite, was *service* or *a helpful/nice staff* and not the physical aspects of the hotels.

Exchange, Transaction and Relationship Marketing

Marketing is based on the concept of exchange. People decide to satisfy needs and wants through the exchange process. Exchange is the act of obtaining a desired object from someone by offering something in return. For exchange to take place, several conditions must be satisfied. There must be two parties and each must have something valued by the other. Each party must want to deal with the other. Each must be free to accept or reject the other's offer. Finally, each party must be able to communicate and deliver. These conditions make exchange possible. A transaction is marketing's unit of measurement; it consists of a trade of value between two parties. A transaction involves at least three things of value, i.e. conditions that are agreed to, a time of agreement and a place of agreement.

While sellers can focus on individual transactions with buyers, smart marketers work at building relationships with valued customers, travel agents, tour operators and tourist offices. Increasingly, marketing is shifting from trying to maximise the profit on each individual transaction to building beneficial relationships with customers and other partners. This is called relationship marketing. It is based on the principle of building good relationships and profits will follow. The concept of relationship marketing is crucial in the tourism and hospitality industries.

Most businesses are finding that they can earn a higher return from investing in repeat sales rather than looking for new customers all the time. Opportunities exist to cross-sell to current customers. More and more companies are forming strategic alliances in tourism and hospitality, making skilled relationship marketing essential. The objectives of relationship marketing are to turn new customers into regular clients, and then progressively move them through being strong supporters of the company and its products to being active and vocal advocates for the business, thus playing an important role as a referral source. In their article, Reicheld and Sasser (1990) showed that the longer customers are retained by a company, the more profitable they become. This is because of increased purchases, reduced operating costs, referrals, price premiums and reduced customer acquisition costs. It is now accepted that it is five times more expensive to attract a new customer than to keep a present one.

Box 1.1 — Challenging Times in Tourism and Hospitality

Vera Feeney, Chairman of the Town and Country Homes Association offers marketing advice to operators:

'Success depends on the individual operator, these are indeed times of changing consumer trends and expectations, and for those who have responded the rewards are great.

A warm welcome, high standards, value for money, time to talk to guests, refreshments on arrival, advice on what to do and see, family support and the declining ingredient of hospitality and spontaneity — these are the basic strengths of running a successful bed and breakfast home.

I do not accept that the traditional warm Irish welcome is on the wane. The attractions of a holiday in our homes are varied, but the bedrock is the quality of the welcome. There are challenging times ahead, so we must not become complacent about the quality of our welcome or the facilities we offer. We have to be better than our competitors.'

Source: Interview with *LINK* magazine, November 1999

WHAT IS A MARKET?

A market is a set of actual and potential buyers who might transact with a seller. The size of a market depends on the number of persons who exhibit a common need, have the money to purchase and are willing to partake in the exchange process. Marketing therefore means working with markets to bring about exchanges for satisfying human needs and wants. Processes facilitating exchanges involve work. Sellers have to search for buyers, identify their needs, design attractive products, promote them, deliver them and set prices. Such activities as product development, market research, communication, distribution and pricing are core marketing activities. Usually we think of marketing as being carried on by sellers, however, buyers carry on marketing when they search for the goods and services they need at prices that they can afford. Travel agents carry out marketing when they track down destinations that are suitable for their clients. Meeting planners carry out marketing when they research hotels to find which ones offer attractive conference packages.

MARKETING MANAGEMENT

Most people think of a marketing manager as someone who finds enough customers to buy the company's current output, i.e. vacant rooms, seats in a restaurant, theatre or airline. This view is too limited. The marketing manager is interested in shaping the level, time and composition of demand for the company's products and services. At any one time there may be no demand, adequate demand, irregular demand or too much demand. One of the most popular parts of Dublin is the Temple Bar district. Restaurants and pubs in the vicinity frequently have a queue outside the door at the weekends. The area became so popular for stag parties, which caused much annoyance to the residents and visitors alike, a programme was put in place to *demarket* the area for stag parties.

The hospitality and tourism industries have incredible peaks and troughs and a key aspect of marketing is to attempt to synchronise supply and demand. Kotler (1996) claims that marketing management is in fact *demand management*. The marketing manager is in charge of not only finding and increasing demand, but also at times with changing or reducing it (demarketing). This can occur when destinations are over-populated with tourists and demand is discouraged at peak times. For example, the Aran Islands in the month of August can have over 4,000 visitors per day to the main island of Inis Mor, yet during the winter months as little as 100 visitors per day.

TOURISM AND HOSPITALITY MARKETING

Marketing is a subject of vital concern in the tourism and hospitality industry because it is the principal management influence which can be brought to bear on the size and behaviour of the vast tourism market. Tourism marketing is best explained as a process of achieving voluntary exchanges between individual parties:

- Customers who buy or use products and services include domestic and international tourists
- Producer organisations which supply and sell tourism products and services including hospitality

This exchange process is continuous with constant tension between a producer's need for profit, the efficient use of assets and the consumers' search for value and satisfaction. This led Kotler (1996) to define marketing as a superior value-delivery system. Thus the market-led tourism business uses its deep knowledge of customers' needs and wants to achieve its objectives, while at the same time developing strategies aimed at long-term customer satisfaction.

MARKETING AS A BUSINESS PHILOSOPHY

Marketing as a business philosophy recognises the importance of the customer and that businesses exist to serve customers. Marketing management, therefore, involves carrying out tasks to achieve desired exchanges with target markets. What philosophy should guide these marketing efforts? There are five alternative philosophies or concepts under which businesses conduct their marketing activities: the production, product, selling, marketing and societal concepts.

1. *The Production Concept:* holds that the consumer will favour products that are available and highly affordable and, therefore, management should focus on improving production and distribution efficiency. Takeaway restaurants often follow this concept, for example, Supermacs focus on providing a range of food products that are low cost and are produced quickly.
2. *The Product Concept:* holds that consumers will favour products that will offer the most quality, performance and innovative features; and that organisations should devote energy to making continuous product improvements. A product orientation in the tourism and hospitality industry can lead businesses to focus only on the product and not realise that they are selling service and hospitality. Many new

hotels and restaurants focus on getting the physical aspects of the product correct but do not budget sufficiently for training and staff development. As a result the quality of the service suffers and occupancy levels drop.

3. *The Selling Concept:* holds that consumers will not buy enough of a business's products or services unless it undertakes a large-scale selling and promotion effort. The concept is typically practiced with unsought goods or services — those that buyers do not normally think of buying or no longer need, for example, a restaurant offering a full *table d'hôte* menu at lunchtime in a busy business district.

4. *The Marketing Concept:* holds that achieving business goals depends on determining the needs and wants of target markets and delivering the desired satisfactions more effectively and efficiently than competitors. The selling and marketing concept are frequently confused. The selling concept takes an *inside-out* perspective. For example, in a restaurant situation it starts with the restaurant focusing on its existing menu and calls for heavy selling and promotion to get customers *in the door*. It focuses on customer conquest — making the sale with little concern about who buys or why. The marketing concept takes an *outside-in* perspective and starts with a well-defined market, focuses on customers' needs, co-ordinates all the marketing activities and makes profits by creating long-term customer relationships based on customer value and satisfaction. Most successful tourism and hospitality operations have adopted the marketing concept including the major hotel chains, fast food restaurants and successful tourism destinations such as Dublin, Killarney and Galway.

5. *The Societal Concept:* holds that the organisation should determine the needs, wants and interests of target markets. It should then deliver the desired satisfactions more effectively and efficiently than competitors in a way that maintains or improves the *consumer's,* and *society's,* wellbeing. This is the newest of the five marketing management philosophies. The societal marketing concept questions whether the pure marketing concept is adequate in an age of environmental problems, resource shortages, worldwide economic problems and neglected social services (Kotler, 1999). It asks if the firm that researches, serves and satisfies individual wants is always doing what is best for consumers and society in the long-run. According to the societal marketing concept, the pure marketing concept overlooks possible conflict between short-term consumer wants and long-term consumer welfare. Consider fast food companies. Most people see them as responsible organisations that have satisfied a need in the market. Yet certain consumer and environmental groups have voiced their concerns that the food produced has little nutritional value, is high in fats and calories, and the packaging adds to the litter problem with disposable containers.

BOX 1.2 — HOW FAST FOOD ADAPTS TO CHANGING LIFESTYLES

Fast food restaurants have been characterised by their limited menus, self-service, high turnover and high percentage of takeaway orders. In the coming years all major chains will have to deal with the ageing European population. As the average age of the consumer increases, a shift away from fast food toward the mid-scale restaurant is a possibility if the fast food restaurants do not meet the needs of this group. One way the industry may adapt to the changing needs of its market is to focus on nutrition. An important aspect of our lifestyles has been an increasing focus on becoming healthier. The changes include more exercise and better eating habits. As all areas of society have changed to reflect this new awareness about health, so too the fast food industry must reposition itself.

Customer satisfaction is the major aim of the marketing concept. First, an organisation must find out what will satisfy customers and with this information it then attempts to create satisfying products and services. The process does not end there. The organisation must continue to alter, adapt and develop products and services to keep pace with changing customers' desires and preferences, see Box 1.2 above to illustrate this point.

MARKETING MIX

The main way that marketing objectives are achieved is through the development of the marketing mix. In simple terms, this means developing the optimum combination of elements, or mix, to develop appropriate products and services to meet tourists' needs, to communicate effectively their benefits to target markets and to ensure that they are available in the right places at the right time. In the purest form, the marketing mix is represented by the four *Ps* — product, price, place and promotion.

PRODUCT

Product is anything that is offered for sale that has value to the consumer. At the most basic level the product should answer the following question: 'What is the buyer really buying?' Every product is a package of problem-solving services, in the hospitality industry this can be referred to as food, beverage, accommodation and service. In tourism the product is frequently a destination that can offer fun, excitement, adventure or peace and relaxation. Thus, marketers view products as a *bundle of benefits* that are offered to the market-place.

PRICE

Price is the amount of money charged for goods or services. It is the only marketing mix element that produces revenue — all others represent cost. Many marketers feel that setting the *right* price is their most difficult task as ultimately the consumer decides if the product is priced right. A pricing mistake can lead to business failure, even when all the other elements of the business are sound.

PLACE (DISTRIBUTION)

Place not only refers to the location of the business but to the distribution systems that provide a steady flow of customers. If we view properties as the heart of a hotel company then distribution systems can be viewed as the company's circulatory system. They usually involve intermediaries that carry out the selling role for the organisation or destination away from the actual location. In tourism we refer to travel agents and tour operators as intermediaries. The Internet is a new powerful means of electronic distribution which is discussed in Chapter 9.

PROMOTION (COMMUNICATION)

Modern marketing calls for more than developing good products, pricing them attractively and making them available to target customers. Businesses must continuously communicate with their present and potential customers. The four main tools used to communicate include: advertising, sales promotion, public relations and personal selling. New forms of promotion are gaining in popularity including database marketing and marketing on the Internet.

SERVICES MARKETING

Some authors have argued that the above elements are too restrictive. In the service area, for example, a number of academics have argued that a broadened marketing mix be recognised to include the unique nature of the services sector.

THE SERVICE PRODUCT

When a manufactured product is purchased the consumer receives something tangible. In the tourism and hospitality industry the product has elements that are intangible, namely the service. A meal in a restaurant may be delicious but if the waiter or waitress is rude then the whole experience is spoilt and the customer is dissatisfied. If a guest is provided with a lovely room but only after a long argument about the room rate or the reservation, the guest stay is marred from the onset.

PERFORMANCE IS PEOPLE INTENSIVE

A service usually involves people, it is a *deed,* a *benefit* or an *activity* that one person bestows on another. Employees are part of the product and so are the guests. Because people are involved on both sides, services are less standardised than are products. Two different members of staff could do a good but somewhat different job in checking-in a guest in a hotel. Highly standardised behaviour is often not possible and frequently undesirable: friendliness and spontaneity are a key strength of Irish people.

PEAKS AND VALLEYS

Service organisations tend to encounter surges in demand that alternate with quiet periods. Tourism businesses are hectic during July and August in Ireland but can be very quiet in January — restaurants are busy at meal times but business is very slow in between meals. Because of the variability in demand, service marketing focuses on *demand management*. This involves managing the marketing mix so that supply and demand are synchronised; sometimes business is moved from peak times to a slower period, for example, a restaurant may offer *early bird specials* to attract customers between 5.30 p.m. and 7.00 p.m.

NO INVENTORY

A service cannot be stored. In manufacturing, products not sold today keep their value and can be sold later. The opportunity to sell a guest room tonight is unique to this night only. The value from a room carried vacant tonight can never be realised in a future time period. Therefore, services are often described as being *time-perishable*. Capacity management is a concern for tourism and hospitality marketers.

CHANNELS OF DISTRIBUTION

Packaged goods make use of traditional channels of distribution such as wholesalers, retailers and shops. In the tourism and hospitality industry the channel members include tour operators, travel agents and tourist information offices. These channels are in the process of rapid change. The global network of reservation systems (discussed in Chapter 9) is changing the way tourism and hospitality services are distributed and will change even more with the growing popularity of the Internet.

BOX 1.3 — THE DISTINCTIVE CHARACTERISTICS OF TOURISM AND HOSPITALITY SERVICES

The Product: The Visitor's Experience
- Largely intangible
- Involves both goods and services
- Visitor is purchasing a 'deed, a performance or an activity'

People Intensive
- Employees are part of the product
- Quality subject to the variability of the individual employee and guest interaction
- Guest is involved in all service transactions

Capacity Management is Crucial
- Variable levels of demand, peaks and valleys
- Time perishable — unused capacity is wasted

Channels of Distribution
- Channels of distribution are increasing in importance
- Channels of distribution are changing rapidly due to developments in technology and telecommunications

Source: Adapted from *Hospitality Marketing* by Tom Powers

In the 1980s the augmented marketing mix was developed to address the above characteristics.

THE AUGMENTED MARKETING MIX

PEOPLE

Tourism is a business where the quality of staff-customer interaction is critical to overall customer satisfaction. Management of one's own staff, and customers' interactions with them, is often a point of differentiation for many tourism enterprises. Family Hotels of Ireland is a marketing consortium open only to family run hotels, and emphasises the resulting personal touch as a key marketing advantage.

PHYSICAL EVIDENCE

The management of all tangible elements of the service offering. Examples include the styling of uniforms, aesthetic design of hotels and restaurants, type of paper used for a brochure and design of company logo.

PROCESSES

The way in which tourism services are delivered are often the cause of either great customer satisfaction or discontent. Examples include the way in which payments for holidays are handled, how customer complaints are addressed and the way in which food is prepared and served in a restaurant.

It has to be acknowledged that other authors question the basis of the augmented mix, arguing that the additional elements are in fact subsets of the product element. Nevertheless, the augmented mix does provide a useful basis for a fuller understanding of the issues to be addressed in marketing strategy development.

Having assessed the environment (Where are we now?) and set marketing objectives (Where do we want to go?) the marketing mix forms the building block for answering the question (How can we get there?) i.e. marketing strategy and tactics.

INTEGRATING THE MARKETING MIX

It is crucial to understand that, although textbooks tend to treat each element of the marketing mix as distinct, each element of the mix is interdependent on the other elements. For example, the level of service in a hotel and the amenities provided to guests have an impact on the price, as well as the decision of where to advertise the hotel.

By integrating the various elements and subelements, of the marketing mix, the chances of inconsistencies or incongruencies occurring is greatly lessened. The elements of the submix are illustrated below, in Figure 1.3.

FIGURE 1.3 — THE SUBMIX ELEMENTS OF THE MARKETING MIX

PRODUCT SUBMIX

Product Policies

Product Life-Cycle (PLC)
Portfolio Analysis
Service Mix

Product Strategy and Tactics

Branding
Customer Care programmes
New Service Development
Screening new services
Licensing/Franchising existing
services

PRODUCT SUBMIX

Pricing Policies

Role of Pricing
Alternative Approaches to
Pricing
Pricing and the PLC
Legal considerations

Pricing Objectives

Pricing Methods and Tactics
Costs
Offensive/Promotional Pricing

**MARKETING ELEMENTS
SUBMIX PLANNING**

DISTRIBUTION SUBMIX

Channels to be used
Direct/Indirect
Technology systems
Speed of response
Intermediary relations
Key account management

PROMOTIONAL SUBMIX

Promotional strategies and tactics:

Advertising
Sales Promotion
Public Relations
Personal Selling
Sponsorship
Direct Marketing
Internet Marketing

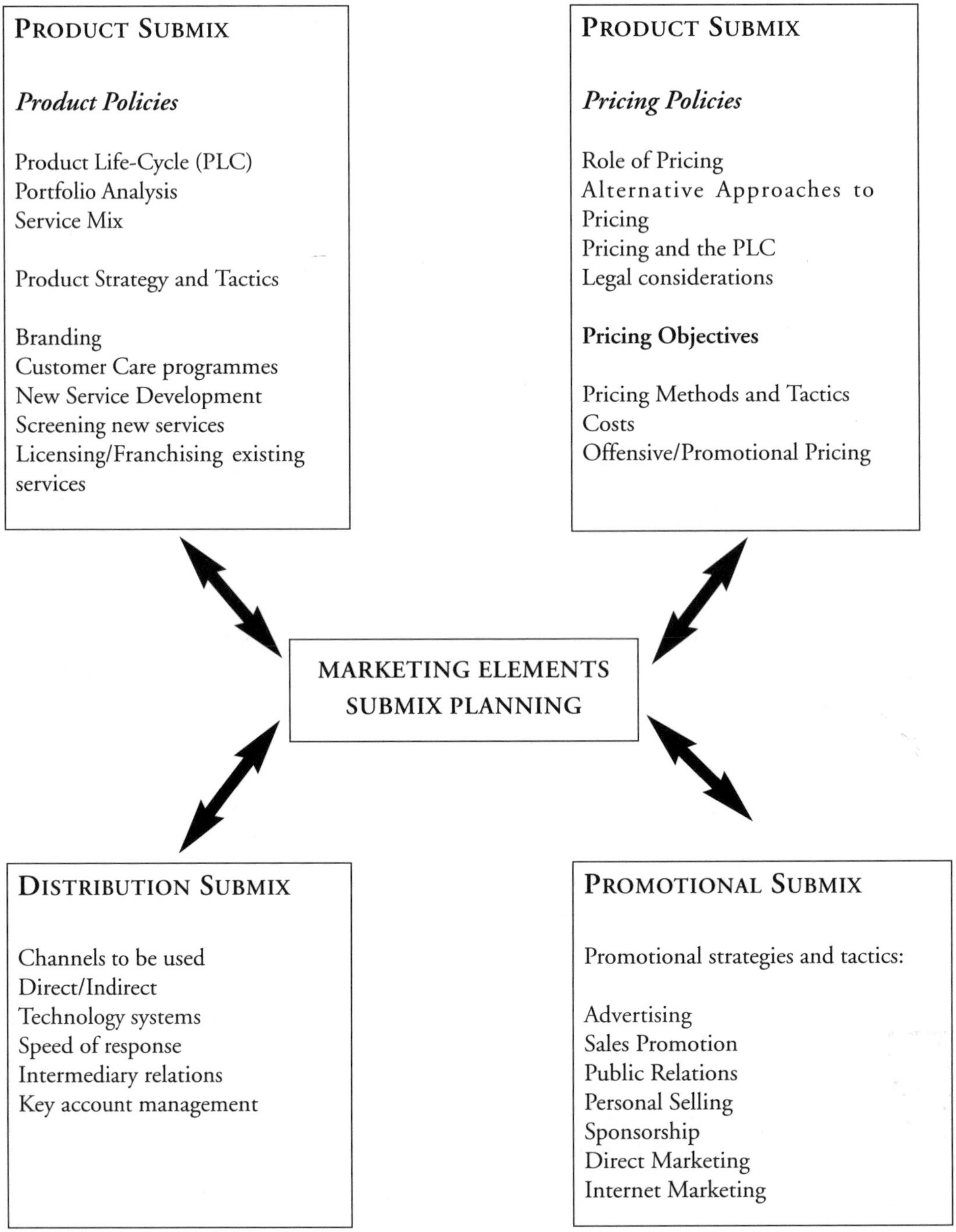

STRATEGIC MARKETING IN TOURISM AND HOSPITALITY

The tourism industry is set to grow five per cent annually (WTO, 1999), and a marketing orientation will be forced upon businesses in competitive markets as a necessary method of survival. A key factor in becoming market-oriented is the practice of target marketing; this involves matching tourists having a particular set of similar needs and wants with a tourism product that can satisfy those needs and wants. Decisions have to be made as to how to serve existing markets, when to enter new markets and when to exit unattractive markets. This is what strategic marketing is all about.

A key requirement for successful marketing is the ability to segment, target and position the various tourism products and services as well as the overall destination. Market segmentation, defined by Kotler (1984) as 'The subdividing of a market into distinct subsets of customers (tourists), where any subset may conceivably be selected as a target market to be reached with a distinct marketing mix.' Segmentation is the cornerstone on which marketing theory is based and a major component of strategic marketing:

'Market segmentation is certainly one of the most important aspects of strategic marketing planning, and it may be the most difficult. When it is done well, it seems obvious.'

Various authorities have used different bases to analyse and segment the tourist market. Tourist markets can be segmented by choice of destination, travel method, demographic characteristics, purpose of visit and benefits sought. Before effective segmentation can take place (and thereafter strategic marketing), detailed research is required on the markets and in many situations this information may be available at a national level.

One of the most useful working definitions of tourism, is given by Mathieson and Wall (1982):

'Tourism is the temporary movement of people to destinations outside their normal places of work and residence, the activities undertaken during their stay in those destinations, and the facilities created to cater for their needs.'

This statement highlights that the supply of, and demand for, tourism takes many forms, each with its own particular spatial and temporal pattern (Davidson and Maitland, 1997).

Marketing focuses on having *the right products in the right place at the right time* and requires careful co-ordination of supplies. What exactly is the *product* supplied to the tourist? Is it the accommodation, food and beverage, attractions or a combination of them all? Kotler (1996) defines a product as 'anything that can be offered to the market-place for attention, acquisition, use or consumption that might satisfy a need or want'. It includes physical objects, services, places, organisations and ideas. Medlik (1991) delves further into the concept of a tourism *product* as the entire experience of the tourist from initial anticipation to postpurchase feelings. In other words, the tourist regards the various elements of transport, accommodation, food and beverage, entertainment and attractions on a macro level as one encounter, experience or product and evaluates it this way.

From a tourism marketing point of view, one way of thinking is to use what Middleton (1994) calls *total tourism product* as a combination of resources and services. Thus, the supply of tourism products must be adapted to meet the ever-changing needs of the market. This is not an easy task; consumers are becoming more sophisticated and demanding (Poon, 1994). Gone are the days of *tinsel and junk* tourism products; instead, the tourist wants a more natural and authentic experience. The challenge to the industry is how to meet these new needs. Some of the answer lies in more detailed market research into travel and identification of preferred visitor markets whose needs match the supply capabilities of the destination.

TOURIST DEMAND

Understanding tourism demand is crucial for successful marketing of tourist destinations. The determinants of that demand may be examined from two different perspectives. Firstly, it is possible to consider the demand for tourism according to the purpose of the visit; the main categories included here are sport and recreation, culture of the destination, visiting friends and relatives and business travel (*see* Table 1.1). Other minor categories exist including health-related purposes, religious and educational. Secondly, demand may be understood through an examination of the various factors, which contribute to the tourist's propensity to travel, i.e. the tourist's motivations. It is generally recognised by writers such as Cooper (1997) that: 'We know relatively little about tourist motivation, and often the reason why a destination is chosen is little understood'.

TABLE 1.1 — TOURIST MOTIVATIONS FOR VISITING IRELAND

	1994	1995	1996	1997	1998	1999
Holiday	41%	42%	42%	41%	39%	37%
VFR*	24%	23%	23%	24%	23%	24%
Business/Conference	20%	21%	21%	21%	24%	25%
Other	15%	14%	14%	14%	14%	14%
	100	100	100	100	100	100

Source: Bord Fáilte Tourism Facts 1999

*Visiting Friends and Relatives.

TOURISM MARKETS

The word *market* has a number of meanings. It is used to refer primarily to the place where goods are bought and sold. It can also refer to a large geographic area. In some cases the word refers to the relationship between the demand for and supply of a specific product, for instance, *the expanding conference market*. Sometimes the word *market* is used for the act of selling something.

Marketing writers view a market in terms of:

'An aggregate of people who, as individuals or in organisations, have need for products in a product class and have the ability, willingness and authority to purchase such products.'

(Dibb, Simpkin, Pride and Ferrell, 1994:63)

Thus, for a group of people to be a market they must need or want a particular product or service, have the ability and authority to purchase the product, and the willingness to use their buying power.

Tourists are consumers who purchase a number of diverse travel and tourism services. If suppliers of these services have a clear understanding of why their products are in demand, they will not only be able to tailor their products more closely to the needs of their clients, but will also understand their decision-making process in choosing a destination or tourism product. Understanding consumer behaviour will allow for effective promotion of tourism products and identification of appropriate imagery. Table 1.2 gives a breakdown of the key tourist markets visiting Ireland and the forecasted percentage change between 1998 and 1999.

TABLE 1.2 — FORECAST NUMBERS TO IRELAND 1999 — PERCENTAGE CHANGE 1999 v 1998 (PROVISIONAL RESULTS)

Markets	Total Visitors	Total Revenue
Britain	+7%	+5%
M. Europe	+5%	+3%
France	+2%	n/a
Germany	-1·6%	n/a
Netherlands	+3·7%	n/a
Italy	+17%	n/a
North America	+10·7%	+13%
Domestic Trips	+5·1%	+17%
Total Out of State	+7·5%	+6·8%

Source: Bord Fáilte Marketing Plan 1999 (forecasts may have been revised in light of further information on 1998 performance)

The actual markets targeted by Bord Fáilte will differ from country to country as the following table shows:

TABLE 1.3 — TARGET MARKETS FOR PROMOTING IRELAND

Country	Target Markets
Britain	ABC1, 35+ years
France	ABC1, 25 to 50 years old
Germany	20 to 69 years, DM3,500+, ABC1, educated to university entry level
US	35+ years, annual salary of $50,000+, major metropolitan areas, past European travellers

Source: Bord Fáilte Marketing Plan 1999

THE HOSPITALITY INDUSTRY IN IRELAND

The hospitality industry in Ireland has a vast range of product types and facilities. The following is a list of the key providers but is not exhaustive.

Hotels

Hotels can be divided into two categories: group owned and individually owned. Irish hotels are a major employer and account for 46,000 jobs — over a third of the total that tourism currently provides (Horwath Bastow Charleton, 1999). The largest groups are Jurys Doyle Hotel Group, Ryan Hotels and Great Southern Hotels. These groups alone account for 4,000 bedrooms. The newer hotels to enter the market include: Quality Hotels, Lynch Hotels, Fitzpatrick Hotels, O'Callaghan Hotels, IBIS and many new individually owned properties in the main city areas of Dublin, Cork, Limerick and Galway.

The majority of hotels in Ireland are run by families or owners. These properties range in size and type, with different marketing strategies. In order to compete against the larger chains these small individually run properties have formed alliances in order to reduce costs and increase their marketing power in a competitive environment. One of the main advantages hotel groups have over individual establishments is that of marketing, as their budgets and expertise far exceed those of the smaller operator. Some of the alliances focus on marketing activities such as Manor House Hotels, Village Inn Hotels and Small Luxury hotels.

Other international groups include: Leading Hotels of the World, *Relais et Chateaux* and Conrad Hilton. Luxury hotels such as the Sheen Falls, the Kildare Hotel and Country Club, the SAS Radisson, the Merrion, Four Seasons and Glenlo Abbey have been built costing millions of pounds and have an international clientele. Other hotels are targeted at the more price sensitive market including Forte Travelodge, Jurys Inns and the Quality Hotel Group. There are indications that the high volume of new development throughout Ireland started to outpace demand growth in 1998 (*see* Box 1.4). The annual hotel survey of Ireland and Northern Ireland indicates a decline in occupancies across all types and sizes of hotels. In Dublin alone, twenty hotels opened or extended in 1998, adding close to 1,500 rooms and bringing the total available rooms supply to 9,200: an increase approaching twenty per cent over rooms available in 1997. Total rooms supply at the end of 1998 is estimated at around 32,500 representing an increase of seven per cent over the previous year (Horwarth et al, 1999). Northern Ireland encountered a ten per cent increase in room availability and almost 900,000 room nights sold. Northern Ireland room occupancies dropped from fifty-eight per cent in 1997 to 56·7 per cent in 1998.

BOX 1.4 — HOTEL INDUSTRY SURVEY 1998

	1996	1997	1998
Room Occupancy Average	69·0%	70·0%	67·0%
Achieved Average Room Rates	£48.61	£53.66	£55.66
Total Revenue per Room	£34,069	£34,042	£36,880
Department Profit per Room	£15,626	£16,145	£16,871
Gross Operating Profit per Room	£7,979	£8,877	£9,203
	23.4%	26.1%	25·0%
Profit before Tax per Room	£4,135	£4,488	£4,461
	12.1%	13.2%	12.1%

Source: Ireland and Northern Ireland Hotel Industry Survey 1998, Horwath Bastow Charleton

Guesthouses, Farmhouses and Bed and Breakfasts

The popularity of guesthouses, farmhouses and bed and breakfast accommodation has grown in recent years. Many visitors who seek a more cultural experience and wish to stay with a *real Irish family* have chosen this type of accommodation. There are 442 registered guesthouses in Ireland, 4,267 farmhouses and Town and Country homes and a large number of unregistered accommodation providers.

- **Self-Catering Guide**
- **Irish Cottage Holiday Homes** — published by Irish Cottage Holiday Homes Association, Dublin
- **Irish Farmhouse Bed and Breakfast Accommodation, Activity Holidays and Self-Catering** — published by Irish Farmhouse Holidays Association, Limerick
- **Irish Country Holidays** — published in association with Bord Fáilte
- **Green Book of Ireland**
- **Conference Ireland** — published by the Convention Bureau of Ireland and the Irish Tourist Board, Dublin
- **The Hidden Ireland:** Accommodation in private heritage houses — published by The Hidden Ireland, Dublin
- **Elegant Ireland** — Castles, Country Houses and Holiday Cottages — published by Elegant Ireland, Dublin
- **Heritage Sites** — published by Duchas The Heritage Service, Dublin
- **Shannon Heritage** — published by Shannon Development, Co. Clare
- **Dining Out in Ireland**
- **Bed and Breakfast Ireland** — published by Town and Country Homes Association
- **Family Homes of Ireland** — published by Family Homes of Ireland Organisation Ltd, Co. Galway
- **Premier Guest Houses** — published by Premier Guesthouses of Ireland, Dublin
- **Other publications** on various regions, cities and towns such as 'An essential Guide to Galway' published by Western Publications Ltd

INTRODUCTION TO THE REMAINING CHAPTERS IN THIS BOOK

Satisfying the customer is a priority in most businesses. In order to prosper, all tourism and hospitality businesses continuously encourage potential customers to buy their products, and they must do this as efficiently as possible. Marketing is not confined to advertising and selling, but covers everything that is related to getting the right product, in the right place, at the right time and at the right price. Marketers must get to know their customers' needs and wants and attempt to deliver satisfying products and services. In tourism and hospitality, our *product* is not just a scenic destination or a beautifully furnished hotel, it is also the delivery of a service. To compete effectively for customers, a business must create a marketing mix that gives their target market more value than their competitor's marketing mix. A key area of competition in the new millennium is in *service*.

In this textbook the principles of marketing are explained, definitions of key terms are given and the theory is then applied to the marketing environment in Ireland. This first chapter introduces key concepts such as definitions of marketing, applying the marketing concept, marketing management and the marketing mix. Each of these key principles are applied to the tourism and hospitality industry in Ireland. Profiles of the tourism and hospitality industry key statistics are introduced.

Chapter 2 examines the marketing environment at a macro and micro level. The key forces that influence Irish tourism and hospitality marketing are identified and include social and cultural changes as well as demographic, economic, technological and ecological changes. The process of environmental scanning is discussed and global tourism trends are examined in detail.

Chapter 3 describes the nature of marketing research, emphasising its role of providing information for marketing decision-making in tourism and hospitality. This chapter contains the key sources of secondary data that exist and are being used by researchers in Ireland today. A key source is Bord Fáilte reports, however, many other sources are examined including government, databases and CD-ROMs, the Internet, European reports, marketing research agencies and the World Tourism Organisation. Guidelines are given for carrying out primary research, and the chapter contains details of how to design a questionnaire.

Chapter 4 seeks to enhance the reader's understanding of principles of consumer behaviour. Consumer behaviour is the study of how and why consumers make purchasing decisions, and this theory is applied to tourists and visitors choosing Ireland as a destination and how they choose between hospitality products. A simple model of consumer behaviour is used and examined in detail. Attention is focused on the individual psychological characteristics of the buyer as well as the external influences on consumers purchasing tourism and hospitality products. The chapter concludes with a theoretical and practical examination of the consumer decision-making process.

Chapter 5 examines the strategic planning process in a tourism or hospitality context. The process of analysis, planning, implementation and control is outlined and key activities such as the marketing audit and SWOT (strengths, weaknesses, opportunities and threats) analysis are examined. Strategic marketing tools such as the Product-Market Opportunity Analysis and the BCG Matrix are explained and applied to a tourism and hospitality situation. Current issues such as strategic alliances in tourism and hospitality are examined and Aer Lingus is used as an example of this process. The chapter concludes with guidelines on the preparation of a marketing plan. Tralee is used as a case-study for strategic market planning.

Chapter 6 examines the process of segmentation, targeting and positioning in marketing. Markets are examined and the bases for segmenting them into smaller groups with similar needs and wants. The requirements for effective segmentation are discussed and the process of target marketing. Numerous examples of Irish tourism and hospitality products and services are given. Positioning strategies are outlined as well as product differentiation.

Chapter 7 views the tourism and hospitality product as the centre of the marketing process. As the product is both a service and a physical product attention is given to new theories in services marketing and, in particular, the extra three *Ps* of the marketing mix: people, process and physical environment. The Product Life-cycle concept is discussed and applied to the industry. An important issue in marketing today is branding and this is examined in detail. The *Fushia Brand* of West Cork is highlighted in a case-study. New product development is discussed as well as the question: 'What is innovation?' in the tourism and hospitality industry. Finally, the issue of service quality is highlighted and examined in the context of rural tourism.

Chapter 8 discusses pricing which is the number one problem for most marketers as it is the only element of the marketing mix that produces revenue. The role and perception of price is looked at from both a buyer's and seller's perspective. Price elasticity of demand is discussed as well as the factors that affect pricing. General approaches to pricing are examined including strategies for introducing new products. Current pricing issues, including yield management and pricing on the Internet, are discussed.

Chapter 9 explains the importance of developing an efficient distribution system in tourism and hospitality. Direct and indirect systems are described, as is the overall management of a distribution channel. Key tourism and hospitality intermediaries are described and emphasis is placed on the greater use of electronic distribution systems. Gulliver, Ireland's electronic distribution system, is studied, as well as distribution systems based on the Internet.

Chapter 10 explores marketing communication today. Components of the marketing communications mix are explored and the communication process is discussed. Advertising as a key form of communication is explored, with details on how to prepare an effective advertising campaign. Public relations, a less-used tool in promotion, is discussed. Details of how to prepare a press release are also included.

Chapter 11 debates the remaining forms of communication including: direct marketing, sales promotion, personal selling and Internet marketing. The advantages and problems of direct marketing are considered, as well as guidelines for planning a campaign. Various types of sales promotions used by the tourism and hospitality industry are cited as well as the impact of Internet marketing in Ireland. Finally, relationship marketing and its vital role is reviewed.

CHAPTER SUMMARY

Today's successful tourism and hospitality operators focus on the customer. The customer is king. Marketing itself is a social and managerial process by which individuals and groups obtain what they need and want through creating and exchanging products and services with others. Marketing is concerned with the key terms: needs, wants, demands, products/services, value, cost and satisfaction, exchange, transactions and relationships. Marketing management involves carrying out tasks to achieve desired exchanges with target markets. The philosophies that guide these marketing efforts include: the production concept, the product concept, the selling concept and the marketing concept. Customer satisfaction is the major aim of the latter concept.

The marketing concept takes an *outside-in* perspective and starts with a well-defined market, focuses on customer needs, co-ordinates all the marketing activities and makes profit by creating long-term customer relationships based on customer value and satisfaction. In order to achieve customer satisfaction, the organisation must have the right goods, in the right place, at the right time and at the right price. This involves developing an appropriate marketing mix, consisting of the four *Ps*: product/service, price, place and promotion. For service industries such as tourism and hospitality this mix is extended and includes: people, process and physical environment. The tourism and hospitality industries are some of the fastest growing industries in the world and operate in a very competitive environment. Understanding tourism demand is crucial for successful marketing and tourism markets must be studied with visitor behaviour being thoroughly understood.

KEY WORDS AND PHRASES

Marketing Defined	Exchange Process
Needs and Wants, Products	Tourism Demand
Marketing Mix	Marketing Management
Value, Cost and Satisfaction	Tourism and Hospitality Marketing
Marketing Management Philosophies	Relationship Marketing

QUESTIONS FOR REVIEW

1. Define Marketing and explain how a business can be market-oriented.
2. What is the exchange process? Explain how this process occurs in our daily lives.
3. Distinguish between needs, wants and demands. Why is it so important for a target market to have sufficient buying power? Give examples of markets with needs but insufficient power.

4. What is the marketing mix?
5. Why is relationship marketing so important in the tourism and hospitality industry?
6. Explain the difference between marketing and selling.
7. Apply the core concepts of marketing (needs, wants, demands, products, exchanges, transactions and markets) to the tourism and hospitality industry.
8. Comment on the trends in the hotel industry as shown in Table 1.1.

QUESTIONS FOR DISCUSSION

1. If you went into a restaurant as a customer, how could you tell if the restaurant had embraced the marketing concept?
2. In order to compete with a price-cutting hotel nearby, a large hotel decides to cut prices even lower. What impact will this have on the other element of the hotel's marketing mix?
3. Apply the seven *Ps* of the marketing mix to a tourism or hospitality business with which you are familiar.
4. Research the level of tourism demand in your local areas. Document the sources of information you used.

REFERENCES AND FURTHER READING

Bord Fáilte, *Tourism Facts '98,* Bord Fáilte Market Research and Planning Department: Dublin 1999.

Bord Fáilte, *Marketing Plan for Irish Tourism 1999,* Bord Fáilte Marketing Planning Department: Dublin 1999.

Bord Fáilte, *A Business Plan for Irish Tourism Marketing 1998–2003,* Bord Fáilte Marketing Planning Department: Dublin 1998.

Cooper, C., Fletcher, J., Gilbert, D. and Wanhill, S. *Tourism Principles and Practice,* 2nd edn., Longman: New York 1998.

Davidson and Maitland, *Tourism Destinations,* Hodder & Stoughton: London 1997.

Dibb, S., Simpkin, L., Pride, W.M. and Ferrell, O.C., *Marketing Concepts and Strategies,* 2nd European edn., Houghton Mifflin: Boston 1994.

Drucker, P., *Management: Tasks, Responsibilities, Practices,* Harper and Row: 1973.

Horwath Bastow Charleton, *Ireland and Northern Ireland Hotel Industry Survey 1998,* Horwath Bastow Charleton: Dublin 1999.

Hotel and Motel Management, 'Study Shows Service Still Stands Supreme', *Hotel and Motel Management,* 15 September: 1997.

Irish Hotel Federation, 'Annual Report', *Irish Hotel Federation:* Dublin 1999.

Kotler, P., *Marketing Management: Analysis, Planning, Implementation and Control,* 5th edn., Prentice Hall: New Jersey 1984.

Kotler, P., *Marketing for Hospitality and Tourism,* Prentice Hall: New Jersey 1996.

Kotler, P., Armstrong, G., Saunders, J. and Wong, V., *Principles of Marketing*, 2nd European edn., Prentice Hall: Europe 1999.

Levitt, T., 'Management Myopia', *Harvard Business Review*, vol. 38, July/August: 1962.

Mathieson and Wall, *Tourism: Economic, Physical and Social Impacts*, Longman: London 1982.

Medlik, S. *Managing Tourism*, Butterworth Heinemann: Oxford 1991.

Middleton, V., *Marketing in Travel and Tourism*, 2nd edn., Butterworth Heinemann: 1994.

Poon, A., *Competitive Strategies in Tourism*: 1994.

Powers, T., *Hospitality Marketing*, 2nd edn., John Wiley & Sons Inc.: New York 1997.

Reicheld, F. and Sasser, W.E., 'Zero Defections: Quality Comes to Services', *Harvard Business Review*, September/October: 1990.

Wearne, N. and Morrison, A., *Hospitality Marketing*, Butterworth Heinemann: 1996.

World Tourism Organisation, *Yearbook of Tourism Statistics*, World Tourism Organisation: Madrid, Spain 1999.

USEFUL WEB SITES

www.IHF.ie	Irish Hotel Federation web site
www.ITAA.ie	Irish Travel Agents Association
www.Ireland.travel.ie	Bord Fáilte's web site for marketing Ireland, Gulliver's site offers 11,000 places to stay and over 10,000 things to see and do
www.NITB.com	Northern Ireland Tourist Board web site, lists details of hotels, guesthouses and B&B occupancy, survey of visitor attractions and local authority estimates for 1998
www.beourguest.ie	Irish Hotel Federation's publication listing hotels and guesthouses in Ireland
www.ebid.ie	Irish online auction site

CHAPTER 2

The Marketing Environment

INTRODUCTION

A tourism and hospitality company can change its own internal policies at will. It can make its own decisions on personnel, financial, operational and marketing issues. However, every company encounters external forces over which it has very limited, if any, control. Some of these forces have a particular and specific impact on the tourism and hospitality sector, such as the development of new airline routes. Others, such as the changing nature of Irish culture, have an impact far beyond the tourism and hospitality sectors. In order to plan effectively companies need to be continually aware of these changes and adopt a structured approach to planning and monitoring.

CHAPTER OBJECTIVES

Following this chapter, students should be able to:

- Distinguish between the internal, macro and microenvironment
- Be familiar with the key forces in the macro and microenvironment for Irish tourism and hospitality marketers
- Understand the process, and alternative methods, of environmental scanning
- Have an insight into trends affecting the global tourism and hospitality sectors

THE MARKETING ENVIRONMENT

Kotler (1996) defines the marketing environment as 'the outside actors and forces that affect a company's ability to develop and maintain successful transactions with its target customers'.

In the marketing environment, forces such as the currency exchange rates, transport developments, changing customer preferences and the Internet all have the potential to have a strong impact on a tourism business, either positively or negatively. The process of continually looking for changes in these uncontrollable forces is called *environmental scanning*. Those companies who have a strong commitment to environmental scanning can expect to be more successful than those who are unstructured or lacking in commitment to the process (Teare and Olsen, 1992).

The marketing environment can be further subdivided into the internal environment, the macroenvironment and the microenvironment as illustrated in Figure 2.1.

FIGURE 2.1 — THE MARKETING ENVIRONMENT

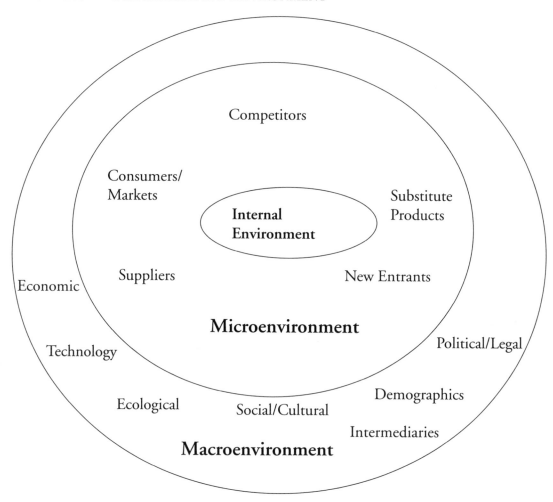

The *internal environment* consists of the other departments that the marketing department must influence in order to plan effectively, such as the operations department, the sales department, the finance and accounts department. With a high degree of integration and interdepartmental co-operation, companies can exert strong control over the internal environment.

The *microenvironment* consists of those factors that are specific to a company and its sector of industry. The microenvironment for tourism consists of the tourist consumer, suppliers (transport suppliers, hotel supplies, building contractors etc.), competitors and intermediaries (tour operators and travel agents). The company may exercise some control over these forces, such as in negotiating with tour operators.

The *macroenvironment* refers to the set of forces that impact across many sectors and industries simultaneously. These factors often have the capacity to make a profound impact on individual businesses, although sometimes the shifts happen in a gradual, rather than a rapid, fashion. Macroenvironmental forces are political, economic, social/cultural, technological, ecological and demographic.

Now let us examine the major forces in the market-place in more detail.

THE MICROENVIRONMENT

The Tourism and Hospitality Market

A market may be defined as potential or actual demand. Those in the tourism and hospitality industry need to be aware of how markets are performing over time, and any noticeable trends. For tourism, several dimensions exist to the term *market*. We may be referring to the global tourism trends, the national position or regional and local trends. We may mean visitor numbers from specific geographic markets, or visitors who are visiting for a specific reason, or to experience specific types of product.

At the macro level, tourism marketers need an overview of the performance of the overall tourism sector. Those who are targeting overseas visitors need to observe the trend in visitor numbers into Ireland and to their particular country or region.

International Tourism Trends

National tourism organisations and large hospitality organisations need to carefully assess the trends happening within tourism internationally. Bord Fáilte and other national tourism organisations need accurate data to identify where the future growth in tourism lies. This forms the basis of strategic marketing efforts. International hotel chains monitor the environment to assess where they need to be investing for future profits.

The World Tourism Organisation (WTO) is the international body responsible for the collation of international visitor statistics. Trends in tourist arrivals over the past ten years make interesting reading. Table 2.1 below charts the main movements in the international arrivals of the leading world destinations.

TABLE 2.1 — WORLD'S TOP TOURISM DESTINATIONS: INTERNATIONAL TOURIST ARRIVALS (EXCLUDING SAME-DAY VISITORS), THOUSANDS OF ARRIVALS — 1998

Rank			Countries	Arrivals 1998 (000s)	% Change 1998/97
1990	1995	1998			
1	1	1	France	70,000	4·7
3	3	2	Spain	47,743	10·0
2	2	3	United States	47,127	−1·3
4	4	4	Italy	34,829	2·2
7	5	5	United Kingdom	25,475	−0·2
12	8	6	China	24,000	1·0
8	7	7	Mexico	19,300	−0·3
27	9	8	Poland	18,820	−3·6
10	11	9	Canada	18,659	7·9
6	10	10	Austria	17,282	3·8
26	25	24	Ireland	6,073	9·3
			World Total	**625,236**	2·4

Source: World Tourism Organisation Press Release, January 1999

The increasing importance of China as a power in the international tourism marketplace is evident from the above table. Some commentators have predicted that China will be the world's number one tourism destination within twenty years (Naisbett, 1994). Within Europe, the position of most countries in the league table has remained relatively stable; with the exception of Poland where, in the wake of communism, enormous progress has been made in developing its tourism industry.

Ireland's share of tourist arrivals has continued to increase. Its 9·3 per cent increase in international tourism arrivals for 1998 is almost four times the international arrivals average increase of 2·4 per cent. The Asian financial crisis of the late 1990s had a dramatic impact on tourism arrivals in countries in this region. This, in turn, served to depress international tourism, leading to the modest overall growth rate. Table 2.2 below isolates the arrival and receipt figures to allow an assessment of Ireland's performance in a European context.

TABLE 2.2 — PERFORMANCE OF GLOBAL REGIONS

1998 Estimates								
	Tourist Arrivals (000s)		% Change		Tourism Receipts (US$ Million)		% Change	
	1997	1998	98/97	97/96	1997	1998	98/97	97/96
World	610,763	635,236	2·4	2·4	435,981	444,741	2·0	0·1
Africa	23,157	24,903	7·5	6·1	9,018	9,551	5·9	3·3
Americas	118,481	120,190	1·4	1·3	118,767	121,225	2·1	5·6
East Asia/Pacific	87,953	86,927	−1·2	−1·2	76,627	73,739	−3·8	−6·9
Europe	361,509	372,523	3·0	3·2	218,155	226,104	3·6	−0·8
Middle East	14,833	15,622	5·3	5·3	9,135	9,722	6·4	10·8
South Asia	4,830	5,071	5·0	8·9	4,279	4,400	2·8	8·4

Source: World Tourism Organisation Press Release, January 1999

As the above table shows, Europe remains the dominant player in tourism arrivals, accounting for more than fifty per cent of total international arrivals. The impact of the Asian financial crisis on their tourism sector is also evident. In the European context, Ireland's growth rate of nine per cent is particularly impressive, at almost four times the European average.

Bord Fáilte publishes a large number of statistical reports based on their surveys and those carried out by the Central Statistics Office. Similar surveys are conducted by the Northern Ireland Tourist Board (NITB). These reports are detailed later in Chapter 3 (Marketing Research in Tourism and Hospitality Industries). It is essential to keep abreast of the trends in the various measures of tourist activity and consumption. The tables below represent the key facts that marketers need to monitor to derive an overview of the tourism market.

As stated above, the marketer needs an overview of the market. A key trend to observe is the total visitor figures, as well as the specific country or region from where the visitor originates. Table 2.3 below shows that Britain remains the most significant source of tourism business for Ireland.

TABLE 2.3 — TOURISM ARRIVALS INTO REPUBLIC OF IRELAND

Numbers (000s)	1988	1995	1996	1997	1998	1999
Britain	1,508	2,285	2,590	2,850	3,199	3,430
Mainland Europe	408	1,101	1,177	1,168	1,255	1,321
Germany	113	319	339	303	310	305
France	111	234	262	250	270	275
Italy	21	112	119	111	141	165
North America	419	641	729	777	858	950
US	385	587	660	718	789	860
Canada	34	54	69	60	69	90
Rest of World	90	204	186	213	221	243
Australia / New Zealand	46	89	88	107	124	136
Japan	n/a	30	33	36	26	28
Other Overseas	44	85	65	71	71	79
Total Overseas	2,425	4,231	4,682	5,007	5,534	5,943
Northern Ireland *	582	587	607	580	530	460
Total Out-of-State **	4,252	4,818	5,289	5,587	6,064	6,403
Domestic Trips ***	4,161	6,924	6,170	6,850	6,934	7,285

Source: Bord FáilteTourism Facts 1999

*   Northern Ireland numbers revised for 1995–1997 inclusive.
**   Marginal discrepancies with *provisional* WTO figures cited in Table 2.2.
*** Domestic trips in 1988 are not comparable due to changes in survey methodology.

Annual variances for smaller markets are subject to lower levels of statistical confidence.

In assessing trends in tourism numbers to Northern Ireland, the Northern Ireland Tourist Board publishes a number of reports annually. Tables 2.4 and 2.5 below show the changes in the number of trips made to Northern Ireland in 1998, from all countries, including the Republic of Ireland.

TABLE 2.4 — VISITORS TO NORTHERN IRELAND IN 1998

		% change with 1997
Trips	1·477 million	+4
Nights	7·835 million	+4
Spend	Stg£217m	+4 (+2 in real terms allowing for inflation)

Source: Northern Ireland Tourism Facts 1998

From Table 2.5 below, the positive impact that the first ceasefire in 1994 had can be seen in the dramatic increase in visitor numbers to Northern Ireland the following year. The collapse of this first ceasefire can be seen to have had the effect of reversing the gains made.

TABLE 2.5 — IMPACT OF CEASEFIRES ON VISITOR NUMBERS

	Trips (000s)	Nights (000s)	Revenue Stg£m
1990	1,153	7,091	153
1991	1,186	7,160	162
1992	1,254	7,466	162
1993	1,262	7,794	173
1994	1,293	7,804	183
1995	1,557	8,500	214
1996	1,436	7,700	206
1997	1,415	7,500	208
1998	1,477	7,835	217

Source: Northern Ireland Tourism Facts 1998

Marketers wishing to assess future opportunities can use the data above to develop trend charts. These can be helpful in making projections about future trends.

Marketers who wish to promote particular products such as angling, cruising and hillwalking are interested to see the overall levels of interest in their particular product and also to glean an insight into the trends. Figure 2.2 below shows that the most popular participation activity for tourists remains walking, with more than a quarter of a million tourists engaging in this activity. Golf tourism is a lucrative source of high-spending tourists and showed the largest increase from 1997 to 1998, with numbers up an impressive twenty-two per cent.

FIGURE 2.2 — TOURIST PARTICIPATION ACTIVITY RATINGS

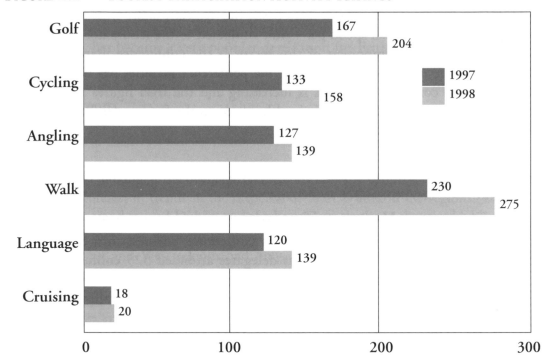

Source: Bord Fáilte Tourism Facts 1998

Geographic Analysis: Numbers

Marketers need to be conscious of the overall trends in tourism internationally. For Ireland, domestic tourism constitutes only a third of the total revenue from tourism. It is therefore essential to keep abreast of the trends in holiday-taking in overseas markets, in Europe and further afield. These form the basis on which projections can be made, recognising that different markets are experiencing different levels of growth. Table 2.6 below shows the percentage of the tourist market accounted for by the major purposes of visit.

TABLE 2.6 — MAIN PURPOSE OF VISIT (PERCENTAGE OF TOURIST ARRIVALS)

	1994	1995	1996	1997	1998	1999
Holiday	41	42	42	41	39	37
VFR *	24	23	23	24	23	24
Business/Conference	20	21	21	21	24	25
Other	15	14	14	14	14	14
	100	100	100	100	100	100

Source: Bord Fáilte Tourism Facts 1999
* Visiting Friends and Relatives.

A Framework for Analysing Competition

International competition for tourist spending power is enormous. National Tourism Organisations (NTOs) must compete vigorously with each other. While the overall size of the tourism cake is increasing there are significant changes taking place, especially at regional level. Competition has the capacity to have a direct, profound and immediate effect on the prospects of a company or destination. Tourism organisations need to monitor the changes in the forces that can influence the long-term attractiveness of their sector. Michael E. Porter of the Harvard Business School identifies five forces that determine the attractiveness of a segment. It is the interplay between these forces, shown in Figure 2.3, that determines the degree of segment attractiveness.

FIGURE 2.3 — PORTER'S FIVE FORCES FRAMEWORK

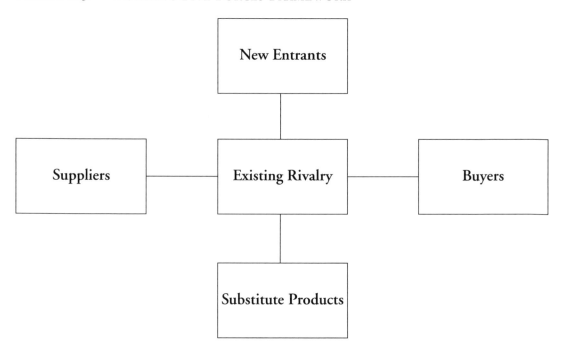

Threat of Intense Segment Rivalry

If a segment already contains numerous competitors, or an expansion in numbers is likely, then this can reduce segment profitability. The case in Exhibit 2.2 illustrates this quite well for the Dublin hotel accommodation segment.

Threat of New Entrants

If it is costly to enter a market (high entry barriers) and easy to leave it (low exit barriers) then the segment will be more profitable than one where the situation is reversed. For international tourist markets, the rise in Asia-Pacific and Eastern European destinations poses an increased threat to the once dominant European players. In Ireland, increased deregulation has led to much greater entry of domestic and foreign competition on existing and new routes. Another example is golf, where Irish and Scottish golf courses now face new competition from Portuguese and Spanish courses to attract golfing tourists.

Threat of Substitute Products

Substitute products give consumers a choice and thus increase their price sensitivity. This, in turn, will depress segment profitability. The opening of the Channel Tunnel led to serious consequences for the existing ferry companies. New technology such as videoconferencing threatens to eliminate the need for certain business trips. This has obvious knock-on effects for hotels and conference centres.

Threat of Suppliers' Growing Bargaining Power

Determining the suppliers in the tourism sector is difficult, as the sector is best understood to be a complex system. Hotels are key suppliers to the sector in that they provide accommodation services, but equally they are themselves buyers of a wide range of services and goods. While airlines are an integral part of the tourism system, they also are a provider of transport services for the rest of the industry. Direct suppliers to the tourist industry include the building sector, which is responsible for the construction of hotels and tourism attractions. Other key suppliers are the labour force who are required on a full- and part-time basis to staff the sector, other suppliers include advertising and marketing services companies such as brochure producers.

If demand for the supplied service exceeds the capacity to supply that service, then this will lead to the increased price of the supplied item. As previously stated, the labour market is a key supplier to the tourism industry. As the demand for labour has not been met with an increased supply, the price (wages) has increased, leading to predictions of reduced profitability in the sector. Companies have to carefully monitor trends in this area. The case-study in Exhibit 2.2 illustrates the challenges involved. Increasingly, the tourism sector has to respond to the requirements of prospective employees for more sympathetic working environments. One example of the industry response to the trend toward increased employee demands is the Irish Hotel Federation's Quality Employer Scheme.

Threat of Buyers' Growing Bargaining Power

The bargaining power of buyers will increase if they become more concentrated in number, if the product is undifferentiated, if the costs of switching supply are low. As buyer bargaining power increases, then there is an increase in competition, and consequent reduction in profitability. European tour operator groups have seen huge merger and acquisition activity in recent years. The Irish tour operator business is now dominated by British companies, most of whom entered the Irish market in recent years by acquisition.

The dynamic nature of these trends needs to be recognised, as does the fact that many are interrelated. For example, changes in economic circumstances affect the tourists' attitudes, as well as behaviour. A feeling that their personal circumstances are improving will often be reflected in a shift from savings to spending. Indeed, in Ireland this is evident in the fact that the Celtic Tiger economy has resulted in increases in demand for specialised types of tourism, such as helicopter tours.

Suppliers

Transport providers are key suppliers to the tourism and hospitality sector. These include the main air carriers such as Aer Lingus, Ryanair, City Jet, British Midland and British Airways. The ferries too provide a useful framework to understand the arrival patterns of the guest. Marketers recognise that changes in the transport infrastructure can have a profound effect on the level and nature of tourism. New routes can have a positive effect in building tourism. Horan Regional Airport in Mayo succeeded in developing new routes between there and Switzerland, where the angling market is particularly targeted.

Aer Lingus introduced a direct service to Los Angeles in May 1999. From the inception of the service it has proved a great success, contributing to a twenty-six per cent increase in transatlantic traffic for the first five months of 1999 compared with the same time period in 1998. Those in the tourism sector recognise the capacity of such routes to open up new opportunities. Hotels and other service providers will have increased opportunities for business from the US West Coast as a result, and many may now develop specific promotions to target this geographic market for the first time.

Aer Rianta, the state controlled airport authority, recorded 7·5 million passengers through Ireland for the first half of 1999, a fourteen per cent increase on the corresponding 1998 figure. The European market accounted for almost thirty per cent of the throughput with a nineteen per cent increase for the half year. Shannon and Cork airports handled 925,879 and 669,482 passengers respectively, both up about seventeen per cent. It's not just a question of new routes opening up. Ryanair has been a classic example of how a completely radical approach to the market has revolutionised their business.

Accommodation

Accommodation is a key component of the tourism and hospitality sector. There have been rapid developments in the numbers of hotels under construction in Ireland. There are significant regional disparities in the types of accommodation available. As can be seen from Table 2.10, the importance of the South-West is evident, with nineteen per cent of hotels and thirty-one per cent of guesthouses.

TABLE 2.10 — PROPERTY TYPE: REGIONAL LOCATION

Region	Hotels	Hotels %	Guest-houses	Guest-houses %	Total	Total %
South-East	94	11	55	11	149	11
South-West	154	19	133	28	287	22
Shannon	108	13	61	13	169	13
Ireland West	137	16	64	13	201	15
North-West	105	12	48	10	153	12
Midlands-East	105	12	33	7	138	10
Dublin	141	17	87	18	228	17
	844	100	481	100	1,325	100

Source: Tourism Quality Services (2000)

It should be noted that Table 2.10 is based on properties, rather than rooms. A more customer-centred perspective would be to assess the usage of accommodation preferences for various individual markets and as a whole. This is illustrated in Table 2.11.

TABLE 2.11 — WHERE OVERSEAS TOURISTS STAY: DISTRIBUTION OF BEDNIGHTS‡

	Total	Britain	Mainland Europe	North America	Rest of World
Hotels	12	15	8	17	7
Guesthouses, B&Bs	18	22	16	20	11
Rented	17	8	24	19	26
Caravan and Camping	3	2	5	*	1
Hostels	5	2	6	5	8
Friends and Relatives	30	44	17	30	24
Other	15	7	24	9	23
Total Bednights (million)	45·3	20·1	13·6	8·9	2·7

Source: Bord Fáilte Tourism Facts 1999

‡ One bednight is deemed to be a visitor staying one night. As an example a couple visiting Ireland for a week would be staying for a total of fourteen bednights.

Also the dynamic nature of the accommodation market, Dublin in particular, has experienced a huge boom in the construction of hotels as well as an expansion of other types of accommodation. This has led some to review the prospects for the sector in the medium term. Exhibit 2.2 outlines the challenges facing Dublin hoteliers.

EXHIBIT 2.2

MARKETING ENVIRONMENT *IN ACTION*

HOTEL CHARGES FALL DUE TO EXCESS CAPACITY

Hotel operators are facing a sharp drop in profits, as the consequences of oversupply in the market become apparent in the near future, according to expert analysis of the industry. The twin pressures of rising staff costs and falling room occupancy levels will impact most strongly in the three-star mid-market sector.

Accountants BDO Simpson Xavier — who have acted as hotel market analyst for many years — predict that even assuming the phenomenal current growth rates in room nights continue, room occupancy in Dublin hotels will fall to fifty-eight per cent by the year 2001. In 1998, occupancy levels in Dublin dropped to seventy-four per cent from the 1997 level of seventy-seven per cent, and indications were that the downward trend would continue in 1999. A drop of the order predicted by BDO Simpson Xavier would put a serious squeeze on profits in many hotels and almost certainly lead to some closures.

Although the building boom in Dublin hotels is showing some signs of slowing down, projects that have recently been completed and those due to come on stream in the near future have produced a glut of available hotel rooms. While visitor numbers to Dublin have also exploded — up from 880,000 in 1988 to three million in 1998 — the rate of increase in hotel rooms has overtaken them. Bord Fáilte figures from October 1998 predicted 2,050 new rooms in 1999 and 1,813 the following year. With an estimated 11,000 rooms in Dublin in 1998, figures of this order represent huge increases.

Hotels due to be completed in Dublin during 1999 included the Four Seasons and Bewley's apart-hotel at the RDS in Ballsbridge, Noel O'Callaghan's project at the corner of Harcourt St. and Cuffe St., the Westin at College St. and a project adjacent to Pearse St. Fire Station. Since the beginning of 1998 hotels have been opened on St Stephens Green (the Fitzwilliam), in Smithfield (Chief O'Neill), Clondalkin (Ibis), Fleet St. (the Morgan), Ormond Quay (the Morrison), Dame St. (Trinity Arch), Camden St. (Camden de Luxe and Camden Court), Pearse St. (Holiday Inn), Northumberland Road (the Schoolhouse), Booterstown (the Radisson/St Helens), Tallaght (Tallaght Plaza), Drumcondra (Regency Airport) and Dublin Airport (Great Southern). According to Ronan

King of BDO Simpson Xavier, by the end of 1999, £708 million will have been spent in hotel development in Dublin since 1992.

Industry sources confirm the trends predicted in the BDO Simpson Xavier report. Michael Governey of the Conrad Hotel on Earlsfort Terrace said: 'In 1994 there were seven 4/5-star hotels in Dublin. There are now sixteen. Next year (2000) there'll be nineteen. Hotels have to be very strong on business planning and marketing. Those that aren't marketing and staff training will be in serious trouble.' The Conrad, he points out, now employs a full-time training officer.

John Power of the Irish Hotels Federation points out that the corporate sector in particular is very strong in Dublin and is anxious to play down reports of a downturn. 'Dublin is still fairly solid,' he said. 'In the rest of the country supply is beginning to have an effect — especially the number of holiday homes that have been built in recent years.'

He agrees that *marketing and staff* will be vital issues for the industry. 'It's no longer a low-pay industry.'

Over the last year wages have increased by seven to eight per cent, he claims, although anecdotal evidence suggests that hotels are finding it harder than ever to hold on to staff.

Source: Adapted and reprinted by permission of Pat Leahy, *Sunday Business Post*, 2 August 1999

THE MACROENVIRONMENT

As stated earlier, the *macroenvironment* refers to the set of forces that impact across many sectors and industries simultaneously. These factors often have the capacity to make profound impact on individual businesses, although sometimes the shifts happen in a gradual, rather than a rapid, fashion. Table 2.12 outlines some of the macro trends that are most pertinent to tourism. Almost all the trends described below are happening on a global scale, while they manifest themselves in slightly different ways in each particular country. As Irish tourism marketers are competing on a global basis, they need to be sensitive to these changes.

TABLE 2.12 — MACROENVIRONMENT FORCES

Macroenvironmental Factor
Demographics
Social and Cultural
Economic
Political and Legal
Technological
Ecological

Demographic Environment

Demographics represent the characteristics of the population and workforce.

Several key demographic trends are evident nationally and internationally. The Central Statistics Office (CSO) is the Government department that compiles the key demographic statistics. Included in the demographic statistics they report on are the population age structure, sex, race, education, language, birth and death rates, geographic distribution and income levels. Detailed below is an extract from the 1996 Census, examining the changing nature of Irish households.

EXHIBIT 2.3

DEMOGRAPHICS *IN ACTION*

HOUSEHOLD SIZE DECREASES — 1996 CENSUS

The average size of private households in permanent housing units in the Republic of Ireland fell from 3·34 in 1991 to 3·14 in 1996, which is the continuation of a long-term decline. The report shows that the average size in 1946 was 4·16. The Census 96 volume also details how the smallest households are to be found in Dublin County Borough with an average of 2·67 people. The largest households were enumerated in South Dublin with an average size of 3·50.

The total number of private households is up from 1·029 million to 1·123 million between 1991 and 1996 — a rise of 94,000 or nine per cent. The average number of children per family has fallen from 2·2 in 1981 to 1·8 in 1996.

Households composed of one person increased by seventeen per cent (+34,274) since 1991 — almost a third of these were in Dublin County and County Borough with 78,913 units. One-person households represent twenty-two per cent of the total number in the State. South Dublin had the lowest figure at twelve per cent.

Census 96 Volume 3 — Household Composition and Family Units also shows that there has been a fifteen per cent increase in the number of lone-parent households with children in the State, from 109,600 in 1991 to 125,500 in 1996. Almost seventy-two per cent of lone-parent households were in urban areas.

People over Sixty-Five Living Alone

One in four people aged sixty-five years and over lived alone in 1996. However, in Leitrim thirty-one per cent of those in that age category lived alone. South Dublin had the lowest percentage of people over sixty-five living alone at twenty per cent. For those aged seventy and over, twenty-eight per cent lived alone. Again Leitrim had the highest percentage at thirty-three per cent.

Source: CSO web site, (www.cso.ie)

The large increase in single person households offers a huge opportunity for tourism marketers, in areas such as packaged holidays targeted at young single people. In the developed world the birth rate is slowing down. This will lead to problems in providing a pool of young labour that is required in the tourism and hospitality sectors.

We are seeing an ageing, but healthier, population in developed countries. The over fifties in particular will become an increasing focus of the tourism marketer's attention because they hold a disproportionate amount of total disposable income.

A continuing increase in urbanisation is leading to new opportunities for short break tourism products and services.

Family structures are changing, as discussed later, in Chapter 4 (Consumer Behaviour). With more double-income households being created, increased participation by women is a pronounced feature in most developed countries. Large opportunities are opening up for those targeting female business travellers. In the US these travellers account for almost fifty per cent of business trips.

Social and Cultural Environment

As discussed in more detail in the following chapter, culture represents a series of learned patterns of behaviour that are shared within a society. Culture is dynamic and constantly evolving. Social norms and patterns of behaviour are also subject to change. The past decade in Ireland is commonly accepted as having witnessed fundamental shifts in attitudes and behaviour. Irish society, like many others, is adapting to an era of global communications, multinational corporations, worker mobility and, quite significantly, tourism and travel. Indeed, many relatively new patterns of culture have been imported to Ireland as a result of exposure to them when on holidays. The *café culture* that is exemplified by Dublin's Temple Bar district bears a striking similarity to that seen in mainland Europe. Food service companies as well as pub and hotel designers have to be particularly sensitive to these shifts in taste.

EXHIBIT 2.4

SOCIAL AND CULTURAL ENVIRONMENT *IN ACTION*

BEWLEY'S

'Inoffensive and boring — the world standard for Cappuccino.'

David Schomer, one of the world's foremost experts on the science and art of espresso preparation, is clear and direct when it comes to the art of making a good cup of coffee. He made the above comment about the poor standards of Cappuccino preparation the world over when he was at an event in Dublin recently to try and increase awareness of properly-made coffee.

'One-third espresso plus five-parts milk in mousse form is best.'

David runs a number of coffee bars in North Seattle under the Espresso Vivace brand and he had plenty to say about his love of good coffee and how little of it is made.

'Blends are best,' he explained. 'Using one bean only is like having a light on a Christmas tree of only the one colour. Coffee flavours are so fragile that the grinder can destroy beans if it gets too hot, for example.' As in the UK, coffee consumption in Ireland is very low compared to our Continental counterparts. The Scandinavians are the biggest consumers.

The event marked the rise in popularity of speciality coffee in Ireland which Bewley's believes is still in its infancy. Here, Bewley's has over sixty per cent of the roasted and ground coffee market in the catering sector. Bewley's now believes that its image is viewed as being too traditional for the young Cappuccino drinker in the twenty-eight- to thirty-five-year-old age group and it has set about doing something to rectify the situation. Thirteen years ago, there were six people in Dublin using the espresso method for preparing coffee; now there are scores of them. The market for speciality coffees is growing at a remarkable rate with espresso coffee now accounting for over six per cent of all coffee consumed in Ireland.

Nevertheless, the idea persists that '*real men* don't drink Cappuccino and that they prefer espresso instead,' explained David McKernan, sales and marketing manager at Bewley's. He is pleased to see that this image is slowly beginning to change with the retailer's help. Café en Seine represents Bewley's biggest volume outlet for its coffee products. 'The Café culture, which mainland Europe has enjoyed for the last ten years or more, has now hit Ireland,' pointed out Patrick Bewley, managing director of Bewley's Coffee. 'Young and old people alike are taking time to experience new culinary tastes in coffee.'

Source: Reprinted by permission: *Licensing World,* 31 March 1998

In our everyday speech, the influence of UK and US sitcoms, and Hollywood films, can be seen in the effect that they have on language usage.

Of course, while Irish culture is changing, it retains many unique dimensions including music, language, sport and the intangible set of attitudes to life that mark out the Irish psyche. It's not all one-way traffic. The Irish pub concept has taken Europe and Asia by storm. In the most unlikely of places the pint of Guinness, the Irish Stew and general good *craic* are to be found.

Economic Environment

Tourism and hospitality is today the single largest industry in the world, and a significant contributor to wealth in Ireland. Globally Bord Fáilte figures suggest that the tourism sector in 1998 accounted for five per cent of exports and some 6·4 per cent of Gross National Product in the Republic of Ireland, providing jobs for 126,000 people in the process. This represented more than one in twelve of the workforce. As tourism is so integral a part of the global economy it is essential to scan a variety of economic trends and indicators that can impact on a business. Key economic trends that should be considered include:

Foreign Exchange Rates — the rate of exchange of one currency for another. When there is a weakening in a country's currency this is usually beneficial for tourism, as it makes the country's services and products cheaper for visitors. The introduction of the Euro has prompted much discussion in the tourism sector. The introduction of the Euro is predicted to have a generally positive impact on tourism as the costs of changing currencies within the Euro region are eliminated. Marketers will also find it easier to forecast arrival numbers from other Euro zone countries. However, Irish tourism will continue to be exposed to fluctuations between the Euro and non-Euro zone members who include our two biggest single sources of tourism revenue (called *source markets*), namely Britain and the United States. Forecasts on likely exchange rate movements should be a feature of any environment scanning process. Such forecasts feature in the *Know your Market* reports produced by Bord Fáilte for a wide variety of source markets.

Gross National Product (GNP) — the total value of all goods and services produced in a country per year and its growth rate. Where the GNP figure is rising strongly this is a good predictor of a strong demand for tourism and hospitality services, as people will have more disposable income to spend. Tourism is said to be highly income elastic, i.e. as income increases demand for tourism increases at an even higher rate — the opposite is also true. As income falls, then tourism expenditure is among the first item to be cut, as witnessed in the Asian crisis discussed earlier in the chapter.

Taxation and Tariffs — taxes on individuals and companies imposed by government. Included in this are port of exit and entry charges which directly impact on the tourism sector. As international governments have woken up to the huge potential of tourism, they have increasingly sought to tax the sector, especially through sales taxes. Some countries and individual regions also impose specific tourist taxes called bednight taxes, where the money is collected from accommodation providers. Proposals to introduce such taxes in Ireland have met with considerable controversy, with many predicting that it would threaten the industry, as illustrated in Exhibit 2.5 below.

EXHIBIT 2.5

ECONOMIC ENVIRONMENT *IN ACTION*

THE TOURIST TAX

In the Autumn of 1998 the Irish Hotels Federation lobbied TDs, Senators and Councillors in a bid to stop the levies on tourists proposed by Government sources, Dublin Corporation and Galway County Council.

In the run-up to the 1998 Budget, three proposals emerged. These were:

- A £5 tax on all incoming visitors which would be used to make up for the expected shortfall in EU funding for tourism promotion
- A £3 per night bed tax in Dublin, proposed by Dublin Corporation, which would be used to develop tourism infrastructure in the city
- A £1 levy on each visitor to the Aran Islands, proposed by Galway County Council, which would be used to fund a waste management project

The Minister for Tourism, Dr Jim McDaid, expressed reservations about the Galway proposal and a number of bodies including the Institute of Chartered Accountants all opposed the three proposals. So too did the chairman of Jurys plc, Walter Beatty, who pointed out that Jurys has an annual rates bill of £450,000 in Dublin alone. The Irish Hotels Federation (IHF) described the taxes as tourist abuse. The IHF rebutted Dublin Corporation's claims that most major cities have tourism taxes. 'This is simply not true', said chief executive, John Power, who argued that visitors to Ireland already pay a disproportionate amount of tax because of our high VAT rates and excise duties.

'Tourists should not be taxed to pay for infrastructural services,' he added.

Hoteliers expressed concerns that if one local authority imposed a tourist levy, others would follow their lead and visitors could end up paying several levies if they travelled to the principal tourist destinations. There was also concern that an initial levy, set at a modest figure, could increase over the years once it had been accepted.

Source: Adapted courtesy of *Hotel and Catering Magazine,* 30: September 1998

While the above mentioned taxes have not been introduced to date, the issue of taxing tourists, particularly as a means of funding international marketing, remains a hotly contested issue.

As the world economy continues to integrate, then the impact of economic change in distant markets will have an ever-increasing bearing on the success of tourism enterprises.

Political and Legal Environment

The political environment includes the following:

Foreign politics — the politics of a local or a host country; host country laws.

Domestic politics — politics that exist in the company's home or parent country; home country laws.

International politics — the interaction of the overall environmental forces of two or more countries; international laws.

For the large international hotel chain, or resort operator, it is particularly important to monitor political developments. Large tourism companies such as Club Med carefully monitor developments in countries where political stability is uncertain, such as Russia. In Ireland, these concerns are of less importance.

European directives do, however, have a direct impact on Irish tourism. The abolition of duty-free sales for intra-EU travel in the summer of 1999 was politically motivated and was predicted to have disastrous consequences. In retrospect, the impact was not as great as feared. Nevertheless such political developments have the capacity to affect marketing plans. Another area where European political developments impact directly on tourism is that of support funding structures from Europe. The Western Seaboard counties, Border counties and Northern Ireland retained their Objective One status for the period of the Operational Plans 1999–2005. This should provide increased opportunities for tourism enterprises in these areas, but may pose a threat to enterprises in counties where assistance will be reduced.

The political environment on the island of Ireland has a direct impact on the tourism sector. Surveys have shown a continuing reluctance among many visitors to visit Ireland, and particularly Northern Ireland, as a result of their anxieties over violence. When these fears are allayed, then the impact on tourism is positive. This was most dramatically evident following the first IRA ceasefire in 1994. Tourism flows to Northern Ireland increased dramatically the following year as seen previously in Table 2.5.

In terms of the legal environment, at national level, the influence of Government in legislative matters can impact both positively and negatively on the tourism sector. Governments take decisions that can have profound direct or indirect impacts on tourism interests. The *Shannon-Stopover* decision is one such instance.

In 1994, the Irish Government abolished the Shannon Stopover. Under this rule all airlines travelling to and from the US to Ireland were obliged to stop-over at Shannon, even if most of their passengers stayed on the plane to disembark at Dublin. Tourism interests in the Mid-West region vehemently opposed the move, arguing that it would have a severe impact on visitor numbers to the entire region. Exhibit 2.6 details the saga.

EXHIBIT 2.6

POLITICAL ENVIRONMENT *IN ACTION*

THE SHANNON AIRPORT STOPOVER

Prophets of doom and gloom were predicting disastrous consequences for Shannon Airport when it lost its exclusive transatlantic status in 1994. Prior to this all transatlantic flights to and from Ireland were obliged to stop-off at Shannon even if their final destination was Dublin.

General Manager, Barry O'Shea, who has spent forty years working at the airport said: 'In…forty years I do not remember a year when there was not some crisis. There always seems to be a crisis. But I have absolute confidence in the staff at Shannon that always rise to the occasion and meet any difficulties that present themselves.'

Aer Rianta set up Shannon Airport Marketing and appointed Martin Moroney as General Manager. Shannon Airport Marketing has a presence in all the airport's main markets, including North America, Germany, France as well as the other main European countries. O'Shea points to the large-scale investment earmarked for the airport and to new services from both the US and Britain. At the same time, Aer Rianta is concerned with more than just upping the tourist numbers. 'We are trying to focus the airport as being a vehicle for traffic in and out,' says O'Shea. 'I keep emphasising traffic rather than just tourism. Nineteen ninety-five was the first full year of the change of transatlantic status. At the end of the year, passenger figures grew by 2·4 per cent, which was very satisfactory given that we had a loss of 150,000 transit passengers,' notes O'Shea.

One of the major problems for Shannon has been the number of Americans who *backtrack* to Ireland. These come via Britain and get cheap flights or ferries and miss out on the West of Ireland altogether. Backtracking was up forty-five per cent last year, despite the fact that many thought getting rid of the Shannon stopover would help to solve the problem.

With two resident Aeroflot aircraft, the Shannon facility is the largest Aeroflot operation outside Russia. Air Ukraine and the Belarus carrier, Belavia, also use Shannon to service five destinations in the CIS and a fourth in the US.

Shannon Airport appears to have weathered the storm caused by the abolition of the stopover, although its growth has been nowhere near as spectacular as that of Dublin airport. By 1998, passenger traffic through Shannon Airport had risen to a record 1·84 million, according to airport manager Barry O'Shea. Terminal traffic was up seven per cent to 1·43 million. Transit traffic, on the other hand, was down fifteen per cent because of fewer Aeroflot flights and the loss of stopovers by TWA and Saudia. Cargo traffic was up twenty-one per cent to 43,000 tonnes.

For Shannon Airport, further political and competitive threats lie ahead if its largest customer, Aer Lingus, joins a strategic alliance involving a large US airline. Many predict that this will happen only after complete deregulation.

In February 1999, a report drawn up for the Shannon Airport Marketing Consultative Committee, among whose members are Shannon Development, Clare County Council and SIPTU, warned of a stark future for Shannon Airport if the proposed link between Aer Lingus and British Airways/American Airlines went ahead. It predicted that transatlantic traffic into Shannon would drop from its current level of 600,000 to 180,000. The report assumed that the country adopted an open skies policy allowing airlines to serve whatever routes they wished. In those circumstances, it says, much of the Shannon traffic would move to Dublin. It urged the government to think seriously about whether an open skies policy was appropriate to accompany the proposed Aer Lingus alliance with other carriers. Many see a consequence of this being a further reduction in flights from Shannon to the US. Clearly the political dimension of the marketing environment is extremely important.

Source: Adapted from the following sources:
28 March 1996, *Business and Finance*
7 January 1999, *Examiner*
30 June 1999, *Irish Independent*

Changes in laws need to be carefully monitored. The tourism sector is continually making representations to government about modifications it would like to see to current legislation or lobbying for the introduction of new laws. A huge variety of laws impact on tourism marketing. We can identify two categories of impact.

Firstly, laws that impact on the tourism sector but which are not specific to the sector, such as laws governing employment practices, competition, EU harmonisation, planning and consumer protection.

Secondly, laws that have a direct and specific impact on the tourism sector. Among the most important are:

Tourist Traffic Acts 1939 — governing, among other things the registration and grading of accommodation.
Intoxicating Liquor Acts 1833–1995 — the retail sale of liquor.
Public Dance Halls Acts — 1935 onwards.
Local Government Planning and Development Acts — 1963 onwards.
Package Holidays and Travel Trade Act 1995.
Transport (Tour Operators and Travel Agents) Act 1982.
Hotel Proprietors Act 1963.
Occupiers Liability Act 1995.

Technological Environment

In the tourism and hospitality industry identifying, and responding to, technological change is identified as one of the key factors for success in the future of most companies. When we hear the term *technology*, images that spring to mind are invariably those associated with the communications and computer industries. However, technology is a much broader concept than computers and communications.

Daft (1989) defines it as 'the utilisation of available knowledge and techniques to produce products and services'.

Stipanuk (1993) argues that there is a danger of seeing technology as being merely a tool of tourism, as is the case with transport technologies such as the Chunnel train linking France and Britain. He argues that we need to adopt a broader perspective of technology, one that recognises technology as being more than a mere tool, but rather as an important creator, protector and destroyer of the tourist experience. When monitoring trends in tourism technology we need to divide technologies into three types as follows:

Hard Technologies

Traditional technologies with an emphasis on physical development. Table 2.13 illustrates the major subcategories of hard technologies and how they manifest themselves in the tourism and hospitality sectors.

Soft Technologies

Managerial systems, ways of planning such as holiday timeshares, hotel franchising, total quality management.

Hard/Soft Technologies

Combinations of hard and soft technologies.

TABLE 2.13 — AREAS OF TECHNOLOGICAL ADVANCEMENT AND EXAMPLES OF IMPORTANT INNOVATIONS FOR THE HOSPITALITY AND TOURISM INDUSTRY

Technology	Example
Communication	Computerised reservation systems (CRS) linking airlines, hotels and car rental structures, fax machines, Internet, telenet, modems, local area networks (LANs), telephone systems and voice mail, e-mail, point-of-sale, touch-screen ordering, voice recognition, videoconferencing, mobile phones

TABLE 2.13 — AREAS OF TECHNOLOGICAL ADVANCEMENT AND EXAMPLES OF IMPORTANT INNOVATIONS FOR THE HOSPITALITY AND TOURISM INDUSTRY *contd.*

Technology	Example
Transportation	High speed and magnet levitation trains, Concorde, airbus, smart roads, Channel Tunnel
Safety and Security	Electronic key access to hotel rooms, credit card locks, biometrics (i.e. identification of hand, fingerprint, retina needed for room access), digital keypads, fire protection systems, infrared sensors, closed circuit television systems
Food and Nutrition	Biotechnology, genetic engineering, seed vaccination technology, fat-free foods, non-nutritive sweeteners
Computers and Software /Electronic Equipment	Computer centres and PCs in hotel rooms, debit or smart card technology, videotext, interactive computer technology, smart hotel rooms, property management systems (PMS), artificial intelligence, decision support systems, database applications, yield management
Robotics	Increased use of robotics and automation in airline catering and hospital food service, sensor fusion technology
Energy	Management controlled computer-aided technologies for electricity and water conservation in hotels, customer-controlled in-room consoles to control comfort level
Layout and Design	Food courts, kiosks, boutique hotels
Equipment	Greater variety of multipurpose food service equipment, point-of-sale food service and hotel technologies, handicap access
Packaging	Controlled and modified atmosphere packaging (CAP and MAP), biosensors, interactive packaging, environmentally friendly and functional packaging, edible cellulose packaging, reusable containers

Source: Adapted from Teare and Olsen, 1992

Ecological Environment

Of increasing concern to today's tourist is the impact that tourism has on the eco-system. Large hotel developments are heavy users of scarce resources such as water and often place intolerable strain on sewerage systems. The building of roads to facilitate tourist access has harmful effects on sensitive wildlife habitats. Tourists themselves contribute to the problem; for example, soil erosion is a feature of many of the most scenic walking and hiking routes. Increasingly tourists are taking stock of the consequences of their choices. This is partly reflected in the huge rise in what is termed ecotourism, where tourists seek to explore natural habitats in a non-intrusive and sustainable way. Tourism organisations are being forced to respond to this increased sensitivity to ecological concerns. Interest in being environmentally sensitive is increasing rapidly. Green Globe is a international membership organisation which tourism enterprises can join provided they meet required environmental standards. Green Globe has developed a number of Priority Action Areas, as identified in *Agenda 21 for the Travel and Tourism Industry: Toward Environmentally Sustainable Development*. This report is produced by the World Travel and Tourism Council, World Tourism Organisation and the Earth Council, to help tourism organisations focus on achievable environmental improvement projects. As a member of Green Globe, companies endeavour to take action in one or more of the following environment related areas:

- Involvement of staff, customers and communities in environmental issues
- Waste minimisation, re-use and recycling
- Energy efficiency, conservation and management
- Management of freshwater resources
- Waste-water management
- Control of hazardous substances
- Transport environment
- Design of sustainability
- Land use and planning
- Protection of air quality
- Noise control
- Environmentally sensitive purchasing
- Environmentally sensitive building, design and construction

Increasingly companies will seek to use their policies for environmental sensitivity as a means of fostering customer support and goodwill. Exhibit 2.7 details the actions taken by the Irish Airport Authority, Aer Rianta in this regard.

EXHIBIT 2.7

ECOLOGICAL ENVIRONMENT *IN ACTION*

ENVIRONMENTAL ISSUES AT AER RIANTA

Aer Rianta is responsible for managing Ireland's major airports at Dublin, Shannon and Cork. The first flight from Dublin took place on 19 January 1940. A record 9·1 million passengers passed through Dublin Airport in 1996 — over one million more than in 1995, giving the airport one of the highest rates of growth in its history. In 1999, it was projected that some eleven million passengers would transit through the airport. Dublin Airport has experienced significant growth over the last few years.

Over the last three years, the traffic figures have grown by one million passengers per annum and it is expected that the airport will handle 11·3 million passengers by the year 2000.

Environmental Issues at Dublin Airport

There are four categories of environmental issues for airport operators:

1. Those arising from the airport's function as a landing and take-off point for aircraft.
2. Those arising from the transport of passengers and accompanying persons to the airport.
3. Commercial operations.
4. Airport related industries, such as aircraft maintenance, cargo handling and transport depots.

The main issues that concern Dublin Airport are as follows:

Air Quality. Emissions from airport sources may be broken down into four main categories — aircraft operations, airside vehicle traffic, airport heating plant and landside vehicle traffic.

Waste. Aer Rianta Dublin Airport handled over ten million passengers in 1998 and this large passenger throughput produced almost two thousand tonnes of waste. The sources of this waste stream are varied and range from cardboard from the Duty Free operation to general office waste.

Energy Management. It is interesting to note that over the last twenty years the airport building has grown in footage by forty-nine per cent, the passenger figures have grown by 164 per cent, but energy consumption has reduced by thirty per cent.

Noise Management. Airlines have to follow designated flight paths to avoid causing noise over densely populated areas.

Water. Surface and ground water pollution at Dublin Airport can arise from the following causes:

- De-icing agents
- Anti-icing agents
- Fuel spillage
- Oil spillage
- Loss of containment of liquid or water-soluble cargo
- Aircraft cleaning
- Surplus fertilisers
- Pesticide residues
- Fire-fighting material
- Aircraft maintenance
- Water treatment chemicals from boiler systems

Visual Impact. As part of the overall programme to improve the aesthetics of the airport there were 15,000 bulbs, 20,000 shrubs and 5,000 trees planted at Dublin Airport in 1996.

Source: Adapted, with permission, from Chapter 10 of *Successful Environmental Management* by Joe Sheerin (Enviro Eire, 1997).

The Process of Environmental Scanning

While the future is uncertain, companies that adopt a structured approach to scanning the environment are more likely to be successful. There are three stages to the environmental scanning process, illustrated in Figure 2.4.

FIGURE 2.4 — THE SCANNING PROCESS

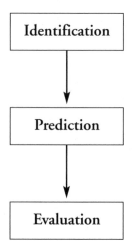

Stage 1: Identification

The company needs to understand what are the key factors that signal threats and opportunities in their sector. For example, hotels would identify computer reservation and Internet technology as factors that need to be carefully monitored, as they play such a critical role in their business. Large theme park operators would carefully assess population shifts of young people, especially children, as this has a bearing on site location and profitability. Airport authorities need to pay particular attention to political developments as discussed earlier in this chapter.

While companies will identify key forces to monitor especially thoroughly, they will continue to monitor all forces.

Stage 2: Prediction

Having identified the relevant forces, companies need to forecast the direction of change taking place and how strong such a change is. They need to assess the exact impact that the trend will have on their operations, and when the impact will be felt. For example, the proportion of people using the Internet to make their travel arrangements is increasing.

Stage 3: Evaluation

Companies need to determine exactly when the trend will occur and what actions it needs to take. Companies need to prioritise their response. Take the example of a theme park. While the trend toward an ageing population is evident and will have a profound effect on such a business, it is not as immediate a threat as the opening of a competitive park in the next year.

Following the three-stage process outlined above will enable companies to develop a more strategic response to the problems they identify.

Environmental Scanning Methods

Companies wishing to scan the environment can use a variety of means to do so. The most common ones are listed in Table 2.14.

TABLE 2.14 — ENVIRONMENTAL SCANNING METHODS

Modelling	Through sophisticated computer analysis, a relationship is established between factors in the environment and the company's performance
Trend Analysis	By examining past data, companies can make an educated forecast of how trends are developing. Usually this involves statistical analysis.

TABLE 2.14 — ENVIRONMENTAL SCANNING METHODS *contd.*

Scenario Analysis	Companies can develop several different scenarios, and develop separate contingency plans accordingly
Delphi Technique	The opinions of experts in a particular area is sought, with a chairperson, called a moderator, having the task of establishing a consensus

The Delphi Method is particularly useful when trying to establish trends for an entire industry. This chapter concludes with a study commissioned by the Pacific Asia Travel Association. The Pacific Asia Travel Association is one of the leading tourism industry associations. It regularly conducts seminars and conferences addressing the major issues and trends that it feels will impact on the industry. This chapter concludes with a considered overview of what the issues and trends will be that will shape the travel and tourism sector into the new millennium. Their prognosis for the tourism industry in the twenty-first century makes interesting reading, and is based on a research project conducted at the World Travel Market in London among leading tourism industry representatives.

EXHIBIT 2.8

GLOBAL TOURISM TRENDS *IN ACTION*

TWENTY-ONE ISSUES AND TRENDS THAT WILL SHAPE TRAVEL AND TOURISM IN THE TWENTY-FIRST CENTURY

FINDING THE RIGHT BALANCE

The travel and tourism buzzword of the twenty-first century will be the search for balance.

The identification, maintenance and management of this threshold of balance will be the single most important requirement for the tourism industry of the twenty-first century. Those companies, institutions and destinations that perform the balancing act well will attain that elusive goal of sustainable development. Those that don't, or won't, will be trapped forever in vicious *boom and bust* cycles.

This balancing act will manifest itself strongly as the following twenty-one critical issues and trends unravel throughout the travel and tourism industry in the twenty-first century. The twenty-one items were identified in research conducted at the November 1998 World Travel Market in London.

1. Economic impact and leakage from tourism
Set to become probably the most significant hot-potato issue in the early twenty-first century. Asian governments will be seeking to maximise that economic impact by keeping more earnings at home and after that, within the region. That will conflict with the increased advances of global multinational groups which will be sending more and more money out in the form of franchise, distribution, management fees and various other forms of earnings. Expect universities, local research think-tanks and regional groupings like the United Nations Economic and Social Commission to focus intensively on this subject.

2. Extension of US influence throughout the travel and tourism industry
The most visible signs of US presence are movies, fast food chains, hotels, airlines, theme parks, credit card companies, media and Internet distribution technology. Over the next two years, these prominent signs of US presence will grow worldwide through equity deals, management and franchise contracts. As tourism is a high-profile industry, the response from local communities could well be unpredictable, especially in places where such images are not popular.

3. Impact of globalisation
Related to the above but impacting on other issues like environmental and consumer protection regulations, changes in currency (such as the recent implementation of the Euro) and aviation policies. While liberalisation of bureaucratic trade practises will continue, NTOs will be under pressure to show that they are not being dictated to by outside powers nor giving more than they are getting.

4. Greater liberalisation of visas, border control formalities and investment opportunities
Several major regional caucuses like the Asia-Pacific Economic Co-operation and ASEAN have these first three issues on their agendas in view of the recognition that they are major impediments to the flow of people and goods. Step-by-step, these barriers will fall as countries adjust to the new realities. However, it is critically important to ensure that countries are encouraged, not pushed, to make the changes.

5. Taxation
Countries, states and even cities that give tax breaks to the tourism industry are advertising it as a promotional tool. In many countries, there is a tendency to do the opposite, i.e. to tax travel and tourism because visitors don't vote. That is a fallacy; visitors vote with their feet. They go elsewhere. Monitoring mechanisms like the World Tourism and Travel Commission's Tax Barometer are keeping a watch on these tax increases in the form of a performance scorecard. In the latest

barometer, released at WTM, Asian destinations hit by currency devaluations did not fare well, mainly because they had to adjust various airport taxes in line with the extent of the devaluation.

6. Social issues

The hardest work for the industry lies in convincing its constituents that it is not an industry created by the rich for the use of the rich. In many parts of the world, luxury hotels are still an incongruous embarrassment in the midst of surrounding poverty. Either ostentation will have to be replaced by modesty or the industry will have to work harder at explaining why it is paying housekeepers as much as it charges guests for twenty cups of coffee. Non-governmental organisations still blame travel and tourism for abetting the problem of child prostitution, even though the industry is working very hard to combat it.

7. Employment

As the industry gains greater respectability and recognition, it will attract more than its fair share of qualified young people seeking to see the world and enjoy the sights and sounds they are exposed to over the Internet. Mobility will increase as Internet web sites allow people to find work in different parts of the world. There will be great demand for people with language skills and the ability to work in different cultures.

8. Safety concerns, crime and political problems, including terrorism

These issues will dominate agendas. In 1998, many destinations suffered from such problems, leading to a marked increase in visitor arrivals in places free of them. Some countries capitalised on the woes of their competitors to stress their political and economic safety in an attempt to regain market share. The struggle to come up with effective crisis management scenarios for the tourism industry continues.

9. Influence of organised crime

There is growing evidence that the cash-rich status of the industry is a convenient channel for global money-laundering rackets, especially through casinos, real estate deals and purchases of luxury items. This is attracting the interest of law enforcement officers and will be the subject of many a scandal in the media as prominent investors are identified as potential suspects.

10. Technology

It is now all but accepted that travel agents are going to become just a regular part of the distribution equation and will have to earn their keep based on their productivity for a supplier. New multichannel strategies are being announced by airlines, and will soon be followed by hotels, which will involve distributing their products through the Internet, direct sales, frequent-flyer databases, corporate suppliers and agents. As one European airline said in announcing the new strategy, 'In a world where 100 per cent of our frequent travellers have a cellular telephone, eighty-five per cent have a PC and over fifty per cent are surfing the Internet a number of times each week, we must adapt our distribution to these new conditions.' Expect to see more Internet auctions of everything from hotel rooms to advertising. Microsoft Expedia has now expanded to Europe — Asia will be next. (Microsoft Expedia is the on-line travel agency set up by global software giant Microsoft. It is reportedly receiving nearly two million hits a month.)

11. Environmental issues

The travel industry has clearly got the message that a strong environmental ethic is at the heart of its survival. Hotel chains, airlines and tour operators are responding energetically to calls for the industry to protect the long-term viability of its lifeline. Travel and tourism's main problem will be the environmental impact of other polluting industries in the neighbourhood.

12. Airlines and aviation

The global power of the airline alliances will begin to manifest itself, leading to code-sharing, joint purchasing, database marketing and more alliances with the smaller airlines. While traffic will take time to recover, capacity has also been reduced due to the huge number of deferred aircraft orders. Airlines are in a heavier cost-cutting mood than ever before. The best that the industry can hope for is that those airlines which cut routes in 1997–8 will reinstate them this year No new destinations are expected to be added. Privatisation of both airports and airlines will continue.

13. Across-the-board alliances

These will happen between the public and private sectors, as well as among them. As access to databases becomes critical, and direct marketing becomes the rage, these alliances will drive the industry as all participants in it seek to attain the highest common denominator. One interesting trend is the growing link between tourism and its associate/supportive industries such as agriculture, textiles, gems and jewellery, retailing and even arts/culture. Expect to see greater realisation that a product sold to a tourist is as good as a product exported.

14. Hotels

Hotels can brace themselves for major takeovers and expansion efforts by the brand-name US-owned chains, especially franchise operators whose offers will be difficult to resist or refuse. As branding gains strength, the unbranded may find themselves increasingly isolated. Branded hotels will receive the backing of marketing and networking power. In the US, some branded hotels are also receiving low-interest or no-interest loans to help them with renovations. But terms and conditions are strict.

15. Cruise and marine tourism
This will take off in a big way throughout the rivers, seas and oceans of the world. In the UK, British Waterways conducted research on how people escape from stress and found that over a quarter of a million people will take a canal boat holiday in the UK in 1998. Canal boating is twice as popular as a day at an amusement park and just as attractive as a weekend at the seaside. One executive commented, 'Certainly one of the fastest ways of slowing down.'

16. Trade shows
The clutter of international trade shows will continue but break up into smaller niche-market shows focusing on both countries and product category. This will open up opportunities for buyers to specialise in various segments but also run the risk of putting all their eggs in one basket. In 1999, Hong Kong will host a new Asia-wide trade show backed by the organisers of ITB Berlin. Reed Travel Exhibitions, organisers of the PATA Travel Mart and the World Travel Market, will organise the first global golf show.

17. Greater focus on regional promotions
To stretch their promotional dollars, groupings such as the South Pacific and Indian Ocean islands, Mekong region countries, African states and others will be stepping up pooling of resources to undertake joint marketing and research efforts. At the WTM, groupings like Caribbean Tourism had a prominent profile, especially as they were seeking to regain market share after the devastating hurricanes of the previous September and November. Other banners are also emerging, such as the 'Silk Road'.

18. Emergence of the Middle East
This area is likely to start running out of oil over the next 20 to 30 years, and with no other resources to sell, many Middle Fast countries are gradually turning to tourism, capitalising on their historic cultures and Islamic traditions. One major UK tour operator announced the start of the first tours to Saudi Arabia. Dubai is as usual at the forefront and will play a prominent role in guiding the tourism destinies of other Gulf countries.

19. Growth in religious tourism
The publicity and promotion of the Bethlehem 2000 project commemorating the birth of Christ is expected to be the major catalyst for a revival in religious tourism globally. Holidays were once purely recreational but in the last ten years

they have moved into physical and mental rejuvenation. Spiritual rejuvenation is quite likely to be next.

20. Holiday trends

A recent study undertaken by the World Tourism Organisation on the impact of global economic changes on employment and holiday-taking patterns concluded that there would be a trend toward more and shorter holidays against fewer and longer holidays, mainly due to time constraints and job insecurities. Though labour laws and working conditions in many countries are moving toward giving more free time, corporate downsizing is leading many executives to work overtime anyway, mostly at home.

21. Emergence of secondary cities, both as source and destinations

So far, most of the world's tourists have originated in the major cities and headed for the major cities, usually as an initial stopping-off point en route to somewhere else. However, worldwide, there are hundreds of state and provincial capitals with sizeable populations, all seeking to get a piece of the action. As these cities emerge from the backwaters, increasing airline and transportation links will help them become inbound/outbound markets in their own right.

Source: Adapted and reprinted by permission of Pacific Asia Travel Association Strategic Information Centre

CHAPTER SUMMARY

Tourism and hospitality companies compete in an environment of macro and micro forces. In the company's microenvironment, the changes at consumer and competitor level deserve particular attention. Today's tourism companies operate in a truly international market-place, and need to have a very broad perspective on continual global changes. Macro forces are constantly changing too, some very quickly such as technology. Other trends, such as the changing demographic structures may occur more slowly, but are no less important in the long run. Companies need to adopt a structured approach to the process of environmental scanning, and follow the identification, prediction and evaluation framework. There are a number of methods that can be used to scan the environment. The major ones are modelling, trend analysis, scenario analysis and the Delphi method.

KEY WORDS AND PHRASES

Marketing Environment	Demographic Forces
Porter's Five Forces	Micro and Macro forces
Competitive Forces	Scanning

QUESTIONS FOR REVIEW

1. Distinguish between macro, micro and internal environmental forces.
2. Describe the five forces (Porter) that determine the competitive environment facing tourism and hospitality firms.
3. Discuss the major methods of environmental scanning.
4. What environmental forces will have an impact on the marketing of Ireland in the twenty-first century?
5. Give an example of a trend in each of the macroenvironmental forces and show how it could affect a tourism or hospitality firm of your choice.

QUESTIONS FOR DISCUSSION

1. Using Figure 2.1, construct a diagram showing the business environment facing the following:

   - A heritage museum
   - A budget airline
   - A zoo
   - A national conference centre

2. Consider the twenty-one trends for the twenty-first century article and explore how these trends will find resonance in the case of Ireland. How would you prioritise them?

REFERENCES AND FURTHER READING

Daft, R.L., *Organisational Theory and Design*, West Publishing Co.: St Paul, Minnesota 1989.

Naisbett, J., *Global Paradox*, BCA: London 1994.

Porter, M., *Competitive Strategy*, Free Press: New York 1980.

Stipanuk, D., 'Tourism and Technology', *Tourism Management*, August, pp. 267–79: 1993.

Teare, R. and Olsen, M., *International Hospitality Management*, Wiley & Sons: New York 1992.

USEFUL WEB SITES

www.pata.org/	Pacific Asia Travel Association
www.greenglobe.org	Green Globe ecology movement
www.cso.ie	The Central Statistics Office, Republic of Ireland
www.nisra.gov.uk	Northern Ireland Statistics and Research Agency
www.bftrade.travel.ie	Trade site of Bord Fáilte — includes latest tourism statistics
www.hotel-online.com	Comprehensive analysis of hospitality trends

CHAPTER 3

Marketing Research in Tourism and Hospitality Industries

INTRODUCTION

Marketing research is one of the most important and fascinating aspects of marketing. In this chapter we describe the nature of marketing research, emphasising its role of providing information for marketing decision-making in tourism, and provide several real life examples to illustrate the basic concepts of marketing research. We give a formal definition of marketing research and show that marketing research is an integral part of marketing information systems and should always assist decision-making. Sources of secondary data in tourism are listed, and for those wishing to carry out primary research the steps in the marketing research process are discussed in detail with guidelines for the design of questionnaires. The ethical aspects of marketing research and the responsibilities that researchers have to themselves, each other and the research project are discussed.

CHAPTER OBJECTIVES

This chapter will help you to:

- Recognise the importance of information to the tourism and hospitality organisation and the role information plays in effective marketing decision-making
- Outline the main sources of secondary data in tourism, understand the role of secondary data and the issues involved in its collection and analysis
- Outline the methods of collecting primary data, understand the role of primary data and the issues involved in its collection and analysis
- Understand the steps in the marketing research process
- How to design a questionnaire, collecting and analysing the data, writing up and presenting the results

WHAT IS MARKETING RESEARCH?

The term marketing research is broad in meaning, and is related to all aspects of marketing. The emphasis in marketing is on the identification and satisfaction of customer needs. To determine customer needs and to implement marketing strategies and programmes aimed at satisfying those needs, marketing personnel need information on customers, competitors, industry trends, long-term forecasts etc. In recent years, the tourism and hospitality industries internationally and domestically have undergone such rapid growth that it is getting more difficult for these businesses to stay up to date with changing trends. As the industries grow, the need for information on larger and more distant markets increases. Tourists have become more affluent and sophisticated, consequently marketing managers need better information on how to respond to competitors and market their products and services more effectively. The tourism environment is changing more rapidly, and tourism businesses need more timely information.

The task of marketing research is to assess the information needs and provide management with relevant, accurate, reliable, valid and current information (Malhotra, 1996). Sound decisions are not solely based on gut feeling, intuition, or even pure judgement, but are subject to research.

DEFINITION OF MARKETING RESEARCH

> **Marketing Research** is the systematic and objective identification, collection, analysis and dissemination of information for the purpose of improving decision-making related to the identification and solution of problems and opportunities in marketing.

Several aspects of this definition are noteworthy:

Firstly, marketing research is systematic, thus planning is required at all stages of the process. The procedures followed at each stage should be methodically sound, well documented and planned in advance as far as possible.

Secondly, marketing research is objective. It attempts to provide accurate information that reflects a true state of affairs. It should be conducted impartially and should be free from the personal or political biases of the researcher or the management. The motto of every researcher should be, 'Find it and tell it like it is', (Malhotra, 1996).

Other definitions include:

> **Marketing Research** is a process that identifies and defines marketing opportunities and problems, monitors and evaluates marketing actions and performance and communicates the findings and implications to management (American Marketing Association, 1987).

> **Marketing Research** is the formalised means of obtaining information to be used in making marketing decisions (The Marketing Institute of Ireland).

Marketing Research is part of a process of having the right information with the right people at the right time. Marketing research is thus a key component of the overall marketing information system for an organisation.

A Marketing Information System (MIS) consists of people, equipment, and procedures to gather, sort, analyse and distribute needed, timely and accurate information to marketing decision-makers. As many organisations in the tourism industry are small in size and may not have dedicated marketing managers, the size and extent of the organisation's information system will vary. However, it is essential that all organisations should keep up to date and have some formal or informal procedures for gathering information.

MARKETING RESEARCH ACTIVITIES

Marketing researchers engage in a variety of activities. Their eight most popular activities are:

- Measurement of market potential
- Market share analysis
- Determination of market characteristics
- Sales analysis
- Studies of business trends
- Short-term forecasting (two to five years)
- Competitive product studies
- Long-range forecasting (over five years)

A company can conduct marketing research by employing its own researcher, involve staff in the process or hiring outside researchers. Large tourism companies may have their own marketing research departments.

Marriott Hotel Group list their research priorities as follows:

- Market segmentation and sizing
- Concept development and testing
- Price sensitivity assessment
- Advertising and promotions assessment
- Market tracking
- Customer satisfaction

SOURCES OF INFORMATION

Internal Sources of Information

Internal Records

Most managers use internal records and reports for making day-to-day planning, implementation and control decisions. Internal records information consists of information gathered from sources within the company to evaluate sales and marketing performance and detect marketing problems and opportunities. Hotel daily reports can include occupancy, number of guests, total revenue, average daily rate, no shows and groups in-house.

BOX 3.1 — SOURCES OF INFORMATION IN A HOTEL

Hotel managers use reservations records and registration information to help in timing their advertising and sales calls. If most tourists book July and August holidays by February, advertising at Easter will be too late.

Reservation records also provide information concerning the hotel's top-producing travel agents and corporate clients. Hotel sales staff can phone, fax or visit the travel agents or corporate clients to inform them of future promotional activities and identify new business opportunities. The sales person can ascertain if the travel agent or corporate client has other needs that the hotel can satisfy e.g. a conference that is just being planned.

Guest History Information

The single most important element in any hospitality-marketing information system is to have a process of capturing and using guest information. This information is vital for improving service, creating effective advertising and sales promotions as well as developing new products and services etc.

Specific guest information needs may include any or all of the information included in Box 3.2.

BOX 3.2 — GUEST INFORMATION

Personal Guest Information
Name
Address
Phone numbers: Work
                   Home
Number in party
Reason for trip
    Business
    Pleasure
    Study
    Other
Name and address of Employer
Occupation

Types of Tourism Products/Services Purchased
    Single/double room suite
    Restaurant
    Room service
    Health club

> **Details of Trip**
>   Length of stay
>   Method of arrival
>   Car/bus/train/taxi
>
> **Method of payment**
>   Credit card/cash/cheque/bill to company
>
> **Membership of frequent guest programme**

Other Sources of Information

Guest Comment Cards. Guest comment cards are often found in guest bedrooms, in dining rooms or handed to departing customers. They provide useful information and can provide insights into problem areas. They can highlight your strengths and weaknesses. However, the problem is that they may not reflect the opinions of the majority of guests, because evidence shows that it is mostly tourists that are very angry or very pleased take the time to complete a card, and it is also important to get information from the 'silent majority'.

Business Cards. Many tourism businesses simply collect business cards from their guests or potential guests and use this information to form a database of customers. Many businesses attending trade fairs such as Holiday World collect business cards from potential customers who have shown an interest in their tourism or hospitality product and use this information to develop the business.

Marketing Intelligence

Marketing intelligence includes everyday information about developments in the business environment that helps managers prepare and adjust marketing plans and short-run tactics. Marketing intelligence systems determine the needed information and collect and deliver it in a useful format for managers. This information can be collected by tourism organisations, service staff, sales staff and sometimes even customers and suppliers can pass on very useful information.

BOX 3.3 — MARKETING INTELLIGENCE AT BORD FÁILTE

> Bord Fáilte marketing team held a number of conferences around Ireland in February 2000. Marketing Plan 2000 was revealed, and a key trend had been identified as a result of their research. The German market was still suffering economic difficulties and as a result no growth was indicated for this market in the following year. Those attending the seminar received this piece of 'intelligence' and made appropriate adjustments to their marketing strategies for the following year.

External Sources of Information

A tourism business must encourage customers, suppliers, tourist information offices, travel agencies and tour operators to pass along important information. It is important for the tourist business to stay in close contact with these people and treat them in a friendly manner. Similarly, members of management should be encouraged to join community and professional organisations where they are likely to obtain essential information. In particular, local marketing organisations such as the Marketing Institute or the HSMA run seminars on various marketing topics that can keep the business person up to date. Seminars aimed at the tourism industry are held each year by Bord Fáilte and the Irish Tourism Industry Confederation. These seminars often highlight trends and forecasts for the tourism industry.

TABLE 3.1 — TYPES AND SOURCES OF INFORMATION FOR THE IRISH TOURISM INDUSTRY

Types of Information	External Sources of Information
Profile of visitors to Ireland	Bord Fáilte
Tourist trends	Department of Tourism
Visitor trends	Regional Tourism Organisations
Tourist expenditure	Chambers of Commerce
Length of stay	Enterprise Boards
Purpose of visit	Tourist Information Offices
Accommodation used	Airlines and Ferry Companies
Food and beverage services used	Associations (hotel, restaurant, hostel, vintners)
	Duchas (OPW)

Sources of Secondary Data

The potential sources of secondary data are vast and it would be impossible to list all sources of data — much depends on the type of project in question. The tourism and hospitality industry in Ireland is fortunate to have an extensive collection of research published by Bord Fáilte (*see* Figure 3.1), however, there are many more sources that can be used at an international, national and regional level.

Government Published Data

Government, through its various departments and agencies, is one of the most important sources of information on general economic, social and tourism statistics. Vast amounts of data in Ireland from national to regional, from urban to rural, are collected and published by the government. This data is generally of high quality and tends to be readily available to the researcher at little or no cost. Tourism reports issued by the government include:

- Improving the Performance of Irish Tourism, September 1987
- Tourism Task Force Report, October 1992
- Operational Programme for Tourism 1994–99
- Statement of Strategy 1998–2001

Central Statistics Office (CSO)

The CSO is the largest gatherer of statistical information in the country. The CSO is the Government agency charged with the responsibility of collecting, compiling and disseminating the results of its statistical inquiries. The most important research survey carried out by the CSO is the Census of Population.

Census of Population (CP). The CP was last carried out in 1996. It contained a detailed questionnaire that was issued to every household and the questions related to topics such as age, marital status, sex, place of birth, principal economic status, occupation and industry. Thus the Census provides valuable marketing information on the Irish market which is useful for domestic tourism. The final Census results include details of:

- Population by area
- Ages and Marital Status
- Household Composition and Family Units
- Principle Economic Status and Industries
- Religion
- Occupations

Household Budget Survey (HBS) 1994–5

The large-scale national HBS covers 7,000–8,000 urban and rural households in Ireland. Estimates are provided for household composition, accommodation facilities, weekly income and weekly expenditure (over three hundred categories of goods and services are distinguished). It shows the actual amount of expenditure and the percentage of the total weekly budget spent on an item. A section of the report focuses on holidays with overnight stays spent in the Republic and elsewhere.

Bord Fáilte: The Irish Tourist Board (ITB)

Bord Fáilte's mission statement is to promote Ireland internationally as a top-quality tourist destination. With a budget of £30 million per year the organisation's main focus is promoting the country. However, Bord Fáilte also undertakes tourism research and publishes an extensive list of reports, some on an annual basis (*see* Figure 3.1). The publications are designed to answer the commonly posed questions from those involved in the tourism industry. The guides are put together by Bord Fáilte staff and other experts, and draw on the research the Bord commissions annually as well as market intelligence supplied by a range of industry sources.

The Irish State Tourism Training Agency (CERT)

CERT is the state agency established in 1963, whose primary function is to co-ordinate the education, recruitment, training and placement of staff at all levels of the Hotel, Catering and Tourism Industry. CERT's programme of research is designed to facilitate accurate forecasting and policy development in relation to the tourism industry. The on-going programme features manpower studies, job content analysis, management research, course evaluation and graduate follow-up studies.

Trade Associations and Other Professionals

Bodies that are organised to represent the interests of their members on a trade and professional basis are an important source of information. Such associations publish or hold detailed information on industry sales, growth patterns, trade members and may hold annual conferences. Special studies relevant to the trade are conducted and this can provide the researcher with useful statistics and tourism data.

Chambers of Commerce

Chambers of Commerce were established for the purpose of acquiring and disseminating useful information on important subjects. Chambers of Commerce and Industry foster and promote business growth and development in the interest of economic progress for the City and the region. Many Chambers have a specific tourism chapter, some Chambers like the Galway Chamber of Commerce and Industry have undertaken research into the local tourism industry and issued reports on the findings (Galway Chamber of Commerce, 1997).

FIGURE 3.1 — SECONDARY SOURCES OF DATA IN TOURISM: BORD FÁILTE PUBLICATIONS

1. **Tourism Facts**   Free
   Outlines the key tourism statistics for previous year. It includes tourism performance, economic benefits, main sources markets, expenditure patterns, regional tourist numbers and revenue, and method of travel and market characteristics.

2. **Marketing for Success**   £75
   A five-part series, in modular form, is designed to build up step-by-step into a programme to assist in improving the marketing activities of a tourism business.
   – Reaching the Customer
   – Contacting the Customer
   – Direct Marketing and the Internet
   – Pricing and Yield Management
   – Customer Care and Relationship Marketing

3. **Know Your Markets (guidebooks)**   £25 each
   This report contains details of the motivations and experiences of overseas holidaymakers to Ireland. Topics such as motivations for choosing Ireland, the holiday planning process, expectations and experiences, ratings of services and facilities in respect of quality, service and price. All the main markets are covered.

4. **The Overseas Market for Seniors**   £20
   This report focuses on the size of the market, traveller characteristics and product requirements and promotional channels.

5. **The Potential for Health Tourism**   £20
   The potential for health tourism is discussed and tour operators listed.

6. **Hotel Survey 1999**   £50
   This is an ongoing survey of bed and room night sales throughout the country.

7. **Operational Programme for Tourism 1994–9**   (file copies only)
   This policy document, drawn up by the Department of Tourism, Recreation and Sport, describes how ERDF funding was directed. The total funds amount to £652m, the largest amount ever spent in Irish tourism.

8. **Bord Fáilte Corporate Strategy 1999–2000**   Free
   An overview of Bord Fáilte's objectives, strategies and ambitions for Irish tourism.

9. **Fáilte Business 2000**   Free
   Details of the tourism industry in Ireland.

10. **Marketing Ireland to World — Annual Review '99 and Outlook 2000**

11. **Bord Fáilte Marketing Plan 2000**   Free
    This report examines the outlook for year 2000 and marketing environment, as well as objectives, funding and marketing strategy for 2000. It examines the main markets to Ireland, and looks at Northern Ireland, regional tourism marketing and special interest product marketing.

12. **Tourism Business Plan 1998–2003** £50

    This plan was intended to set out the growth which Irish tourism could achieve between 1998 and 2003. It contains a performance review, a situational analysis, selection of markets for prioritisation, targets and an overview of planning and funding.

13. **Visitor Attitudes Survey 1999** £25

    This report examines what motivates consumers in choosing Ireland for a holiday, what sources of information they use, and to what extent did their holiday experience in Ireland match their expectations.

14. **Trade and Consumer Promotions Calendar 2000** Free

    This document lists all the major trade and consumer fairs held throughout the world. It lists the event, the date and location, a brief description, Bord Fáilte involvement and cost of participation.

15. **Link Magazine** Free

    Link magazine connects suppliers and the trade by keeping them up to date. The magazine focuses on current issues facing the industry, interviews with industry experts, calendar of promotions, new research data, and market updates.

The Marketing Institute

The Marketing Institute is the representative body for the marketing profession in Ireland. It is a national organisation with seven regional councils, and produces a number of publications each year including:

- *MII News*
- *The Marketing Review*
- Programme of Events
- Yearbook and Diary
- Also ad hoc publications such as *Sources of Market Information* edited by Jane Williams

The Institute runs specialist seminars by top-calibre national and international practitioners and academics — tourism is frequently the topic of these seminars.

Other Professional Bodies

There are numerous bodies and some of these are listed below:

- Irish Hotel Federation (IHF)
- Irish Hotel and Catering Industry (IHCI)
- Irish Country Houses and Restaurants Association
- Town and Country Homes Association
- Irish Farmhouse Holidays Association
- Irish Cottage Holiday Homes Association

- Incoming Tour Operators Association
- Car Rental Council of Ireland
- Hotel Sales and Marketing Association (HSMAI)
- Vintners Association

Databases and CD-ROMs

The most dramatic development in secondary data has been the application of the computer to data collection, storage and transmission. This includes CD-ROMs, on-line and off-line databases, the Internet and the Worldwide Web (WWW). Technology, used in this way is transforming the world of marketing research.

Databases are software that let you enter information into one large, structured file so that it can then be searched. There are computer-stored issues of journal articles, newspapers, conference proceedings, trade statistics and other official publications on a wide range of topics including tourism.

Some widely used databases include:

Gulliver

Gulliver is Ireland's electronic tourism information and reservation system (*see* Chapter 9 on Distribution in Tourism and Hospitality). It was developed jointly by Bord Fáilte and the Northern Irish Tourist Board and in 1998 was sold to FEXCO. Gulliver is a vast database that provides the tourist and travel organiser with details of a wide range of services including accommodation, places to visit, entertainment, activities, events, transport and other general information. Gulliver is linked to the two major airline computer reservation systems in Europe: Galileo and Amadeus, thus serving travel agents throughout the world.

Anbar Abstracts

A CD-ROM database covering a range of topics including marketing and distribution, information management and technology.

Business Eye

A CD-ROM which includes full text of business and finance plus other Irish publications; abstracts of business items from the Irish Times; overviews of 2,200 companies and an index to market research studies and reports.

ABI Inform

A global business database on CD-ROM covering journal literature in business and management. Over 800 journals are abstracted, and brief summaries of the articles included.

Textline
An on-line record of all major worldwide publications. It allows the operator to search for any reference to a person, company, market or product in any period over the last ten years.

WHATT
A CD-ROM database covering a wide range of tourism publications.

World Tourism Organisation (WTO)
WTO offers an interactive database of tourism statistics and market trends. This service is fee based.

The Internet and the Worldwide Web

The Internet is a worldwide information highway based upon information technology — a global network of computers and communication. It is a huge global electronic library that never closes and is available twenty-four hours a day (Domegan and Flemming, 1999). An enormous breadth and depth of tourism related information is available including: company/product information, tourism destinations (Bord Fáilte has an award-winning web site), use of technology in tourism, tourism conferences/seminars, tourism publications, etc.

See end of chapter for Useful Web Sites.

EU and European Reports

Over the years, the EU has become a major provider of secondary data on its member states. The statistics office of the EU, EUROSTAT, publishes statistics for European countries including Ireland. Some of the reports focusing on tourism include:

European Information Centres
There are six European Information Centres (EICs) in Ireland, with the aim of improving the information flow to the business sector. They are based in and run by existing business organisations (mainly the Chambers of Commerce). Access to information is freely given.

Market Research Agencies

A number of specialist providers of market information have emerged. They often sell the information on a subscription basis. A number of the important providers in Europe are:

Euromonitor Publications is a major provider of reports and statistics across Europe.

The Economist Intelligence Unit (EIU) produces market research reports on a variety of issues including tourism.

Providers of research reports in Ireland include:

Landsdowne Marketing Research. This company has produced a number of tourism reports including *Tourist Views on Litter — August 1996*, other reports include *The JNRR Survey* (Joint National Readership Research) which provides a profile of products and services used by Irish consumers including holiday trips and locations chosen for home holidays.

Behaviour and Attitudes Ltd. This agency produced a survey of attitudes in Ireland during the Spring of 1995. The report documented Irish attitudes toward diet and health, shopping habits, response to promotions and direct marketing, people's tastes in relation to newspaper features, music and TV programmes and our attitudes toward advertising.

Tourism and Leisure Partners. Tourism and Leisure Partners have conducted a number of important surveys for the Irish Tourism Industry Confederation (ITIC) over the last few years including:

- Changing Distribution of Irish Tourism, 1996
- Strategy for Growth Beyond 2000, 1998

Tourism Development International (TDI) have also issued reports and carry out consultancy work for the tourism industry. A widely used report produced by TDI is the *Visitor Attractions Survey*, last produced for 1997. This report audits 257 fee-paying attractions and produces visitor numbers, trends, marketing, infrastructure and facilities as well as a detailed profile of visitors.

Horwath Bastow Charleton, carry out annual research on the hotel market in Ireland and Northern Ireland. Their annual report *Ireland and Northern Ireland Hotel Industry Survey 1999*, is an excellent source of information on the industry. The information contained in the report includes: tourism and accommodation statistics, survey results by hotel size and hotel classification and results by region. Valuable information such as the main source of hotel business, overall performance measurements, payroll and related expenses and general market data is presented.

McConnells. McConnells advertising services produce *Media Facts* which focuses on advertising statistics for Ireland, taking information from sources North and South. It includes information on advertising media rates.

Wilson Hartnell Advertising produces *The Irish Market: Facts and Figures*. This booklet gives statistics on advertising, population, consumer expenditure including leisure time.

MRBI. MRBI have also conducted reports on the tourism industry.

World Tourism Statistics

The most comprehensive source of tourism statistics is the World Tourism Organisation (WTO), located in Madrid, Spain. Each year this organisation collects, analyses and publishes reports on international tourism flows, forecasts and trends in the industry, such as:

- *Yearbook of Tourism Statistics*
- *Compendium of Tourism Statistics*
- *Travel and Tourism Barometer* (three each year)
- *Tourism Market Trends* (by region)

WTO's statistics section provides a rapid data response service that offers customised statistical reports on requests from members.

Organisation for Economic Co-operation and Development (OECD)

The OECD compiles data relating to tourism and tourism policy in OECD member countries. OECD has issued a number of specific reports on tourism in its member countries. In 1997, it issued a report on International Tourism in the OECD area and highlighted key trends in tourism.

Miscellaneous Sources

There is a virtually endless array of books, leaflets, brochures, dissertations, newspapers and magazines that contain relevant information for tourism marketing. Some are not specifically published for the tourism industry but are very useful for studying the Irish market and include:

- *Tourism Policy and Performance: The Irish Experience* — a textbook by James Deegan and Donal Dineen
- *The Irish Consumer Market* — a textbook by Professor Mary Lamkin
- *The Irish Market — A Profile* — a textbook by Edel Foley
- *The Irish Market Facts and Figures* — a booklet by Wilson and Hartnell

Note: An excellent book on marketing research is *Marketing Research in Ireland: Theory and Practice,* C. Domegan and D. Fleming, Gill & Macmillan, 1999

PLANNING PRIMARY DATA COLLECTION

Once the decision to use primary research has been made, researchers have to define what data needs to be collected and how. The data needed may be drawn from personal interviews, telephone or mail surveys, involving tourists, airlines, travel agents, tour operators or any other group of interest. Casually collected data can be useless or misleading. Designing a plan for primary data collection calls for decisions about research approaches, contact methods, a sampling plan and research instruments.

The Origins of Research Data

There are two types of data, which are generated by fundamentally different research approaches.

1. Qualitative Research

Qualitative research involves the collection of data that is open to interpretation, for example, people's opinions; where there is no intention of establishing statistical validity. This type of research is especially useful for investigating tourist motivation, attitudes, beliefs and intentions. The research is often based on small samples, and as a result cannot be generalised in numerical terms. A range of methods can be adopted including: survey research/questionnaires, focus groups, in-depth interviews, observational techniques and experimentation. An example of qualitative research is the research by Overseas Tourism Marketing Initiative (OTMI) group into perceptions of Ireland as a tourist destination.

BOX 3.4 — VISITOR SATISFACTION WITH IRELAND

Bord Fáilte has been conducting the Visitor Attitudes Survey on a biannual basis for many years. The objectives of the research are as follows:

- To examine what motivates consumers in choosing Ireland for a holiday
- What were the main sources of information they used for both choosing the destination and planning the holiday
- The extent to which the pre-visit expectations in respect of their Irish holdiay were matched by their experiences
- To measure their satisfaction with the Irish tourism product

The survey is conducted amongst overseas visitors whose main purpose in visiting Ireland was for a holiday, while excluding those who were born in Ireland.

2. Quantitative Research

Quantitative research involves the collection of information that is quantifiable and can be expressed statistically. It includes data such as sales figures, market share, market size and turnover. An example of quantitative research is *Tourism Facts* produced by Bord Fáilte annually.

Research Approaches

The choice of research approaches is closely tied to the type of research design that is being followed. Generally focus group and in-depth-interviews are associated with qualitative research. *A focus group* consists of eight to twelve participants who are led by a moderator in an in-depth discussion on a particular topic or concept. The main purpose of the focus group is to gain insights by listening to a group of people for the appropriate target market. Feargal Quinn made focus groups popular in Ireland by inviting regular shoppers from his Superquinn Stores to participate in these discussions. *In-depth interviews* are another way of obtaining qualitative data. The interviews are unstructured and are conducted on a one-to-one basis. The technique uses extensive probing to get a respondent to reveal motivations, beliefs, attitudes and feelings on a topic. Three basic research approaches are observations, surveys and experiments.

Observational Research

This is the gathering of primary data by observing relevant people, actions and situations. A restaurant evaluates possible new locations by researching the locations of competing restaurants, traffic patterns and housing developments in the area. A hotel chain sends a *mystery shopper* posing as a guest to check on the quality of the services and friendliness of the staff.

Observational research can produce information that people are normally unwilling or unable to provide. However, this approach is limited as feelings, beliefs and attitudes that motivate tourists' buying behaviour cannot be observed. Long-run or infrequent behaviour is also difficult to observe. Because of these limitations, researchers often supplement observation with survey research.

Mystery shopper

This is an observation technique that is popular in tourism and hospitality operations. The researcher poses as a customer to experience the normal interaction between customer and organisation. According to Domegan and Fleming (1999), mystery shopping has changed dramatically in the past ten years from being used as a hiring-and-firing technique to a *nurturing* and learning tool. Researchers and management in tourism and hospitality are now using it as a means of identifying weaknesses that require improvements over time. See Figure 3.2 for an example of the type of checklist that a mystery shopper could use when evaluating all the attributes of the restaurant dining experience.

FIGURE 3.2 — MYSTERY SHOPPER'S CHECKLIST FOR RESTAURANT

Pre-Visit
Signage
- *Visible*   Yes ☐   No ☐
- *Illuminated*   Yes ☐   No ☐
Promotions
- *Visible*   Yes ☐   No ☐
- *Readable*   Yes ☐   No ☐
- *Enticing*   Yes ☐   No ☐
Overall Pre-Visit Rating (0–10)   ☐
(Note: 0 denotes poor, 10 denotes excellent)

Arrival
- General appearance   Good ☐   Poor ☐
- Customer flow   Good ☐   Poor ☐
- Adequate lighting   Yes ☐   No ☐
- Sense of space   Yes ☐   No ☐
- Exterior cleanliness   Yes ☐   No ☐
    Tidiness   Yes ☐   No ☐
    Spillages   Yes ☐   No ☐
- Visibility of menu board   Yes ☐   No ☐
Overall Arrival Rating (0–10)   ☐

Interior Cleanliness
- *Floors*   Yes ☐   No ☐
- *Chairs*   Yes ☐   No ☐
- *Tables*   Yes ☐   No ☐
- *Walls*   Yes ☐   No ☐
- *Odours*   Yes ☐   No ☐
Overall Cleanliness Rating (0–10)   ☐

Guest Experience
- Friendly customer greeting   Yes ☐   No ☐
- Appropriate time of wait from arrival to
  order being taken   Yes ☐   No ☐
- Assistance when order taken   Yes ☐   No ☐
- Appropriate time of wait for order arrival   Yes ☐   No ☐
    Level of business   Quiet ☐   Busy ☐

- Staff personal hygiene   Good ❏   Poor ❏
Overall Guest Experience Rating (0–10)   ❏

Meal Experience
- Menu item availability   Yes ❏   No ❏
- Accuracy of order   Yes ❏   No ❏
- Food quality   Yes ❏   No ❏
    Match to menu specification   Yes ❏   No ❏
    Appearance   Good ❏   Poor ❏
    Taste   Good ❏   Poor ❏
    Texture   Good ❏   Poor ❏
    Temperature   Good ❏   Poor ❏
    Quantity/Value   Good ❏   Poor ❏
    Adequate accompaniments   Yes ❏   No ❏
Overall Meal Experience Rating (0–10)   ❏

Payment
- Correct change   Yes ❏   No ❏
- Friendly customer interaction   Yes ❏   No ❏
Overall Payment Rating (0–10)   ❏

Follow-Up
- Treatment of repeat customers   Yes ❏   No ❏
- Complaint/Suggestion procedure   Yes ❏   No ❏
Overall Follow-Up Rating (0–10)   ❏

Rate Overall Restaurant Experience (0–10)   ❏

Other Comments: ....

Source: Richard Nielsen, Lecturer at the Galway-Mayo Institute of Technology

Survey Research

This is the approach best suited to gathering descriptive information. The major advantage of survey research is its flexibility. It can be used to obtain many different kinds of information in many different tourism marketing situations. Surveys are used extensively by Bord Fáilte to obtain a detailed profile of tourists to Ireland each year; one large survey is carried out on tourists departing the country and is known as the SOT (survey of tourists) survey.

Experimental Research

This approach is best suited for gathering causal information. Experiments involve selecting matched groups of subjects, giving them different treatments, controlling unrelated factors and checking for different group responses.

MARKETING RESEARCH PROCESS

The Marketing Research Process presents a logical five-step approach to marketing research. The steps are outlined in Box 3.5 below:

BOX 3.5 — MARKETING RESEARCH PROCESS

1. **Identifying and defining the problem or opportunity**
2. **Developing the research plan**
3. **Collecting the data**
4. **Implementing the research**
5. **Interpreting and reporting the findings**

If the findings are to be accurate and objective, the researcher must be orderly and rational in his/her approach, be thorough and precise and interpret the findings honestly.

STEP 1: IDENTIFYING AND DEFINING THE PROBLEM OR OPPORTUNITY

No research project can begin until the nature of the problem or opportunity has been clearly defined. Identifying and defining the problem is the first step in the process of finding a solution. A poor diagnosis will lead to an ineffective solution.

For example, a manager of a heritage centre hired a researcher to determine the centre's level of awareness among incoming tour operators and travel agents. The manager felt that lack of awareness explained the low turnover of tour groups each summer. The researcher found to the contrary, that many people were aware of the centre. Further exploratory research revealed that travel agents perceived the centre to have poor parking facilities for buses and no restaurant, thus the agents were reluctant to include it on the itineraries. The manager had initially incorrectly defined the problem and research objectives.

STEP 2: DEVELOPING THE RESEARCH PLAN

Assuming that the problem is well defined, the next stage is to choose a research design. A research design is an overall blueprint, guideline, plan of action or framework for the rest of the research process to facilitate later decisions that need to be made (Domegan and Flemming, 1999). One way to classify the nature of the required information, and hence the research designs, is according to the three terms: exploratory, descriptive and causal.

Exploratory research gathers information that will help define the problem and suggest hypotheses (statements that the research will prove or disprove). *Descriptive research* describes size and composition of the market and *Causal research* tests the cause-and-effect relationships between two variables such as price and demand. Projects tend to start with exploratory research and later follow with descriptive and/or causal research.

The second step calls for determining the needed information and developing a plan for collecting the data. The research design is the *grand plan* for the project; it specifies the data that is needed and the procedures for collecting, processing and analysing that data.

Researchers distinguish between primary data and secondary data.

Primary data is data collected for a specific purpose. The data must not have been collected previously.

The big advantage of primary data is that it relates specifically to the problem at hand, while the disadvantages are in the cost and time required to collect it.

Secondary data is data that was previously collected; it is data already in existence somewhere, having been collected for another purpose.

Secondary data is usually cheaper and faster to collect, but researchers must always consider its relevance, accuracy, credibility and timeliness. When a tourism organisation uses Bord Fáilte's *Tourism Facts* it is using secondary data.

Designing the Data Collection Instrument

Marketing researchers use two main types of instruments for collecting primary data: mechanical/electronic devices and questionnaires.

1. Mechanical and Electronic Devices

Among the mechanical and electronic devices available for collecting primary data are the turnstile counters that monitor visitor numbers at tourist attractions and which are often found at tourist information centres. More and more interviewers are carrying pen-based computers. The interviewers ask respondents questions and check off answers on the screen. Personal computers can also be used to interview people. Software can be used to design questions that are based on previous answers. Many researchers believe that respondents will provide more private information to a computer than they will in a face-to-face interview.

2. Questionnaires

The questionnaire is the most common method for gathering primary data. In designing a questionnaire, researchers must exercise great care in:

1. Which questions to ask
2. In what form to ask the question
3. How to word the question
4. How to sequence the questions
5. Layout and physical presentation of the questionnaire

The research **objectives** should guide decisions about which questions to ask. Questions that are likely to create suspicion and antagonism should be avoided. Similarly, questions that confuse the respondent or that require the respondent to complete detailed mental calculations are not recommended — for example, questions on tourists' expenditure patterns need to be broken down into a number of separate questions as it requires mental calculations. Care is needed to avoid asking questions that require information not readily available to respondents.

The **form** in which the questions are presented is very important. Open-ended questions, such as shown in Figure 3.3 do not provide the respondent with a choice of answers. Instead, respondents formulate their own answers in their own words. Closed-ended questions give respondents all the possible answers to each question, respondents simply choose one. Closed-ended questions can be as simple as *yes* or *no* answers.

Choice of words can make the difference between a good and a poor questionnaire. Words should be simple and unambiguous so that they will mean the same thing to all respondents. They should not be biased, create misunderstandings, or lead respondents into giving the answer the researcher wants.

The **sequencing of the questions** should be carefully planned. Starting off with difficult and highly personal questions such as the respondents' age or income earned can antagonise them and lead to refusals to participate. Pre-testing a questionnaire on a sample of respondents before using it in the full survey is always advisable.

The **physical layout** of a questionnaire can influence the participation in the survey. Questionnaires should always be neatly typed, clearly laid out and easy to follow. Good quality paper should be used, especially for postal questionnaires. There should be no grammar or spelling errors.

Validity and Reliability

These criteria should always be considered in questionnaire development. Validity is a measurement instrument's (usually a questionnaire) ability to measure what it is supposed to measure. Reliability is a measurement instrument's ability to produce essentially identical results after repeated use. It indicates the extent to which a measure is free from random error and yields consistent results. The validity and reliability of data can easily be compromised if respondents cannot answer the questions accurately. This is important in tourism research as it cannot be assumed that all tourists speak English and frequently the questionnaires have to be translated and interpreted for the tourist.

FIGURE 3.3 — EXAMPLES OF OPEN-ENDED QUESTIONS, CLOSED-ENDED QUESTIONS AND FAULTY QUESTIONS

1. **Totally Open**
   'What is your opinion of Aer Lingus?'

2. **Sentence Completion**
   'When choosing an airline, the most important consideration in my decision is…' _____

3. **Word Association**
   'What is the first word that comes to mind when you hear the following?'
   Travel… _____
   Airline… _____
   Airline food… _____

4. **Dichotomous (a question offering two answer choices)**
   'In arranging this trip did you contact Bord Fáilte?'   Yes ❏   No ❏

5. **Multiple choice**
   'What age group are you in?'
20 or under ____	30–39 ____	50–59 ____
21–29 ____	40–49 ____	60 or over ____

6. **Semantic Differential Scale**
   'Galway Crystal Heritage Centre is'
   Large _____ Small
   Interesting _____ Boring

7. **Rating Scale**
   'Customer service at the Blarney Park Hotel is…' _____
1. excellent	4. average	7. very poor
2. very good	5. fair	
3. good	6. poor	

8. **Faulty Question**
   'How often do you eat out?'
   The question is ambiguous. It does not specify the meal or the type of restaurant. This question could be improved by adding response categories such as 'daily' or 'once a week'.

9. **Leading Question**
   'Do you think fast food is bad for your health?'

Designing the Sampling Plan

In tourism marketing particularly, time and cost constraints mean that it is impractical to include every single tourist in any research project. Instead, a carefully chosen representative *sample* of the entire population of tourists will be enough to give the researchers confidence that they are getting a true picture that can be generalised. In most cases, researchers are able to draw conclusions about the whole population (i.e. the tourists or visitors) based on the study of a sample. A **sample** is a set of units, or items, selected from a population. Most customer satisfaction research is based on use of sampling techniques.

The Sampling Process

A good sampling plan will produce a sample that is representative of the characteristics of the population from which it is drawn. Designing a sample calls for three decisions. Firstly, **who** will be surveyed? This is not always obvious. For example, to study the decision-making process of a family holiday, should the researcher interview the husband, wife, children, travel agent or all of these? The researcher must decide what type of information is needed and who is most likely to have it.

Secondly, **how many people should be surveyed**? Large samples give more reliable results than small samples. However, it is not necessary to sample every tourist to obtain reliable results. If well chosen, samples of less than one per cent of a population can give good reliability (Kotler et al, 1996).

Thirdly, **how should the sample be chosen**? Sample members might be chosen at random from the entire population (a probability sample), or the researcher might select people who are easiest to obtain information from (a non-probability sample called a *convenience* sample). Or the researcher might choose a specified number of participants from each of several demographic groups such as English, French or American tourists. A quota for the number of tourists to be surveyed is set for each group. These and other ways of drawing samples have different cost and time limitations and varying accuracy and statistical properties. The needs of the research project will determine which method is most effective.

STEP 3: COLLECT THE DATA

Interviews and surveys involve the collection of information from individuals. This may be direct face-to-face personal interviews, either individually or in a group, by telephone or mail (postal) questionnaire.

BOX 3.6 — DATA COLLECTION METHODS

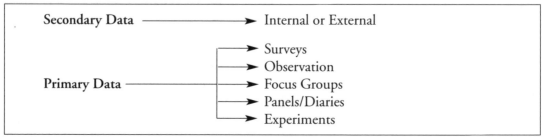

Source: Adapted from *Marketing Research in Ireland: Theory and Practice,* Domegan and Fleming, Gill & Macmillan, 1999

Personal Interviews. The most direct type of survey is the personal interview because the respondent and the interviewer are in face-to-face-contact. Individual interviewing is conducted on a one-to-one basis in the respondent's home, on the street or in a shopping centre. Group interviewing is usually referred to as *focus group interviewing.* A focus group interview is an in-depth interview in which a moderator meets with eight to twelve participants and leads them through a discussion on a given topic.

BOX 3.7 — PERCEPTIONS OF IRELAND

In 1996, Bord Fáilte undertook the repositioning of Ireland as a tourism destination. The director of marketing undertook research into tourists' perceptions of Ireland as a destination. The research included holding seventeen focus groups across the world, with many different nationalities. The results proved interesting: Ireland was perceived to be a *macho* destination, more suited for men, with little to offer families!

STEP 4: IMPLEMENTING THE RESEARCH PLAN

The researcher puts the marketing research plan into action by collecting, processing, and analysing the information.

The data collection step is often the most costly; the potential for error is also very high. The researcher must monitor every phase. If a personal interview survey is used, for example, it is very important to monitor the fieldwork (i.e. the interviewers) and carry out spot checks on the work being performed. Problems can occur in contacting respondents, for example, some may refuse to co-operate or give dishonest answers. The researcher might take a sample of completed questionnaires and call the respondents to verify they were, in fact, interviewed. Data from questionnaires are checked for accuracy and completeness and coded for computer analysis. The researcher applies standard computer programmes to prepare tabulation of results and compute averages and other statistical measures. A number of software packages can be used such as Microsoft Excel, Microsoft Access or Statistical Package for the Social Sciences (SPSS).

STEP 5: INTERPRETING AND REPORTING THE FINDINGS

The final step in the research process involves the researcher interpreting the findings, drawing conclusions and reporting them to management. Researchers should avoid overwhelming managers with numbers and complex statistical techniques. Instead, management needs results presenting in a way that will be easy to understand and will help in decision-making.

Report. A report that is too complex is of limited use. Clear language and the use of visual aids, such as graphs and charts, are critical elements in the presentation and interpretation of research reports. Various software packages, such as Microsoft Powerpoint, greatly assist presentation of data. Although a verbal presentation can make an important contribution to the understanding process, it is the report itself that has the power to influence thinking. There are no standard report formats, however, the following headings are frequently included in research reports:

Title Page. This includes details of the report title, the client, the researchers and the date of completion.

Table of Contents. This contains the main heading and subheadings of the report. It should convey the structure of the report and where to find the relevant sections.

Executive Summary. Busy executives do not have time to read the full report. The executive summary should highlight the main points of the research and draw the reader's attention to the main conclusions and recommendations.

Introduction. The introduction should set the background for the report, why the research was undertaken and outline the marketing problems requiring solutions.

Research Methods. This section explains how the research aims were approached, why particular techniques were chosen and how they were put into action. Details of primary and secondary research methods used and why.

Findings. These constitute the body of the report and what the client is really interested in. The findings should be in sufficient detail to enable the reader to assess the information, to check its accuracy and validity and to understand what has been generated. A full range of presentation techniques may be used to present the findings, also consider heavy use of appendices for information too detailed to be included in the body of the report.

Conclusions. The conclusion is the creative part for the researchers as they must now interpret the results of the research.

Recommendations. Depending on the nature of the research objectives it may be necessary for the researcher to move beyond the findings and conclusions and give firm recommendations to the client for future action.

Appendices. The appendices contain data that may be relevant to a detailed understanding of the research. Appendices should always relate back to key parts of the text to guide the interested reader. Often items such as the questionnaire, tables, literature, sampling methods and so on are found in this section.

ETHICS IN MARKETING RESEARCH

The ethical concerns surrounding market research have been the subject of an ongoing debate in the industry for a long time. It is essential that the researchers' credibility is maintained and that the highest standards of professional practice are demonstrated. This is vital if researchers are to maintain the confidence of their clients, as well as that of the general public and the government. The European Society for Opinion and Marketing Research (ESOMAR), a leading research association, is actively trying to encourage members to practice ethical research, and to stamp out practices such as *slugging* (selling under the guise of market research), through an agreed code of practice.

EXHIBIT 3.1

MARKETING RESEARCH *IN ACTION*

GENERAL TRENDS IN MARKETING RESEARCH

Just as marketing exists in an ever-changing world, so too does marketing research. More so than ever before, research is experiencing tremendous changes. Problem definition becomes more complex and complicated in the global village and in the face of intense competition. As the abundance of internal and external secondary sources of data continues to grow, the issue confronting managers is not lack of information per se, but lack of relevant information and information overload. A number of trends are affecting marketing research worldwide. To keep up to date with such developments, you are recommended to join a professional research or marketing association, such as The Marketing Society of Ireland, the Marketing Institute of Ireland (MII), the Market Society (UK) and ESOMAR. For the present, an overview of the major trends will provide the necessary background against which the more detailed trends are set.

Summary of Overall Trends in Marketing Research

1. Traditional marketing research broadens into relationship and extended marketing research, as the business world becomes more complex and dynamic.
2. Continued growth and augmentation of exploratory research.

---

3. More use of research methods to get into customer shoes.

4. Increased penetration of information technologies into all marketing functions, especially marketing information and information management.

5. Concentrated efforts and focus upon ethics and code of conduct within the industry.

We will now outline each of these trends.

Types of Research

With the advent of customer service and *relationship marketing*, more and more research studies look to the criteria necessary for building long-term relationships with some market segments. This results in detailed *psychographic* information about customer preferences, lifestyles and personalities to augment the existing demographic data which many companies tend to have. Dubbed as *relationship marketing research*, Pat Cody, Director of Kompass, Ireland, predicts that this trend will continue, as 'detailed information gathering will soon become as routine as bookkeeping; marketing will move away from average customers and toward individual customer analysis to facilitate one-to-one marketing'. Guinness discovered, through research, that because of the specialised nature of their new brand of beers — St James' Gate Beers — drinkers want to be engaged in a dialogue with the brand in order to feel more involved with it. Hence, Guinness plans to establish a one-to-one relationship with St James' Gate beer drinkers through an innovative relationship marketing campaign.

Coupled with this, in an accelerating competitive environment, companies have to keep in touch with other external agents in their environment. For example, Digital, in researching the environmental technology in Europe, included the suppliers as well as the users of such technology to ensure a profitable market existed. This is referred to as *extended research* and can be expected to continue to grow as markets become less clear and as macroenvironmental factors impact on marketing strategy more and more.

Data Collection Methods

Traditionally, marketing research has been dominated by descriptive research. Describing a customer's age, income level, social class and occupation has enabled firms to better segment markets and fine-tune their offer to these segments. However, shorter product life-cycles, intense competition, outsourcing of raw material and deregulation has led to the need for more detailed, exploratory or *soft* data about customer needs, preferences, expectations and motivations. This has led to a rise in the use of data collection methods such as focus groups and in-depth interviews. This trend toward greater utilisation of exploratory research designs and related data collection methods will continue to evolve. Such data once generated and gathered, can then be used to feed into more sophisticated marketing computer models, to generate satisfaction models and scenarios of different strategies for companies.

The new interest in exploratory research does not imply a neglect of descriptive or causal research. On the contrary, exploratory research can be undertaken and complemented with a follow-up descriptive study.

One further trend, though focus groups and in-depth interviews are generally associated with exploratory research, there has been a strong trend in the 1990s to use focus groups and in-depth interviews to generate descriptive data.

Technology and Research
Marketing and Marketing Research is being transformed like never before with the advent of new technologies. MRNet, or marketing research in cyberspace, is a new departure for many practitioners. *Infosurfing* (secondary research medium) and *cyberesearch* (through the on-line world at household and individual level) offer new ways of accessing, storing, collecting, generating, processing and reporting data and information. Thus, it comes as no surprise that every phase of marketing research is being influenced by information technology. Nowhere is the technology effect more evident than in secondary sources of data. The advent of the Internet, web sites and on-line databases is transforming desk research, as discussed in Chapter 4, giving rise to what many call the digital age of information.

In this vein, researchers have better storage and analysis tools to apply to qualitative and quantitative data, e.g. the recent introduction of a new statistical software package in Ireland specifically aimed at researchers who conduct exploratory research. Other packages, such as Quantum and SAS, can be used for developing and processing questionnaires.

With sophisticated computer hardware and software readily available and becoming more affordable every week, marketing models will become more popular and market behaviour will be mathematically modelled. Many computer packages are readily available for assisting with the interviewing process, (referred to as CATI, computer-aided telephone interviewing).

Source: This exhibit has been prepared by Christine Domegan and Declan Fleming; lecturers at NUI, Galway

CHAPTER SUMMARY

As the tourism and hospitality industry grows, the need for information increases and it is getting more difficult for businesses to stay up to date with changing trends. As visitors become more affluent and sophisticated, marketing managers need better information on how to respond to competitors and market their products and services more effectively. It is important for the marketer to be familiar with the main sources of information. These can be divided into internal and external sources.

When a research project has to be carried out, there is a logical five-step approach to the process consisting of: identifying and defining the problem or opportunity; developing the research plan; collection of the data; analysis of the data and ending with preparation of the final report. Distinction is made between the different types of data such as qualitative and quantitative data, as well as different sources such as secondary data and primary data. Secondary sources of data are quite extensive in tourism and hospitality and should include the newer sources such as database research and use of the Internet. If a survey is to be carried out then much time and effort will be spent on questionnaire design and the fieldwork involved. The data is analysed, usually using a software package such as SPSS. Finally, a report is prepared and presented.

KEY WORDS AND PHRASES

Marketing Information	System
Marketing Research	Research Design
Primary Data	Secondary Data
Observational Research	Experimental Research
Survey Research	Focus Group Interview
Validity	Reliability
Sample	Probability or Random Sample
Non-Probability Sample	

QUESTIONS FOR REVIEW

1. Why is marketing research an essential tool for the tourism marketing manager?
2. What is the difference between primary and secondary research?
3. What kinds of marketing problems might be addressed through:
   (a) exploratory research
   (b) descriptive research
   (c) causal research
4. What are the criteria for evaluating secondary sources of data? List five main tourism reports published by Bord Fáilte.
5. What is observational research and in what circumstances might it be more appropriate than interviews or surveys?
6. What are the main decisions in developing a sampling plan? Why is it so important to accurately pick a sample?
7. Describe the steps in the marketing research process.

QUESTIONS FOR DISCUSSION

Without looking back, how many sources of secondary data in Irish tourism can you list? Investigate what your library has to offer.

Design a questionnaire. It should contain about twenty questions, and you should use as many different types of questions as possible. The objective is to develop a profile of tourists to your area. Pilot your questionnaire on twelve to fifteen people (outside your college), analyse the results and make any adjustments. Be prepared to discuss the rationale behind your questionnaire, the outcomes, and any data analysis problems.

Why is a systematic approach to marketing research important?

REFERENCES AND FURTHER READING

Domegan, C. and Fleming, D., *Marketing Research in Ireland: Theory and Practice*, Gill & Macmillan: Dublin 1999.

Brunt, P., *Market Research in Travel and Tourism*, Butterworth Heinemann: 1997.

Brassington, F. and Pettitt, S., *Principles of Marketing*, Pitman Publishing: 1997.

Kotler, P., Bowen, J. and Makens, J., *Marketing for Hospitality and Tourism*, 2nd ed., Prentice Hall: New Jersey 1999.

Malhotra, M., *Marketing Research*, Prentice Hall: New Jersey 1996.

USEFUL WEB SITES

www.cso.ie	CSO
www.ireland.travel.ie	Bord Fáilte
www.world-tourism.org/	World Tourism Organisation
www.nua.ie	Internet Research Information
www.gmarketing.com	More effective use of the web
www.wttc.org/	World Travel and Tourism Council
www.ttra.com	Travel and Tourism Research Association
http://tinet.ita.doc.gov	Tourism Statistics on America
www.amarach.com	Market Research on Business Forecasting

CHAPTER 4

Consumer Behaviour

INTRODUCTION

Consumers seldom behave in a predictable and rational way. Just when marketers feel that they can anticipate what consumers will do, they behave in the opposite way. Understanding such patterns of behaviour is a difficult task. This chapter seeks to enhance your understanding of the principles of consumer behaviour. Consumer behaviour is the study of how and why consumers make purchasing decisions. It involves not just the study of what has been bought, but also the reasons that have led to such a purchase. It explores the uniquely individual psychological factors that shape our behaviour such as personality and motivational state. It seeks to give marketers an insight into how their products and promotional messages are perceived, and how consumers develop favourable or unfavourable attitudes. Our behaviour is invariably shaped by societal and family influences. To be more effective marketers need a more thorough understanding of this complex series of personal, psychological and external influences.

CHAPTER OBJECTIVES

Following this chapter, students should be able to:

- Understand a basic model of consumer behaviour
- Recognise the internal and external influences on tourist buyer behaviour
- Understand the consumer decision-making process
- Be able to apply consumer behaviour theory in a tourism and hospitality context

DEFINITION OF CONSUMER BEHAVIOUR

'Consumer behaviour reflects the totality of consumers' decisions with respect to the acquisition, consumption, and disposition of goods, services, time and ideas by (human) decision-making units over time.'

(Jacoby, 1976)

The term customer behaviour is somewhat misleading. As the above definition remind us, to be true to the principle of the marketing concept as described in Chapter 1, we need to constantly strive to focus on a total understanding of the customer, not just their observable behaviour.

We need a full understanding of the influences on their behaviour and the process of such behaviour. The following are illustrative examples of questions, which are regularly asked in order to get such an understanding:

- What are the roles played by family members in choosing where to go and what to do, on holiday?
- What motivates an individual to take a holiday; to choose a particular type of holiday?
- What perceptions do tourists have of a destination before they visit it; and how are these opinions developed?
- How do consumers search for information about destinations, activities and hotels?
- On what basis do tourists make a final decision on where to holiday?

The above definitions point to the fact that:

Consumer behaviour is dynamic — customer preferences and attitudes are in a constant state of change. Large shifts in Irish and global culture are affecting demand for all types of services and products, including tourism. Lifestyle changes have led to an increasing interest in adventure tourism such as that offered in the Delphi Adventure Centre in Mayo. Rising living standards, combined with smaller families have led to increasing numbers of Irish people choosing foreign holidays. As people become older and their individual circumstances change, their attitudes and behaviour are also subject to change. The way that people search for information about tourism is changing radically. In the past, Irish people relied on the opinions of friends or newspaper advertising to find out about holiday choices; today a much wider source of information is available such as the Internet, teletext and holiday fairs such as Holidayworld.

Consumer behaviour involves interactions — any study of consumer behaviour needs to focus on what consumers think (cognition), what they feel (affect) and what they do (behaviour). Tourism and hospitality consumer behaviour is an area where many people are involved. The annual holiday can involve the opinions of all the family. A company day outing is typically a collective decision. A tour operator choosing a hotel for his coach party will consult with fellow executives and other people. Some people may act as the information gatherer (by going to a travel agent to collect brochures), others may take the role of influencer (by virtue of their extensive travelling experience), others may make the actual purchase (because they have a credit card), while others may be users (young children use the product although they seldom play other roles).

In helping us to understand consumer motivation we can propose a simple model of consumer behaviour depicted in Figure 4.1.

FIGURE 4.1 — A SIMPLE MODEL OF CONSUMER BEHAVIOUR

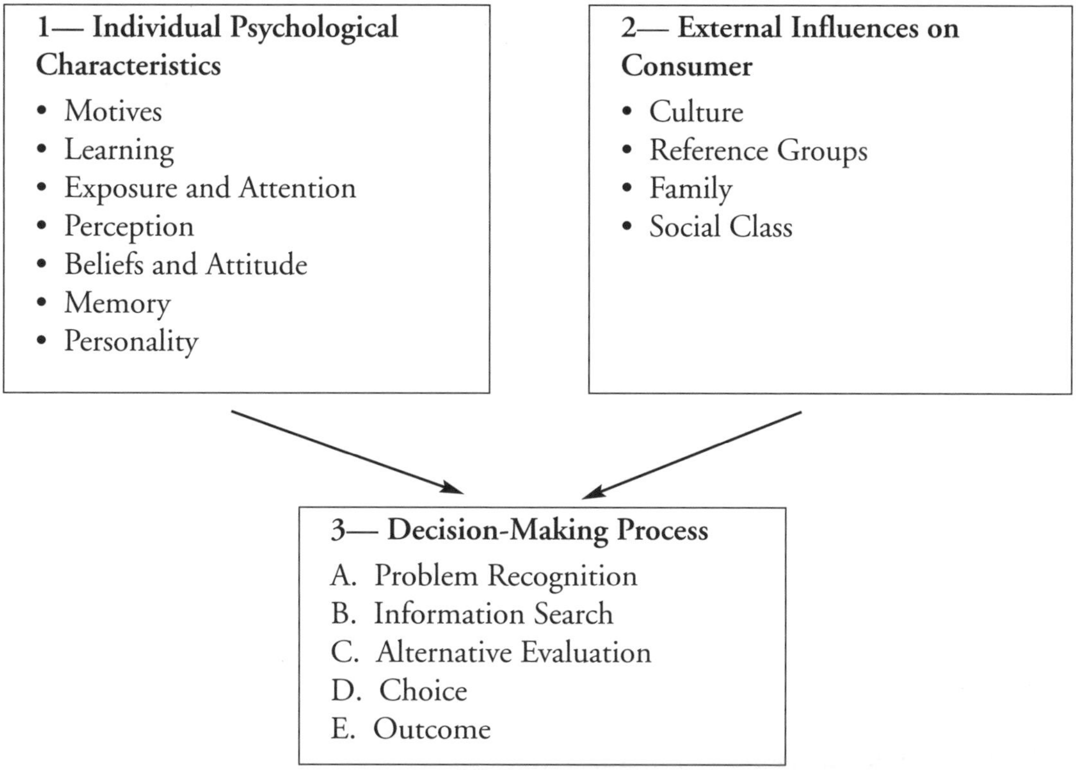

1— Individual Psychological Characteristics

- Motives
- Learning
- Exposure and Attention
- Perception
- Beliefs and Attitude
- Memory
- Personality

2— External Influences on Consumer

- Culture
- Reference Groups
- Family
- Social Class

3— Decision-Making Process
A. Problem Recognition
B. Information Search
C. Alternative Evaluation
D. Choice
E. Outcome

From the above model we can see that consumer behaviour is the outcome of a combination of individual characteristics of the customer and the external influences on that consumer, impacting on the decision process of the customer.

Let us consider each of these factors in turn.

1. INDIVIDUAL PSYCHOLOGICAL CHARACTERISTICS

MOTIVES

Motives may be defined as: 'enduring predispositions that direct behaviour toward certain goals' (Engel and Blackwell, 1982). Such motives are particular to an individual, but there are enough sufficiently broad motives to enable marketing people to identify segments who share similar motives. Abraham Maslow's theory of motivation is the best-known model for grouping people's needs. He argued that consumers were driven, or motivated, to satisfy a hierarchy of needs. At the most basic level are universal needs such as the need to satisfy hunger and thirst — these needs are basic and instinctive. Further up the hierarchy of needs, are those needs that are learnt by us as part of a family, society and culture. Maslow argued that as needs at lower levels were satisfied, then the customer was motivated to satisfy higher order needs.

FIGURE 4.2 — MASLOW'S HIERARCHY OF NEEDS MODEL

Self-Actualisation:
Desire for fulfilment e.g. painting weekends

Esteem/status:
e.g. Ski holidays, staying in luxury hotel

Belongingness:
Need to be part of a group e.g. Butlin's holidays

Safety:
Need to have personal security e.g. closed circuit TV
monitored hotel corridors, safe beaches (Blue Flag etc.)

Physiological:
Basic, instinctual requirements
Adequate food provision

The model can be criticised for being untested and not incorporating sufficiently certain needs that may be important in tourism, such as the need for knowledge. The model's implication, of people moving upwards in terms of their needs, does not acknowledge that people will simultaneously require higher order and lower order needs to be satisfied.

LEARNING

The concept of learning refers to the way in which visitors receive and interpret a variety of stimuli. Among the ways people *learn* about holidays are through their previous experiences with a destination, through a discussion with friends who have visited a destination, or through reading a brochure. A recent survey of visitors to Galway examined the most important sources of information for visitors to Galway.

TABLE 4.1 — MAIN SOURCES OF INFORMATION ABOUT GALWAY

Heard About Galway from:	%
Friends/Relatives	52
Bord Fáilte Literature	11
Brochures/Posters/Leaflets	9
Tour Operator/Travel Agent	9
Commercial Guidebooks	8
Newspapers/Magazines	4
Tourist Offices	4
Other	2

Source: Galway Tourism Research Report, 1997

The important role of the family and friends in helping people decide on, or confirm, their travel plans is highlighted by this survey. The above table points to the critical role of ensuring positive word-of-mouth communication, whether that be via friends/relatives or tour operators.

EXPOSURE AND ATTENTION

Potential tourists have to be exposed to a message (e.g. an advertisement) about products before they can be expected to notice it. Exposure is achieved when it is *possible* for a tourist to see or hear a message. It refers to the process by which the consumer comes in physical contact with the stimulus (brochure, press advertisement, Internet site etc.). If a hotel wants to publicise its golfing breaks, it needs to consider which magazines, which special newspaper supplements, which Internet sites will enable the maximum potential number of the target market, i.e. golfers, to see it.

Just because a golfer is exposed to an advertisement for a hotel, because they buy the golf magazine it is advertised in, it does not automatically follow that the advertisement will be noticed (attended to). Attention refers to *the process by which an individual allocates part of their mental resources to a stimulus.* The extent to which attention to a message occurs depends on the nature of the stimulus (advertisement), the nature of the receiver (golfer) and personal relevance (importance of message to golfer).

PERCEPTION

Perception refers to the way that people filter the huge amount of information they receive and fit it into their understanding of the world. People will subconsciously organise messages into a way that makes it easier and quicker for them to make judgements on people, issues, companies, destinations etc. This often leads to distortions from the truth. Tourist Boards everywhere struggle to challenge stereotypes of their country or people. The market research conducted by Bord Fáilte in 1996 as part of the Tourism Brand Ireland project revealed critical misconceptions about Ireland. In Britain, especially among females, there was a perception that Ireland was a destination offering little of interest to families, with activities revolving around pubs. Continental Europeans, especially the French, felt that Ireland's restaurants and food options were limited. US consumers retained an idealised sense of Ireland as a land of unbounded welcome. Marketers need to have an understanding of how their product is perceived by customers.

BELIEFS AND ATTITUDES

Customers hold a wide variety of beliefs about tourism offerings. They may consider hotels to be sophisticated, destinations to be inaccessible, skiing to be fashionable, resorts to be unsuitable for families etc. It is important to distinguish between attitude and belief. Belief is concerned with the perceived presence of an attribute or characteristic. For example, a hotel is either seen to offer room service or it is not; a museum is perceived as being conveniently located or it is not, and so on. Attitude differs from belief because belief is neutral, whereas attitude contains belief and *opinion*. Let us take the example of a resort. Two people may share a *belief* that the resort is not suitable for children, but one person may have a favourable opinion of this (because they don't like the noise disruption of children), and the other person may have an unfavourable opinion (because they enjoy taking their children on holidays with them).

Attitudes have three components: cognitive, affective and conative. Taking the example above of a tourist considering a weekend away, Table 4.2 illustrates these three components.

TABLE 4.2 — COMPONENTS OF ATTITUDES

Component	Definition	Context	Example
Cognitive	Perceptual component of attitude	The conscious part of the attitude, involving beliefs, awareness, knowledge	A potential tourist may believe that Dublin has a wide variety of cultural tourism attractions

TABLE 4.2 — COMPONENTS OF ATTITUDES *contd.*

Component	Definition	Context	Example
Affective	Evaluative component of attitude	The feelings and emotions that the tourist has toward the object — these may not always be based on objective reality	Previous visitors to Dublin may have an affectionate recollection of holidays spent there, those who have not yet visited may have romantic images of the city through its famed literature etc.
Conative	Behavioural intention	The extent to which we are likely to act, whether to buy a product, or reject a product. It is not the same as actual behaviour, but rather intention to act.	The tourist, having formed a positive image of a weekend visit to Dublin, forms an intention to visit the city. This is the conation.

As mentioned in the above table, although someone has a positive attitude toward going to Dublin for a weekend break, it does not automatically follow that they will do so. They may have second thoughts nearer the time, financial circumstances may change, or partners may influence the person to choose another destination.

Changing Attitudes

Bringing about a change in attitude is difficult, especially if relates to an area of importance to a consumer. While an advertiser might be able to make a person switch brand of toothpaste quite easily, it is much more difficult to change attitudes in fundamental areas of life such as religion and politics. Changing attitudes to holiday destinations is also quite a challenge. Negative attitudes can stem from personal experience, media coverage or the word of mouth influence of others, making a shift in attitudes difficult.

To change attitudes three basic strategies exist, and these are related to the components of an attitude.

Change the beliefs: The Bord Fáilte campaigns have sought to change beliefs among some, most notably British, markets that Ireland is very pub oriented in its entertainment for tourists. The television commercials featured stunning landscapes and people in a variety of fun scenes.

Change the evaluative criteria: This involves the attempt to encourage customers to consider other evaluative criteria. If people feel a hotel is very expensive, the hotel might not be able to change this *belief,* but it could encourage the potential guest to consider other evaluative criteria, such as the value that is being offered.

Introduce new evaluative criteria: A hotel might, through new product introductions, give the potential guest other factors to consider when making their choice.

MEMORY

One view of memory is that it is comprised of three components or storage systems, as depicted in Figure 4.3.

FIGURE 4.3 — MEMORY COMPONENTS/STORAGE SYSTEMS

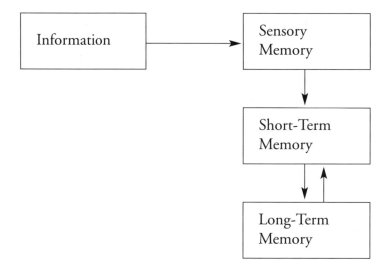

Memory is assumed to function as follows:

1. The stimulus enters and is processed first in the sensory ~~/~~ extracted about colour, contour and so on. No meaning i~~/~~ this stage.
2. The input then goes to short-term memory where it is held ⌐ is analysed for meaning. The input fades from short-term memoi₊₎ rehearsed. Advertisers can help this process of rehearsing by ensuring thaᴛ consumer is exposed several times to a message, such as in a Jurys' *Treasure Your Leisure* radio campaign, the objective of which is to ensure that, over time, the audience associates the Jurys name with leisure breaks.
3. Information that is rehearsed is then transferred to long-term memory where it is stored permanently. It may be retrieved later, such as when we are considering a city break and we recall seeing some programme about Barcelona on television. Forgetting occurs when means of retrieval are lost or when new information provides interference. This is a real problem in tourism advertising, as so many tourism organisations and destinations are now competing for people's attention.

PERSONALITY

Personality may be defined as the distinctive psychological characteristics, or *traits*, which are evident in the unique behaviour of each individual. These characteristics are what make each person unique. Numerous studies have been conducted to categorise people by personality and to explore the marketing effectiveness of such a categorisation. One of the most common viewpoints is to view people as having introverted or extroverted and stable or unstable personality traits. Generally, it is felt that the application of personality in tourism marketing is limited, largely because of the problem of targeting on the basis of personality.

Rather than try to use personality as a basis for segmenting markets, a more common approach has been to develop typologies, or groupings of tourists based on common attitudes and behaviours in respect of tourism. A survey by American Express in 1989 identified five *typologies*, or groupings, of tourists.

TABLE 4.3 — TYPOLOGIES OF TOURISTS

Category	Description
Adventurers	Adventurers are independent and confident. They like to try new activities, meet new people and experience different cultures. Generally, they are better educated and more affluent than the members of other groups. For the adventurers, travel plays a central

.3 — TYPOLOGIES OF TOURISTS *contd.*

Category	Description
	role in their lives. Besides, the adventurers are predominantly male and they tend to be younger than other travellers, with 44 per cent of the group being between the ages of 18 and 34.
Worriers	Worriers experience considerable anxiety from the perceived stresses of travel, have little confidence in their ability to make travel decisions and are generally afraid to fly. Overall, worriers tend to be less educated and less affluent than other travellers in their country. Moreover, this category travels the least of the five groups and, when they do, they are more likely to travel domestically. Worriers are predominantly female and rather older travellers, nearly half are over the age of 50.
Dreamers	Dreamers are intrigued with the idea of travel and attach great importance to the meaning it can bring to their lives. Despite reading and talking a lot about new destinations, they have travel experiences that are usually less remarkable than their ideas and more often oriented toward relaxation than adventure. The dreamers belong to the modest income and education categories and they are usually women aged 50 and over. Most dreamers rely on maps and guidebooks when they travel to new places.
Economisers	Economisers. Travel provides economisers with a routine outlet for relaxation and is not perceived as an experience that adds meaning to their lives. The economisers seek value in travel and they do not think it is worth paying extra for specialist amenities and services, even if they can afford them. Economisers are more likely to be men than women and they are slightly older than their travelling counterparts. These people have an average income level and are slightly less educated. They take an average of two trips per year.

TABLE 4.3 — TYPOLOGIES OF TOURISTS *contd.*

Category	Description
Indulgers	Indulgers are generally wealthier than other travellers and they are willing to pay for additional comfort and better service when they travel. The indulgers are more likely than other travellers to stay in large hotels because they like to be pampered. This group of travellers are second only to adventurers in the amount they travel and they are equally divided between men and women.

Source: American Express 1989: cited in Lumsden 1997

2. EXTERNAL INFLUENCES ON CONSUMER

It is essential for tourism marketers to identify the complex range of external influences that affect the individual choices of the consumer. Knowing what these influences are is of crucial benefit in identifying where to concentrate marketing effort. By targeting and using these influences, such as family members, social groupings or work colleagues, marketers can achieve that which their own messages alone cannot.

CULTURE

Culture may be defined as 'a set of beliefs, values, attitudes, habits and forms of behaviour that are shared by a society and are transmitted from generation to generation' (Bennett and Kassarjian, 1972).

There are several dimensions of culture that are reflected in the above definition.

Firstly, culture is *shared.* Common rituals and customs, languages and dialects that are commonly held mark each society. At an aggregate level we can say that culture is visible at the level of the country. Foreign tourists often cite the attraction of Irish culture as a motivator to come here. Irish culture has been the focus of numerous studies. Irish people are regarded as gregarious, sport loving, spiritual and having a strong sense of pride in their heritage: including arts, native sports and music. These *traits* continue to have an enduring appeal to foreign visitors.

A second important dimension to culture is the fact that it is *learnt.* Through the process of *socialisation,* individuals develop specific patterns of behaviour and attitudes, which are part of a broader social system.

Although culture is passed from generation to generation, it should be acknowledged that culture is *dynamic,* with rapid changes evident in many aspects of culture. Many of these changes are driven by an ever-expanding global culture, which is in turn influenced by the rapid emergence of a common global communications media such as Internet and

Satellite TV. Certain US soap operas have become a staple part of peoples' lives across the globe, as has the huge impact that Hollywood has on a common global culture.

Culture has many influences on consumer behaviour. Hoteliers know only too well that wide differences exist in the behaviour patterns of different nationalities among their guest list. Being sensitive to these differences is increasingly important in marketing internationally.

In certain countries family togetherness is extremely powerful. In France, it is the norm for all family members to dine out as a unit on a weekly basis. Similarly, the importance attaching to food and the social dimension of eating out is a strong dimension to most Mediterranean countries. This is reflected in the particularly strong interest in cuisine quality as a deciding factor in destination choice. Bord Fáilte's television advertisements in the French market have a special emphasis on showing the natural food quality on offer.

In many countries, Ireland included, socialising is assigned a strong part of the cultural make-up. Indeed, a defining dimension of Irishness for many commentators is our famed *pub culture*. In other countries, particularly in the Mediterranean, it is the café culture that dominates. In most countries in Europe it is commonplace to have a beer with each meal — hence in France McDonald's includes lager on its menu. In Asia, the concept of the group is of central importance, particularly the loyalty employees feel to their company. It is very common to see Japanese tourists in Europe being led by a flag-waving leader around various tourism attractions. With respect to complaining, certain cultures, especially Asian ones, are notoriously reluctant to complain, being reluctant to have the server *lose face*. Their displeasure is evident only later, when they refuse to return to a destination and disparage it when they return home. This makes it difficult to assess exactly how satisfied certain nationalities are. US visitors, by way of contrast, are renowned by their willingness to assert their right to the highest service standards, a reflection of their culture's premium attached to individual rights.

Tourism itself has been a *shaper of culture* in two ways.

Firstly, visiting tourists have impacts, both damaging and beneficial, on the culture of the countries being visited. Tourism's potential to enhance cultures is evident in Ireland with the rise in popularity of traditional music, and arts and crafts, in many respects facilitated by tourism demand. Festivals, celebrating Irish culture in all its diversity, have been recognised as having a huge potential to attract overseas visitors. Of course, the negative impact of tourism can be seen too, in the impact that it has on indigenous cultures. This is most evident in underdeveloped countries, where tourism development has damaged the physical environment of native communities, and in extreme cases led to serious crime problems. Publicans in Dublin's Temple Bar cultural quarter have in recent times called for a curtailment of the activities of visiting British *stag* parties, citing their negative effect on the cultural ambience of the area.

Secondly, tourism shapes culture by virtue of the impact travel has on changing peoples' attitudes and behaviour. The *café culture* that we see today in many large Irish towns and cities, has been strongly influenced by the large numbers of Irish people who have enjoyed the atmosphere in Continental Europe. This more extensive travel experience is also reflected in a much wider choice of cuisine being sampled by Irish people.

Today's tourism marketers also need to recognise the existence of a wide variety of subcultures. These are cultural groups that operate within a larger cultural context. Ireland is a relatively homogeneous culture by international standards. Countries, such as Britain, which have a wide ethnic mix, need to recognise the subcultural influences and adapt their communication and products accordingly. Youth subculture is a particularly difficult one for marketers to tap into. The Club 25 brand is an example of an Irish tour operator that specifically targets the youth market, with an unashamed appeal to their chosen market.

FIGURE 4.4 — ADVERTISEMENT FOR CLUB 25

SOCIAL INTERACTION

In addition to the impact that living in a particular culture has on the individual, the individual interacts with a wide variety of groups and individuals on a daily basis. These interactions have a profound effect in shaping their behaviour.

We can identify three groups as having particular relevance: *reference groups,* the *family* and *social class.*

REFERENCE GROUPS

A reference group may be defined as *a group from which the individual gains direction and influences behaviour and attitudes.*

A reference group is so called because it *acts as a point of reference for an individual.* Sometimes the individual will use a particular group as a point of reference in defining what they do not want to be. Such groups are called *dissociative groups.* More commonly, reference groups to which an individual would like to belong are called aspirational groups. The launch of the VIP magazine in Ireland is one example of the strong interest in many people in studying, and emulating, the lifestyles of the rich and famous.

Reference groups act in two ways.

Firstly, they act in establishing *norms.* Norms are behavioural standards that are set by the group. Secondly, the group acts as a basis for the individual to make comparisons. The desire to conform to groups is quite strong. By showing the product or service in use or recommended by specific reference groups, marketers can make the product or service seem more attractive to potential buyers.

The degree to which a reference group acts on an individual depends on several factors. The more cohesive a group the more likely it is that the individual will adhere to the group norms. The more an individual wants to become a member of reference group the more likely it is that they will be influenced by that group. Not all services are equally prone to reference group influence. Holidays are often influenced because of the high degree of social visibility attaching to them. Certain people are strongly influenced by others to go on certain types of holiday. Take the example of holiday packages targeting singles: whether to go skiing or to choose a sunshine type of holiday is highly likely to be influenced by a reference group. The influence of the reference group may be quite strong in terms of the type of holiday chosen, but less so in the case of brand or tour operator/travel agent used.

In the world of business the choice of a conference venue is often highly influenced by the word-of-mouth influence of influential sources, called *opinion leaders.* Exhibit 4.1 examines the use of opinion leaders to help promote tourism in Waterford.

EXHIBIT 4.1

OPINION LEADERSHIP *IN ACTION*

WATERFORD TOURISM

Waterford Tourism have been very successful in their attempts to use opinion leaders when targeting the domestic tourist market. Throughout the summer of 1999, they ran a campaign of forty-eight spots on national radio and sixty spots on local radio stations across Ireland. All the advertisements were based on the testimonials of three well-known personalities with Waterford connections. Des Smith, designer of Waterford Castle Golf Course, was chosen to promote the great golf courses in Waterford. Mick McCarthy, with family connections in West Waterford, promoted Waterford as a great family destination. Finally, balladeer Liam Clancy promoted the beautiful west of the county, and gave a special mention to the new visitor attraction *Waterford Treasures at the Granary*.

As a further example, Waterford Tourism teamed up with the Waterford Lions to make a pitch for the year 2000 Lions Conference. Lions clubs are voluntary clubs of business people who fundraise for charities. As part of their campaign to attract the conference to Waterford the chief executive of Waterford Crystal, Michael Kenny, featured in a specially commissioned promotional video. This is an example of the use of a high profile and credible person to attract visitors. Waterford Tourism were successful in their efforts in bringing more than 300 delegates to the conference.

Source: Waterford Tourism newsletters

While Waterford Tourism have been successful in attracting Irish conference delegates to their county, the Convention Bureau of Ireland plays the leading role in developing international conference business. It has developed a pioneering concept, based on reference group theory, to attract more conferences to Ireland.

EXHIBIT 4.2

REFERENCE GROUPS *IN ACTION*

CONVENTION BUREAU OF IRELAND

Convention Bureau of Ireland's most successful marketing ploy comes at a very low cost and is very effective — the Conference Ambassador Programme. Quite simply, leading academic, professional and business personalities are actively encouraged to bring conference, incentive or meeting business to Ireland. The idea is simple. An Irish person attending a conference abroad can invite the organisers to run their next available conference in Ireland. Similarly, Irish managers of multinational companies can suggest that their international colleagues hold meetings in Ireland or have Ireland included on the list for incentive rewards. 'Irish people are great at bidding for conference and meeting business,' says Bernard McMahon, CBI chief executive, who also argues that there is a benefit for the individual involved. 'Without a doubt, the Irish person who brings a conference or meeting to Ireland increases his or her standing within their association, organisation or business,' he says.

The CBI supports inspection visits to Ireland by convention organisers and advises on the organisation of the event. It also acts as a bridge to suppliers of convention services and, where appropriate, arranges Government or municipal involvement.

In a new marketing initiative, the CBI is presently seeking to appoint 1,000 of the top Irish American business men and women to become *Ambassadors for Ireland*. The campaign is designed to replicate the Conference Ambassador scheme that has worked so well in Irish academic, professional and business circles. The literature that accompanies the invitation to become an Ambassador for Ireland makes its case succinctly: 'Your status in major business circles and your history of unselfish service to Ireland establish you as a key influence whose ideas and suggestions are greatly valued by your peers and associates. By endorsing Ireland, you help many to experience all that is uniquely beautiful about Ireland, as well as helping to create sound business opportunities between our countries.'

Source: 'Growth In Conference Business Continues', *Business and Finance,* 22 May 1997

THE FAMILY

From the point of view of tourism, the family is an extremely important *unit of consumption.* The family remains a dominant purchaser of tourism services. Many Irish seaside resorts are almost completely dependent on the attraction they hold for families. Today these seaside resorts face increased international competition from countries such as Spain and France, which have become annual destinations for thousands of Irish families. Certain Irish hotel chains have responded in kind, most notably Ryans, who specifically target families in their advertising and have developed attractions designed to appeal to the entire family.

FIGURE 4.5 — RYANS ADVERTISEMENT

Understanding how families purchase holidays is therefore of great importance to marketers.

At the micro level (the individual family) identifying the complex interactions and degrees of influence that exist within families can pay handsome rewards. We need to know the relative influence of different family members at various stages of the purchasing process; who collects the information, who has most influence on when and how long to holiday for, do children exert much influence etc.

At the macro level (society) marketers are interested in understanding the rapidly changing nature of the modern family. Traditional families, with predictable purchasing patterns, are increasingly hard to find. A more sophisticated, and sensitive, response is required in developing products, services and communication.

The term family is particularly difficult to define because it is in such a state of flux. The contemporary family consists of a wide variety of combinations of people. A traditional definition by Shiffman and Kanuk (1998) is as follows:

'A family is defined as two or more persons related by blood, marriage, or adoption who reside together.'

Families may be included as a subset of *households*. A household includes people residing together who are not related by blood, marriage or adoption. In Ireland there has been a rapid rise in such households, led by an increase in cohabiting couples and single people sharing accommodation. A particular trend has been the increase in single person households.

Three types of family have been identified. These are:

The *married couple* — husband and wife, includes those couples who have recently married and have no children and older couples whose children have left home.

The *nuclear family* — husband, wife and one or more children. This family unit actually comprises only one quarter of all Irish households and has been in decline in recent years.

The *extended family* — comprises the nuclear family, together with at least one grandparent in residence.

Both the nuclear and the extended family have been in decline as the rate of divorce, separation, and out-of-wedlock births increase in Ireland. This phenomenon mirrors trends in Europe and America.

This increase in single person and non-traditional households is reflected in Table 4.4.

TABLE 4.4 — ADAPTED FROM CSO: CENSUS 1996. PRINCIPAL DEMOGRAPHIC RESULTS

Years	Single %	Married %	Separated %	Widowed/Divorced %
1986	39·3	51·8	1·5	7·4
1991	39·2	51·4	2·1	7·3
1996	41·4	48·8	3·2	6·6

When studying the composition of families in society, we can observe that they pass through well-defined stages. These stages are important to tourism marketers because they often pose constraints on purchasing and have a strong impact on the nature of the products consumed, as well as on the role of individual family members.

Family Life-cycle

The *family life-cycle* describes the various stages that the family passes through with the passage of time. The changes in society discussed earlier have led to the development of the modernised family life-cycle as shown in Table 4.5.

TABLE 4.5 — FAMILY LIFE-CYCLE

Stage	Typical Items of Expenditure
Young single adult	Clothing, entertainment, car
Unmarried couples	Low-cost furniture, budget travel
Newly married family, no children	Furniture, appliances, entertainment
Married without children	Design furniture, entertainment, smaller homes, sports cars, business suits
Family with young children at home	Insurance, medical expenses, children's clothing, toys
Family with older children at home	Personal electronic items, holidays, larger homes
Single parents	Low-cost housing, discount food, inexpensive clothing
Divorced couples without children	Apartments, small packages, dating services, clubs
Family, children left home (empty nest)	Travel, hobbies, home improvement
Family, main wage earner retired	Medicines, smaller residences, jewellery
Solitary survivor	Medical expenses, restaurants, apartments

Family Roles

There are five key roles that family members can play in the decision-making process. These are outlined in Table 4.6 below.

TABLE 4.6 — FAMILY BUYING ROLES

Role Played	Nature of Involvement
Influencers	These family members provide information about a product or service. One person may volunteer to go to the travel agents to collect the required brochures, or to visit a travel show to talk to service providers.
Gatekeepers	These family members control the flow of information about a product or service.
Decision-makers	The person(s) who make the ultimate decision on various dimensions of the purchase decision; the time to holiday, duration, destination, budget, accommodation type etc.
Buyers (Purchasers)	The person(s) who make the actual purchase. One person may have a credit card and therefore they actually pay for the holiday. There may be only one wage earner in the family and they may pay.
Users	The person(s) who use or consume the particular product or service. The whole family may holiday together and therefore all members are users.

The importance of the decision may affect who has influence in the decision-making process. Choosing a holiday destination probably falls into this category and therefore we can expect to see most influence being exerted by parents. Children's influence is quite strong in areas of particular relevance to them. For example, children will have a strong influence on day-trip activities, but quite a weak one on holiday budgets or accommodation types. Other factors also impact on the nature of decision-making.

The relative influence of different family members is a continuing source of study for market researchers. In traditional families purchase decisions fall into four broad categories:

- *Husband-dominated* decisions are typically found in purchase categories such as DIY tools and financial matters.
- *Wife-dominated* decisions are found in food and clothing.
- *Joint* or *Syncretic* purchasing can be found in several categories, including tourism. In fact, decisions concerning holidays are among the most syncretically based.

Other categories where joint decision-making is evident include home decoration, children's education and house purchase.

- Either husband or wife can take *autonomic* decisions. Categories where this is seen include toiletries, men's suits and alcoholic beverages.

It is important to note that the purchasing roles are influenced by the different stages of the decision-making process. The decision-making process involves several stages: problem recognition, information search, alternative evaluation and choice. Davis and Rigaux (1974) established that the wife has a stronger influence in recognising the need for products and services than the husband, who does play a more important role in the evaluation of competing offerings. As can be seen in Table 4.7, in the decision-making stage there is an increase in syncretic purchasing behaviour. With regard to children's impact in the holiday decision process, Holdert and Antonides (1997) found that they have a greater influence in the alternative evaluation and choice stages than they do in problem recognition or information search.

TABLE 4.7 — INFLUENCE OF HUSBAND AND WIFE IN DECISION-MAKING, DAVIS AND RIGAUX, 1974

	Problem Recognition %	Orientation %	Decision %
Husband-dominant	8	12	8
Wife-dominant	24	28	20
Autonomous	40	36	20
Syncretic	28	24	52

Several factors influence the nature of the different roles:

Social Class. A person's social class is influential in buying styles. In middle-class households there is more joint decision-making. In higher income families the occurrence of two income-earners is higher leading to more autonomic purchasing, whereas in lower social class units roles are more clearly defined and either husband or wife are dominant.

Perceived Risk. Increased financial, social or physical risk associated with a purchase usually leads to an increase in syncretic purchasing. Holidays are usually the most expensive annual expenditure item, as well as carrying degrees of social risk.

Time Pressures. These are having an impact in reducing the amount of time available for joint decision-making. Today's hectic lifestyles are perhaps responsible for an increased incidence of autonomic purchasing.

The stage in the family life-cycle is also a factor. Couples who are just married have not developed *role specialisations.* Over time, experience dictates that certain roles may be assigned to one partner or the other.

SOCIAL CLASS

Social class can be seen as the division of society into different status groupings and strata, where people in each stratum share similar rank. People in different social classes share similar preferences, financial circumstances and behaviours. Social classes are considered more or less permanent and homogenous categories in society. Measurement of social class is typically measured in terms of the occupation of the head of household. The Central Statistics Office classifies the Irish population into the following social groups.

TABLE 4.8 — IRISH SOCIO-ECONOMIC GROUPS

Socio-Economic Group	Population %
A. Employers and Managers	11·4
B. Higher Professional	4·4
C. Lower Professional	8·0
D. Non-manual	17·0
E. Manual skilled	14·2
F. Semi-skilled	9·5
G. Unskilled	7·6
H. Own account workers	5·6
I. Farmers	8·5
Z. All others/unknown	11·7

Source: Principal Socio-Economic Results, Central Statistics Office, 1996

For marketing purposes the more common basis is to use a more simplified scale as shown in Table 4.9. This scale is based on the occupation status of the head of the household. These classifications are popular as the various media outlets in Ireland are monitored every six months in terms of the social class profile of their readers.

TABLE 4.9 — IRISH SOCIAL CLASS COMPOSITION

Grade	% of Population	Class Description
A, B	12·1	Upper, Upper Middle
C1	20·0	Lower Middle
C2	24·0	Skilled Working
D, E	27·0	Unskilled Working
F1	9·6	Large Farmers >50acres
F2	6·3	Small Farmers <50 acres, Farm Labourers

Source: Joint National Listenership Research/Market Research Bureau of Ireland, 1997

3. THE DECISION-MAKING PROCESS

The final part of the simple model of consumer behaviour, outlined earlier in figure 4.1, is the decision-making process. Consumers pass through a number of stages when purchasing any product or service. Choosing an annual holiday location is often a long process with a high degree of risk involved. There is the obvious financial cost, but equally there are other risks such as safety and the social implications of choosing certain destinations.

The decision-making process follows from the individual pyschological differences and the external influences on the consumer outlined previously in this chapter. The stages follow logically from each other and the marketer needs to be sensitive to the stage that an individual is at, in order to organise the most effective marketing campaigns.

FIGURE 4.6 — STAGES INVOLVED IN THE CONSUMER DECISION-MAKING PROCESS

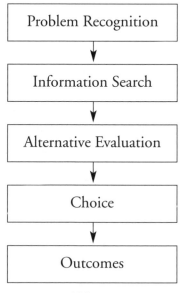

PROBLEM RECOGNITION

The decision-making process begins when the customer is aware of a need that requires satisfying. Recognition of a problem can be internal, such as when we are hungry or tired and need food, or sleep, respectively. The problem may be generated externally too, as when family members may discuss the option of a short break holiday and need to select a destination. A company executive may be instructed to go to Berlin to a crucial meeting and will need to find a suitable hotel. As discussed earlier, we have a complex series of motives that drive our behaviour. In advertising, marketers can seek to stimulate recognition of needs through imagery and persuasive messages.

INFORMATION SEARCH

Having established the need for a tourism product, the consumer must search for information to make a suitable choice. Internal search means that the consumer relies only on their long-term memory store. If we are familiar and happy with the place we usually go to on holidays, then there will be no need for external search. External search in the tourism and hospitality sector is often quite extensive. We should not forget that the most commonly consulted source for information remains friends and relatives, particularly for leisure tourism. Consumers also rely on information from guidebooks and travel programmes on television. Marketers have only a limited degree of influence over this type of information search. Consumers will sometimes pay to search for information about tourism and hospitality services, as is the case with holiday fairs discussed later in this book. Other marketer-influenced sources of information include television and radio advertising. As will be discussed later in this book, the Internet is rapidly becoming a very important source of travel and hospitality information.

ALTERNATIVE EVALUATION

Having searched for information about alternative destinations or products, the consumer will normally have just a few to choose from. This group is known as the *consideration set.*

Consumers form attitudes about the alternatives on offer. Often a mental trade-off has to be made. While destination A may have a fantastic beach, it may be lacking in night life, when compared to destination B. Marketers need to be aware of the factors, or evaluative criteria as discussed earlier, that are used to make a choice between destinations or holiday types. Price is usually a key criteria, as is shown in Exhibit 4.3 later in this chapter.

CHOICE

Having evaluated between alternatives, and considered them, the consumer makes a choice. Sometimes this choice may be heavily influenced by circumstances. A planned holiday in the US may be postponed in favour of a break in Ireland, due to unexpected financial pressures. The choice may be brought into effect in a number of ways. When consumers make a choice with a high degree of risk, and following a period of extensive search, they often experience a degree of anxiety about their choice. They will be conscious of the positive aspects of the alternatives they rejected.

This anxiety is known as *cognitive dissonance*, and marketers can take advantage of it by reassuring the customer that they have made the right choice. Often consumers will actively seek out information that will support the choice that they have made. By sending brochures and information packs to tourists before they arrive in Ireland, companies can go a long way to providing the necessary reassurance.

OUTCOMES

Two outcomes are possible following the tourism and hospitality experience; satisfaction or dissatisfaction. Much research today in the tourism and hospitality sector is centred in gaining a deeper understanding of what contributes to a satisfactory experience on the part of the guest.

The decision process is a complicated one and needs careful research on the part of the marketer. Exhibit 4.3 below examines some of the issues in the decision process in the context of the promotion of the Shannon-Erne Waterway.

EXHIBIT 4.3

CONSUMER BEHAVIOUR *IN ACTION*

SHANNON-ERNE WATERWAY

The Shannon-Erne Waterway links the majestic expanse of Upper and Lower Lough Erne in Northern Ireland to the mighty Shannon River in the Republic of Ireland, creating Europe's longest navigable leisure waterway (750 km). The Shannon-Erne Waterway project involved the reopening of the historic Ballinamore-Ballyconnell Canal that links Ireland's two greatest waterways, the Shannon and Erne river systems.

Many parts of the canal itself, together with a number of locks which had been closed for many years, were rebuilt to open up a section of navigable water stretching some 200 miles from Fermanagh in Northern Ireland to Limerick in the South.

The British and Irish Governments envisaged the restoration of the Shannon-Erne Waterway as being the *flagship* cross-border tourism project. So far it has brought development, prosperity and real co-operation among people and organisations from the public, private and community sector on both sides of the border.

The Waterway

The original Waterway was constructed between 1846 and 1860 to link the Shannon and Erne navigation for commercial traffic. It was closed and abandoned in 1869. The reconstruction and restoration took place between 1991 and 1993 exclusively as a tourist and leisure amenity under a joint initiative by the Irish and British Governments. Total investment in the project amounted to some IR£30 million.

Care of the Waterway is now a function of the Office of Public Works, Dublin, and the Department of Agriculture, Northern Ireland. As part of the Belfast Agreement a separate North-South body was established to take control of the running of the Waterway.

The total length of Shannon-Erne Waterway is 62·5 km and it traverses 11·5 km of lake, 42·5 km of canalised river and 8·5 km of still-water canal.

The development has prompted a host of complementary projects. For example, a new marina for commercial cruisers has been established in Belturbet,

Co. Cavan. New restaurants have been opened in villages in County Leitrim; a hostel and coffee shop were opened in Ballinamore and a number of other services have also started such as taxis, home baking and a new air charter service direct from Switzerland to Fermanagh.

When the restoration project was undertaken at the beginning of the 1990s, 120 years of neglect had reduced the Waterway to a sad, weed-choked channel of broken bridges and missing locks. Using the original sites and stonework, the bridges are now restored, the Waterway is navigable for modern pleasure cruisers and the new locks are operated by a push-button electro-hydraulic system.

No large cities or major industries mar the landscape along the canal's pleasant course. Reed banks thrive in the lakes and hedgerows parcel the pleasant fields, providing refuge for a great variety of wildlife. Wild flora decorates the banks and moors, delighting the senses. Long before recorded history, early man marked the landscape with mysterious monuments in stone. These, together with early Christian establishments, punctuate the landscape.

Facilities

Perches (fixed stakes with a top-mark) mark the navigation channel throughout. The conventional markings used on the Erne system apply from the Erne through Woodford Reach to the mid-point of Summit Reach, thereafter the conventions of the Shannon Navigation apply. There are six modern public moorings at Leitrim, Lough Scur (near Keshcarrigan), Ballinamore, Lough Garadice (at Haughton's Shore), Ballyconnell and Aghalane. Standard amenities at all moorings include slipway, car park, telephone, toilets, showers, fresh water and pump-out facility. Additional facilities are being developed.

Cruisers are available for charter at Enniskillen, Belturbet and Carrick On Shannon. The area is well supplied with excellent accommodation for visitors, mainly in guesthouses, and is noted for its abundance of comfortable bed and breakfasts. Several good restaurants lie within easy reach of the Waterway.

The Waterway is already well established with anglers for trout and coarse fish: reconstruction has improved the fishing grounds and brown trout have been restocked. Wildlife includes badgers, otters, foxes, kingfishers, mute swans, whooper swans and many migratory species of duck. Other leisure amenities include local golf facilities ranging from championship eighteen-hole standard to attractive nine-hole courses. Several riding stables provide tuition, hacking and trekking. Canoes and bicycles are also available for hire. Full tourist information facilities are located at Ballinamore, Carrick-On-Shannon and Enniskillen.

Shannon-Erne Waterway Promotions Ltd

Shannon-Erne Waterway Promotions Ltd is the generic marketing organisation responsible for promoting the Waterway. Its objective is to introduce as many

people at home and abroad to the Waterway and to get more Waterway traffic moving from north to south and south to north. They work closely with the entire cruise hire fleets in Ireland helping to sell a quality fleet to those people wishing to have a memorable holiday experience. Since the canal opened in 1994 an average of 15,000 visitors per year have passed through the Waterway. It is calculated that the impact of this on the region has created 300 sustainable jobs.

The marketing manager of Shannon-Erne Waterways Promotions Ltd is Alan Hill. He has observed interesting aspects of consumer behaviour among those who use the Waterway.

Market Characteristics

One group who use the Waterway heavily are the *Shogun anglers,* named after their preference for four-wheel-drive vehicles. These are mostly from the UK and particularly enjoy the access to towns and villages, they don't mind spending money in local villages and they can get back to the jetty in the evening. For this group the social aspect of cruising on the Waterway is of prime importance. It offers a relaxing way to mingle with friends and enjoy the local pubs en route. According to Alan Hill the ecological aspect is of minimum importance to this group, who are typically from the top ten per cent of the social class spectrum.

The Irish market is changing very rapidly with a change in holidaying patterns toward short breaks at home. There is a direct correlation in the rise in income and the preference for short breaks. One of the major cruiser hire companies now finds that the Irish market is second only to the German market, which has been suffering in recent years.

The Irish market has a tendency to book extremely late. The industry does not like this, money is not a problem, but they tend to leave it very late. Alan Hill says, 'Back in 1970 there were 500 private craft, by 1998 that number had gone up to well over 2,500. A lot of the people who would have taken a craft are now in a position to buy their own craft. It's the younger set who is renting.'

Alan Hill has noticed a trend among Irish people to use a cruise on the Shannon as a solution to their need for a short break. 'One family had booked short weekends — it was their fourth weekend of the summer. I think you will see much more of this. Up until now the sector hasn't needed the domestic market — the industry did not bother informing the domestic market of the potential of the Irish waterways as a holiday experience...it's only now that people are looking in a strategic way at the potential of the domestic market to account for twenty-five per cent of the market.'

While the Irish market is set to become the most important one, Alan Hill is concerned that use of the Waterway should not become the preserve of the well-to-do. 'The Irish are more self-confident and are very critical of those presenting something as a super premium product. I would hate to see anybody trying to elevate the waterways...to be outside the reach of the majority of Irish people. We have to maintain a very tight control of the environment, sorting out bottlenecks such as a lack of mooring facilities. There is almost boat rage now on the Shannon!'

In terms of the information seeking phase of the decision-making process, Alan Hill has some interesting observations.

Information sources consulted vary widely between nationalities. Eighty-five per cent of Germans book through tour operators. They remain a vital point of first contact for either repeat or first-timers. They pick up a programme for large tour operators such as DER tours. At present some twenty-eight German tour operators feature Irish waterways, ahead of any other Irish product featured, including Dublin. In 1970 some forty per cent of all people on the Shannon and Erne were British, by 1973 this had fallen to thirteen per cent following the outbreak of the Troubles. The Irish industry had to desperately find new markets. It was established that the German market loved Ireland and so became the focus of marketing activity. British consumers are more likely to make enquiries as a result of seeing advertising in the press and magazines.

In their evaluation between holiday alternatives, Alan Hill emphasises the important role of price. 'I think price is very important. Even though you may have a very high earning middle-class couple who can go to Dar-es-Salaam or Bali, money's no problem, when you really scratch below the surface, money is always a primary issue in a holiday with…ninety-five per cent of people who buy holidays. It would be easy to create the illusion that it [Waterway Holidays] is not price sensitive. I would say it is very price sensitive.'

Waterways are not isolated from competition. It's not just a case of getting a message across and they will come. Alan Hill points out that a French customer could have bought two weeks on Canada's waterways for the price of one week in Ireland in 1999. 'Their [Canada's] season is half of the Irish season. They are iced up. The same is true of Scandinavia, particularly.'

The marketing approach of Shannon-Erne Promotions is to broaden the appeal of using the Waterway. 'We are deliberately getting away from aiming our holiday at boaty people, people who wear Timberland shoes and funny hats . . . . The boaty message will attract one per cent of those who might be interested. Moving it into the mainstream is the objective,' says Hill.

'The accommodation is on your boat, it's simple to drive your boat, you go thought beautiful unspoilt parts of Ireland, you're using scheduled flights into Ireland and you've a private transfer. For a party of six people it represents good value, you are moving that percentage from one per cent to two or three per cent effectively trebling the business.'

Source: Personal Interview with Alan Hill and Shannon-Erne web site

CHAPTER SUMMARY

Consumer behaviour is a very complex phenomenon. The consumer must process advertising and other commercial messages. This process is subject to internal influences that include psychological forces such as motivation, perception and attitudes. Marketers are particularly interested in the application of learning theory to help them understand how consumers process advertisements. Consumers are part of a social system, which exerts huge influences on their behaviour. The family, in particular, is important both as a shaper of our behaviour and as a buying unit in its own right.

KEY WORDS AND PHRASES

Psychological Forces	Culture
Motivation	Perception
External Influences	Cognitive Dissonance
Attitudes	Decision Process
Learning	

QUESTIONS FOR REVIEW

1. Discuss the individual psychological influences on consumer behaviour.
2. Discuss the external influences on consumer behaviour.
3. Describe the alternative roles that can be played in the family decision-making process.
4. How useful is Maslow's *Hierarchy of Needs* model in explaining tourist buying behaviour?

QUESTIONS FOR DISCUSSION

1. Consider any holiday you have spent with your family. Who acted as influencer, information gatherer, etc.
2. Consider the cultural forces that might affect a company seeking to expand an Irish Pub brand into overseas markets.
3. Apply the five stages of the decision process to the selection of a holiday destination for a short break.
4. Conduct an exercise on your group's perceptions of three countries as holiday destinations. How have your perceptions about the destination developed? What accounts for any individual differences in perception, if any, in your group?

REFERENCES AND FURTHER READING

Bennett, P.D. and Kassarjian, H.J., *Consumer Behaviour*, Prentice Hall: Englewood Cliffs, New Jersey 1972.

Davis, H.L. and Rigaux B.P., 'Perception of marital roles in decision processes', *Journal of Consumer Research*, 1, pp. 51–61: 1974.

Engel, J. and Blackwell, R., *Consumer Behaviour*, 4th edn., Holt-Saunders: New York 1982.

Galway Chamber of Commerce, *Galway Tourism Research Report*, Galway Regional Technical College: 1997.

Holdert, F. and Antonides, G., 'Family type effects on household decision-making', *Advances in Consumer Research*, 24, pp. 48–54: 1997.

Jacoby, J., 'Consumer Psychology: An Octenium', eds. Paul Mussen and Mark Rosenweig, *Annual Review of Psychology*: 1976.

Murray, J. and O'Driscoll, A., *Managing Marketing: Concepts and Irish Cases*, 2nd edn., Gill & Macmillan: Dublin 1999.

USEFUL WEB SITES

www.globalchange.com   Details on changing cultures

www.shannon-erne.com   Shannon-Erne web site

CHAPTER 5

Strategic Market Planning

INTRODUCTION

So far, this book examines the practical aspects of marketing, from identifying consumers' needs and wants through to designing and delivering a product or service that aims to meet those needs and wants, and maintains customer loyalty despite the efforts of the competition. The tools that make up the marketing mix (seven *Ps*) are critical for implementing the marketing concept in a tourism and hospitality business. Each one adds value to the overall offering, contributing toward competitive advantage that will attract the target market. What constitutes the best mix to adopt varies from business to business and must be subject to research, experimentation and judgement. Marketing managers in the tourism and hospitality industries must ask the strategic questions:

- What business are we in?
- Which markets should we be in?
- What does our business have that will give it a competitive advantage?
- Do we have the resources, skills and assets to reach our objectives?
- Where do we want to be in five years' time?
- What will our competitors be doing in five years' time?

These concerns are strategic, not operational, as they affect the whole organisation and provide a framework for operational decisions. They focus on the future, aligning the whole organisation to new opportunities and challenges within the changing marketing environment. Thus, strategic market planning may have long-term implications for the direction and shape of the whole business, rather than just impacting on the operational management of the marketing mix elements themselves.

CHAPTER OBJECTIVES

After studying this chapter, you will be able to:

- Define strategic planning and understand the stages in the process
- Identify strategic business units and perform a situation analysis on a tourism and hospitality operation

- Establish objectives and formulate strategies for a business and understand the process of implementation and control
- Fully appreciate the potential use of strategic tools such as the BCG Matrix, and the Product-Market Matrix
- Prepare a marketing plan for a tourism or hospitality operation

DEFINITION OF STRATEGIC PLANNING

One of the major challenges facing today's tourism and hospitality companies is how to build and maintain viable businesses in a rapidly changing market-place and business environment. In the 1950s, the answer was thought to lie in increasing production efficiency. In the 1960s and 1970s, companies sought growth and profits through acquisitions and diversification. In the 1980s, companies decided to *stick to their knitting* and stay in businesses they knew well. The concepts that underlie strategic planning emerged in the 1970s as a result of a number of shock waves that affected world economies including an energy crisis, high inflation, economic stagnation and deregulation of key industries. Strategic planning replaced conventional long-range planning. Today the goal of strategic planning is to help a company select and organise its businesses in a way that will keep the company healthy, even when unexpected events upset any of its specific businesses or product lines.

Kotler (1999) has defined strategic planning as:

'Market-oriented strategic planning is the managerial process of developing and maintaining a viable fit between the organisation's objectives, skills and resources and its changing market opportunities. The aim of strategic planning is to shape and reshape the company's businesses and products so that they will yield target profits and growth.'

Kotler claims that strategic planning calls for action in three areas:

The first area requires *managing a company's businesses as an investment portfolio*. Each business has a different profit potential and the company resources should be allocated accordingly.

The second area involves *assessing each business accurately by examining the market's growth rate and the company's position and fit in the market*. It is not sufficient to use current sales or profits as a guide. If Jurys Hotel Group had not looked at the emerging trend toward budget accommodation they would never have developed the very profitable 'Inn' Group, and would have simply poured cash into the traditional hotels which existed in saturated markets.

The third key area of strategic planning is *strategy*. For each of its businesses, the company must develop a game plan for achieving its long-run objectives. Because there is no one strategy that is optimal for all companies in that business, each company must determine what makes most sense in the light of its industry position, objectives, opportunities, skills and resources. Thus in the hospitality industry, the Merrion Hotel is pursuing a quality strategy, the Quality hotels are positioning themselves on value for money, while the Conrad Hilton follows a service orientation.

Strategic planning differs from the production of the marketing plan and these issues are dealt with separately in this chapter. The marketing plan is the working document that the hospitality enterprise develops for action for the forthcoming year. The plan flows from the mission statement and strategy formulation stages of strategic planning. In many tourism and hospitality operations in Ireland, the corporate level and the business unit level are one and the same. This does not negate the need for strategic planning. On the other hand, many hospitality and tourism businesses do not do strategic planning or develop annual marketing plans. This can be a mistake. Marketing plans are crucial in a competitive environment and are a necessary part of business success.

Figure 5.1 — Strategic Planning Process

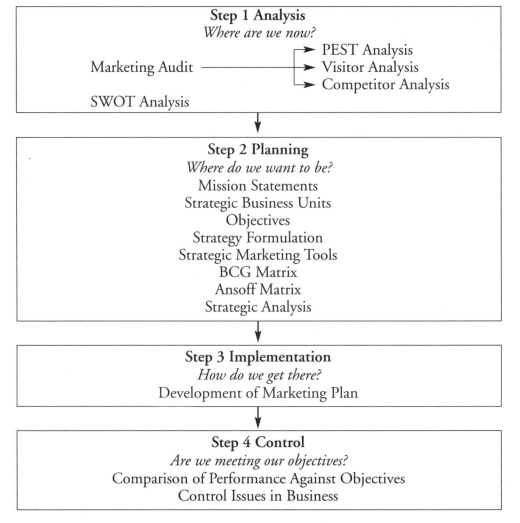

Step 1 Analysis
Where are we now?

Marketing Audit ————→ PEST Analysis
————→ Visitor Analysis
————→ Competitor Analysis

SWOT Analysis

Step 2 Planning
Where do we want to be?
Mission Statements
Strategic Business Units
Objectives
Strategy Formulation
Strategic Marketing Tools
BCG Matrix
Ansoff Matrix
Strategic Analysis

Step 3 Implementation
How do we get there?
Development of Marketing Plan

Step 4 Control
Are we meeting our objectives?
Comparison of Performance Against Objectives
Control Issues in Business

INTRODUCTION TO PLANNING

Management has the responsibility for setting into motion the strategic planning process. By preparing mission statements, policy, strategy and goals, management establishes the framework within which the divisions and business units prepare their plans. Some companies give a lot of freedom to their business units to set their own sales and profit goals and strategies. Others hold a tighter rein and all major decisions are made at headquarters. In Ireland, only a few of the larger tourism and hospitality organisations have a corporate headquarters. Therefore the subject of planning will not be separated into corporate and divisional planning, but discussed under the overall heading of planning.

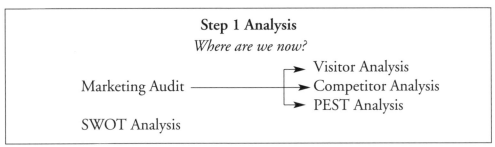

Step 1 Analysis
Where are we now?

Marketing Audit ————————→ Visitor Analysis
⟶ Competitor Analysis
⟶ PEST Analysis

SWOT Analysis

Step 1: Analysis

The Marketing Audit

The marketing audit is the 'means by which a company can identify its own strengths and weaknesses as they relate to external opportunities and threats' (McDonald, 1995). It involves an analysis of the marketing environment, that is the uncontrollable external factors that can affect the company's performance and the resource capacity of the business. It usually includes the following three key external dimensions: Visitor Analysis, Competitor Analysis and the Political, Economic, Social/Cultural and Technological (PEST) Analysis.

1. Visitor Analysis

A detailed analysis of customers or visitors is vital to the formation of a strategy, in that the organisation needs to know the size, structure and dynamics of the market, as well as the types of customers and their desires. Lumsdon (1997) outlines a market assessment as follows:

- *Volume and value of current visitor/customer base.* For example, a hotel will need to know the types of guests staying there: male, female, families, elderly couples. They will also need information on different rates being paid by different segments of the market including: group rates, corporate rates, conference rates, tour and travel rates and the level of revenue that each segment is producing.

- *Benefits sought.* Understanding the main motivation factors attracting different visitors to the business. For example, visitors can be motivated to visit an interpretative centre for educational reasons, interest in culture, a venue to bring friends or a place for meeting people.
- *Visitor profiles.* The characteristics of visitors by location, social class, lifestyle, etc. Not only are individual businesses looking at visitor profiles but tourism destinations are also gathering data on visitors and establishing detailed profiles.
- *Segmentation.* Can the overall market for the business be readily segmented into measurable groups such as domestic versus international tourists, by country of origin, age, stage in the life-cycle, rate of usage or lifestyles?
- *Nature of the buying process.* A review of how the visitor ends up purchasing the product or service. What percentage of visitors use travel agents or tourist offices? What percentage purchase directly via the internet?

2. Competitor Analysis

Competitor analysis looks at the level of direct and indirect competition. Analysis of direct competition looks at similar products or services i.e. competing hotels, restaurants, museums or tourist destinations that have similar facilities or image. Generally a SWOT analysis is carried out which examines the strengths, weaknesses, opportunities and threats of the business (*see* Box 5.1). A SWOT can also be carried out on each competitor, using ranking criteria such as resource availability, performance and strategic planning and an assessment of marketing mix activities.

A wider audit of the indirect competition can be carried out. Substitute products can be examined such as home-based entertainment or other forms of leisure activities. In the case of business travel the Internet can be considered as a form of indirect competition because it is forecasted that many business trips will no longer be necessary due to easy communication via the Internet.

The outcome of such a competitor analysis is to seek ways to gain competitive advantage 'by finding an aspect of differentiation that targeted customers will perceive as superior value and that cannot be duplicated by the competition' (Craven, 1994). The two key aspects of differentiation are first, non-price benefits, such as a visitor's perception of a destination or a hotel as easily accessible in comparison with a competitor's. Secondly, the price comparison between the two products or services.

3. Political, Economic, Social/Cultural and Technological (PEST) Analysis

This is the general examination of the broad trends in a country, region or on a world level. It examines factors that the business does not have direct control over, but can provide business opportunities or threats in the future.

Political Factors: these range from politics in the generating country e.g. if America is voting for a new president then overseas travel is reduced. It can include civil unrest in the receiving country e.g. Northern Ireland's tourism industry has been badly damaged by the Troubles since 1969. There are also legal matters to consider such as visas as an entry requirement to certain countries.

Economic Factors: these could include the effects of a tourist tax on exiting Ireland as has been discussed recently by the government. It can also include exchange rates and the overall economy of the generating country. Ireland has seen no growth in the German market in the last two to three years as a result of economic problems in Germany. It should also include an assessment of income distribution, levels of discretionary incomes available in the generating country, patterns of consumer spending and emergence of home-based spending opportunities.

Social and Cultural Factors: these factors greatly affect our lifestyles and therefore how we spend our leisure time. Recent trends include a growing interest in environmentally sensitive holidays, healthy living, activities and sports holidays which all affect the tourism and hospitality industry. Other trends include changing family patterns from the extended and nuclear family toward a higher percentage of single parent households. The traditional four-week holiday in August is being replaced by several short breaks throughout the year. Dublin has tapped into this trend and is one of the most popular short-visit destinations in Europe.

Technological Factors: these have resulted in the stimulation of the markets. Better telecommunications have resulted in exotic destinations such as Bali becoming a household name. Better transport means the distant destinations are *closer* and easier to reach. The development of computer reservation systems (CRS) and global distribution systems (GDS) have changed the market-place for booking holidays. The effects of the Internet are already being felt by the tourism and hospitality suppliers that have tapped into this means of promotion and distribution.

Strengths, Weaknesses, Opportunities and Threats (SWOT) Analysis

Another way to sum up the components of SWOT is internal and external analyses. The strengths and weaknesses of the business need to be examined in a candid fashion. For instance, the quality of the product (rooms, food, entertainment, transportation, etc.), service and facilities should be reviewed. It is always appropriate to recognise strengths and to develop ways to capitalise on them. A unique strength of a business can be developed to become its competitive advantage in the future. Ryanair has a competitive advantage due to its ability to undercut the prices of competitors and this is its major strength. Negative internal factors are the weaknesses of the business. Weaknesses should be carefully examined with the aim to minimise them when planning future strategies.

Opportunities and threats facing the business are typically found in the external environment. Opportunities form the basis of future success for an organisation. An upswing in the economy, for example, could provide opportunity to a marketer of luxury cruises on the Shannon. Opportunities, however, are most often realised only if the marketer takes advantage of them. Threats are problems that must be dealt with if the business is to improve its performance. A trend toward greater use of teleconferencing could be considered a threat to a conference centre. The threat of an outbreak of violence in Northern Ireland is a constant threat to tourism in the North and South. Many times, the impact of an external factor could be characterised as either an opportunity or a threat depending on how the marketer responds to it. A national trend toward healthier eating could threaten the fast food industry in Ireland. However, they may respond by introducing new menu items that are considered healthy and low in calories. Box 5.1 (page 137) shows an example of the SWOT analysis of Ireland as a tourist destination.

> **Step 2 Planning**
> *Where do we want to be?*
> Mission Statements
> Strategic Business Units
> Objectives
> Strategy Formulation
> Strategic Marketing Tools
> BCG Matrix
> Ansoff Matrix
> Strategic Analysis

STEP 2: PLANNING

The Mission Statement

Every successful business has a vision of what it is all about. The organisation's business definition, also called the mission statement, answers the question 'What business are we in?' It provides thrust and direction to the organisation and is the cornerstone of its marketing strategy. A firm's business mission, of course, may change over time. Such changes are typically reflected in changes in marketing strategy as well.

Components of a Good Business Definition

A good business definition should be:

- Specific enough to impact the behaviour of the organisation
- Focused more upon the satisfaction of customer needs than the characteristics of the company's product
- Able to reflect the essential skills of the organisation
- Attainable
- Flexible

Box 5.1 — SWOT of Ireland as a Tourist Destination

Strengths
- superb scenic landscapes
- a friendly, welcoming and convivial people
- a green *unspoiled* environment
- relaxing pace of life
- good quality tourism infrastructure (accommodation and other facilities)
- excellent location for outdoor activities and sports
- a distinctive heritage and culture

Weaknesses
- the weather
- political insecurity due to Northern Ireland
- poor image of Irish food
- insufficient sophisticated shopping
- limited entertainment for older or more *up-market* tourists
- perceived as a *male orientated* destination with little for families to do

Opportunities
- 70 million people worldwide who can trace their ancestral lineage to Ireland
- growth in tourism worldwide
- to attract *empty nesters* as a key growth segment
- fashionability of Irish culture including Riverdance, Irish music and Irish fashion
- joint marketing opportunities exist with certain consumer goods suppliers from alcohol to financial services
- a willingness to exploit technology
- relationship marketing and loyalty programmes
- competitive access fares
- foreign investment could result in greater corporate travel to Ireland

Threats
- cost-competitiveness of Irish tourism as a result of the Celtic Tiger and abolition of intra-European duty free facilities in 1999
- euro could be a threat if exchange rates change with England
- quality of the Irish product may diminish if the industry can no longer attract Irish people to work in it
- size of the Irish market has discouraged the larger international leisure brands from entering the Irish market
- competitors including Britain and in particular Scotland, as well as Eastern and Central European destinations

Source: Adapted from: 'A Business Plan for Irish Tourism Marketing 1998–2003', *Bord Fáilte, 1998*

Strategic Business Units

Many companies in tourism and hospitality are diversified into a number of different businesses and still more have a number of different products. All of the various businesses or products should, of course, be consistent with the organisation's business definition or mission statement. To facilitate strategic market planning, however, such companies often view themselves as comprised of separate business units. A strategic business unit (SBU) is a self-contained part of a larger organisation. Each SBU has its own set of customers and competitors, separate costs and a distinct marketing strategy. It can be a company division, a product line within a division or a single product.

Disney is an example of an international company that has a number of SBUs, each representing a distinct business, though all fall under the general business definition of providing quality entertainment for the entire family.

Disney owns theme parks in America and Europe, movie studios, a cable television station, retail stores and a record company.

In Ireland organisations such as Campbell Catering or Fitzpatrick Hotels could view each of their divisions as SBUs. Within a single business, each product could be viewed as an SBU, thus a hotel may view its restaurants, banqueting facilities, leisure facilities, rooms division and bars each as an SBU.

Having completed the mission statement the next step in the planning process is the formation of goals.

Establishing Objectives

Having studied the threats and opportunities, the manager can now set objectives and consider issues that will affect them. The objectives should be stated as goals the company would like to reach during the plan's term and should be set in light of the information uncovered by the marketing audit.

Good objectives must:

1. specify exactly what is to be accomplished
2. designate a quantitative level to be attained
3. specify a time frame for meeting the objective

For example, if a hospitality business sets the objective *to increase return on investment* this objective does not meet the criteria of level and time. But the statement *to increase our food sales by four per cent over the next twelve months* does meet all three criteria.

Objectives provide the baseline against which actual performance is measured and as such, they are necessary to control the business. Therefore, it is necessary that objectives be attainable. Most organisations have multiple objectives. When this is the case, it is necessary for objectives to be consistent with each other. A business may wish to increase its customer base while reducing the amount spent on promotion. These are typically inconsistent with each other, because it generally takes considerable funds to increase a base of customers and build awareness that the organisation exists and make known what it has to offer.

In summary, objectives should be:

- Precise and quantified in term of sales volume, revenue and market share
- Specific in terms of products and services and market segments
- Time periods stated in which they are to be achieved
- Realistic in terms of market trends and in relation to budget available
- Agreed and accepted by management and staff
- Measurable

BOX 5.2 — PLANNING PROCESS

The marketing planning process asks an organisation to restate the following fundamental questions:

What is our current position?
Example: A hotel group that has ten medium-size hotels of which six are profitable and four are marginal performers.

Where does the organisation aim to be?
Example: A hotel group with twelve medium- to large-scale hotels of which all are profitable.

Which is the best route to follow?
Example: Sell four of the current smaller hotels to finance an acquisition of another company with an appropriate portfolio of properties.

How do we arrive at our preferred position?
Example: Prepare detailed plans for disposal of existing assets, purchase of a new hotel group, corporate and brand restructuring, internal marketing, promotional campaign and new market development with business clients.

How should the plan be implemented?
Example: Execution of detailed programmes of work such as establishing a project team to undertake disposals and acquisitions, devising a detailed internal marketing exercise to advise staff through the transitional period. This would be followed by a major external communications exercise with existing and potential customers.

Have we arrived?
Example: Monitoring the progress and applying control measures where necessary. Have the sales of properties executed to secure working capital towards the purchase of new hotels? Has there been minimal disturbance to the core customer base?

Source: Adapted from *Tourism Marketing*, Les Lumsdon, 1997

Strategy Formulation

Objectives indicate what a business wants to achieve; strategy is a game plan for how to get there. Every business must tailor a strategy for achieving its goals or objectives. Although many types of strategies are available, Michael Porter has condensed them into three generic types as follows:

Overall Cost Leadership

Here the business works hard to achieve the lowest production and distribution costs so that it can price lower than its competitors and win a large market share. This is a common strategy among the large tour operators and travel agents competing for market share and leadership. Firms pursuing this strategy must be good at dealing with large volumes of travellers and keep their costs at a minimum. Direct Holidays have just entered the Irish market offering the lowest price holidays and undercutting more established travel agents. The problem with this strategy is that it is easy to copy and other firms will emerge with still lower prices. The real key is for the firm to achieve the lowest cost among those competitors adopting a similar differentiation or focus strategy.

Logos from the distinctive brands within the same company: Jurys Hotel Group and Jurys Inns.

Differentiation

Here the business concentrates on achieving superior performance in an important customer benefit valued by a large part of the market. It can strive to be the service leader, the quality leader and the style leader etc., but it is not possible to be all of those things. For example, the Morrisson Hotel in Dublin strives to be the style leader, the Sheen Falls Lodge and the Mount Juliet strive to be the quality leaders, while many small family-run hotels focus on service quality and attention to detail. Cromleagh Lodge has won numerous prizes for the quality of its service and it has the advantage of being owner-operated and can get to know each of its guests on an individual basis.

Focus

Here the business focuses on one or more narrow market segments rather than going after a large market. The firm gets to know the segment needs and pursues either cost leadership or a form of differentiation within the target segment. The aim of the strategy is almost total immersion in terms of one market segment by developing strong relationships with existing and potential customers. This allows a special service offering to be developed and aimed at the target market. Many businesses catering toward activity-based tourism follow a focus strategy and target specific segments or niches, such as those interested in walking, golfing or fishing.

According to Porter, those firms pursuing the same strategy directed to the same target market or segment constituted a *strategic group*. Firms that do not pursue a clear strategy — *middle of the roaders* — do the worst. Porter's strategic framework has been widely accepted and many tourism and hospitality companies appear to pursue a low-cost differentiation strategy, this combines two of the three generic options.

Forming a Marketing Strategy

After forming objectives, the marketing manager is ready to plan a strategy to accomplish those objectives. Marketing strategy is the long-term plan for developing a marketing mix which will achieve the organisation's objectives by meeting the target market needs. Marketing strategy begins with the identification of the target market. The questions 'Who is the intended audience of the marketing mix?' and 'What are its basic requirements?' should be answered.

Once the target market has been identified, the marketing manager plans the marketing mix. The mix can be defined as everything the organisation can do to influence demand for its products and services. When working in the service industry it has been found useful to expand the marketing mix from the four *Ps* of product, price, place and promotion; to the services' marketing mix with the additional categories: people, process and physical environment.

Marketing strategy should define the product and its characteristics (product decisions). It should explain how the product is to be brought to the user (distribution decisions). It should describe how the target market will be made aware of the product or service and persuaded to buy it (promotion decisions). Finally, it should specify the relative value of the offer vis-à-vis alternatives (price decisions). In the service industry, marketing strategy must emphasise the importance of the service provider and how they interact with the customer (people decisions). It must outline the exact procedures that are to be followed for the delivery of the service, and to ensure that the same standard of service is received by every customer (process decisions). Finally, the marketing strategy must acknowledge the importance of the physical environment and any tangible offerings that the customer views and uses to make a judgement regarding the service (physical evidence). The case-study on Tralee (at the end of this chapter), shows how the town uses strategic planning to address its problems and develop solutions.

EXHIBIT 5.1

STRATEGIC TOURISM PLANNING *IN ACTION*

NORTHERN IRELAND

The Northern Ireland tourist industry earned £280m in 1998 (£268m in 1997), of which £217m came from staying visitors in Northern Ireland and £63m from domestic holiday spending. Spending by staying visitors and residents on holiday in the province accounted for approximately 1·6 per cent of GDP. The level of employment stemming from tourism is estimated at around 15,000.

Visitor tourism to Northern Ireland increased by four per cent in 1998 over the previous year, primarily as a result of an upturn in visitor numbers from Great Britain (five per cent) and the Republic of Ireland (four per cent). A rise in visitor numbers from overseas markets was also experienced. The European market grew by three per cent, mainly attributable to a significant expansion in business traffic. Total visitors from North America increased by six per cent. Some 277,000 of all trips were made by pure holidaymakers. This figure represents nineteen per cent of all visitors in 1998 and an increase of five per cent in this market sector over the previous year.

TABLE 5.1 — NORTHERN IRELAND'S KEY MARKETS

	Visitor Numbers	% change with 1997
Great Britain	838,000	+5
Republic of Ireland	360,000	+4
Europe	108,000	+3
North America	115,000	+6
Other Overseas	56,000	–2

TABLE 5.2 — DOMESTIC HOLIDAYS IN NORTHERN IRELAND

		% change with 1997
TRIPS	543,000	–5
NIGHTS	2,040,000	0
SPEND	£63.0m	+5 (+2 in real terms)

TABLE 5.3 — WHAT PERCENTAGE OF THE MARKET DID EACH COUNTRY TAKE?

	1972	1994	1995	1996	1997	1998
number of trips	435,000	1,293,900	1,557,000	1,436,000	1,415,000	1,477,000
Origin total = 100%	100%	100%	100%	100%	100%
England	46	41	38	41	41	39
(London and South-East)	(17)	(14)	(15)	(16)	(16)	(16)
Scotland	11	13	13	15	15	17
Wales	1	1	1	1	1	1
(Great Britain)	(58)	(55)	(52)	(57)	(57)	(57)
Republic of Ireland	31	30	30	26	24	24
North America	5	6	8	7	8	8
Europe	3	7	7	7	7	7
Other Overseas	3	2	3	3	4	4

Source: Northern Ireland Tourist Board (NITB) Tourism Facts, 1998

Northern Ireland has much to offer as a tourist destination, large tracts of unspoilt countryside, areas of outstanding beauty, a rich cultural heritage, along with a friendly people, are just some of the area's greatest strengths. However, this idyllic view is not what most people perceive of Northern Ireland. Unfortunately, scenes of bombing, killing and political instability are what have been shown on television screens around the world. The Troubles of the past thirty years have been a major contributor to the decline of the tourism industry in the region.

The ceasefire which began on 31 August 1994, and lasted until February 1996, brought much needed optimism to the tourism industry. It was during these months, and in particular the summer of 1995, that the industry briefly experienced the potential the region had as a tourist destination if a long-term solution to the Troubles could be found (*see* Table 5.4). During this time an acute lack of accommodation was experienced in most areas, as a result of unprecedented demand.

TABLE 5.4 — THE TOTAL STAYING VISITOR FIGURES AND REVENUE

	Trips (000s)	Nights (000s)	Revenue £m
1963	704·6	7,670·9	10·14
1967	1,080·0	8,679·4	16·94
1972	435·0	3,499·4	8·64
1988	930·4	6,673·9	97·00
1989	1,090·6	6,636·4	136·31
1990	1,152·8	7,091·0	153·09
1991	1,186·1	7,160·0	162·00
1992	1,254·5	7,466·6	161·67
1993	1,262·0	7,794·0	173·00
1994	1,293·9	7,804·0	183·00
1995	1,557·0	8,500·0	214·00
1996	1,436·0	7,700·0	206·00
1997	1,415·0	7,500·0	208·00
1998	1,477·0	7,835·0	217·00

Source: NITB, Tourism Facts 1998

Most economists state peace and political stability as being very important to the production of tourism. Since 1968 there has been civil unrest in Northern Ireland, known as the Troubles. Lennon and Titterington (1996) claim that 'with the beginning of the Troubles in 1969, Northern Ireland lost most if not all of its attractions as a significant tourist destination.' Potential tourists were fed a regular diet of new stories chronicling regular bombings, sectarian killings, street disturbances and political tension and instability. Tourism marketing has well documented evidence of the need for a favourable image when promoting a tourist destination. Having unfavourable images beamed across the world means that even those who are not afraid of terrorism will be discouraged from taking a holiday in Northern Ireland. Most research on tourist motivations points to fear and insecurity as a major barrier to travel, and thus a major limitation on the growth of the industry. In 1986, Richter and Waugh stated, 'Unfortunately, many national leaders and planners either do not understand or will not accept the fact that political serenity, not scenic or cultural attraction, constitute the first and central requirement of tourism.'

The market segment which has declined the most during the Troubles have been the British (Buckley and Klemm, 1993), showing a fall in numbers of thirty-five per cent. Northern Ireland Tourist Board (NITB) set about the task of developing tourism in Northern Ireland (NI). The NITB produced a number of documents starting with *Tourism into the '90s*, which targeted increasing the contribution of tourism to the local economy and the overall effectiveness of tourism promotion. This was followed by *Tourism in NI – a view to the future*. The objectives were mainly to improve the image and increase the awareness of NI as a tourist destination: improving the marketing of the tourism product, improving the transport linkages to the Province and developing an improved tourist organisation.

The Northern Ireland Tourist Board (NITB)

The NITB is a non-departmental public body of the Department of Economic Development (DED) constituted under the *Tourism (Northern Ireland) Order 1992*. It has responsibility for developing tourism in Northern Ireland and for promoting the area as a tourist destination. It also advises the DED on the formulation and implementation of policy in relation to the development of tourism. As one of the DED's agencies, NITB is represented on the management board and contributes to the core policy-making. In delivering its services, NITB works in close co-operation with the other DED businesses, in particular the Training and Employment Agency (T&EA), the Industrial Development Board (IDB) and the Local Enterprise Development Unit (LEDU). NITB also works closely with other government departments, with the tourism industry in Northern Ireland and with its counterparts elsewhere in the UK and in the Republic of Ireland. Its board is made up of business people with knowledge and expertise in the areas of tourism, marketing and commerce.

NITB's Mission

A Strategy for the Development of Tourism in Northern Ireland established a new agenda for tourism based on the views of the industry in its widest sense. Fundamental to the future success of tourism is a clear shared goal. The agreed goal is to increase the contribution that tourism makes to the economy in a way that responds to the needs of visitors, respects the environment, is acceptable to the people who live here and is economically viable in the long term. The Corporate Plan provides NITB with the opportunity to detail its role in moving toward the realisation of this goal. While acknowledging that the ability to deliver success resides principally with those individuals involved in the industry, it is nevertheless critical that through its Corporate Plan, NITB should seek to explain its role in ensuring that the necessary supportive environment is developed to enable tourism to flourish. This qualification of its role described in terms of a mission statement, key and supporting objectives must necessarily be accompanied by some attempt to quantify the impact of that role. It is important that all aspects of the agreed goal for tourism are reflected in NITB's objectives. It is also necessary to identify a series of basic principles which will underpin all their activities in pursuit of these objectives and to set targets that enable them to chart their progress initially toward those objectives and ultimately toward the agreed goal.

NITB's mission statement is:

'To optimise the tourism industry's potential as a significant creator of sustainable wealth and jobs by marketing and developing Northern Ireland as a high-quality competitive tourist destination through proactive partnerships.'

NITB's Key Objectives

1. **To increase visitor expenditure.** This means achieving real increases in visitor expenditure from which net growth of tourism-related employment can follow. It will call for volume increases in pure holiday and first-time visitors in key market segments, secured through targeted marketing to deliver increased revenue. It will also call for higher per capita spend by visitors.
2. **To spread the benefits of tourism.** This means developing, through effective partnerships, regional tourism organisations which not only offer the opportunity for a customer-focused, co-ordinated approach but also provide the scope to align marketing initiatives more closely with the ability to manage the product in terms of both the natural and built environment.
3. **To maximise the effectiveness of NITB and its people.** This means recognising that staff are NITB's most valuable resource and that their development needs are afforded priority.

The process of marketing Ireland (north and south) as one destination has already produced tangible benefits. The successful launch of Tourism Brand Ireland in November 1996 has assisted in the marketing of the region. Since then Bord Fáilte and NITB have worked together on a number of projects promoting the country as a whole such as the Shannon-Erne Waterway. Likewise co-operation exists in the conference market where the Northern Ireland Conference Bureau (NICB) and the Conference Bureau of Ireland (CBI) work together. Northern Ireland has a number of ideal settings for conferences and the Hastings

Hotel Group, the largest in Northern Ireland, offers seventy conference rooms and 700 bedrooms, while the Waterfront Hall in Belfast can hold up to 2,000 people. The Group has just announced a £12 million investment programme for its three Belfast hotels, this is a good indication of the confidence in the tourism industry for the future.

Following the ceasefires, there has been extensive investment by Northern Ireland hoteliers in their facilities. At least fifteen hotels have upgraded their facilities recently. The growing attractiveness of Northern Ireland as a holiday and business destination has also seen the arrival of leading hotel chains including the Radisson and the Holiday Inn operations.

TABLE 5.5 — HOW BUSY ARE NORTHERN IRELAND'S HOTELS AND GUESTHOUSES?

HOTEL OCCUPANCY				GUESTHOUSE/B&B OCCUPANCY			
Jan–Dec Period	Room	Bedspace	Visitor Content	Apr–Sep Period	Room	Bedspace	Visitor Content
1973	31	22	51	1973	n/a	n/a	n/a
1986	43	29	54	1986	38	30	45
1987	47	32	55	1987	42	34	46
1988	45	30	54	1988	39	31	44
1989	50	33	55	1989	40	34	39
1990	50	34	57	1990	39	34	51
1991	49	33	56	1991	39	33	49
1992	47	32	54	1992	41	34	52
1993	48	32	61	1993	37	31	60
1994	51	31	61	1994	39	32	51
1995	62	41	68	1995	51	45	70
1996	56	35	65	1996	38	31	65
1997	53	33	62	1997	33	26	67
1998	53	32	62	1998	32	25	67

The occupancy rate represents the number of rooms or bedspaces taken in a given period as a percentage of the total rooms or bedspaces on offer. Double or twin-bedded rooms count as having two bedspaces. (Visitor content = percentage of all guests registered who come from outside Northern Ireland.)

To conclude, the future of tourism in Northern Ireland looks good providing that peace and stability remain in the region. While tourism is the world's fastest growing industry with WTO forecasts projecting arrivals to reach 1,005 million in 2010, the industry is very volatile and political stability is crucial for the successful marketing of a tourist destination.

Source: this case-study was prepared with the assistance of Orla Doherty, Lecturer at the Galway-Mayo Institute of Technology. *NITB Tourism Facts 1998* was also used extensively.

Strategic Marketing Tools

One of the purposes of strategic planning is to identify the strong elements of the business from the weak ones, and to develop separate strategies and assign appropriate funding. Most management will recognise its portfolio of businesses usually includes a number of what Kotler calls 'yesterday's has-beens' as well as 'tomorrow's breadwinners'. But it cannot rely just on impressions; it needs analytical tools for classifying its businesses by profit potential. One of the best known business portfolio evaluation models is the Boston Consulting Group model known as the BCG Matrix.

1. BCG Matrix

The Boston Consulting Group are a leading management consulting firm, they developed the growth-share matrix in Figure 5.2. The location of each business unit indicates its market growth rate and relative market share.

FIGURE 5.2 — BCG GROWTH-SHARE MATRIX

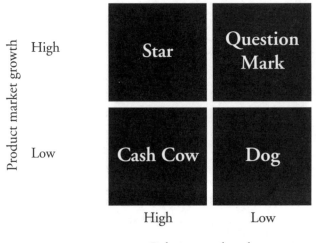

The market growth rate in the vertical axis indicates the annual growth rate of the market. For example the lowest level of growth is zero and the highest level is twenty per cent. Thus the higher the growth rate the more attractive the market. The horizontal axis indicates relative market share. It allows the marketer to plot the market share of each service product relative to its largest competitor, providing a yardstick for competitive growth. It serves as a measure of the company's strength in the relative market. A relative market share of 0.1 means that the company's sales volume is only ten per cent of the leader's sales volume; a relative share of ten means that the business is the leader and has ten times the sales of the next strongest competitor. Relative market share is divided into high and low share, using 1.0 as the dividing line.

The growth-share matrix is divided into four cells, each indicating a different type of business with different potential:

1. *Question Marks:* Question marks are businesses that operate in high-growth markets but have low relative market shares. Most businesses start off as question marks as the company tries to enter a high-growth market in which there is already a market leader. A question mark requires a lot of cash because the company has to spend money on equipment and personnel to keep up with the fast-growing market, and because it wants to overtake the leader. Question marks require substantial investment, generate limited cash-flows and therefore offer low or negative profitability. They are a *question mark* because the marketing team has to decide whether to increase investment to build market share or to plan a withdrawal from the market. Having too many question marks is not good planning and the company might be better off investing more cash in one or two of these businesses instead of spreading its cash over a number of them.

2. *Stars:* If the question-mark business is successful, it becomes a star. A star is the market leader in a high-growth market. A star does not necessarily produce a positive cash-flow for the company. The company must spend substantial funds to keep up with the high market growth and fight off competitors' attacks. A company should be concerned if it has no stars.

3. *Cash Cows:* When a market's annual growth rate falls to less than ten per cent, the star becomes a cash cow if it still has the largest market share. A cash cow produces a lot of cash for the company. In mature markets, where growth rates have slowed, cash cows bring great returns without heavy investment. Since the business is the market leader, it enjoys economies of scale and higher profit margins. The company uses its cash cows businesses to pay its bills and support other business such as the question marks. Having only one cash cow leaves a company vulnerable, if this cash cow starts losing market share the company will have to pump enough money into it to maintain market leadership. If it uses all the cash to support its other businesses, its strong cash cow may become a dog.

4. *Dogs:* Dogs are businesses that have weak market shares in low-growth markets. They typically generate low profits or losses, but may generate some cash-flow. If a company has a number of dogs it should reconsider the reasons it is holding on to these dogs: is it for good business reasons such as an expected turnaround in the market growth rate or for sentimental reasons? Dogs often consume more management time than they are worth and need to be phased down or out.

Having plotted the various businesses in the growth-share matrix, management must determine whether the portfolio is healthy or not. An unbalanced portfolio would have too many dogs or question marks and too few stars and cash cows.

The company's next task is to determine what objective, strategy and budget to assign to each business. Four strategies can be pursued:

1. *Build:* The objective is to increase the market share of the businesses and is appropriate for question marks whose market share must grow if they are to become stars.
2. *Hold:* The objective is to preserve the businesses' market share. This strategy is appropriate for strong cash cows if they are to continue yielding a large positive cash-flow.
3. *Harvest:* The objective is to increase the businesses' short-term cash-flow regardless of long-term effects. Harvesting involves a decision to eventually withdraw from a business by implementing a programme of cost reduction. The hope is to reduce costs at a rate faster than any potential drop in sales. It usually involves reducing advertising expenses, cutting research and development, reducing the sales staff, etc. This strategy is appropriate for weak cash cows whose future is dim. Harvesting can also be used with question marks and dogs.
4. *Divest:* The objective is to sell or liquidate the business because resources can be used better elsewhere. This strategy is used for dogs or question marks that show little or no promise.

It should be noted that businesses change their position in the matrix. Successful businesses have a life-cycle consisting of introduction, growth, maturity and decline stages. Likewise in the matrix they start as question marks, become stars, then cash cows and finally dogs. Companies should not only examine the present positions on the matrix but also their moving positions. Each business should be reviewed as to where it was in past years and where it will probably move in future years. It is important that a company plans its portfolio carefully. Kotler claims that the worst mistake a company could make is to require all its businesses to aim for the same growth rate or return level. The very point of the analysis is that each business has a different potential and requires its own strategy.

Critique of the BCG Matrix

Portfolio models help managers think more strategically, understand the economies of their businesses better, improve the quality of their plans, improve communication between businesses, eliminate weak businesses and strengthen their investment in the stronger businesses. However, the models must be used with caution. One of the main frustrations about the BCG matrix is that unless you are in full possession of the data pertaining to a particular product or service and have similar data about the main competitors in the market-place, it is almost impossible to use in the way it was intended. The model has also been criticised because it ignores the dynamism of the markets. What is the time period over which the market should be investigated? Some markets change rapidly, such as the fast food market, while others move slowly such as national parks. Secondly, the model ignores the level of competitor activity in the market-place and this will always have a major bearing on the strategy chosen. Thirdly, the matrix does not take into account the interrelationship between tourism and hospitality offerings which are so important for building strategy. Service offerings might be complementary or one product an essential component in developing another. For example, hotels can have loss-making areas such as the leisure centre but this facility is necessary to attract the weekend family market as well as the business executive.

To conclude, marketers use models such as the BCG matrix as diagnostic tools and combine them with experience, business flair and common sense to develop appropriate strategies for their businesses. In terms of simplicity the matrix scores well, but should be used in conjunction with other tools and viewed as a method of analysis.

2. Product-Market Opportunity Analysis

When an organisation's stated objectives are related to growth, the product-market opportunity analysis can be useful in plotting the appropriate strategy. This is probably the most commonly used of the strategic matrices and is named after the author (Ansoff) who first devised the framework in the 1950s. The simple structure is demonstrated in Figure 5.3. The analysis is performed through the use of a classification scheme that represents alternative growth strategies a firm might implement. The dimensions in the matrix are markets and products. An organisation can choose to grow by building a relationship with existing or new groups in either category.

FIGURE 5.3 — ANSOFF'S PRODUCT/MARKET EXPANSION GRID

	Product	
	Present	New
Market Present	**Market Penetration**	**Product Development**
Market New	**Market Development**	**Diversification**

The strategy implied when the decision is to focus growth efforts on existing markets and existing products is **Market Penetration**. With this strategy the company considers whether it could gain more market share with its current products in their current markets. For example, a restaurant might attempt to increase its market share through effective advertising and encourage more frequent patronage of the business. Market penetration represents a relatively low-risk strategy for the firm. The organisation is not breaking new ground in terms of people or products. While the low risk aspect of market penetration may be appealing to an organisation, it is true that the opportunity for significant growth may not be great. In other words it can be a slow means of growth. Other examples of market penetration strategy are airline frequent-flyer programmes such as Aer Lingus programmed *TAB*. The major hotel chains have developed loyalty programmes including Holiday Inn *Priority Club*.

The aim of this strategy is to increase the frequency by which the consumer uses the service, to increase the amount purchased or to introduce the present consumer to a new aspect of the product or service.

TAB Aer Lingus Frequent-Flyer Programme

Market Development increases sales by taking present products to new markets. New markets may be found in many places like other segments of the population or by expanding overseas. Supermacs fast food restaurants aims to practice market development and have an outlet in every major town in Ireland. Firms sometimes find that market development can be accomplished expediently by working with another company that is familiar with the new market and forming an alliance with them (*see* section on Strategic Alliances in Tourism and Hospitality later in this chapter). Not all market development is accomplished through overseas expansions, sometimes there are new markets on our *doorstep* that we have not considered before. Many hospitality companies are targeting children, who offer the double benefit of money to spend now and the hope of becoming future customers. Ryan Hotels has used this strategy with its Friendly Fellows who provide special services to children who are guests of the hotel.

The opposite of market development is **Product Development**. With this strategy sales are increased by introducing new products into present markets. The two main fast food chains in Ireland: Supermacs and McDonald's have introduced a number of new food items including pizzas, salads, barbecued foods and new variations of hamburgers including the *vegetarian hamburger*. The aim was to increase sales by offering more products to the same market, now parents found foods that appealed to them and not just their children. Both market development and product development are higher risk growth strategies than market penetration. In both cases the organisation is exploring new ground and they are viewed as medium risk strategies.

Diversification is the final growth strategy. With this strategy, sales are increased by introducing new products into new markets. Diversification clearly carries the highest risk of the four strategies. The organisation is breaking new ground in the area of product and market! The organisation may choose to manage and minimise the risk of diversification by acquisition, thus the company grows by buying an existing firm that specialised in the product/market they are interested in entering. In this type of situation, diversification allows the firm to expand into new products and markets while building on the strengths and skills of the organisation. Sometimes diversification can prove to be too great of a challenge. Coca-Cola's failure with Taylor wines have been attributed to the fact that wine production and marketing were too different from soft drink production and marketing for Coke to be able to make it a success.

A marketing manager who uses product-market opportunity analysis in planning a growth strategy in tourism and hospitality must consider the resources of the firm, the potential for growth vis-à-vis the firm's objectives, and the amount of risk the firm is willing to incur.

Step 3 Implementation
How do we get there?
Development of Marketing Plan
Costing of Programmes

STEP 3: IMPLEMENTATION

Implementing Marketing Tactics

Having a marketing strategy does not guarantee success. The strategy itself may be badly designed, and there are many ways to implement it. While strategy provides guidance regarding how to accomplish objectives, the business must make specific decisions about each element of the marketing mix before implementation, these are called marketing tactics. Marketing tactics bring an organisation's strategy to life. Tactics form the heart of the organisation's short-term marketing plan. This plan develops detailed executions on each marketing mix element and becomes the blueprint for implementation. For example, tactical decisions in the area of the product would include specifications regarding the number of different types of products and services on offer. In a restaurant this will outline the type of food served, special menu items, theme nights, special offers for children, etc.

The importance of effective marketing tactics should not be underestimated. A carefully thought-out marketing strategy that does not translate to equally well thought-out tactics has little chance of success.

Strategic Alliances in Tourism and Hospitality

'Collaboration between competitors is in fashion.'

(Hamel, Doz and Prahalad, 1989)

Global competition is forcing industries to review their management philosophies and strategic planning. Manufacturing has already embraced the idea of alliances, joint ventures and collaboration, with many of the world's leading companies now *co-operating* in order to achieve a competitive advantage. A prime example of this is IBM: in the United States it has few allies but in Japan it has teamed up with just about every ally possible. The logic of forming strategic alliances is spreading and the tourism industry, as it becomes more competitive, is beginning to see the benefits of strategic alliances.

As Kenichi Ohmae (1993) proclaimed, 'Companies are just beginning to learn what nations have always known: in a complex, uncertain world filled with dangerous opponents, it is best not to go-it-alone'. Companies are learning to co-operate as it allows them to share costs, skills and to access markets. Alliances are an important strategic option because the reality of being in business today means being part of a global market, co-operation is essential for survival.

The tourism industry has always had a tradition of co-operation but not always of a strategic nature. In the travel industry, which is global by nature, we are witnessing the formation of global alliances between firms of different types as well as similar businesses (Dev, 1993). Alliances are another form of contractual agreement, they are developed to allow two organisations to benefit from each other's strengths (Kotler, Bowen and Makens, 1996).

Tourism textbooks such as Medlik (1991), Teare (1992), Poon (1993), and Holloway (1994) devote little or no attention to strategic alliances, yet collaboration is occurring almost daily in the industry. Research has mainly focused on the manufacturing industry with detailed analysis of Japanese-American alliances particularly in the car manufacturing sector.

Alliances in tourism, while not the focus of much academic research, are a major challenge for the manager of most tourism products or services today. Alliances in tourism are defined as, 'organisational arrangements and operating policies through which separate arrangements share administrative authority and form social links through more open-ended contractual arrangements as opposed to very specific, arm's lengths contracts' (Go and Hedges, 1995). Such corporate relationships often violate much of what has been taught in business school, such as the importance of control. It is for this reason managers have been slow to experiment with genuinely strategic alliances.

Distinctive Competencies

In order to survive in a competitive environment it is suggested that every viable business has some *distinctive competence*, something at which it is peculiarly effective (Selznick, 1957). It may not be unique and the firm may not be the best, but at least, in some aspect, it must be better than its competitors.

For the distinctive competence to be of any strategic value it must be embodied in the product the customer buys. It can then create what Drucker (1964) calls a 'leadership position'. Leadership, according to Drucker is the ability of the organisation to produce 'something of value to the customer'. It might be in service or distribution or even relate to the firm's ability *to convert ideas to saleable products*.

Sustainable Competitive Advantage

Selznick's idea of distinctive competencies was further developed by Prahalad and Hamel (1990), who saw core competencies as not simply the possession of a particular technology or managerial capability but as a combination of such capabilities which provide the firm with a leadership position in the development of certain generic or core products. This is what gives the business a *sustainable competitive advantage*. Every management needs to know what competencies form the foundation of its most successful products, so that they can develop those competencies and the future people on whom they depend. Hospitality organisations are forming alliances to benefit from the advantages that competitors possess. The famous Sandals Resorts International have formed a strategic alliance with the Ramada Group and benefit from Ramada's Best Hospitality Training for its resorts throughout the Caribbean (Andorka, 1998).

Collaborating with Your Competitor in Tourism and Hospitality

International co-operation in tourism has been evident for more than fifty years via various tourism organisations. However alliances in the private sector are of a strategic nature rather than a simple partnership for the purpose of achieving short-term objectives.

Alliances in tourism are emphasising the move away from volume strategy to value-added strategy an example of this has occurred in the airline industry (Go and Hedges,

1994). These moves involve airlines building brand equity through the development of global airline brands, the exchange of facilities and expertise (crews); combining frequent-flyer plans which retain passengers on a select number of airlines anywhere in the world. In addition, benefits can involve combining network development of routes and information; development of cost-control methodology and systems which can include joint ownership of aircraft and computerised reservation systems, as well as code sharing, either as blocked space or joint marketing of services. (*see* Exhibit 5.2, Aer Lingus alliance with Delta and 'Oneworld').

Alliances exist between many other areas of the travel industry including hotels, car rental companies, travel agents, coach hire, tour operators and marketing organisations. Networks have been developed to raise standards, to co-ordinate efforts and to market the small individual tourist suppliers who often have neither the resources nor the expertise to market their own individual products. Such alliances have been extremely successful and have been useful in niche marketing. An example of a successful alliance is the Overseas Tourist Marketing Initiative presently being co-ordinated by Bord Fáilte. In this partnership the private sector and government combine additional funds to finance a direct response consumer-driven advertising campaign in the US and mainland Europe. The initiative is unique as it is marketing the Island of Ireland as an entity for the first time to the world's major travel markets.

EXHIBIT 5.2

STRATEGIC ALLIANCES *IN ACTION*

AER LINGUS — DELTA AND 'ONEWORLD' ALLIANCE

Aer Lingus entered its first strategic alliance with the US carrier Delta, this alliance began on 1 May 1996 and involved Delta and Aer Lingus in a code-sharing/blocked-space agreement. This meant that Delta purchased seats on Aer Lingus daily flights between New York (John F. Kennedy), Shannon and Dublin airports.

Delta served Shannon and Dublin from Atlanta with an all-year service, and with added access to New York, Delta passengers had direct service to both leading US gateways. In exchange, Aer Lingus had access to Delta's extensive operations in the US. Delta carried more passengers worldwide than any other airline and flew into cities that had a strong ethnic Irish population, allowing it to draw passengers from other areas via the Delta connection. It was envisaged that this would provide a significant boost to revenues from the North American market. Delta and its strategic partners, which included Aer Lingus, operated more than 4,900 flights each day to over 300 cities and thirty-two countries. Reports claimed that the

---

relationship with Delta was instrumental in Aer Lingus securing a deal worth $500,000 per annum with US mail. The *hub and spoke* strategy adopted by American Airlines when flying into Europe offered another possibility of forging a stronger alliance between the two airlines. Delta's use of Dublin as a hub from which its flights into Europe could be directed was a profitable decision for the airport. In addition, it involved Team Aer Lingus carrying out some of Delta's aircraft maintenance work.

The advantages to both parties were many, and as the industry analysts' predictions were toward the development of *mega-carriers* it was important for Aer Lingus to get a strong foothold in many markets in order to strengthen its industry position. Already British Airways and American Airlines have agreed to combine large parts of their business to form the world's largest and most powerful airline alliance *Oneworld*. This alliance not only involved joint marketing, code sharing, ticketing, integrating of frequent-flyer programmes, sharing of routes and facilities but also profit sharing which is a first for two international airlines.

Aer Lingus, on 1 June 2000, joined *Oneworld* global alliance. Together with their new partner airlines, American Airlines, British Airways, Cathay Pacific, Finnair, Iberia, Quantas and LanChile, the airline offers its customers greater travel options and a seamless service across the network of all the member airlines.

The member airlines carry 200 million passengers throughout a network of over 550 destinations across the globe. Aer Lingus group executive, Larry Stanley, claims that 'exposing the Irish market to this massive global audience will reap benefits for Ireland beyond the normal tourism and commercial business markets'.

Entry to *Oneworld* global alliance has come at a crucial stage in the commercial development of Aer Lingus and the additional traffic accruing will further boost the strong growth achieved by the airline in recent years.

Source: Richardson O'Hara, J., Delta's Sales Manager for Ireland, *Press Release*, 12 April 1996. Harding, T., 'Aer Lingus dispute prompts concern over Delta Alliance', *Sunday Tribune*, 9 June 1996. Thomson and Ashworth, 'BA in biggest global Link', *The Times*, 11 June 1996.

Development of a Marketing Plan

The strategic plan defines the company's mission and objectives within each business unit and a marketing plan must be prepared. The marketing plan is a document which formulates a plan for marketing the business's products and services. Why is it needed?

In highly competitive times it is necessary to be able to use *marketing* to channel *sales* in the right direction. As a document with a formal structure, a marketing plan disciplines the writer to put their feelings and thoughts, facts and conclusions down in a logical manner that can be followed by others. The written plan should be clear, concise, simply written and easy to understand. It should not be cluttered with excessive or irrelevant information and should be up to date.

Components of a plan:

1. Executive Summary
2. Current Market Situation
3. Strengths, Weaknesses, Threats and Opportunities (SWOT)
4. Objectives and Issues
5. Marketing Strategies
6. Action Plans
7. Budgets
8. Controls

Current Market Situation

The current market situation describes the target market and the company's position in it. The marketer needs information about the market, product/service performance, pricing structures, competition and distribution. It should include a market description that defines the market and the major segments. A product review can be included showing sales, prices and gross margins of the major products and services. A section on competitors identifies major competitors and their strategies. It should also show the market share held by the company and each competitor. Finally, a section on distribution describes sales trends and developments in the major distribution channels.

Strengths, Weaknesses, Threats and Opportunities (SWOT)

Strengths are inherited advantages for the organisation in relation to competitors, for example, Jurys Inns have the advantage of dominance in the budget accommodation sector in Ireland. Once identified, these strengths can be developed into competitive advantages and promoted to potential customers.

Weaknesses range from ageing products, e.g. hotels that are in need of refurbishment, poor locations or surly staff. Once identified they may be subject to management action designed to minimise their impact, e.g. training of all staff in customer care, or to remove them where possible. Marketers must look ahead for major threats and opportunities that the product or service might face. A marketing opportunity is an attractive arena for marketing action in which the company would enjoy a competitive advantage. Developing opportunities involves risks. When evaluating opportunities, the marketing manger must decide whether the expected returns justify these risks. Threats can be presented by internal elements within the businesses control or by external events. In Ireland we are threatened by the outbreak of violence in Northern Ireland which would greatly reduce the number of visitors entering the country.

Objectives and Issues

After the marketing manager has reviewed the issues involved with the product and service, they must decide the organisation's objectives. Objectives must be stated clearly and if possible in quantitative terms, e.g. to increase our base of customers by ten per cent or to expand consumer awareness from fifteen per cent to thirty per cent over the next twelve months. Hospitality operations frequently set objectives that focus on average rate and occupancy.

Marketing Strategies

The marketer outlines the broad marketing strategy or *game plan* for attaining objectives. It consists of specific strategies for target markets and detailed descriptions of the marketing mix. It should spell out the market segments which the company will target. The marketing strategy can be presented under the following headings:

- Target Market
- Positioning Strategy
- Marketing Research
- Products/Services Offered
- New Product Development (if applicable)
- Price Strategy
- Distribution Strategy
- Promotions
  - Advertising Strategy
  - Sales Promotions Strategy
  - Public Relations Strategy
  - Personal Selling Strategy
  - Internet Marketing Strategy
  - Database Marketing Strategy

In developing the strategies, the marketer must talk to all the necessary *production* people, in hotels this would include the front-office manager, head housekeeper, food and beverage manager and head chef. Finance would have an important role also, to make sure enough advertising and promotion funds will be available.

Action Plans

The marketing plan must specify the marketing programmes or action plans designed to achieve the business objectives. Each element of the marketing strategy must now be examined to answer the following questions: What will be done? When will it be done? Who will do it? How much will it cost?

Frequently, the action plans will end up as very detailed, documenting all the planned marketing activities for a full twelve months, sometimes week by week if not month by month. Each action may have a person assigned to carry out the task and the date by which it should be completed.

Costing of Programmes

Action plans allow the marketer to establish a budget. Each action is costed and the total costs per month projected. On the revenue side, the forecasted sales turnover is shown, as well as average rates and occupancy levels. Once the budget has been prepared, top management will review it and approve or modify it. This stage can take some time because there can be much discussion between the marketing department and top management.

Once approved, the budget is the basis for developing plans and schedules for purchasing, recruitment, staff scheduling and marketing operations. Typically the budget acts as a control mechanism for monitoring the marketing plan's progress. Top management can review the results each month and identify sectors of their business that are not reaching their goals.

Step 4 Control
Are we meeting our objectives?
Comparison of Performance Against Objectives
Development of Contingency Plans

STEP 4: CONTROL

Marketing Control

The marketing manager must control marketing plans once they have been implemented. The function of marketing control is to give the manager feedback on how the plans are progressing. The purpose of marketing control is to maximise the probability that the organisation's objectives will be achieved. With the feedback that marketing control provides, the manager is in a position to know whether adjustments are needed. Box 5.3 illustrates the control issues.

BOX 5.3 — CONTROL ISSUES IN BUSINESS

What do we want to achieve? ——————————▶	Goal Setting
What is happening? ——————————————▶	Performance Measurement
Why is it happening? ————————————▶	Performance Diagnosis
What should we do about it? ——————▶	Corrective Action

Source: Adopted from *Principles of Marketing,* Kinnear, Berhardt Krentler, HarperCollins, 1995

Control is most often accomplished through the use of various sales and profitability measures. Such measures include:

- *Revenue analysis* — the measurement and evaluation of actual revenue in relation to objectives set. The most common measure is sales turnover. Depending on the organisation this figure can be broken down by department or by activity.
- *Market share analysis* — is consideration of how the firm is doing in comparison to competitors. In Ireland it is extremely difficult to get operating data on competitors and instead many marketing managers use industry reports to make comparisons.
- *Expenses-to-sales analysis* — compares the ratio of various marketing expenses such as advertising and personal selling to the sales being generated.

The results of these analyses should be available on a monthly basis.

EXHIBIT 5.3

STRATEGIC MARKET PLANNING *IN ACTION*
DEVELOPING TOURISM IN TRALEE

Tralee, the capital town of County Kerry, lies on the south-west coast of Ireland at the gateway to the Dingle Peninsula. The town has a population of approximately 20,000 and is the administrative centre of the county. It serves as the focal point for retailing and is the location of some of its premier industries.

However, in the late 1980s and early 1990s, considerable employment contraction occurred as a number of industries closed or were curtailed. This situation gave rise to substantial concern and a desire for new development. Tourism was identified as the major window of opportunity for Tralee.

Tourism by its nature is a spatially distributed industry and has, without doubt, an important contribution to make to regional development. Tralee is located at the hub of two of the most important tourism regions in Ireland — The Cork-Kerry Region (Counties Cork and South Kerry) and the Shannon

Region (Counties North Kerry, Limerick, Clare, North Tipperary and South Offaly). These are the regional classifications as defined by Bord Fáilte. In 1998, the regions attracted more tourists and generated more revenue than any other part of the country. The South-West and Shannon Regions combined accounted for twenty-nine per cent of all tourist numbers and thirty per cent of all revenue generated. By comparison, Dublin, the most popular single region accounted for twenty-five per cent of tourist numbers and twenty-five per cent of revenue.

TABLE 5.6 — TOURISM NUMBERS AND REGIONAL REVENUES FOR 1998

	Numbers (000s)	Revenue (£m)
Ireland	16,460	2,552·3
South-West	2,790	508·3
Shannon Region	1,988	266·9
Total	4,778	775·2

Source: Bord Fáilte Tourism Facts 1998 (These figures include overseas, domestic and Northern Ireland tourists)

Bord Fáilte (1994) estimated that investment in tourism in the Cork-Kerry region was £175 million in the period 1989–94. Ambitious growth targets for the region were set. The achievement of these targets was contingent on an investment of £250m over the period 1994–9 and would support an estimated 23,000 jobs in the region.

TABLE 5.7 — GROWTH TARGETS — CORK-KERRY REGION

	£m
Overseas Tourism Revenue	340
Domestic and Northern Ireland Revenue	195
Total	535

Source: Developing Sustainable Tourism — Tourism Development Plan 1994–1999, Bord Fáilte, 1994

At the same time, targets were set for the Shannon Region. Investment in the period 1989–94 was £120 million. Achievement of growth targets in this region required an investment of £150 million over the period 1994–9, and would support an estimated 14,000 jobs.

TABLE 5.8 — GROWTH TARGETS — SHANNON REGION

Kerry Perspective

	£m
Overseas Tourism Revenue	200
Domestic and Northern Ireland Revenue	125
Total	**325**

County Kerry plays a dominant role in the Irish tourist industry as it contains an international portfolio of natural tourism attractions such as The Lakes of Killarney, The Ring of Kerry and The Dingle Peninsula. A tradition of tourism has been established in the county, and visitors find a warm and welcoming social climate.

According to the Tralee Task Force (1992), in 1988 total visitor revenue was estimated at £150 million in Kerry, representing a fifteen per cent share of the total visitor revenue in Ireland.

Kerry County Council (1994), estimated that tourism revenue for County Kerry had reached £160 million in 1991, well over half of which was received from out-of-state tourism.

A report by Tourism Development International (1995), stated that tourism revenue had increased to over £166 million by 1994 and the county was attracting 1.7 million visitors annually. The report further outlined that the projected growth of tourism in Kerry would see an increase in visitors from 1,949 million in 1996 to 2,177 million in 1998.

Tralee Perspective

In the 1980s, Tralee as a tourism base had limited appeal. Apart from *Siamsa Tíre*, the National Folk Theatre of Ireland and a limited accommodation supply, Tralee offered little to encourage visitors to the town. The main tourism flagship was the International Rose of Tralee Festival, which combined with Tralee Races, brought both national and international visitors to the town. By 1989, the festival was thirty years in operation and was beginning to face stiff competition from a number of other national festivals.

At this time, the backbone of the tourism industry in the town was the coach tour business and some day-trippers. This tour business came to Tralee at *rock bottom prices* and spent little time or money in the town. There were few independent travellers or families visiting Tralee as a holiday destination.

The lack of recording procedures makes it difficult to obtain tourism statistics specific to a particular town. However, it is recorded that in 1991 there were approximately 62,000 personal callers to Tralee tourist information office. (Shannon Development, 1999.)

A year into its existence the group consulted with Shannon Development and determined that their present structure prohibited further development. Based on a co-operative and consultative approach, it was determined that the establishment of a task force which consisted of a number of personnel representing the private and public sector was required. These included representatives from Tralee Urban District Council, the business community and Shannon Development.

The Tralee Task Force recognised the need for a strategic approach and engaged an experienced and well-respected tourism consultant to provide an assessment of the tourism potential of the town. This report combined with a number of other surveys and consultations led to the development, in 1992, of the *Tralee 2000* Report, which outlined a strategy for tourism in Tralee town. Within this report, the goal of Tralee Task Force was identified:

'Our goal is to secure Tralee as an internationally renowned tourism centre. Tralee will serve as a major centre for touring, a natural gateway to the South-West and a destination attraction in its own right. The town will contain a range of international-level visitor attractions, substantial and varied accommodation facilities, an urban environment worth staying in, together with complementary leisure facilities.'

At this stage a SWOT analysis was conducted by Tralee Task Force and concluded that Tralee possessed the following strengths, weaknesses, opportunities and threats:

Strengths

- Location as a hub for the entire south-west of Ireland
- Recently developed tourist attractions
- The Rose of Tralee Festival
- The high levels of local initiative, drive and enthusiasm

We would have identified further strengths of Tralee at the time as:
The home of *Siamsa Tíre*, The National Folk Theatre of Ireland.
Tralee as the capital of the region with a reasonable base of retail outlets.

Weaknesses

- Tralee's image as a market town with little experience in catering for tourists
- Accommodation shortages

- Poor standard of physical environment
- Lack of tourist infrastructure

A further weakness we perceived was:
The lack of a planned and cohesive marketing strategy at that time.

Opportunities

- The growth in tourism globally

Other factors we have identified from that period include:

- The framework adopted by the Government for tourism development in Ireland
- The expansion of Kerry Airport providing direct access to Tralee
- The growth of activity-based holidays such as golf and Tralee's proximity to the world-renowned Ballybunion Golf Club
- Access to an established market base in Killarney, one of Ireland's premier tourist destinations, situated just nineteen miles from Tralee

Threats

- Tourism is a highly competitive business

Other factors that deserved consideration at the time include:

- Political unrest in Northern Ireland
- Increasing demands from other centres for structural funds for tourism development
- Tralee's peripheral location on the western seaboard
- Killarney's strong position in the international tourism market and the difficulties of competing with this established name

In mid-1992, following this analysis, the Tralee Task Force formulated a tourism development strategy for Tralee for the period 1992–2000. They identified a number of categories of visitor that could be attracted to the town, including small touring groups such as families, activity holidaymakers and independent travellers.

Broad strategies were suggested, which formed the basis for development over the following decade. These included:

- Product Development
- Expanded Accommodation
- Enhanced Physical Environment
- Marketing
- Access Improvement
- Promotion of Culture of International Tourism

The task force anticipated that the proposed tourism developments in Tralee could push annual visitor revenue in Kerry to £300 million per annum.

The development of Tralee as tourism destination had now commenced in earnest.

A number of initiatives were undertaken under the broad strategies mentioned above.

Product Development

Since 1987 there has been considerable investment in tourist attractions in Tralee based on the premise that there was a need for a cluster of high quality, weather independent amenities focused on activity and heritage/cultural tourism. These products include:

- Geraldine Experience
- Kerry County Museum
- Blennerville Centre
- Tralee to Blennerville Steam Train
- *Siamsa Tíre* (new purpose-built centre)
- Tralee Golf Club (new course and clubhouse)
- Aquadome
- Bowling Alley
- Jungle Jim's Adventure Centre
- Kennedy's Equine Centre
- Tralee Regional Sports and Leisure Centre
- Multi-Screen Cinema
- Jeannie Johnston
- Georgian House Visitor Centre

One of the guiding principles behind this cluster approach was that the increase in the number of visitors to Tralee town would spark investment in accommodation, as businesses would feel confident in their investment in this sector. It was also felt that the above product mix combined with a quality accommodation base would make Tralee attractive as a family holiday destination.

Product development for the town is continuing and includes:

- Lee Valley Development
- Tralee Ship Canal
- Adventure Golf

Expanded Accommodation

The development of visitor attractions in Tralee led to the expansion of the accommodation base in the town. In 1990, it was reported that there were just 422 hotel rooms in Tralee (Keane, 1990). From 1992 onwards, accommodation began to grow vigorously in all categories as illustrated by the following examples:

TABLE 5.9 — SAMPLE ACCOMMODATION DEVELOPMENTS IN TRALEE

Year	Development	Accommodation Type
1992	Tralee Holiday Homes	11 houses (self-catering)
1993	Brandon Place Holiday Homes	12 houses (self-catering)
1994	Brandon Court Hotel	49 rooms
1995	Abbeygate Hotel	100 rooms
1995	Tralee Holiday Apartments	54 apartments
1996	Brandon Hotel	25 additional rooms and suites
1997	Tralee Court Hotel	45 rooms
1997	Westwood Court	43 rooms (hostel)
1997	Earl of Desmond Hotel	120 additional rooms
1999	The Johnston Marina Hotel	35 rooms

Planned investment includes the development of three new hotels in the near future. Bed and breakfast accommodation also continues to expand at a considerable pace with a move toward purpose-built houses.

Enhanced Physical Environment

Tralee Urban District Council is committed toward the development of Tralee as a sustainable tourism destination and over the past decade has facilitated this process through its development plan. Measures taken include:

- Improving the appearance of access points to and from the town by measures such as planting of trees, flowers and shrubs
- Pedestrianising areas of the town centre
- Provision of seating areas
- Development of Tralee town park

- Removal of overhead electrical cables
- Representation on Tidy Towns Associations
- Limited provision of *old-style* street lamps
- Protection of listed buildings of historical significance
- Provision of quality public restrooms

Tralee Urban District Council aims to continue its support of tourism in the town by recognising the historic character of Tralee's environment as important in achieving sustainable tourism. Planned future initiatives include:

- To consolidate the tourism/leisure zone being developed in the Lee Valley area of the town
- To develop an attractive *speciality shopping precinct* which would have appeal to tourists and locals in the old market area of the town
- To develop an existing derelict mill to house a *Centre of Excellence* in Kerry crafts and farmhouse products

Marketing

At the beginning of the decade, the marketing of Tralee as a tourist destination was limited. The town failed to identify its unique selling propositions and marketing was conducted on an individual as opposed to a co-operative basis. Consequently the town did not adopt a clear positioning strategy. One of the first groups established to address this issue, was Tralee Tourism Ltd, which was incorporated in June 1992. The focus of the group was to promote and encourage the development of tourism traffic to Tralee. Sample activities include the yearly production of a full colour brochure produced in a number of different languages, cinema advertising and attendance at holiday fairs.

The Tralee Task Force also initiated the development of a marketing body called Holiday Tralee. Marketing activities undertaken by this body include newspaper, journal and radio advertising, shopping centre promotions, attendance at holiday and trade fairs and market research. This body currently employs a full-time marketing executive.

There is also ongoing marketing by Shannon Development including the establishment of a tourism web site, and financial and administrative support for various projects such as The North Kerry Good Food Dining Circle and the North Kerry Walks.

Access Improvement

In improving accessibility to Tralee town over the past decade a number of initiatives have been adopted. These include:

- Improved facilities at Kerry Airport to include:
  - Twice daily flights from Dublin to Kerry, facilitating direct access to the county from international destinations
  - Two major carriers servicing the airport — Aer Lingus and Ryanair
  - Potential for expanding transatlantic flights which have to date been facilitated on a limited basis
- Upgrading of the Dublin to Kerry and Cork to Kerry rail network
- Continued investment in the regional and national road networks

Promotion of Culture of International Tourism

Over the past decade significant progress has been made in the transition of Tralee from a market and commercial town to the position of a national and international tourism destination. Specific steps were necessary to facilitate this transition and included providing information, education and training. Some of the initiatives that have contributed to this transition are:

- Further development of tourism and hospitality courses at the Institute of Technology, Tralee
- Education programmes aimed at the second-level sector such as CERT (State Tourism Training Agency) open days and Tourism Awareness programmes during transition year
- A partnership approach toward tourism development in the town. An example is the development of the Aquadome where matching funds were raised through contributions from the business and householders of Tralee town. This strategy created a sense of ownership of the project by the residents of the town and appears to have developed a sense of understanding and appreciation of the social and economic contribution of tourism to the area
- The local culture has, to a certain degree, been developed to cater for the diverse needs of the various market segments by, for example, including alternative cuisine in menu offerings, providing varied entertainment and leisure facilities and developing language skills.

Performance Indicators

The number of tourists visiting Tralee has continued to increase since the inception of Tralee Task Force. Tralee tourist office indicates an increase in visitor numbers from approximately 62,000 visitors in 1991 to circa 108,052 in 1998 (Shannon Development, 1999). A more accurate assessment of visitor growth is reflected in the visitor numbers of the main tourist attractions. In 1991, 106,000 visitors were recorded and in 1997 the statistics indicated that this figure had grown to 520,000 visitors.

TABLE 5.10 — VISITOR NUMBERS TO TRALEE 1991-7

Year	Enquiries to Tourist Office	Visitor Numbers to Attractions	Estimated Visitor Numbers to Tralee
1991	62,000	106,000	151,429
1992	63,000	176,000	251,429
1993	68,681	247,000	352,857
1994	71,474	467,000	667,143
1995	86,952	510,000	728,571
1996	77,729	530,000	757,143
1997	89,122	520,000	742,857
1998	108,052	n/a	n/a

Source: Shannon Development, 1999

There are no officially recorded visitor numbers to Tralee. Research undertaken by Reuter (1998), estimated that the percentage of visitors to Tralee that did not visit any of the tourist attractions was thirty per cent. Therefore, estimated visitor numbers to Tralee given above are based on the assumption that visitors to tourist attractions represent seventy per cent of the total visitor numbers to the town. These figures do not include visitors who come to the town because of festivals or other special events. For example, The Rose of Tralee Festival alone is estimated to attract 100,000 visitors.

There is no official data available concerning the average length of stay by tourists in Tralee in the late 1980s and early 1990s. However, anecdotal evidence suggests that the market primarily consisted of day-trippers and coach tours spending one night in the town. Research by Reuter (1998) shows the average length of stay as 3·16 nights in 1998.

Tralee Today

Today, Tralee is a town of real tourism opportunity. It combines the vibrancy and bustle of a thriving and growing tourism centre with a range of recreational amenities, which makes it an ideal holiday destination. It has become a very cosmopolitan town with a strong sense of community and purpose. The town has shown what can be done when individuals get together with the specific aim of improving the quality of the tourism product. The buoyancy of tourism development has created the impetus for further investment and development.

This Exhibit has been prepared by Tony Donovan, Eileen Maher and Brid McElligott, lecturers at the Institute of Technology, Tralee, Co. Kerry. The case was presented at the TTRA Conference (Dublin) in September 1999.

CHAPTER SUMMARY

One of the major challenges facing today's tourism and hospitality operations is how to build and maintain viable businesses in a rapidly changing market-place. Strategic market planning aims to help a company select and organise its business in a way that will keep the company healthy even when unexpected events occur. Strategic market planning focuses on four main steps:

Analysis: this answers the question 'Where are we now?' and involves the development of a marketing audit and SWOT analysis.

Planning: this answers the question 'Where do we want to be?' The stages involved in this process include the mission statement, setting objectives and identification and evaluation of alternatives.

Implementation: answers the question 'How do we get there?' This involves the development of action programmes and costing them.

Control: this answers the question 'Are we meeting our objectives?' This involves the comparison of performance achieved against the objectives set. It may also involve the development of contingency plans.

Strategic tools that can be used to carry market planning include Portfolio Analysis, using a model such as the BCG Matrix. Other tools include the Product-Market Opportunity Analysis. Both of these tools simply help the tourism and hospitality marketer to view their business(es) in a more strategic way.

A key issue that faces all businesses today is competition and, during the 1990s, strategic alliances were offered as a possible solution to fighting off competitors. In other words business were collaborating in order to compete.

The process of strategic market planning ends with the production of the Marketing Plan. This document simply formulates a plan for marketing the businesses' products and services. The written plan should be clear, concise and easy to understand. The content of a plan can include: executive summary, current market situation, SWOT analysis, marketing objectives, marketing strategies, action plans, budgets and control.

KEY WORDS AND PHRASES

Strategic Planning	Marketing Audit	Mission Statement
Objectives	Strategic Business Unit (SBU)	PEST
SWOT	Objectives	Strategies
Marketing Tactics	BCG Matrix	Ansoff Matrix
Strategic Alliances	Marketing Plan	Competitive Advantage

REFERENCES AND FURTHER READING

Andorka, F., 'Ramada helps Sandals put "Personal Best" foot forward', *Hotel and Management*, p. 4, vol. 213, Iss: 6: 1998.

Ansoff, I., 'Strategies for Diversification', *Harvard Business Review*, September/October, p. 114: 1957.

Buckley, P.J. and Klemm, M., 'The decline of tourism in NI — the causes', *Tourism Management*, June: 1993.

Craven, D.W., *Strategic Marketing*, Irwin: Illinois 1994.

Dev, C. and Klein, S., 'Strategic Alliances in the Hotel Industry', *The Cornell H.R.A. Quarterly:* 1993.

Dibb, Simpkin, Pride, and Ferrell, *Marketing Concepts and Strategies*, 2nd European edn., Houghton Mifflin: Boston 1994.

Drucker, P.F., *Managing for Results,* Harper Row: New York 1964.

Go, F.M. and Hedges, *Strategic Alliance in Tourism Marketing and Management Handbook*, 2nd edn., Prentice Hall: New York 1994.

Hamel, G., Doz, Y. and Prahalad, C.K., 'Collaborate with your Competitors — and Win', *Harvard Business Review:* 1989.

Holloway, C. *The Business of Tourism*, 4th edn., Pitman Publishing: 1994.

Keane, C., 'North Kerry needs more accommodation for tourists', *Kerryman Newspaper:* 1990.

Kotler, P., Armstrong, G., Saunders, J. and Wong, V., *Principles of Marketing*, 2nd European edn., Prentice Hall Europe: 1999.

Lennon, R. and Titterington, A.J., 'The prospects for tourism in NI', *International Journal and Contemporary Hospitality Management*, vol. 8, No. 3, pp. 11–17: 1996.

Lumsdon, L., *Tourism Marketing*, Thomson Business Press: London 1997.

Medlik, S., *Managing Tourism,* Butterworth-Heinemann Ltd: 1991.

McDonald, M.H.B., *Marketing Plans, How to Prepare Them, How to Use Them*, 2nd edn., Butterworth Heinemann: Oxford 1995.

Ohmae, K., *The Global Logic of Strategic Alliances in Collaborating to Compete by Bleeke and Ernst,* John Wiley & Sons Inc: 1993.

Poon, A., *Tourism, Technology and Competitive Strategies,* CAB International: 1993.

Prahalad, C.K., and Hamel, G., 'The Core Competence of the Organisation', *Harvard Business Review:* 1990.

Reuter, A., 'The Impact of Tourism on the Local Economy with Special Reference to Tralee (Ireland)', unpublished under-graduate thesis: 1998.

Richter, L.K. and Waugh, W.L. Jr., 'Terrorism and tourism as logical companions', *Tourism Management*, Dec: 1986.

Selznick, P., *Leadership and Administration*, Harper & Row: New York 1957.

Shannon Development, Number of Calls to Tourist Information Offices: 1999.

Teare, R. and Olsen, M., *International Hospitality Management,* John Wiley and Sons Inc: 1992.

Tourism Development International, Review of Tourism Development and Marketing Plan for Kerry County Council: 1995.

Wearne, N. and Morrison, A., *Hospitality Marketing*, Butterworth Heinemann: 1996.

USEFUL WEB SITES

www.ft.com	Financial Times
www.aerlingus.ie	Aer Lingus
www.atlas.ie	Atlas Travel Service
www.budgettravel.ie	Budget Travel
www.travelocity.com	Travel site

CHAPTER 6

Market Segmentation, Targeting and Positioning

INTRODUCTION

To be able to serve a market, it is important for a marketer to describe the market accurately. It is also important for the marketer to understand the diversity in the market. Marketers have found that greater success comes from breaking up a large market into smaller segments. This approach is called *market segmentation*. Each of these segments will have similar needs and wants and will respond similarly to marketing mix offerings. Segmentation allows marketers to develop products and services that are uniquely positioned to meet the needs of a particular segment. This process involves deciding which segments to target. Once target segments have been selected, the marketers must then decide how they wish the target market to perceive the product or service. This involves positioning the product or service. Thus the process of segmentation, targeting and positioning are very important concepts in tourism and hospitality marketing today.

CHAPTER OBJECTIVES

After studying this chapter you will be able to:

- Explain the concepts of segmentation, targeting and positioning
- Understand how companies segment markets
- Decide what criteria a company can use to choose the most attractive target market
- Understand how to position a product or service in a tourism or hospitality market

WHAT IS A MARKET?

When marketers set out to sell a product or service, one of the most important things they must do is identify their market by determining who their potential customers are. To qualify as potential customers, persons or businesses must meet each of the four criteria:

1. They must need or want the product or service
2. They must be interested or potentially interested in buying the product or service
3. They must have enough money or credit to buy the product or service
4. They must be willing to buy the product or service

A market consists of people or businesses with the interest or potential interest, the purchasing power and the willingness to buy a product or service that satisfies a need or desire.

Today, many companies are moving away from focusing on large mass markets to smaller *niche* markets. The steps in this process are called market segmentation, targeting and positioning, (*see* Figure 6.1). The process of dividing up a market and choosing the preferred segments is often referred to as *target marketing*. As a result of the fragmentation of the tourism and hospitality markets into hundreds of micro-markets, each with different needs and lifestyles, target marketing is crucial.

FIGURE 6.1 — STEPS IN SEGMENTATION, TARGETING AND POSITIONING

Market Segmentation

1. Identify bases for segmenting the market

2. Develop profiles of the resulting segments

Market Targeting

3. Evaluate the attractiveness of each segment

4. Select the target segments

Market Positioning

5. Identify possible positioning concepts for each target segment (target market)

6. Develop marketing mix for target market

Adapted from *Marketing for Hospitality and Tourism,* Kotler et al, 1996

MARKET SEGMENTATION

There is no single best way to segment the market, but there is no shortage of different ways to do it. The more commonly used segmentation variables include geographic, demographic, behavioural and psychographic variables.

BASES OF SEGMENTATION

Markets vary greatly. Some are comprised of people or businesses that have very similar needs, preferences, and desires. These homogeneous markets are fairly easy for the marketer to please. A single marketing mix can be developed to satisfy everyone in the market. Most tourism and hospitality markets are heterogeneous (i.e. the consumers differ greatly), for example, a family market differs from a business market. Meeting the needs of these markets is a challenge to marketers. As previously mentioned, one way to do this is to segment the market. The goal is to identify market segments with similar characteristics and therefore similar needs.

Just about any human characteristic can be used as a variable to subdivide a large potential market into homogeneous market segments that differ from one another in terms of that characteristic, e.g. age. However, not all identifiable characteristics make good segmentation variables, e.g. trying to divide a market based on the colour of people's hair! When deciding which variables to use to segment markets, the marketing manager's goal should be to identify market segments that differ from one another in the ways that they respond to a particular marketing mix. For example, Michael Gibbons owns the Connemara Walking Centre in Clifden, Co. Galway. Michael's goal is to segment the overseas tourist market into those interested in walking and those that are not. A number of characteristics are used as segmentation variables for the tourism and hospitality markets.

Tour Operators Panorama clearly segment their holiday market and effectively promote a different marketing mix to each segment.

Geographic Segmentation

Geographic segmentation calls for dividing the total market into segments on the basis of location. Many types of location can be used: countries, regions, counties, cities or towns and even neighbourhoods. Even McDonald's, who traditionally did not differentiate its products from country to country now offer wine in France and rice in Japan. Newspapers publish different editions to accommodate the needs of different readers in different areas or countries, e.g. *The Sunday Times* has an Irish edition. In tourism, Bord Fáilte segment the overseas market by using geographic segmentation as is shown in Table 6.1.

TABLE 6.1 — GEOGRAPHIC SEGMENTATION OF OVERSEAS MARKET TO IRELAND

Numbers (000s)	1998	1999
Britain	3,199	3,430
Mainland Europe	1,255	1,321
Germany	310	305
France	270	275
Italy	141	165
Netherlands	134	139
Belgium/Luxembourg	71	71
Spain	82	78
Denmark	30	39
Norway/Sweden	67	81
Switzerland	54	60
Other Europe	97	108
North America	858	950
US	789	860
Canada	69	90
Rest of World	221	243
Australia/New Zealand	124	136
Japan	26	28
Other Overseas	71	79
Total Overseas	5,534	5,943
Northern Ireland	530	460
Total Out of State	6,064	6,403
Domestic Trips	6,934	7,285

Source: CSO/Bord Fáilte/NITB, 2000

Demographic Segmentation

Dividing the total market into segmentation on the basis of such demographic variables as age, gender, income, occupation, education, race, nationality and social class is called demographic segmentation. This is one of the most popular methods by which marketers segment tourism and hospitality markets. Demographic segmentation is widely used for two reasons, first, the consumers' wants and needs are often closely associated with their demographic characteristics. For example, age is an important segmentation variable used by Club Med, while gender is used to segment markets for cosmetics.

OIDEAS GAEL offers study programmes for universities, companies, social clubs and other organisations who would like specialist courses on the Irish language, culture, archaeology, environment, folklore, weaving or other disciplines. Combination courses are also organised by special arrangement. Accommodation and travel can be arranged to suit particular requirements.

New for 2000! Cultural Tours of Donegal, Ireland's Gaelic Heartland! **The tours include hotel accommodation and full itinerary of activities.**

Both GaelSaoire and Oideas Gael segment the market and target those interested in learning the Irish Language and about Irish Culture.

AGE AND LIFE-CYCLE STAGE

Consumers needs and wants change with age. Some companies offer different products or marketing strategies to penetrate various age and life-cycle segments. For example,

Supermacs offers happy meals that include toys, aimed at young children. These toys are often part of a series, encouraging children to return until they have completed the entire set. The chain has added new food items including salads, pizza and barbecued foods to attract an older and health conscious market.

TABLE 6.2 — LIFE-CYCLE STAGES

Bachelor stage (young single people not living with parents)

Newly married couples without children

Full nest I (youngest child under 6)

Full nest II (youngest child 6 or over)

Full nest III (older married couple with dependent children)

Empty nest I (no children living at home, family head in work)

Empty nest II (family head retired)

Solitary survivor (in work)

Solitary survivor (retired)

Source: 'Life-cycle Stages', *Consumer Market Research Handbook*, Wells and Gubar, 1986

A mistake can be made in tourism and hospitality to assume that older people do not enjoy travel and are not adventuresome. Many hotels offer *golden oldies* programmes targeting elderly people who now have the time and interest to travel. This group is frequently referred to as *empty nesters* as their children have usually left home. This strategy has proved very successful for group hotels who fill quiet months such as November, February and March by targeting this segment. Full marketing mixes are designed and include an itinerary of activities for the elderly travellers, (*see* Great Southern Hotels promotion aimed at the elderly).

Golden Breaks

Corrib, Torc, Rosslare, Great Southern Hotels

People of all ages are welcome the year round at Great Southern Hotels, but on certain days midweek during the Spring, Summer and Autumn, there is an extra-special welcome for senior guests — the fun-loving over fifty-fives.

Our standard Gold Programme includes:

- Three nights bed and breakfast (Tuesday, Wednesday, Thursday) and superb five-course dinner each evening
- Get-together welcome reception
- Free half-day coach tour
- Card games
- Free collection to and from the train or bus station (just let us know your time of arrival when you book)
- Short-mat bowling
- Complimentary three-minute phone call to anywhere in Ireland, so you can keep in touch with home
- Optional coach tour (small additional charge)
- Complimentary coffee and tea service in the lounge throughout your stay
- Use of all your hotel's leisure facilities free of charge
- Evening entertainment
- Optional quiz night
- Four- and five-night programmes also available
- For further details and a copy of our Golden Breaks brochure call 01 2808031

Great Southern Hotels have segmented their markets by age and are targeting the elderly with the Golden Breaks Package.

GENDER

Gender segmentation has been used in marketing clothes, hairdressing, cosmetics and magazines. The tourism and hospitality sector is now beginning to use it. In America women in the past accounted for only one per cent of all business travellers, today it is over forty per cent. Hotel companies now design hotels with women in mind and use women in their advertising. Kotler et al (1996), claims that researchers discovered that a single woman living in a large Canadian city is more likely than her male counterparts, or her married friends, to increase her spending in restaurants as a result of a pay increase.

INCOME AND OCCUPATION

Segmentation by income and occupation have been used by marketers of products and services such as clothing, cars and travel. Country clubs often use income and occupation to identify potential members for their direct mail campaign. One aspect of the Celtic Tiger economy has been the *new* wealth that it has created. Some of the higher incomes being earned are not by the *traditional* professions such as doctors or teachers, but by innovators in the area of information technology, by tradesmen, property owners and developers. Income does not always predict which customers will buy a given product or service. Single people in America spend more than half of their food budget dining out, while married couples spend only thirty-seven per cent. It is important to remember that the significance of income will vary from market to market. A study of Galway as a tourist destination showed that *income* was not as strong a segmentation variable as *purpose of visit*. Galway City attracts a market that consists of a wide range of incomes and occupations.

TABLE 6.3 — DEMOGRAPHIC SEGMENTATION

Category	Profile	Examples
Young children (4–11)	Parents influenced by desires of small children	Ryan Hotels packages featuring *friendly helpers*, EuroDisney
Young people (11–18)	Adventure holidays but with parental approval, guidance	Youth hostels associations, Adventure Centres such as Delphi and Killary
Young couples, groups and singles (18–30)	Good fun, flexible, fast paced holidays, night clubs, adventure	Club Med. Temple Bar in Dublin, Galway
Family Holidays (25–50 with younger children)	Children are key to the holiday; activities and relaxation	Butlins, Trabollgin, child friendly resorts
Empty Nester Holiday (45–60)	Active ex parents — discovering new tourism destinations, pastimes without children	Cruise market, special interest and activity oriented, painting, creative writing, hiking
Senior citizens (55+)	Older people, singles and couples, seeking holidays which include culture, but not paced intineraries	Golden breaks at Great Southern Hotels.

Source: Adapted from *Tourism Marketing*, Lumsdon, L., 1997

GEODEMOGRAPHICS

This technique enhances geographic segmentation in that it classifies potential market segments according to residential neighbourhoods in which they live. The market leader in the UK is a system known as ACORN (A Classification of Residential Neighbourhoods). It assesses segmentation areas according to forty variables combined with analysis of the census and other commercial market intelligence which is then collated. Similar databases are available in a number of countries, either derived from census data on households, or based on telephone ownership. Companies then use such systems to target likely customers for such products as overseas holidays or timeshares. Geodemographic segmentation is starting to become popular in Ireland as the range and variety of data collected by government bodies increases.

PSYCHOGRAPHIC SEGMENTATION

Another way markets are segmented is through the use of psychographics, segmentation variables based on consumers' personality characteristics and lifestyle. Lifestyle refers to a set of values or tastes exhibited by a group of consumers, especially as they are reflected in consumption patterns. A good way to understand the conceptual differences between the bases of segmentation that have been discussed and psychographics, is to think of the former as states of *being* and the latter as states of *mind*. One of the most common ways of identifying psychographic variables is the AIO (activities, interests and opinions) inventory. Such inventories are typically gathered from surveys where the researchers ask consumers to respond to questions that provide insight into the consumers' interests, opinions and the types of activities they engage in. Figure 6.2 provides an example of the types of questions that might be included on a typical AIO inventory.

FIGURE 6.2 — TYPICAL AIO INVENTORY STATEMENTS

Statements — Agree or Disagree?
My greatest achievements are still ahead of me
Five years from now, my income will probably be a lot higher than it is now
I'd like to spend a year in Japan
I like to be considered a leader
I don't like to take chances
I like parties where there is lots of music and talk
I always have the car radio on when I drive
Cosmopolitan is one of my favourite magazines
I like driving fast
Liquor is a curse on Irish life
People should be banned from smoking in public

Source: Adapted from *Principles of Marketing*, Kinnear, Bernhardt and Krentler, 1995

One of the most prominent users of psychographic analysis (or lifestyle analysis) has been a research firm called SRI International. They have developed a programme called VALS (values and lifestyles). The programme classifies the American population into nine segments based on diversity of values and lifestyles. The lifestyle characteristics include: the fulfilleds, the believers, the actualisers, the achievers, the strivers, the strugglers, the experiencers and the makers. The eight segments are grouped into three categories based on principles, status and action. Fulfilleds and believers make up the principle-oriented category. Actualisers, achievers, strivers and strugglers belong to the status-oriented category. Experiencers and makers comprise the action-oriented category. American Airlines has used VALS to identify its frequent-flyer customer group, the business traveller, as achievers. Please refer to Chapter 4 on Consumer Behaviour for further details on VALS.

BEHAVIOURAL SEGMENTATION

In behaviour segmentation, market segments are identified according to the actual behaviour of consumers in the market-place. Included in this category are usage rate, brand loyalty, readiness stage and benefits sought.

Usage Rate

The frequency with which consumers buy or use a product or service is its 'usage rate'. In many cases, twenty per cent of the users account for close to eighty per cent of the sales. This is often referred to as the eighty/twenty rule. When marketers choose usage rate as a segmentation variable, they first divide the market into three categories: heavy users, light users and non-users. To more easily identify the three segments, a marketer may attempt to find demographic characteristics that correlate with usage rate. A *heavy user* of a hotel may be sales people between the ages of twenty-one and forty, who stay mostly mid-week and spend an average of £60 a night.

Different marketing mix strategies are directed toward each segment. Beer and stout producers might use price promotions to attract the heavy-user segment (likely to be sensitive to price), while they target light consumers through emphasising the taste of a new high-priced beer. Light users might also be a good market for smaller units: six or eight ounce bottles or cans. Non-users might be attracted by the introduction of non-alcoholic beer. A marketer might decide instead to concentrate on just the heavy-user segment and ignore the other two segments.

In the hospitality and airline industry the use of frequent-flyer and frequent-guest programmes is aimed at identifying heavy users and keeping them loyal to the business by offering rewards for frequent usage. These programmes are expensive to maintain but appear to be successful in keeping a large portion of the business-travel market coming back to those hotels and airlines that offer the programmes. Recent research on the major hotel chains indicates that these programmes are still being used as a key aspect of marketing strategy. Individual chains of hotels are being forced to maintain them as a means of encouraging and maintaining customer loyalty.

Marketers should identify heavy users and build a marketing mix to attract them. Kotler (1996) claims too many firms spread their marketing resources evenly across all potential customers. Seasoned marketers identify heavy users and focus marketing strategies toward them.

Brand Loyalty

Consumers show different degrees of brand loyalty. Loyalty refers to a consumer's consistent purchase of a product or service that he or she prefers. For instance, some travellers will always stay at Lynch Hotels if possible, some will stay at Ryans if it is convenient, some will switch hotels for the sake of variety, and some will try to avoid hotels and may stay at bed and breakfast operations. Brand-loyal consumers are a valuable commodity to an organisation. In addition to requiring less promotion, sales transactions with brand-loyal customers takes less time and generally results in greater purchases.

Marketers are also interested in encouraging consumers who are prone to switch brands to become loyal to one brand. Frequent-flyer programmes and frequent-guest programmes, as already discussed, aim to achieve this. In the hospitality and tourism industries, marketers attempt to build brand loyalty through relationship marketing. Hotels use guest histories to build a database of customers and use this information to customise offers and customer communications. A restaurant may keep a list of its frequent customers with details of the favourite tables and special billing arrangements. Some restaurants offer customers a VIP reservation phone number or special offers such as a complimentary bottle of wine to loyal customers.

Readiness Stage

At any given time, people are in different stages of readiness to buy a product or service. Some are unaware of the product; some are aware; some are informed; some want the product or service and some intend to buy. The relative number in each stage makes a big difference in designing a marketing programme. There are over forty million people in America of Irish descent. Many of them want to visit Ireland and intend to purchase a holiday in the future. In order to encourage them, Bord Fáilte and the Overseas Tourism Marketing Initiative (OTMI), launched an intensive advertising campaign targeting Irish Americans. As a result of the campaign thousands of call were received through the toll-free number and these were converted into actual bookings.

Benefits Segmentation

Buyers can be grouped according to the product/service benefits they seek. Visitors seek different benefits from a holiday, a hotel or a meal in a restaurant. Some prefer more education than entertainment, others status through pursuit of a pastime and other visitors enjoy the convenience of a hotel by the beach. They place different emphasis on different aspects of the product, (*see* Table 6.4 below).

Knowing the benefits sought by customers is useful in two ways. First, tourism and hospitality marketers know what to provide and promote in order to attract a specific segment. Second, identification of customer types is possible. The current customers can be studied to identify potential customers and this will save energy and resources from being wasted in the future.

Table 6.4 — Benefit Segmentation in Tourism and Hospitality

Relaxation

Health

Fun and freedom

Adventure and challenge

Closeness to nature

Eroticism/sexual gratification

Education (culture vulture)

Sun seeking

Companionship

Discovery

Source: Adapted from *Tourism Marketing*, Lumsdon, L., 1997

Promotions by Panorama Holidays emphasise the benefits of purchasing one of their ski packages.

REQUIREMENTS FOR EFFECTIVE SEGMENTATION

There are four basic criteria for segmentation. A good segment will be identifiable, measurable, of adequate size and accessible.

Identifiable. The degree to which effective marketing mixes can be designed for attracting and servicing segments. A small airline like *City Jet* could identify a number of segments it would like to attract but due to small staffing numbers and limited budgets it would not be able to develop a separate marketing mix for each one.

Measurable. The degree to which the segment's size and purchasing power can be measured. Certain segmentation variables are difficult to measure, such as the size of the teenage market who purchase their own clothes.

Adequate Size. The degree to which segments are large or profitable enough to serve as markets. A segment should be the largest possible homogeneous group economically viable to support a marketing programme. For example, large Irish cities such as Dublin, Cork, Galway, Limerick and Belfast can support many different ethnic restaurants such as Thai, Chinese and Indian, but these restaurants would not survive in small towns.

Accessible. The degree to which the segments can be accessed and served. It must be possible and economically feasible to reach this segment. People feeling like a weekend splurge sounds like an attractive segment in hospitality but how would you find them?

Segmentation is not done for its own sake; instead, it is done to understand consumers.

EXHIBIT 6.1

MARKET SEGMENTATION *IN ACTION*

CLONMACNOISE

The ancient monastic site of Clonmacnoise is situated at the crossroads of Ireland in County Offaly and dates back almost 1,500 years. St Ciaran, the son of an Ulsterman who had settled in Connaught, chose the site in A.D. 545 because of its ideal location at the junction of river and road travel in Celtic Ireland. There is a wealth of history in Clonmacnoise, dating from its humble beginnings in the mid-sixth century when St Ciaran first founded a church here. Today the noble ruins of seven churches, two round towers, grave stones and high crosses stand testimony to the proud history of Clonmacnoise — the most famous of all Irish monasteries.

The monastery attracted many of the scholars of Ireland and from across Europe. It was to become the most illustrious school in Europe, the precursor to universities perhaps? It was a Scriptorium from the eighth to the tenth century, and many scribes toiled long and arduous hours learning the skills which were to become world-renowned in works such as the Book of Kells and Durrow.

Clonmacnoise lay in decay until the Office of Public Works began the arduous task of turning this place into one of Ireland's most famous visitor centres.

Clonmacnoise as a Cultural Attraction

Today Clonmacnoise features as a tourist attraction in the Midland East Region, attracting 140,000 visitors in 1997. The site, for statistical records, is classified as a *fee-paying* monument and is one of nineteen such attractions in Ireland. This classification of attraction is six per cent of the total supply of fee-paying attractions while interpretative centres/museums are forty per cent and historic houses/castles are twenty-six per cent.

In 1997, five million visitors came to Ireland and just under one million visited monuments. Only twelve per cent of the total visitors came to the *Midland East* region of Ireland despite the fact there are twenty-two per cent of the *fee-paying* attractions here. Clearly, visitor numbers are determined not by attractions but by the overall attractiveness of the region in question.

Cultural Tourism in Ireland

Cultural tourism as a recognised form of tourism is a recent phenomenon in Ireland. Traditionally, the vast majority of visitors to Ireland may not have specifically chosen to come here solely because of the historical and cultural attractions, it was probably implicit in their perception of Ireland that such aspects would form an intrinsic part of the holiday experience.

In 1992, the then Director General of Bord Fáilte, Martin Dully, stated that 'There are people all over the world in search of cultural experience who are eager to enrich their knowledge about other lands and other people's way of life, tradition and customs. Some are interested in archaeology, historic buildings and ruins, others in museums and galleries, concerts, operas or traditional dancing and you will always find people who want to trace their ancestors.' The emerging significance of *cultural tourism* in the Ireland of the 1990s is reflected by:

- Operational Programme 1994–9 for tourism where natural and cultural tourism developments received £94,000,000 under European Regional Development Fund (ERDF) funding
- The creation of a new government department, then known as the Department of Arts, Culture and the Gaeltacht, with responsibility for administrating funding for natural/cultural/tourism projects
- The formulation of the Heritage Council under the Heritage Act, 1995, to propose policies and priorities for the identification, protection, presentation and enhancement of the national heritage

Visitor Satisfaction

A successful attraction is rewarding to the participants. Of course, attendance figures alone do not reveal the depth of user satisfaction. This is a major challenge in designing and establishing attractions. If a visitor leaves feeling disappointed, uninterested or even defrauded, the attraction may have succeeded in attracting but not in carrying out its complete function. If a developer is to produce successful attractions, the plans and establishments must elicit user satisfaction. To achieve this objective a thorough understanding of the target market is required.

In Ireland, while satisfaction still exists with internal facilities at fee-charging visitor attractions, there has been a noticeable drop in visitors claiming to be *satisfied* with all of the core facilities.

Tourism Markets

In 1997, the Irish Tourism Industry generated a total of £2·8 billion in revenue within the state. It attracted over five million overseas visitors whose expenditure represented £2·1 billion in foreign earnings. Of this five million, 1·7 million tourists engaged in some form of heritage/cultural activity. Over 1·3 million visiting houses and castles and just under a million visiting monuments.

Ireland has a rich supply of cultural and heritage attractions. An audit of Irish National Heritage in 1985 indicated the existence of 200,000 known archaeological sites and monuments and 60,000 buildings of architectural or historic interest. In 1997, Tourism Development International Ltd, a leading independent tourism research consultancy group in Ireland produced the fourth biannual Visitor Attractions Survey which identified that many aspects of our culture, be it tangible or intangible, are of significance when it comes to the decision to visit Ireland. In 1997, there were an estimated 10·3 million visits to fee-charging attractions in the Republic of Ireland. This represented a growth of twenty-five per cent since 1995, when the previous survey was carried out.

FIGURE 6.3 — VISITS TO FEE-CHARGING ATTRACTIONS — REPUBLIC OF IRELAND

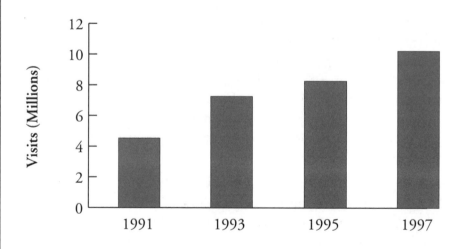

Of the total increase in visits recorded between 1995 and 1997, an estimated 550,000 visits were made to newly opened attractions. The table (Table 6.5) below identifies the five main types of visitor attractions in the Republic of Ireland.

TABLE 6.5 — VISITS TO ATTRACTIONS — REPUBLIC OF IRELAND

	1995	1996	1997	% Growth (1995–7)
Historic houses/castles	2,378,345	2,659,464	2,711,012	+ 14
Interpretative centres/museums	2,652,024	3,362,047	3,620,380	+ 36
Parks	706,241	693,663	689,912	– 2
Historic monuments	653,424	745,265	774,180	+ 18
Gardens	410,369	434,635	505,533	+ 23
Other attractions	1,360,450	1,875,791	1,958,892	+ 44
Total	**8,160,450**	**9,770,865**	**10,259,909**	**+ 26**

In 1997, more than 3·6 million visitors were attracted to interpretative centres and museums. This growing importance of interpretative centres can be attributed to the sustained, high level of investment and development that has taken place throughout the decade. Just over one quarter (twenty-six per cent) of all visits took place at historic houses/castles (2·7 million visitors) making it the second most significant category. Historic monuments also recorded a substantial increase in visitor numbers of eighteen per cent since 1995.

FIGURE 6.4 — PROFILE OF VISITORS TO FEE-CHARGING ATTRACTIONS — MARKET AREA — REPUBLIC OF IRELAND

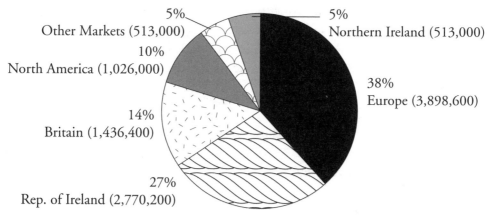

5%
Other Markets (513,000)

10%
North America (1,026,000)

14%
Britain (1,436,400)

27%
Rep. of Ireland (2,770,200)

5%
Northern Ireland (513,000)

38%
Europe (3,898,600)

Culture is less important as a motive for domestic tourism in Ireland. The domestic market representing twenty-seven per cent and out-of-state visitors reaching seventy-three per cent. Mainland Europe (thirty-eight per cent) is the most significant source market for fee-charging attractions in the Republic of Ireland (ROI). Europe is particularly important to attractions in the South-West and West regions of Ireland where it accounts for forty-seven per cent and forty-nine per cent respectively. All regions in Ireland have seen strong growth in numbers visiting attractions. Dublin has experienced a forty-one per cent growth in numbers. This is partly due to the Dublin region receiving more grant aid for visitor attractions than any other region over the period of the two Operational Programmes 1989–99. This explains the strong position of attractions like Dublin Zoo, Trinity College, Guinness Hop Store and Powerscourt Gardens which are listed among the top ten attractions. Law (1991) suggests that this growth is due to the increase in the number of people taking short breaks for cultural experience in urban areas.

Market Segments Visiting Clonmacnoise

A survey was carried out on visitors to Clonmacnoise in 1997. The findings showed that the market for Clonmacnoise can be segmented geographically with Mainland European (thirty-one per cent) and North American (twenty-four per cent) as the dominant segments. The domestic market was dominated by families and school tours.

The market could also be segmented by the benefits sought and level of interest in culture. The visitors to the site were asked about the importance of the site. A majority (thirty-six per cent) felt it was very important, thirty per cent important, twenty-three per cent neutral, six per cent unimportant and five per cent very unimportant. The majority of the visitors had no advance booking arrangements and seemed to be simply passing through the area on their way to another destination. Only one per cent of visitors were spending five nights in the area, and forty-five per cent were going elsewhere. The majority of visitors showed an interested in culture with seventy-one per cent having visited or were planning to visit another cultural attraction in Ireland.

It appears that the Australians (four per cent), New Zealanders (two per cent) and South Africans (one per cent) tourists are the most interested and have the greatest respect for Clonmacnoise.

Marketing Cultural Attractions

The process of marketing Ireland as a tourist destination is now firmly based on partnership between the state sector and the industry In addition, four heritage marketing groups have been assisted with heritage-focused funding from the

ERDF marketing board over the past few years. These groups include Heritage Island, Great Houses, Castles and Gardens of Ireland, Heritage Towns and Culture Ireland. The government division responsible for the marketing of national monuments comes under Dúchas the heritage service. It is obvious that much more research is needed into the cultural tourism market, their motivation and the type of products that satisfy their needs. The research at Clonmacnoise indicates that cultural attractions in Ireland are attracting a percentage of visitors that can have little or no interest in these sites.

Source: This exhibit was prepared by Frances McGettigan, Lecturer in Tourism, Athlone Institute of Technology, and Kevin Byrnes, Lecturer in Hotel Operations, Dundalk Institute of Technology.

MARKET TARGETING

Market Targeting is the logical action step that follows after segmentation. Having clearly identified a number of segments, marketers choose those segments they can best serve based on what the company's product is and on their competitive situation.

The outcome is that an organisation decides to pursue one of the three following strategies:

UNDIFFERENTIATED MARKETING (MASS MARKETING)

The business ignores market segmentation differences and goes after the whole market with one marketing offer. It focuses on the common needs of consumers, rather than on differences. It designs a marketing plan that will reach the greatest number of buyers. Mass distribution and mass advertising serve as the basic tools to create a superior image in the consumers' minds. Undifferentiated marketing is the least popular strategy, however, it can be sensible in some situations such as the marketing of capital cities where the appeal is very broad. Nevertheless, individual tourism and hospitality suppliers will segment their markets to meet the needs and desires of different visitors such as business travellers, study groups and the family market.

DIFFERENTIATED MARKETING

Using a differentiated marketing strategy, the firm targets several market segments and designs separate offers for each. Accor hotels in France, operate under twelve trade names and manage several brands and types of hotels including Novotel, Ibis and Formula One. Jurys Hotel Group adopted this strategy by developing *Jury Inns* targeting the more price-sensitive traveller that does not require the services of a four-star hotel. Differentiated marketing occurs at many destinations where different features or sectors of a resort are targeted to different segments. Wexford, for example, is a popular destination for families, it also attracts opera buffs during the famous Wexford Opera Festival each year.

CONCENTRATED MARKETING

This strategy is suited to the small tourism or hospitality business as it requires less resources. Instead of going for a small share of a large market, the firm pursues a large share of one or more small markets. The firm aims to dominate a small market niche that others do not consider worthwhile. This strategy is practised in the activity holiday market where there are numerous specialists offering packages aimed at those who enjoy canoeing, painting, hill walking and fishing. The main disadvantage of this strategy is the risk involved. The particular market segment can turn sour. Many companies, therefore, prefer to operate in more than one segment. Exhibit 6.2 below outlines how Dvblinia markets to two quite distinct segments.

EXHIBIT 6.2

TARGETING *IN ACTION*

DVBLINIA — A BRIDGE TO THE MEDIEVAL PAST

Dvblinia, the medieval heritage centre, is located in the Synod Hall beside Dublin's Christ Church Cathedral. It tells the story of the development of Dublin from the arrival of Strongbow and his Anglo-Norman knights in the twelfth century to the era of Henry VIII in the sixteenth century.

On arrival each visitor is provided with a personal cassette player to take them on a *Journey Through Time* which guides them through ten memorable episodes in Dublin's medieval history. Events such as the building of Dublin Castle, the Black Death, the crowning of Lambert Simnel (pretender to the English throne), the Feast of Corpus Christi and performances of Biblical plays by members of trade guilds are depicted through sets and models.

The first floor houses life-size reconstructions of medieval interiors and the artefacts from the Wood Quay excavations (*see also* Dublin's Viking Adventure).

A thirteenth-century dockside, a leather worker outside his timber-frame house and a fifteenth-century merchant's kitchen all help bring history to life. Wine from Bordeaux, pottery from Saintonge and spices from the Orient demonstrate that Medieval Dubliners appreciated the finer things in life.

Visitors may then climb the ninety-six steps to the top of the seventeenth-century St Michael's Tower, admire the view, and compare old Dublin with the new. The realities of life long ago can be experienced by trying on parts of a suit of armour or dressing up in medieval robes. A reconstruction of a medieval market has recently been added to the range of attractions.

Target Markets

Dvblinia has a number of specific targets. Two that are particularly important are the educational market and the corporate/business market.

Targeting the Educational Market

Hundreds of schools, both from Dublin and nationwide, visit the capital every year on educational trips. In order to encourage teachers to put Dvblinia on their tour itinerary they are provided with a number of educational tools to help prepare for a visit. Groups who wish to increase their historical knowledge of Dublin and Ireland are offered a wealth of information.

Information is available in English, French, German, Italian and Spanish. A detailed teacher's pack including an eight-page history of Medieval Dublin is available for primary and secondary school teachers. It includes a list of recommended reading, together with worksheets for students. Teachers are entitled to a free preliminary visit on request, and an Education Officer is on-site to answer questions.

The Malton Room Coffee Shop contains original eighteenth-century prints by James Malton, portraying medieval life in Dublin. The Great Hall was originally used for the ecclesiastical meetings (Synods) of the bishops and the Council of the Diocese.

A short walking tour through the heart of Medieval Dublin has been developed to enable visitors to discover the fragmented remains of the medieval town (information on this is available from the Curator). Two other tours in Dublin related to Medieval Dublin are the Wood Quay Walk, showing artwork inspired by Dublin's past, and the Malton Trail that passes the most beautiful buildings in Dublin.

Targeting the Corporate/Business Market

A less obvious market for Dvblinia is that of the corporate/business sector. The Great Hall at Dvblinia is a unique venue for corporate entertainment and product launches. Built in the 1870s this magnificent Victorian Hall, with its renowned pine floors and arched ceilings, is ideal for an evening's entertainment.

Between 150 and 200 seated guests can be accommodated in splendid surroundings and caterers and entertainment companies are used to make corporate entertainment a truly memorable event. Bailey's, who are sponsors of Dvblinia, are regular users of the Hall for promotional events. The Hospitality Sales and Marketing Association have held their annual marketing awards ceremony there on a number of occasions.

Adjacent to the Great Hall is the Civic Room with its magnificent stained glass window, commissioned by the Medieval Trust, creating a unique background for your pre-dinner drinks reception, your special product display units or alternatively, for an intimate dinner for up to thirty guests. A specific brochure has been produced to promote the use of Dvblinia for corporate markets.

While their requirements are quite different from schools, targeting the corporate sector makes sense, as they are using a facility in the evenings and are therefore maximising the revenue to Dvblinia.

MARKET POSITIONING

A product's position is the way the product is defined by consumers on important attributes — the place the product occupies in consumers' minds relative to competing products. Consumers are overloaded with information about products and services. They cannot re-evaluate products every time they make a buying decision. To simplify buying decision-making, consumers organise products into categories — they position products, companies and destinations in their minds. Positioning is the way in which a company, tourism offering, destination or country is viewed, in relation to other companies or organisations, by customer segments.

Positioning lies ultimately in the eyes of the consumer: it refers to how the market perceives the organisation, rather than how it perceives itself. Marketers do not want to leave their products' position to chance. They plan positions that will give their products the greatest advantage in selected target markets and then design marketing mixes to create the planned positions.

POSITIONING STRATEGIES

Marketers can follow several positioning strategies. They can position product bases on specific product attributes or features. The Morrisson Hotel promotes its unique design. Products can be positioned relative to the needs they meet or the benefits they offer. Bars in the trendy Temple Bar area of Dublin promote their image as meeting places for members of the opposite sex. A product can be positioned against an existing competitor. In the airline war between Aer Lingus and Ryanair, both airlines battle it out in the national newspapers with advertisements. Finally, products can be positioned against another product class. Restaurant advertising campaigns can entice a customer to eat out rather than cook at home. Budget hotels have positioned themselves against bed and breakfast operations, and cruise boats position themselves against other forms of leisure activities.

When two or more firms pursue the same position, each must seek to differentiate further, such as a family destination at a lower cost or a family destination with great shopping. Each business must build a unique bundle of competitive advantages that appeals to a substantial group within the segment. This subpositioning is often called *niche marketing.*

In terms of destinations, positioning is equally important. Each country, region and county seeks differential advantage through positioning. Ireland undertook to reposition itself in 1996 and Bord Fáilte developed Tourism Brand Ireland (*see* Exhibit 6.3). Various counties have attempted to position themselves as attractive tourism destinations including Donegal, who developed the motto of 'It's different up here'.

CHOOSING AND IMPLEMENTING A POSITIONING STRATEGY

The task of positioning a tourism or hospitality business consists of three steps:

1. Identifying a set of possible competitive advantages upon which to build a position
2. Selecting the right competitive advantage
3. Effectively communicating and delivering the chosen position to a carefully selected target market

A company can differentiate itself by bundling competitive advantages (Kotler et al, 1996). It gains competitive advantage by offering customers lower prices than competitors for similar products, or by providing more benefits to justify higher prices. Thus, a company must compare its prices and products to those of competitors and continuously look for possible improvements. To the extent that it can do better than its competitors, the company has achieved a competitive advantage. It is important to remember that few companies can achieve a permanent advantage. Destinations, hotels and restaurants sometimes believe that their locations on a beach, near an airport or a conference hall gives them a permanent advantage. This is not so, beaches can get polluted, airports can face competition and conference halls can become run down. Permanent advantages may only be temporary advantages.

EXHIBIT 6.3

MARKET POSITIONING *IN ACTION*
TOURISM BRAND IRELAND

By any standards it was a daunting challenge. Following an extensive consultation and research process, stretching back over the previous twelve months, decision time had arrived. Noel Toolan, the newly appointed International Marketing Director at Bord Fáilte (the Irish Tourist Board) had only been appointed in May 1995 and now, just eight weeks later, a decision had to be made on the choice of market positioning for the Irish tourism product.

Positioning Concepts

The research process carried out by Bord Fáilte as it sought to assess the views of respondents to four positioning concepts that had been developed by the Branding Committee during the preceding months.

All four of the positionings were represented by *concept advertising campaigns.* The campaigns were presented in a relatively finished visual form. The language used in the concept advertising was appropriate to the territory under review. Respondents were able to visit and spend some time examining the positioning boards that were located in the corners of the interview room. This enabled them to consider the concepts in some detail as well as merely give an assessment of the visual and written executions. When respondents had spent sufficient time in becoming familiar with each of the executions, response to them was evaluated with the moderator in the group forum.

The four separate positioning concepts developed were chosen on the basis that they were already in use in existing markets. A key objective of the research was to identify a positioning route that would offer the possibility of being used across all the key target markets, although it was anticipated that some concepts might have more appeal in some countries than others.

The current status where the communications strategy for each market was different carried obvious advantages in being sensitive to the local market conditions. However, the desire to develop a strong brand identity for Ireland meant that consideration had to be given to the possibilities of a standardised approach to positioning, and perhaps also to marketing communications. While there were likely to be requirements for executional changes in the different markets there was a desire on the part of the Branding Committee to explore the extent to which a relatively consistent positioning for Ireland could be achieved across the major markets. Following prolonged debate four positioning concepts emerged that were felt to offer real prospects of such a standardised approach.

Magical Island

This positioning concept emerged as the favoured position from the exploratory research. It was felt to offer real advantages as it had received a favourable response and was felt to reflect some of the brand attributes that would be required. It was felt that the idea of Magical Island had reference values that had been lost in other more industrialised countries. This positioning had been used for several years previously in Germany, albeit in a slightly modified form as discussed earlier. It was envisaged that the concept would lead to consumers interpreting the message as reflecting magical personal experiences of pleasure and enjoyment and a sense of touching their deeper spiritual selves. From the research it emerged that the idea of Magical Island could be interpreted as Mythical Island, something that was considered a strong attribute.

Come for the Landscape — Experience the People

It was very evident from all previous research that landscapes, including nature, and people were key factors in the brand appeal of Ireland. The positioning option reflected the reality for holidaymakers to Ireland. Moreover, this appeal had historically featured in the majority of promotional campaigns. It was clear that the landscapes and people of Ireland did form a strong image in the mind of overseas visitors and had a degree of motivating power. It was the images of Irish landscapes which most strongly attracted visitors, but it was the Irish people, in terms of their friendliness, warmth and hospitality to visitors which made the most impact on visitors while they were in Ireland. As the recent visitor enquirer research had shown, friendliness of people was a strong image, although among non-enquirers it was significantly weaker. A key question surrounded the extent to which these features were distinct to Ireland. Nonetheless, landscape and people images had dominated in previous research among respondents — choosing this as the positioning route was seen as offering the prospect of truthfully reflecting the brand appeal of Ireland.

Emotional Experience

This positioning was based on an assessment of the benefits derived from taking a holiday in Ireland. It was based on the assessment that the core essence of the brand was the deep and pleasurable holiday experiences of holidaying in Ireland. These experiences included the possibilities of *escaping* from everyday pressures; being somewhere new; *sharing* the good times with special people; *discovering* the new, exciting and the different; the *freedom* from structures; *controlling* one's holiday time and *involvement* with the open and welcoming Irish people. Many prior research studies had indicated a deep feeling of affinity between visitors and Ireland. This reflected itself in an emotional attachment to Ireland, and that was reflected in a feeling of individual discovery and pleasure together with a sense that visitors could really have a *dialogue* with the brand. The positioning was felt to have a strong motivational power and to be credible. One concern that emerged was that this positioning might be off-putting to some visitors if it was interpreted as suggesting Ireland was a *retreat* destination. The research indicated that translating the concept into a series of commercials was something that might prove a real challenge

(Ancient) Birthplace of Good Times

This positioning strategy was already in place in the North American market, where it struck a chord with the key, ethnic Irish who formed the bulk of visitors from that region. The concept rationalised and explained why Ireland was the original birthplace of good times and defined the distinctive good times to be enjoyed by visitors to Ireland. Among the research groups it reflected well the acknowledged sense of zest for living that the Irish were perceived as having. In the United States, in particular, it met with a high level of consumer demand. It reflected the current perceptions of the Irish identity and clearly emphasised the attributes of tradition, simplicity, history and culture. The US market was a very important one and the research groups there responded very favourably to this positioning strategy. What was less certain from the research was the extent to which the positioning would be motivating, especially among the European markets.

This exhibit is adapted from *Tourism Brand Ireland Case-Study*, written by Alex Gibson, in *Case Studies in Marketing*, Marketing Institute of Ireland, 1997.

PRODUCT DIFFERENTIATION

A company can differentiate its product or offer products similar to competitors. Today most tourism and hospitality operations try to differentiate themselves from their competition. A company can differentiate along the lines of physical attributes, services, personnel, location or image.

Physical Attributes or Features

Businesses can differentiate themselves in many ways, castle hotels such as Waterford Castle Hotel offers glimpses of the past, Modern hotels frequently use popular designers to differentiate themselves. Planet Hollywood uses its memorabilia from the film industry to create a novel atmosphere.

Service Differentiation

Some companies differentiate themselves on service, in particular five-star hotels and exclusive resorts. By providing services that will benefit its target market, a company can achieve differentiation.

Personnel Differentiation

Companies can achieve a stronger competitive advantage through hiring and training better people. Ritz Carlton Hotels are famous worldwide for their ability to select, train and motivate personnel that excel at delivering good service. Personnel differentiation requires that a company select its customer-contact personnel carefully and train them. Superquinn is well known in Ireland for following this positioning. This is getting increasingly difficult in Ireland due to shortage of labour. Many tourism and hospitality operations are recruiting young Europeans to work in their businesses.

Location Differentiation

The famous hotelier, Statler, claimed the secret to success in the hotel business was 'location, location, location'. Many country house hotels have beautiful rural settings that give them an advantage for the leisure market. The newer budget hotels that have been built recently focus on a good location for the business traveller and are often close to business districts or major motorways or airports.

Image Differentiation

Even when competing products or services look the same, buyers may perceive a difference based on company or brand images. Thus, companies need to work to establish images that differentiate them from competitors. Developing a strong and distinctive image calls for creating a singular distinctive message that communicates the product's major benefits and positioning. This is a slow process and will not be achieved overnight, it is not achieved by a slick advertising campaign. The image must be supported by everything the company says and does.

Price Differentiation

Price is a powerful positioning tool because it is perceived to say a great deal about the product. High prices indicate a high quality/status product or service. The power of price positioning is one reason that up-market hotel groups such as Leading Hotels of the World maintain high rack rates. To lower the published rate is perceived as lowering the image and positioning downmarket.

TABLE 6.6 — ALTERNATIVE POSITION STRATEGIES IN TOURISM AND HOSPITALITY

Market share leader	The biggest
Quality leader	The best/most reliable products and services
Service leader	The best qualified staff
Technology leader	The first to develop new technology
Innovation leader	The most creative in applying it
Relationship leader	The most committed to customer's success
Prestige leader	The most exclusive
Bargain leader	The lowest price
Value leader	The best price performance

Source: Adapted from *Corporate Planning*, Kosnick, T.J., 1989

EXHIBIT 6.4

PRODUCT DIFFERENTIATION *IN ACTION*
CASTLE LESLIE IN THE KINGDOM OF ORIEL

Castle Leslie in the Kingdom of Oriel, just two hours from Dublin has been in the Leslie family for over 300 years. It is a very special place that has changed little since the present Castle was built. The Castle is set in an estate that covers 1,000 acres beside the picturesque cut-stone village of Glaslough. On arrival guests will not find a front-of-house reception desk but a welcoming oak-panelled hall and afternoon tea in the Drawing Room.

The beauty of Castle Leslie is that in spite of its rich history and Victorian splendour it is one of the most informal of the Great Houses of Ireland. The Castle is like a step back in time with all the glory of a bygone era. There are no phones, televisions or clocks in the rooms and the only concessions made to the twentieth century is lots of hot water and plenty of heating. The original furniture, family portraits and books fill every room enhancing the Castle's homely atmosphere. The family live in the servants' wing so guests can enjoy the Castle for themselves. Due to the nature of the Castle it is unsuitable for children, but a wonderful refuge for grown-ups from the outside world.

PROBLEMS OF POSITIONING

The major positioning problems are:

- Lack of resources to sustain the position for any length of time
- Lack of clarity in terms of communication, thus leading to a mismatch between the image the company intends to project and the image interpreted by the consumer segment
- Competitors adopt the same positioning strategy. Scotland is attempting to position itself similarly to Tourism Brand Ireland

WHICH DIFFERENCES TO PROMOTE?

Not all differences are meaningful or worthwhile. Not every difference makes a good differentiator. Each difference has the potential to create company costs as well as customer benefits. Therefore, the company should carefully select the ways in which it will distinguish itself from competitors. A difference is worth establishing to the extent that it satisfies the following criteria:

- *Important.* The difference delivers a highly valued benefit to target buyers
- *Distinctive.* Competitors do not offer the difference, or the company can offer it in a more distinctive way
- *Superior.* The difference is superior to other ways that customers might obtain the same benefit
- *Communicable.* The difference is communicable and visible to buyers
- *Pre-emptive.* Competitors cannot easily copy the difference
- *Affordable.* Buyers can afford to pay for the difference
- *Profitable.* The company can introduce the difference profitably

Many companies have introduced differentiations that failed one or more of these tests. Some companies advantages may be quickly ruled out because they are too slight, too costly to develop, or too inconsistent with the company's profile. Careful consideration must be given to the chosen position and the choice should be based on market research.

REPOSITIONING

Repositioning, as the name implies, constitutes changing a position or image in the market-place. The process is the same as the initial positioning process with the addition of one other element: removing the old positioning image. There may be a number of reasons for wanting to reposition: the business may be occupying an unsuccessful position in the first place, it may have tried and failed to fully achieve a desired position, or it may have perceived a new niche opportunity of which it wishes to take advantage. All of these situations are relatively common in the tourism and hospitality industry.

Repositioning might also be used to appeal to a new segment while holding on to an old one, or to increase the size of a segment. Finally, repositioning would be called for in developing a new concept or upgrading a new property which has been refurbished.

EXHIBIT 6.5

NICHE MARKETING *IN ACTION*

POSITIONING *LOUTHIANA*

In April 1999, the printing firm, Dundalgan Press (W. Tempest) Ltd, of Francis St., Dundalk, announced their intention of reprinting a mid-eighteenth-century book on the archaeology of Co. Louth. The text in question was *Louthiana*, an illustrated antiquarian work published in London in 1748. Aiming at the upper end of the book market, the company sought to exploit the growing interest in Irish heritage, in particular, antiquarian texts on archaeology, linking it with the perennial interest in fine quality, exclusive reprints of old books. With a minimum of marketing, and a deliberate avoidance of the usual retail outlets, the company completely sold out a limited facsimile edition of 250 leather-bound reprints, priced at £95–125 each, between April and November 1999.

The Concept

In 1748, Thomas Wright, a Durham astronomer and landscape gardener was invited to Ireland by his patron Lord Limerick. The ostensible reason for the visit appears to have been the landscaping of Lord Limerick's demesnes at Tollymore, Co. Down and Dundalk Co. Louth. However, its most lasting legacy was *Louthiana, or an Introduction to the Antiquities of Ireland*, a 178-page book on the archaeological monuments of Co. Louth. Although a second edition appeared in 1758, the book has been out of print for almost 250 years. Its academic importance lies in the fact that it was the first detailed survey of archaeological monuments in Ireland. But its modern appeal lies in its copious illustrations; fine copperplate drawings which delight the eye. This, and its rarity, have meant that is has become a sought-after work on the antiquarian book market, where it is currently listed at £500–600 in booksellers catalogues.

The idea of reprinting *Louthiana* arose from discussions between Mr Liam Gaynor, a staff member of Dundalgan Press and Mr Paul Gosling, lecturer in Heritage Studies at the Galway-Mayo Institute of Technology in 1997. By focusing on the upper end of the reprint market, it was argued that a quality reprint could be successfully marketed and sold in a short period of time. Founded in 1859, Dundalgan Press (W. Tempest) Ltd have long been associated with the publishing and printing of academic texts. In the mid-twentieth century, in particular, the company had been responsible for the publication of a number of seminal works: for instance, H.G. Leask's *Irish Castles and Castellated Houses* (1941) and Estyn Evan's *The Mourne Country* (1951), both of which are still in print! However, since the death of the founder's son, Harold Tempest, in the mid-1960s, the company has tended to concentrate on the general printing trade rather than on book publishing. In March 1999, Mr Gerry Gormley, Managing Director, decided to proceed with the venture, astutely linking its marketing to the Millennium and the company's own 140th anniversary. As a reputable printing firm, with a strong skills base in quality printing, Dundalgan Press was well placed to capitalise on this publishing opportunity.

The Product

In order to enhance the retail value and maximise the attractiveness of *Louthiana* as a product, the company decided that it should be printed on high quality paper, leather bound and sold directly to the customer through specifically targeted marketing.

Target Market

The publishers sought to target a very specific market, comprising three segments:

(a) Members of the local archaeological and historical societies in Co. Louth, whose combined membership totals almost 800 individuals
(b) Book collectors with an interest in limited editions as investments
(c) Prominent social and business figures in north Leinster

Promotion

The actual promotion took the form of a *flier*: a six-page, A4 size, two-colour brochure in landscape orientation detailing the product. This was inserted into the spring issues of *Archaeology Ireland* and *History Ireland*, the two most widely circulating popular magazines on Ireland's human heritage. It was supplemented by a mailshot to a selected list of potential customers. The publication was also highlighted through a couple of feature articles in the local newspapers. Finally, a number of strategically placed letters in the national press also assisted in highlighting the forthcoming reprint.

Unique Selling Points

The promotion of the book focused on the exclusivity of the reprinted product, as follows (the quotations are taken from the *flier* issued by Dundalgan Press in April 1999):

a) The importance of the original publication, 'Louthiana…is regarded as a landmark publication…in the awakening of antiquarian interest in eighteenth-century Ireland'

b) The quality of the reproduction, 'a facsimile edition…printed on 15 gms acid-free wove'

c) The quality of the binding, 'half bound in leather with marbled boards and blocked spine in a size of $11^1/_2" \times 8^{11}/_{12}"$

d) The fact that it was to be a limited print run of 250

e) The individual numbering of the copies

f) The inclusion of the purchasers' names in a List of Subscribers in the new edition: 'as was the case with the first edition'

g) The linking of the book's republication with the Millennium, 'Millennium Facsimile Edition'. The reprint is dated MM, the Roman numerals for 2000

h) A pre-publication offer comprising a pre-launch purchase price of £95 which would rise to £125 thereafter

Profit

While the detailed costings for the reprint of *Louthiana* are obviously a confidential matter, the total printing and marketing costs were in the region of £16,000. Of this, the single greatest cost was the leather binding — around £35 per copy — due to the fact that it was done by hand. As the sales figures below indicate, the book had effectively broken even by 14 July 1999, and the gross profit on the whole venture was in the region of thirty-five per cent.

The Launch

The book was launched by Dr Peter Harbison, archaeologist, on 7 October 1999 in the County Museum, Dundalk. The launch, which included a wine reception and exhibition, was hosted by Dundalgan Press. It was by invitation only, and was used as a vehicle to distribute the publication, thus saving on postage costs.

Sales Turnover

The copies sold by the 14 July 1999 numbered 181, the cut-off point for having one's name included in the List of Subscribers. By the time of the book's launch, on 7 October 1999, some thirty additional copies had been sold and about a dozen further copies were purchased at the launch itself. The remaining copies were sold directly from the publisher's premises. The whole run was completely sold out by mid-November, 1999.

Source: This exhibit has been contributed by Paul Gosling, Lecturer in Heritage Studies, Galway-Mayo Institute of Technology and Eamon Mathews, Dundalgan Press Ltd.

POSITIONING AND THE MARKETING MIX

Having chosen the position in the market-place for the tourism or hospitality product, the company must decide on an appropriate marketing mix. All of a company's marketing mix efforts must support its positioning strategy. John Fitzpatrick, CEO of Fitzpatrick Family Group of Hotels, dedicated the penthouse suite of his newest property, The Fitzpatrick Grand Central, to actor Liam Neeson. The Neeson Penthouse comprises a larger main suite and two garden rooms, all of which have separate terraces overlooking the New York skyline. The suites are furnished in traditional Irish fashion with canopied beds in elegant damask and jacquard, Navan carpeting, Waterford crystal chandeliers and Irish linens and towels. In addition, the suites are adorned with autographed photographs from the actor's most famous films. The price to rent this penthouse is $2,000 a night. The rooms can be booked separately: $1,000 for the main suite and £500 a night for each garden room.

Companies normally develop a memorable statement to communicate their desired position. Avis Rent-a-Car became famous for its positioning statement 'We're only number two, so we try harder'. This statement positioned them with the number one company Hertz and away from the other competitors. A company's positioning decisions determine who its competitors will be. When setting its positioning strategy, the company should review its competitive strengths and weaknesses, review its research on the market-place and select a position that places it in a superior position vis-à-vis its chosen competitor.

CHAPTER SUMMARY

A key cornerstone to successful marketing is the process of segmentation, targeting and positioning. Markets vary greatly. Most tourism and hospitality operations today recognise the need to segment markets. The goal is to identify market segments with similar characteristics and therefore similar needs. The most popular bases for segmentation are geographic, demographic, behavioural and psychographic. There are four basic criteria for segmentation. A good segment will be identifiable, measurable, of adequate size and accessible.

Target marketing is the logical step that follows segmentation. Marketers choose those segments they can best serve, usually the choice is between three strategies: undifferentiated marketing, differentiated marketing and concentrated marketing.

The third step in the process is choosing the product's position — the place the product occupies in consumers' minds relative to competing products. Due to inform-ation overload, consumers organise products into categories — they position products, companies and destinations in their minds. Thus, position lies ultimately in the eyes of the consumer. There are a number of positioning strategies that marketers can follow. The most popular ways to position a product and differentiate it from competitors is to choose a unique position. A company can differentiate along the lines of physical features or attributes, services, personnel, location or image. Not all differences are meaningful or worthwhile and they must be carefully chosen. Finally the business must communicate their position to target customers.

KEY WORDS AND PHRASES

Market Segmentation	Target Marketing
Positioning Strategy	Life-cycle
Psychographic Segmentation	Geodemographic Segmentation
Usage Rate	Brand Loyalty
Readiness Stage	Differentiated Marketing
Concentrated Strategy	Concentrated Marketing
Undifferentiated Marketing	

QUESTIONS FOR REVIEW

1. Explain the process of market segmentation, market targeting, and market positioning.
2. What variables are used for market segmentation in restaurants? Are the same variables used for market segmentation by Bord Fáilte?
3. Chose a major Irish hotel group and explain how their marketing efforts meet the wants of their target market.
4. Why is usage rate an important segmentation variable in tourism and hospitality marketing?

5. Some hotels want to develop a hotel with something for everyone. Why can this be a dangerous policy?

6. Explain the advantages and disadvantages of undifferentiated, differentiated and concentrated marketing. Can you think of an example when each might be appropriate for a tourism destination?

QUESTIONS FOR DISCUSSION

1. Suggest a useful way to segment the markets for the following products:
   - cars
   - breakfast cereals
   - heritage centres
   - hotels
   - restaurants
   - airlines
2. Evaluate the pros and cons of tourism marketing on a regional basis.

REFERENCES AND FURTHER READING

Holloway, C. and Plant, R., *Marketing for Tourism*, Pitman: London 1992.

Kotler, P., Armstrong, G., Saunders, J. and Wong, V., *Principles of Marketing*, 2nd European edn., Prentice Hall: Europe 1999.

Kotler, P., Bowens, J. and Makens, J., *Marketing for Hospitality and Tourism*, Prentice Hall: New Jersey 1996.

Laws, E., *Tourism Marketing: Service and Quality Management Perspectives*, Stanley Thornes: UK 1991.

Lewis, R.C., Chambers, R.E. and Chacko, H.E., *Marketing Leadership in Hospitality: Foundations and Practices*, 2nd edn., Van Nostrand Reinhold: New York 1995.

Lumsdon, L., *Tourism Marketing*, Thomson Business Press: London 1997.

Powers, T., *Marketing Hospitality*, 2nd edn., John Wiley & Sons: New York 1997.

USEFUL WEB SITES

www.ireland.travel.ie	Bord Fáilte's web site
www.travelocity.com	Destination information
www.travigator.com	Links to thousands of travel sites

CHAPTER 7

The Tourism and Hospitality Product

INTRODUCTION

The product is at the centre of the marketing management process. No amount of advertising, or low prices, will compensate for a product that does not meet consumer needs and wants more effectively than competitors. Unless the product delivers real benefits to the consumer by meeting core needs, it is unlikely to be a success. Because consumer preferences are constantly changing and new sources of competition are emerging, continual adaptation of the product and introduction of new products is a key task for marketers. Different marketing strategies will be called for, depending on the stage of development of the product. These decisions extend far beyond the physical nature of the product. Marketers also have to consider the brand identity of the product and the largely intangible nature of service quality.

CHAPTER OBJECTIVES

Following this chapter, students should be able to:

- Identify the unique characteristics of services
- Distinguish between core, tangible and augmented components of the tourism and hospitality product
- Understand the concept of the tourism area life-cycle
- Recognise the stages involved in new service development
- Appreciate the growing importance of branding in the tourism and hospitality sector
- Identify the determinants of quality in tourism and hospitality organisations

DEFINITIONS

Holloway and Robinson (1995) define the product as: 'anything that is offered to a market to satisfy a want or need. The term therefore includes tangible goods, services, people, places, organisations or ideas.'

According to Murray and O'Driscoll (1996) the product is: 'a bundle of physical, service and psychological benefits designed to satisfy a customer's needs and related wants'.

The above definitions have a common emphasis in the fact that the product is not merely something physical or tangible. For marketers, it is more important to focus on the fact that the product is actually a solution to a set of personal needs and wants. Indeed, if marketers only focus on the physical side of things they can adopt too narrow a perspective of what business they really are in. This shortsightness, or myopia, was examined by Theodore Levitt in 1960 in one of the most published marketing articles *Marketing Myopia*. Levitt cited the example of the railroad companies in the US in the 1930s as having a truly short-sighted vision of their product.

When faced with the opportunity of entering the burgeoning airline transport business, the railroads rejected the chance, arguing that they were in the railroad business. A definition of their business that was more reflective of customer needs would undoubtedly have led these companies to recognise that they were, in fact, in the *transportation* business. The subsequent demise of the railroad companies would most likely, never have occurred, had such a more benefits-oriented perspective been adopted.

Both the prior definitions of product distinguish between a product and a service, although in reality the terms are used interchangeably in the area of tourism marketing. Nonetheless, it is worth reflecting on the fact that there has been an enormous amount of research and literature on the specific nature and characteristics of services.

THE SERVICE PRODUCT

A useful starting point is to examine various definitions of the service.

Stanton (1981) offers the following comprehensive definition of a service:

'Services are those separately identifiable, essentially intangible activities which provide want-satisfaction, and that are not necessarily tied to the sale of product or another service. To produce a service may or may not require the use of tangible goods. However, when such use is required, there is no transfer of title (permanent ownership) to these tangible goods.'

The above definition serves to focus on the fact that services are *delivered* to the customer who may indeed take ownership of tangible goods, such as a hotel room, but such ownership is of a purely temporary nature. This perspective is echoed in the Kotler (1996) definition below:

'A service is any activity or benefit that one party can offer to another, which is essentially intangible and does not result in the ownership of anything. Its production may, or may not, be tied to a physical product. Activities such as renting a hotel room, depositing money in a bank, travelling on an aeroplane, visiting a doctor, getting a haircut, having a car repaired, watching a professional sport, seeing a movie, having clothes cleaned at a dry cleaner, getting advice from a lawyer — all involve buying a service.'

The above definitions point to the fact that services have characteristics that distinguish them from products. These characteristics have to be managed carefully by marketers. The main distinguishing characteristics of services are *intangibility, inseparability, variability, perishability* and *lack of ownership*.

INTANGIBILITY

Services cannot be seen, or displayed, and therefore cannot be easily examined by the customer in advance of the purchase. Many services, including many tourism and hospitality services, are sold to customers on the basis of a promise of a special experience. These cannot be sampled in advance, as might be the case for a new wine or cheese, which are regularly sampled in supermarkets. Other products, such as tea and soaps, can be distributed door-to-door in special *trial packs* for customers to assess the product. For tourism services there are more difficulties. A hotel wanting to communicate its warmth of welcome and personalised attention, needs to develop other ways of communicating these benefits.

To achieve this, tangible *cues*, or indicators of service quality, are used. In advertisements, a hotel may feature smiling employees and guests, or may feature letters of recommendation from previously satisfied guests. Aer Lingus's most recent television commercials featured their staff in various interactions with customers. Using the concept of recognising the customer's *True Colours*, the commercials were designed to reflect the desire on the part of travellers to be recognised as individuals, with a complex set of needs.

The *physical evidence* dimension of the marketing mix is critically important. The uniforms that staff wear are an important signal to customers who use such signs as a means of forming quality impressions. Aer Lingus have used the services of internationally renowned designer Paul Costello to design their uniforms to reflect the airline's image. Another way in which the intangible nature of services is addressed is through the name of the service. Several international hotel chains have developed brand names to reflect the various quality levels they provide. The US-based Choice International hotel chain has recently undergone a major expansion programme in Ireland. Their brand names reflect the various quality levels:

- **Clarion:** the highest standard level, usually based in city centre locations
- **Comfort:** hotels that offer comfortable accommodation to business and leisure travellers alike
- **Sleep Inns:** the most basic level of quality. Clean, comfortable rooms designed for those who don't require a full range of hotel services, but have more fundamental requirements i.e. rest and rejuvenation

INSEPARABILITY

Services provision cannot be separated from the service provider. For example, for a hotel guest to receive a meal, the waiting staff and chef must be present. It can't be stored for later distribution. Where people are central to the service provision, as in the case of entertaining tourists, then constraints are placed on the extent to which a service can be provided. The Bunratty Banquet is uniquely location-bound. In the retailing industry, Superquinn's expansion from its Dublin base has been deliberate, with Fergal Quinn citing his regular visits to the stores as a key to optimising quality levels. Obviously, if marketers can separate the producer from the service, then there are opportunities to grow the business. An example of this is the Riverdance musical. Riverdance, the Irish dancing phenomenon might have been assumed to be inexorably linked with the personalities of Michael Flatley and Jean Butler, who took the arts by storm when the show began its initial run. However, following the success of the initial shows, promoters John McColgan and Moya Doherty have been successful in replicating the concept with new performers. The measure of their success is the fact that there are now four Riverdance productions touring the world.

Another feature of inseparability that needs to be addressed is the provider-customer interaction which needs to be carefully managed. Customer-care programmes have become a feature of the tourism and hospitality sector and are primarily designed to address this issue.

Furthermore, there are other guests that form part of the service delivery system that need to be managed. An individual's enjoyment of a meal is determined not only by the interaction with staff, but also by the other customers in the restaurant. Noisy or boisterous customers can greatly affect the meal experience.

VARIABILITY

Services are constantly subject to variability, or *heterogeneity*, because of the high level of people involvement in their provision. Unlike machines, people vary in terms of ability, commitment and motivational state. As well as differences between people, individuals may provide differing levels of service at different times due to a variety of pressures, both work related and personal. Service quality can also vary because of the existence of other customers in the service environment.

Because hotels employ large numbers of temporary staff, at several locations, often across international borders and cultures, there are particular concerns to ensure as much consistency across their service provision as possible. They are continually implementing quality monitoring and improvement programmes. These quality management programmes are often run to the specific service standards of the hotel company involved, but there are also national and international quality standards to be attained, for example, the ISO 9002 which is the international standard for service quality, and the Quality Mark which is a national designation. In addition to training service employees to provide more consistent levels of service, tourism companies are also looking at ways of substituting equipment for people. Many budget hotels use credit card check-in facilities, as well as food and drink vending machines.

PERISHABILITY

Services are perishable and cannot be stored. A Connemara hotel with empty rooms in February cannot store this unsold inventory in order to sell them at a later stage in the year. Likewise a city tour bus which is only fifty per cent booked has lost the revenue from the unsold seats forever. For manufacturers and retailers there is the opportunity to hold unsold stock and sell it later when demand is higher. However, those in the tourism industry have no such fallback position. Moreover, the sector is notoriously seasonal in nature, with severe peaks in the summer season and troughs in the off-season. Demand also fluctuates widely according to the day of the week. Weekends are normally much busier than midweek for most accommodation providers.

Exceptions to this include five-star hotels targeting the business community. In this sector the challenge is one of keeping occupancy high at the weekends. To try to smooth demand many hotels now employ sophisticated computer programmes to maximise the revenue, or yield, based on a detailed understanding of past demand levels for specific days. This process is called *yield management* and can often result in several different prices being charged for the same night's accommodation. This practice has been in widespread use for many years in the airline industry.

In the absence of such yield management systems, many tourism companies use a wide variety of discounts, special offers and incentives to boost demand at slack periods. They also ensure that the maximum rate is charged at time periods of high demand. When rugby internationals are held in Dublin, hotel rooms are booked for months in advance, with customers being forced to pay the published price with no discounts available. This price is called the *rack rate*.

Table 7.1 details some of the marketing actions taken for various tourism sectors to moderate the effect of fluctuating demand.

TABLE 7.1 — COPING WITH FLUCTUATING DEMAND

Sector	Action
Airlines	Saturday Night stop-over fares
Hotels	Midweek specials, senior persons' discounts, off-season specials
Visitor Attractions	Off-season specials, midweek specials
Retail outlets	Summer sales
Train/Bus/Ferry transport	Midweek special return fares
Entertainment	Matinee specials

LACK OF OWNERSHIP

When purchasing a service, the customer has no ownership of the product. Where physical products are involved, such as a hotel room, the facility is being rented for a specified time period. This means that the customer has many restrictions on the use of the service. For tourists, the memory of the experiences they had on holiday is what they retain, with souvenirs and photography being important.

While the above service characteristics have been examined in many contexts, there has been a limited debate on the application of the above characteristics to tourism marketing. Service characteristics have to be recognised in the process of marketing planning. However, the fact is that the distinction between services and goods is not a simple one.

It is fair to say that the existence of either pure products or pure services is questionable. There is, however, a perspective that what we are really discussing is a continuum of offerings with either tangible or intangible dominant features. The work of Shostack (1977) has been very influential in the proposition of a *continuum of tangibility*, illustrated below in Figure 7.1.

FIGURE 7.1 — CONTINUUM OF TANGIBILITY

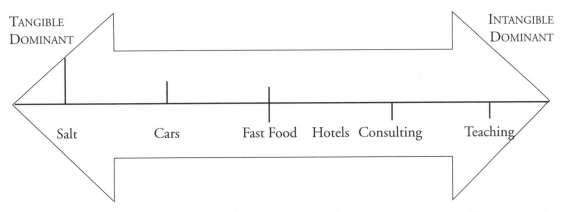

Source: Adapted from Shostack G.L., 'Breaking Free from Product Marketing', *Journal of Marketing*, vol. 41, No. 2, April 1977, American Marketing Association

The above figure illustrates the point that, in reality, there are few *pure* products and *pure* services. The hospitality sector is comprised of many offerings that have both high degrees of tangibility and intangibility. A stay in a hotel is intangible dominant, in that there is no transfer of ownership to the guest. But it has a very high level of tangibles associated with it, from the décor of the hotel room, to the appearance of staff to the physical amenities available to guests.

ELEMENTS OF THE TOURISM PRODUCT

While there are many tangible items associated with it, the tourism product is largely a series of experiences. These experiences can be particularly individual, such as the feeling of freedom and discovery associated with much travel. Sometimes they may be collective experiences, such as the pleasant interaction with friends and fellow holidaymakers. Marketers need to manage these essential, or core, experiences and identify what are the basic needs that they are satisfying with their product.

In many instances marketers can provide numerous physical goods and processes to meet the same basic need. We can identify three *elements* to the product: core, tangible and augmented.

FIGURE 7.2 — ELEMENTS OF THE PRODUCT

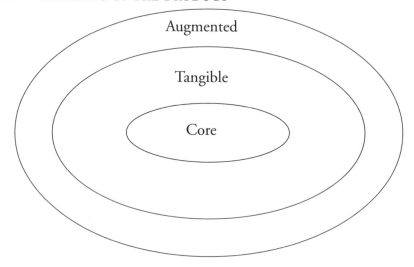

THE CORE PRODUCT

The *core* product refers to the essential benefit for which the customer is looking. Rather than focus on the physical product, the most astute marketers have a superior understanding of the real benefits sought by consumers. Charles Revlon, the founder of Revlon cosmetics, is reported to have said, 'In the factory we make lipstick, in the drugstore we sell hope.' Tourism marketers need to display an equal insight into the minds of their customers. For each tourism offering the marketer needs to have a basic understanding of the needs being satisfied. The Maslow *Hierarchy of Needs Model*, discussed in Chapter 4, is a useful framework for such an analysis. Table 7.2 illustrates the possible core products for a number of tourism offerings.

TABLE 7.2 — POSSIBLE CORE PRODUCTS FOR VARIOUS TOURISM OFFERINGS

Tourism Offering	Core Product
International Conference Centre	Opportunity to meet people, opportunity to efficiently market to key opinion formers, interesting location
Ecotours of the Burren	Education, relaxation, interaction with other nationalities, value for money
Language courses	Education, authentic cultural experience
Sun holiday	Relaxation, social interaction
Painting holiday	Relaxation, self-expression
Activity holidays	Rejuvenation, social interaction

As the above table shows, marketers need to be aware of the many benefits that each offering serves to satisfy. Additionally, we need to recognise that in a single group of tourists, on the same holiday, many different needs may be served. Some people go on painting holidays primarily to meet other people, while for others the attraction of such a holiday is the opportunity that it provides to fulfil their quest for artistic expression. As we move from mass to one-to-one marketing, greater attention will be required to identify individual differences in tourist motivations.

THE TANGIBLE PRODUCT

The *tangible* product is that part of the offering that can be seen, touched, tasted etc. It includes not just equipment and buildings, but also the people providing the service and their appearance. The tangible aspects of the product, such as the uniforms people wear, the appearance of the signage on a hotel and the cutlery used in a restaurant are all important means by which customers make comparisons between competing offerings.

TABLE 7.3 — THE TANGIBLE PRODUCT

Offering	Tangible Product
International Conference Centre	Amphitheatre, audiovisual equipment, catering facilities
Ecotours of the Burren	Burren, bus, maps, guesthouse
Language courses	School, teacher, workbooks
Sun holiday	Beach, hotel, pubs
Painting holiday	Painting materials, accommodation, instructor
Activity holidays	Equipment, physical environment, instructor

THE AUGMENTED PRODUCT

The *augmented* product consists of aspects of the offering that are peripheral to the core product. They are nonetheless important to overall satisfaction with the service and often are the basis on which one service is distinguished from another. The augmented product is often the basis by which tourism companies seek to distinguish themselves from the competition. Possible bases on which a competitive advantage through augmentation can be secured are itemised in Table 7.4.

TABLE 7.4 — THE AUGMENTED PRODUCT

Tourism Offering	Augmented Product
International Conference Centre	Quality of conference speeches, attitudes of conference staff to customers
Ecotours of the Burren	Knowledge of the tour guide, accessibility to the landscape
Language courses	Quality of interaction with other students
Sun holiday	General atmosphere in resort, quality of night life, ambience in restaurants
Painting holiday	Enthusiasm of instructor, student-instructor interaction
Activity holidays	General involvement of fellow tourist, expertise of instructor

The preceding discussion leads us to recognise that the tourism product, or *offering* as it should more correctly be termed, is a complex concept. In particular, the role of the customer-provider interaction is critical, and often serves as a basis for distinguishing one company from another.

As described in Chapter 1, the tourism system is a complex one, with many inter-dependent elements. Each of these elements constitutes a part of the tourism product, whether that is accommodation, destinations, transport providers etc. Moreover, each element can be purchased in isolation from another. The hotel product can be bought as a package, but equally we can pay separately for use of the entertainment, pub, restaurant and even leisure facilities. But it is the identification and management of the core benefits that must be managed.

As discussed earlier in this book, the product component of the extended services mix is often further split into three dimensions:

- Physical Evidence
- Process
- People

Lumsden (1997) incorporates these elements into a model for the management of the tourism product.

FIGURE 7.3 — THE MANAGEMENT OF THE TOURISM PRODUCT

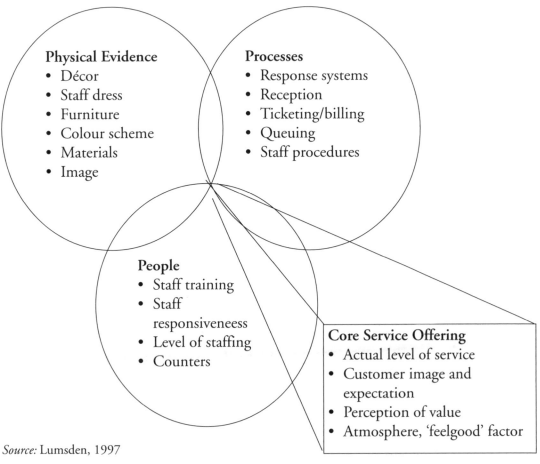

Physical Evidence
- Décor
- Staff dress
- Furniture
- Colour scheme
- Materials
- Image

Processes
- Response systems
- Reception
- Ticketing/billing
- Queuing
- Staff procedures

People
- Staff training
- Staff responsiveneess
- Level of staffing
- Counters

Core Service Offering
- Actual level of service
- Customer image and expectation
- Perception of value
- Atmosphere, 'feelgood' factor

Source: Lumsden, 1997

The model is useful in that it reminds us that, while marketers need to target each of the three *P*s, any improvements in them need to reflect the broader core service offering.

THE PRODUCT LIFE-CYCLE (PLC)

One of the most widely used planning tools to help marketers is the concept of the PLC. It features widely in marketing literature, as well as being used by practitioners in product planning. The PLC refers to the fact that products, including tourism and hospitality products, pass through a series of identifiable and predictable stages over time. The concept of the Tourism Area Life-cycle is an application of the PLC to the tourism and hospitality sector, and recognises that entire destinations pass through periods of varying popularity. Irish seaside resorts have seen the number of visitors decline during the 1980s and 1990s under pressure from cheaper foreign holidays, rising living standards and consumer demand for novelty. The stages of the classic, or *S-shaped*, PLC are as follows:

FIGURE 7.4 — THE PRODUCT LIFE-CYCLE

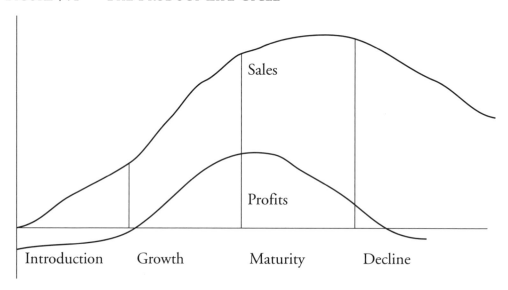

Sales

Profits

Introduction   Growth   Maturity   Decline

INTRODUCTION STAGE

Sales of products and services build slowly at the start. Whether the product is a destination, a new visitor attraction, a new hotel or a new amenity for hotel guests there is a degree of risk on the part of the consumer. This uncertainty is increased if a new technology is involved, or if there are economic or social risks involved. Another reason for slower sales of products at the introduction stage is that distributors are often reluctant to stock a new product initially. When Dublin was promoted in Iceland as a shopping destination, there was a very slow start to the flow of visitors. Now, every Christmas, thousands flock to Dublin to avail themselves of the value and range of facilities on offer. In the case of tourism a new hotel may initially only feature in a few tour operators' brochures until it establishes itself. During the introduction stage, profits are negligible or non-existent, due to the heavy start-up costs required at the product's launch. New hotels can cost up to £100,000 per room to construct. In addition to these costs, advertising, as well as recruitment and training of personnel, are also particularly costly at this early stage.

GROWTH STAGE

During the growth stages, sales begin to expand at their fastest rate. Competitors enter the market and more sophisticated products are developed to target different segments.

More distributors gain confidence in the product and its availability widens. At this stage, the profit levels are at their highest, as higher volumes result in cost economies.

MATURITY STAGE

At this stage the sales increase slows down and eventually peaks. Most people have tried the product and sales are comprised mainly of repeat purchases. Any growth in the sales is dependent on the market itself growing, for example, through population growth. Profits at this stage begin to decline because of the large number of competitors, and the difficulty of continuing to extract cost efficiencies. At the end of the 1990s, it was clear that Dublin was entering a mature phase in its life-cycle, following a decade of rapid expansion as a tourism destination. (Magee, 1998)

DECLINE STAGE

Sales decline due to many factors. The product may go out of fashion, superior technologies may be developed, or customer tastes may alter. Not surprisingly, profits decline as a crowded market-place leads to competitor price battles. Seaside resorts around the Irish coast have suffered from falling visitor numbers for over two decades, as people take advantage of cheaper overseas holidays with more dependable weather. Resorts have had to invest heavily in all-weather facilities such as the Waterpoint facility in Enniscrone, Co. Sligo.

USING THE PRODUCT LIFE-CYCLE

The PLC is a useful tool for diagnosing the position of a company's product, or range of products. Knowing what stage a product is at in its life-cycle is useful, particularly in helping develop strategies appropriate for each stage. The introduction stage requires heavy investment in advertising to promote awareness and trial of the product. As the product enters the growth phase, a different set of strategies is required, focusing on the building of market share. At maturity, maintaining share is critical and there is a need for innovative pricing alternatives combined with a need to develop different product versions for different segments.

Knowing that a product is entering the decline stage is important, as the company can plan replacement products, or a campaign to revive interest and sales in the struggling product or service. Butlin's, part of the huge Rank leisure and entertainment group, is a good example of how a product such as holiday camps can be revitalised though new attractions, improvements to accommodation and re-branding. The term *holiday camp* has been replaced by *Family Resorts*, more national and international music acts entertain holidaymakers, and branded food outlets such as Burger King have been introduced in many of their sites. They have also targeted new consumer groups, such as the teenage market, by hosting Ireland's largest dance music weekend at Butlin's Mosney, Co. Meath in September, 1999.

The person who buys the product at the introduction stage may differ significantly from those who first buy a product as it enters its maturity or decline phase. Some people are constantly looking for new activities and destinations and are the first to try new exotic locations These people, called *early adopters,* are likely to be more confident in the product category than those who are latecomers, known as *laggards.* Different marketing mix strategies will be required for each group.

CRITICISMS OF THE PRODUCT LIFE-CYCLE

The PLC is regarded as a *normative* model, i.e. a model of what *should* happen in an ideal world. This rarely happens. The classic, S-shaped curve depicted in Figure 7.4 is, in practice, uncommon. Take the example of a tourist resort. Many Irish seaside resorts suffered steep, rather than gradual declines in their visitor numbers in the 1970s and 1980s, as package holiday destinations in the sun became available as a cheaper alternative. Conversely, these same resorts have recently seen their PLC rejuvenated with increasing visitor numbers, with special tax-break led investment leading to renewed visitor numbers. Other tourism products, most notably events and festivals, are characterised by rapid growth phases and equally rapid declines. An example would be the Cutty Sark Tall Ships visit to Dublin in 1998. The life-cycle pattern is called a *fad* life-cycle. This is illustrated in Figure 7.5

FIGURE 7.5 — THE FAD LIFE-CYCLE

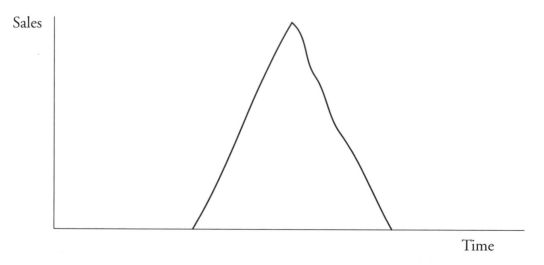

Another major criticism of the model is that it is often used in isolation from other techniques, and that marketers are too quick to propose actions based on a superficial, and generalised, assessment of a product's stage in the PLC. Many people mistakenly see time as the agent of change in the PLC. Although the changes take place with the *passage* of time, it is not time per se that brings about these changes, but rather what *occurs* over the passage of time.

Some actions are within the control of the marketer, most notably the marketing strategy being pursued. If the company launches a product with heavy advertising and very low prices, then the shape of the PLC will differ significantly from that of the company who has a higher-price entry point and lighter advertising support. Other factors that influence the shape and length of the PLC include:

- The *nature of the product.* Complex products that require a degree of consumer learning will have a slower growth phase than products whose benefits are easily communicable to consumers.
- The *competitive environment.* The degree and intensity of competition will affect the speed of the adoption of the product.
- The *social, economic and cultural climate.* In economic boom times new innovations are likely to be tried more readily. Certain cultures are more open to change and innovation than others.
- The concept of the PLC has been applied to areas or destinations, with the sales revenue axis being replaced by visitor numbers. This is known as the *Tourism Area Life-cycle.*

BRANDING

INTRODUCTION

The brand is at the centre of our lives today. For many people the brands they buy form a basis on which they express themselves. The creation of strong brand identities has been well established in the cosmetics, clothing and drinks sectors. Brands such as Tommy Hilfiger, Tango Orange and Virgin lead their respective sectors despite a relatively short market presence. Their strength lies in the continual investment in developing and maintaining a clear identity in the market. In other sectors, leading brands have been around for generations, such as Kodak, McDonald's and Disney. Tourism companies have also begun to take a greater interest in the branding process. More recently the branding of tourism destinations has become a subject of intense interest and debate.

A brand may be defined as a 'name, sign, symbol or design, or combination of these, intended to identify the products of an organisation and distinguish them from those of competitors', (Holloway and Robinson, 1995). The combination of the brand name in a specific typeface and the identifying logo, if any, is known as the *marque.* This marque can be legally registered in order to protect the company's asset.

A renewed interest in brands is evident, not least in the tourism sector. The potential for developing international brands is greater than before with trade and political barriers being reduced.

WHY BRAND?

Historically branding was used as a *basis of identification*. Most produce was in commodity format such as tea, coffee, sugar etc. In order to attribute ownership, companies *branded* their products, just as cattle were literally branded with a sign to represent their owner.

Subsequently, the brand became a useful *quality indicator* for the consumer. Where a product had proved satisfactory in the past, the consumer could easily locate it among competitive offerings. Today the brand remains a strong indication of a specific quality level. Customers can develop a clear set of expectations about the product or service based on their prior experience of a product. Furthermore, new products can be more easily introduced if associated with an established and credible brand name. An example of this is the Hot Press Music Hall of Fame attraction in Dublin. The established reputation of the magazine has been attached to the new attraction and should help develop its identity.

Brands are also useful for the *status that they confer* on their user. Today, the *symbolic* (what it means) as well as *functional* (what it does) dimension of the brand is being recognised. Through advertising, especially television and magazines, it is possible to create a *brand personality*. Brands that have had significant marketing investment have clear profiles in the minds of the customers. Some are seen as conservative, secure, energetic, outrageous, friendly — all personality traits. Indeed, in qualitative research studies respondents are often able link brands in various product categories to well-known television soap characters. Understanding the mental images conveyed in the brand is therefore critical in marketing.

BRAND EQUITY

Because successful brands have strong symbolic and functional characteristics there has been increased interest in viewing the brand as an asset. Just as the physical goods and inventory can be valued, it is argued that the assets attaching to the brand name are also of worth. Indeed, in some instances the brand assets may be more valuable than the physical products.

Aaker (1996) calls the assets of the brand its *brand equity*. Brand equity can be viewed as being 'a set of assets (and liabilities) linked to a brand's name and symbol that adds to (or subtracts from) the value provided by a product or service to a firm and/or that firm's customers'. Aaker contends that the major asset categories are:

Brand Name Awareness

Brands that have a high level of awareness generally have a higher degree of positive consumer feelings. Familiar brand names can provide a degree of reassurance to the consumer. Microsoft is one of the world's leading brands. Its venture into the travel and tourism sector via the Expedia network (www.expedia.com) is likely to prove successful. Tourists, who are reluctant to make bookings using their credit card, are likely to be reassured by the backing of the Microsoft name.

Brand Loyalty

Where there is a group of loyal customers a company can protect itself against competitor threats. A loyal group of customers can also act as brand ambassadors to others to try the product or service. Aer Lingus has a strong following among the Irish business community. Through the TAB frequent-flier programme and the provision of special Gold Circle lounges, the company strives to maintain a close relationship with this lucrative segment of the market.

Perceived Quality

Brands that have a strong quality image can effect price increases more easily, give people a strong reason to buy the product. The reputation of luxury country house hotels such as Ashford Castle and Dromoland Castle enable them to weather economic downturns easier than other companies.

Brand Associations

If a brand has a strong point, or points, of distinction they can use these images to introduce new product lines or brand extensions as they are called. Cadbury is synonymous with chocolate. This has enabled the company to launch a wide variety of confectionery lines and enter related markets such as cakes, biscuits and liqueurs. Disney is acknowledged as one of the most powerful brands in the world. It has very positive associations built up over half a century. A reputation for fun, entertainment and excellence in storytelling has enabled the brand to be used in a variety of sectors including tourism with their theme parks in the US, France and Japan. The Disney cruise ships have been a remarkable success, as has the move to develop conference centres at their theme parks.

As will be seen later in this chapter, the positive images of Ireland for friendly people and outstanding scenery have the potential to become the basis for the development of a brand identity of Ireland. Indeed, the potential to brand a destination has generated a high degree of interest.

BRANDING DESTINATIONS

One of the earliest attempts at destination branding was the I♥NY campaign, developed for the city of New York in the 1980s. The campaign was developed to counteract the image of the city as a crime-ridden, tourist-unfriendly city. Indeed the campaign's simple message led to the slogan being adopted, in copycat fashion, for a host of other products and destinations.

Internationally, there is huge potential in destination branding. This interest extends from National Tourism Offices seeking to develop brand identities for a country, to the attempts by villages and counties to establish an identity for their area. In Ireland today, most county tourism boards have developed their own county brand identity:

Sligo	*Land of Hearts Desire*
Waterford	*The Crystal County*
Donegal	*It's Different Up Here*

In West Cork, there has been a particularly novel attempt to brand the area as both a tourism destination and as a location of natural quality food produce.

Fuchsia Brands Limited have developed a brand identity for the West Cork area, designed to reinforce the perception of the area as a distinctive one, with a reputation for authenticity and natural ingredients. Using the slogan *A Place Apart* and the image of the prominent, native fuchsia flower, the logo features on a wide variety of tourism providers' literature and amenities.

EXHIBIT 7.1

BRANDING *IN ACTION: 1*

THE FUCHSIA BRAND OF WEST CORK

West Cork, the most southern area of Ireland, is renowned for the gentility of its people and the rugged spectacle of the landscape. With a rich diversity of flora and fauna unique to this region, West Cork retains the unspoilt flavour of an ancient Ireland. From the culinary delights of a cobblestoned Kinsale to the rugged splendour of the Beara Peninsula, West Cork remains an area of unparalleled beauty. Its landscape is complemented by a multitude of activities and attractions catering for all interests and ages. West Cork boasts miles of unspoilt, golden beaches, some of the most renowned fishing waters in Western Europe, sites of international archaeological interest and a host of traditions and customs that make an unsurpassed holiday destination.

Today, a more professional approach is being taken to the development of a brand identity for the area. Branding is an important aspect in developing any product and the tourism industry is no exception. Fuchsia Brands Ltd was established to oversee the strategic direction and implementation of the West Cork Brand, and may be seen as a perfect example of an organisation that has successfully used branding as part of its competitive advantage.

The origins of Fuchsia Brands may be traced back to the EU rural development programme LEADER. After conducting an extensive audit of the area, tourism and food were identified as key competencies within the region.

The idea of developing a single regional brand was a visionary idea and had the possibility of ensuring a competitive advantage to the region.

The West Cork LEADER group decided it was essential that a planned and managed approach had to be implemented in developing a brand. It was important to note that they wanted to develop a brand and not just a visual logo. Time and resources needed to be invested into the idea. The focus of the Fuchsia project was to promote, package and brand both tourism and food products within the area.

The LEADER Two programme was able to provide Fuchsia Brands Ltd with the opportunity to access funding that could make the idea of developing a brand a reality. The West Cork LEADER Co-operative is the largest LEADER group in the country and, as a consequence, were able to allocate a substantial budget to the concept of developing a brand. After two years of development and planning Fuchsia Brands Ltd was launched in 1998.

Companies and individuals involved in the tourism and food sectors needed to be encouraged to get involved in developing a regional identity. More importantly these people needed to recognise the value a West Cork *brand* could play in the marketing of their individual businesses. To bring two diverse sectors together was a difficult task. According to an executive with Fuchsia Brands, Ian Dempsey, the challenge was to give people what they wanted within the needs of their business, while taking into consideration the overall development of the brand.

The process of developing the brand involved many stages:

1. A full-time manager was put in place to manage the development of the brand.
2. Financial resources were required to develop the brand. This funding was sourced through the LEADER Two programme and with donations from industry.
3. Values that harnessed the area and characteristics of the region had to be identified, such as unspoilt environment, scenery, quality and innovation. These needed to be incorporated in an image that reflected the area.
4. A selection of visual images were created and the symbol chosen for the West Cork brand was the *Fuchsia* flower which has been patented by Fuchsia Brands Ltd.

Initially, these images would be incorporated for both sectors using differing *tag lines*, or slogans.

For Tourism Providers   *'West Cork a place apart'*
For Food Providers   *'A taste of West Cork'*

In order to use the brand logos and participate fully as part of the West Cork marketing effort, certain criteria for accreditation were developed.

The key problem in developing the food and tourism sectors was trying to satisfy two different sets of needs. In the initial stages the two sectors had to be brought along on an individual basis and in the latter stages of development were brought together to unite under Fuchsia Brands.

To become accredited the *tourism provider* must adhere to Fuchsia Brands Code of Best Practice, key elements of which are listed below:

- Commitment to meeting and exceeding customer expectations in terms of product quality and safety
- Commitment to continuous improvement and innovation in regard to product quality, marketing and customer service
- Commitment to and adoption of Best Practice with regard to marketing and promotion
- Commitment to continuous upgrading of employee skills
- Commitment to co-operate, within the limits of normal competition, with other members of Fuchsia Brands Ltd, to achieve common objectives through exchange of information, group training initiatives and co-operative marketing

Due to the unique characteristics of the tourism industry, accreditation to become a member of Fuchsia Brands involves commitment and investment in terms of time from the tourism providers.

As part of the conditions to become a member accredited to Fuchsia Brands tourism providers must:

- Partake in training programmes developed for Fuchsia Brands. Modules include Customer Care, Sales and Marketing, Modern Kitchen Management, Food Hygiene, Principle of Quality, Professional Hospitality, Chefs' Workshop. The number of modules required is dependent on the type of tourism business.
- Have reached the standards as identified by the relevant national tourism statutory bodies
- Become a fully paid-up member of West Cork Tourism, and be actively involved in marketing West Cork as a tourism destination

- Provide all customers to their establishment with Customer Response Cards — Fuchsia Brands monitor the standards and experience of the customer in all accredited tourism establishments. Fuchsia Brands Ltd issue Customer Response Cards as part of its monitoring mechanism. All cards are coded as a linking mechanism to tourism providers and are returned to Fuchsia Brands in prepaid envelopes, where all responses are monitored.

The benefits to the branding of tourism have been evident within the region. Money has been invested in developing a niche tourism market based on a rural community. From a marketing perspective, the branding has led to an improvement in product quality, a cohesive, consistent identity and co-operative marketing. Access has also been made possible to trade and consumer and, of course, the unique linkage of two different sectors utilising the one brand.

Finally to the concept of branding West Cork — has it worked? The changes according to John Connolly, manager of Fuchsia Brands Ltd, have been exceptional. The concept of developing the West Cork brand has allowed for co-operative structures, a proactive marketing role for members, a vast improvement in quality standards in both food and tourism sectors, the development of a brand that will make a difference in the market-place and visually an identity that is a most useful marketing tool.

Members affiliated to Fuchsia Brands have experienced the value of the brand and understand fully that as producers of either tourism or food products, they represent the brand

As for the future, proactive marketing and visionary management still remain a focus with Fuchsia brands, and plans are in place for accrediting more members and developing the use of the brand in other sectors. It is a firm belief in West Cork that the brand is making, and will continue to make, a difference in the market-place.

Source: Exhibit contributed by Gráinne Daly, Lecturer in Marketing, Cork Institute of Technology

The principles of branding can also be applied to that of an entire country, as well as a region. Exhibit 7.2 below details the challenges involved in positioning Ireland as a tourism destination.

EXHIBIT 7.2

BRANDING *IN ACTION: 2*

TOURISM BRAND IRELAND: POSITIONING A COUNTRY

A strategic appraisal by Bord Fáilte of the state of the sector had revealed that many of the factors that led to success might not be guaranteed into the future. Among the imponderables clouding the immediate future were:

- Product development investment in Ireland had reached very high levels by international standards
- The *Peace Dividend* brought about by the IRA ceasefire in August 1994 had been reflected in a return to healthy visitor and inquiry levels from Britain, but was still a fragile situation
- Ireland's major competitors were not standing still
- A major factor accounting for the phenomenal growth in tourist arrivals to Ireland had been the undoubted fashionability of the country
- Finally, it was apparent that some areas in Ireland were in danger of suffering from an over-concentration of visitors at certain times of the year, particularly in the peak season of July and August

It was in the context of this strategic reappraisal of performance and business environment, that the decision was made by Bord Fáilte and the wider tourism industry, to investigate the feasibility of a brand identity for Ireland as a tourism destination.

Any proposal to develop a brand identity would require careful consideration to be made of the impact that this would have on the current advertising and communication strategies in the major source markets. To implement a common brand identity across the various markets would require an initial understanding of the current nature of promotional activity in each market.

Promotional Activity in General

In the past, Bord Fáilte's communication campaigns had been tailored to each of the major source markets such as Britain, United States, France and Germany. The creative direction of the campaigns had, in recent years, been overseen by the representatives in each country of the Overseas Tourism Marketing Initiative. A common theme running through all the campaigns, however, had been a depiction of Ireland as a market with landscapes and people that were distinct, with specific positionings being developed in each country depending on market behaviour and perceptions. Each market had distinctive characteristics and was managed by dedicated Bord Fáilte offices in the respective country. Britain remained the major source market for overseas tourists, accounting for fifty-five out of every 100 tourists arriving in Ireland in 1994.

Promotional Activity in Britain

Two major promotional campaigns had been run in Britain in the 1990s. The first campaign running in 1992 and 1993 featured the food and drink television personality, Keith Floyd, in a series of TV and Press advertisements. The campaign, using a strong overt humour appeal, achieved high awareness levels but was discontinued when the view emerged that the narrow focus on food and drink needed to be expanded.

The second campaign had begun in 1994 emphasising the range of activities that were possible in Ireland, the relaxed pace of life, together with the intangible nature of the atmosphere available in entertainment and socialising in Ireland — the *craic* as it was known in Ireland.

Promotional Activity in North America

North America had, in 1994, achieved a significant increase of 17·2 per cent in revenue to £213·4 million and 17·1 per cent in tourist numbers to 494,000. Of the visitor numbers, 350,000 could be classified as pure holidaymakers (as opposed to those visiting friends, on business etc.). The general appeal of advertising to the North American positioned Ireland as a country with a rich and varied heritage and sought to exploit the huge potential market of people with ethnic ties to Ireland. This positioning was neatly reflected in the advertising slogan, *Ireland — The Ancient Birthplace of Good Times.*

Promotional Activity in France

In 1994, visitor numbers were down 4·5 per cent on the previous year to 121,000 with revenue down nineteen per cent to £74 million. The French outbound market was distinctly depressed.

Each year Bord Fáilte ran a major advertising campaign in France in co-operation with the major air and sea carriers. In previous years TV had been the main medium, but in 1994 print was the main focus. The campaign was designed to portray Ireland as a country that possessed *dépaysement* and a friendly ambience, and as a place where a warm welcome could be expected. Playing on this theme the campaign had successfully used the same slogan for several years — 'You will have come for Ireland, you will come back for the Irish.'

Promotional Activity in Germany

In 1994, the market had seen a modest 1·5 per cent increase in visitor numbers to 269,000, but revenue had dropped by six per cent to £110 million. The primary motivating factors for the Germans who had visited Ireland were contact with locals, cultural pastimes, the atmosphere and the opportunity to be active and participate in sports.

The German market absorbed about thirty per cent of Bord Fáilte's mainland European budget, predominantly spent nationwide using black and white press advertisements. Some colour advertisements were used in magazines as campaign openers. The main objectives of the German campaign were to enhance the image of Ireland as well as to provide information on the range of activities, regions, products and prices.

The primary images of Ireland focused on its unspoiled nature and landscapes. Almost uniquely among the European markets, Ireland was seen as a somewhat magical and mystical island. Its positioning differed from that of France in that this magical quality was reflected in Ireland's positioning. The headline *Europe's Green Holiday Island* had featured in advertising and reflected the positioning of Ireland as a place to spend a quiet, relaxed time in an unspoilt environment.

It was clear that differences, some subtle and some more significant, existed in the positioning strategies that had been adopted in the major markets. The initial research into the feasibility of branding had yielded encouraging results. However, to gain a more informed picture of the perceptions of the markets, it was felt essential to commission an extensive piece of *consumer* research.

Consumer Research

An international consumer research study, looking at the development of a brand identity for Irish tourism was commissioned in the summer of 1995. The research took the form of qualitative research groups in June and July 1995. The following countries were targeted: United States, Britain, Germany, France, the Netherlands and Ireland.

The respondents were asked to study a number of concept positionings in the form of *advertising campaigns* and to discuss their reactions to the messages behind the campaigns. Some of the *advertisements* used in the research had been used in the past to promote Ireland in overseas markets, but most were specially designed for the research project.

In addition to the main research, the research groups' responses to a number of logos and shamrocks, most of which were specially designed, were also examined. The objective of this part of the research was to see what could be learned at this stage about the possible development of a new symbolic representation for Ireland.

Perceptions of Ireland

Entertainment, things to do and see and the expectation of *fun* on one's holiday were critical ingredients in selecting holiday destinations, and recent research indicated that overseas consumers thought that Ireland might not always deliver in these areas. This suggested that Irish tourism still had a lot more to do to spread the good news about the huge investment that had taken place in the previous few years.

Another interesting point revealed in the research was that evening-time activities in Ireland were still seen to centre on the pub and drinking, and while the pub culture had certain appeals, there were some indications that it diminished the appeal of Ireland to women. This resulted in Ireland being perceived mainly as an adult, male-oriented destination not really suitable for women and children.

Consumers in all countries, including Ireland, didn't spontaneously think of Ireland as an island. This gave rise to a situation, especially overseas, where there was no real appreciation of Ireland's beautiful beaches, seascapes and seafood. Notwithstanding this, the research revealed that when consumers thought of Ireland as a holiday destination they thought of the whole island and not just the twenty-six counties of the Republic. While cities generally didn't figure in consumers' images of Ireland, Dublin proved to be the exception everywhere, suggesting that it could be developed as a separate sub-brand, building on the reputation it had gained in the previous couple of years as a trendy and hip place to visit.

However, in spite of all these positives, the research strongly suggested that the image of Ireland in the consumers' minds lacked clarity and distinctiveness vis-à-vis competitor destinations. In broad terms the research suggested that some sort of visual identity or logo would help overcome this, but that it didn't necessarily have to be dominated by green shamrock images. The shamrock was strongly associated with Ireland and featured widely as a representation of the country, not least in Bord Fáilte's own logo.

According to the majority of consumers who participated in the research, the significant point of distinction between Ireland and other places lay in the very deep and unique experience which they thought they could enjoy in Ireland: summed up nicely in the words of one of the research respondents 'everything else you can buy somewhere else'.

Positioning Concepts

The research process also sought to assess the views of respondents to four positioning concepts that had been developed by the Branding Committee during the preceding months.

Magical Island

This positioning concept emerged as the favoured position from the exploratory research. It was felt to offer real advantages as it had received a favourable response and was felt to reflect some of the brand attributes that would be required. It was felt that the idea of Magical Island had reference values that had been lost in other more industrialised countries. This positioning had been used for several years previously in Germany, albeit in a slightly modified form as discussed earlier. It was envisaged that the concept would lead to consumers interpreting the message as reflecting magical personal experiences of pleasure and enjoyment, and a sense of touching their deeper spiritual selves.

Come for the Landscape — Experience the People

It was very evident from all previous research that landscapes, including nature, and people were key factors in the brand appeal of Ireland. The positioning option reflected the reality for holidaymakers to Ireland. Moreover, this appeal had historically featured in the majority of promotional campaigns. It was clear that the landscapes and people of Ireland did form a strong image in the mind of overseas visitors and had a degree of motivating power.

Emotional Experience

This positioning was based on an assessment of the benefits derived from taking a holiday in Ireland. It was based on the assessment that the core essence of the brand was the deep and pleasurable holiday experiences of holidaying in Ireland. These experiences included the possibilities of *escaping* from everyday pressures, being somewhere new, *sharing* the good times with special people, *discovering* the new, exciting, the different, the *freedom* from structures, controlling one's holiday-time and *involvement* with the open and welcoming Irish people. Many prior research studies had indicated a deep feeling of affinity between visitors and Ireland. This reflected itself in an emotional attachment to Ireland, which was reflected in a feeling of individual discovery and pleasure together with a sense that visitors could really have a *dialogue* with the brand.

(Ancient) Birthplace of Good Times

This positioning strategy was that already in place in the North American market, where it struck a chord with the key ethnic-Irish who formed the bulk of visitors from that region. The concept rationalised and explained why Ireland was the original birthplace of good times — and defined the distinctive good times to be enjoyed by visitors to Ireland. Among the research groups it reflected well the acknowledged sense of zest for living that the Irish were perceived as having.

Bord Fáilte's choice was that of the *emotional* positioning route. The research pointed to the motivating power of this positioning across all the various markets surveyed. Of greater importance though, was the fact that it could form the basis for a distinctive position for Ireland in an increasingly competitive arena. The concept of magical Ireland was strong and has subsequently found itself included in much of the television advertisements as a subtheme rather than a primary one.

The key sequence of events following the choice of positioning in Summer 1995 were:

- *October 1995* — the presentation of the positioning strategy to sixty representatives of the tourism sector for endorsement of *Ireland — An Emotional Experience* strategy
- *February–March 1996* — fifty agencies asked to compete, or *pitch,* for the advertising campaign — ten were shortlisted for detailed briefing sessions
- *May 1996* — Peter Owens/DDB emerge as winners of creative pitch process. Initial visual identity brief is issued to twenty-two Irish design agencies, four shortlisted by May.
- *June 1996* — Designworks agency won the creative pitch for the visual identity work. Advertising concepts were presented to key industry representatives. Northern Ireland Tourist Board *buy in* to an all-island brand approach
- *July 1996* — Wide-ranging consumer research (seventeen focus groups in five countries) takes place to test alternative advertising concepts
- *September 1996* — Shooting of the television commercials took place in several locations in Ireland, over a three-week period
- *November 1996* — The Campaign including new Visual Identity and Advertising Commercials for key markets was launched simultaneously in Dublin, London and New York. The advertising reflected a common positioning with the emotional experience of visiting Ireland being encapsulated in the theme of *living a different life in Ireland*. The majority of images and visual characteristics of the advertisements were standardised.

However, a degree of customisation of each advertisement was made to reflect the different perceptions and motivations of various source markets. Hence, the advertisements for the US depicted castles and emphasised the quality of service, while the slogan *Live a Different Life* that was used in Britain, was amended to *Awaken to a Different World*. The French commercials depicted images of Irish food and shopping facilities, again to reflect key motivators in that country. These are examples of the need to be sensitive to local market conditions, even when following an essentially standardised approach to marketing communications.

DEVELOPING NEW TOURISM PRODUCTS

The need to introduce new products and services is obvious when the theory of the product life-cycle is considered. The fact that a series of factors can lead to a decline in sales of products means that companies need to be continually looking for ways to improve on their current offerings, and of developing new ones. Companies need to remain competitive and recognise that customers are continually looking for new solutions to their problems. Unfortunately, in the Irish tourism industry, there has been insufficient attention paid to developing a professional and structured approach to new service development. The Tourism Task Force report of 1992 was highly critical of the lack of innovation among Irish tourism companies. Just what constitutes new has been the subject of much academic discussion. Most new products and services are to a degree, adaptations of existing services. We can identify several types of newness. Table 7.5 indicates a number of types of tourism innovations.

TABLE 7.5 — TYPES OF INNOVATION

Types of Innovation	Category
Entirely new tourism offering	Submarine tourism — Visit the Titanic
New additions to existing destinations/attraction	'Honey, I Shrunk the Audience' — new Disneyland attraction, new international conference centre in Dublin, Waterpoint facility in Enniscrone, Co. Sligo
Technology enhancements	On-line booking of holidays through travel Internet sites (e.g. www.ireland-travel.com, www.visitbritain.com)
Service quality improvements	Newer conference facilities, improved campsite facilities

Whatever the degree of newness, companies should adopt a logical and structured approach to the development of new services.

THE NEW SERVICE DEVELOPMENT PROCESS

The most commonly cited process of new service development is that of Booz, Allen and Hamilton (1982). They propose a structured framework to service development.

FIGURE 7.6 — THE PRODUCT DEVELOPMENT PROCESS

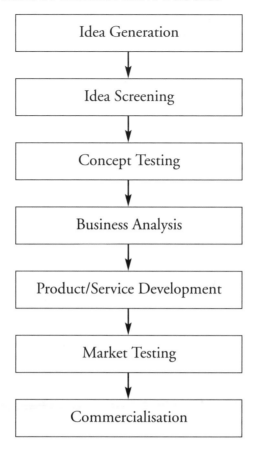

Idea Generation

The first stage of the new service development process is to generate as many ideas as possible. The main objective at this stage is to maximise the *quantity* of ideas generated without making any judgement on their usefulness.

Potential sources of new ideas:

- *Brainstorming*: Using a range of psychological and creative techniques, groups of company employees are encouraged to propose a large number of possible solutions to a predetermined problem
- *Personal visits*: many of today's tourism and hospitality products owe their origins to an overseas visit, where new approaches may have been seen to succeed
- *Customers*: many companies actively encourage customers to generate new ideas through suggestion boxes and comment cards
- *Trade press and magazines*: these are a good source of new ideas, particularly if they have a focus on international developments

- *Specialised reports on markets and products*: These are a useful way of generating ideas on very specialised topics. Many of the major external sources are discussed in Chapter 3 (Marketing Research in Tourism and Hospitality Industries).

EXHIBIT 7.3

IDEA GENERATION *IN ACTION*

POWERSCOURT ESTATE

Powerscourt Estate, located near Enniskerry, Co. Wicklow, is one of Ireland's largest privately owned heritage attractions. The former seat of the Wingfield family, it was acquired in 1961 by the Slazenger family, who remain the owners today. Powerscourt comprises the magnificent Powerscourt House, the ornate gardens surrounding the house, and the larger estate grounds where Ireland's largest waterfall can be found.

Following the tragic fire of 1974, which destroyed most of the historic eighteenth-century mansion, plans were drawn up to restore the buildings. By 1996, enough funds has been raised to rebuild the roof of the building. This was a priority, both in terms of preserving the buildings, but also to act as the starting point to develop new ways of increasing revenue. Sarah Slazenger, Sales and Marketing Manager, oversaw the idea generation process. Ideas which have come to fruition include a garden centre, a golf course and exclusive apartments in the grounds. Concession retail outlets have been taken up by leading retailers of Irish goods in an impressive shopping area in the main house.

Source: Extract from Sara Slazenger, presentation to TTRA European Conference, Dublin, October 1999.

Idea Screening

During this stage the large number of ideas generated in stage one are filtered down to a more manageable number. During this stage each idea is assessed against a number of criteria, each with separate importance weightings. For tourism projects, typical criteria include the market size, market potential, competition level, fit with existing products and services, the level of financial, managerial and technical investment required, etc.

Concept Testing

This involves developing a concept, or outline, of what the finished product or services will be like, and presenting them in the form of *concept boards* for consumers to assess. Usually this is done in the form of concept testing to gauge the likely acceptance of the concept. In very large companies, concept testing may involve surveying a statistically significant sample of the target market. Respondents may use a scale indicating purchase likelihood ranging from *definitely will buy* to *definitely will not buy*. Results may then be projected to the whole population. More commonly, however, resources do not permit this, and many tourism companies do not follow this stage. Ultimately, skipping this stage can prove a false economy. Many tourism failures, such as the now closed Celtworld Celtic mythology centre might have benefited from a more thorough appraisal of the concept.

Business Analysis

Those proposals that have a strong concept proceed to the business analysis stage. During this stage, management has to estimate likely sales revenues and costs. Revenues will be projected on the basis of market size, growth rate and market share that can be achieved. Costs include product and service costs, as well as marketing investment required at the start. *Sensitivity analysis* is the term used to describe the practice where the best- and worst-case scenarios are examined. For larger projects, a detailed feasibility study is called for, to determine the market and financial viability of a proposal. Often specialised consultancy companies are used to conduct such studies, especially if the project hopes to attract Government, or European Union, grant aid.

Product/Service Development

During this stage, the company seeks to develop a finished product or service. For a hotel, this might involve asking the chef to prepare a new restaurant menu or in the case of very large groups the development of a prototype of a new room layout. The largest international hotel chains have sufficient resources to build entire floors, or even individual hotels, as a prototype. For a tour operator this stage may mean putting together a sample tour itinerary in consultation with all the suppliers of services.

Market Testing

The tourism company may wish to launch the product in a limited geographic area only, to gauge reactions of customers and competitors before the *rollout* of the product or service to the ultimate market. This gives the company the opportunity to iron out any service or product glitches. During this stage the product positioning, pricing, service levels and customer reactions are all monitored. The market testing stage is not too common in Ireland's tourism industry, but can be seen in the food and drinks sector.

Commercialisation

In Irish tourism projects it is not uncommon to proceed directly from business analysis to the launch of the product or service. The small scale and fragmented nature of the tourism and hospitality sector mean that there are limited resources for detailed testing in advance of launch. Often it is a case of trial and error. Companies learn as they introduce new products.

Nevertheless, even at the launch stage, the company does need to consider exactly when to launch. The seasonal and economic cycles should be carefully assessed. Ideally hotels and tourism operators would like to have their operations running efficiently in plenty of time to meet the busy summer season. Tour operators have strict schedules to meet when putting together packages — if hotels open even a week behind schedule it can mean a full year's delay in featuring in a tour operator's brochure.

A precise implementation schedule needs to be drawn up to include the finalised marketing mix. In the following case-study the process of developing a new tourism product is detailed.

EXHIBIT 7.4

INNOVATION *IN ACTION: 1*

CEOL MUSICAL HERITAGE CENTRE

A visitor attraction based on Irish music, an observation platform on top of a distillery chimney, a themed cafe and bar and a seventy-four bedroom hotel are all part of a £44 million development built at Smithfield, Dublin. The landmark development by the Devey Group was designed to develop this area of Viking Dublin into a leisure and visitor centre, which included the new National Museum and the Irish Distillers' Heritage Centre.

The leisure facilities, being developed by Devey Leisure Ltd, a company headed by Gerry Fagan, the former chief executive of Campbell Catering, represent an investment of £22 million and were launched in September 1998. The hotel and café bar which is called *Chief O'Neill's*, after a Chicago Irish-American police chief, who was a keen promoter of traditional music in the US. It offers 'four-star standard at three-star prices', according to operations director Alan Hand, 'and it features a high standard of décor and innovative design'.

Glass-walled bathrooms are located in the centre of some guest rooms while three *attic suites* have their own roof gardens. The new hotel does not have its own dining facilities, apart from breakfast service in the guest rooms, but it is on the same campus as the café bar also to be called *Chief O'Neill's*, which is on three levels and has 100 covers capacity. Guests also have access to a new large Leisure Centre which forms part of the development. This has its own membership, with

---

the legal profession from the nearby Four Courts, a prime target market.

The entire development occupies a two-acre site stretching from the Children's Court to the corner of Smithfield. It includes 244 apartments, thirty-nine of which have been earmarked as an *aparthotel* — a hotel with accommodation similar to apartments including a small kitchen.

'One of the most exciting features of the development is Ceol — a visitor attraction based on the rich heritage of Irish music', says Dominic Francis, a director of Devey Leisure. 'It incorporates a theatre, the first 180-degree movie screen in Ireland and interactive audiovisual displays reflecting the many facets of Irish music.' The central feature of the theatre show is a film showing the rich tapestry of the Irish countryside, which has been made during months of shooting scenes from a helicopter. It is accompanied by a specially written musical soundtrack and projected onto the 180-degree screen. The complex also includes a performance/rehearsal space for young musicians.

Visitors to the new Smithfield Village also get a bird's eye view of Dublin, if they ride to the top of the Distillery Chimney on the outside lift which runs to an observation platform. At a later date, they will be able to shop in a new retail area which is to be incorporated in the development, and which will have speciality shops selling everything from crafts and souvenirs, to fine foods and spices.

Source: Hotel and Catering Review, 31 March 1998, adapted from original article.
Personal interview with Sally Buckley, Sales and Marketing Manager, September 1999.

The process of innovation has been the subject of considerable interest by those in charge of planning in the sector. One concern has been that much of the development in tourism that has occurred has been imitative rather than sufficiently new enough to attract completely new target markets to visit. Exhibit 7.5 below explores some of the concepts in innovation and applies them to the Irish situation.

EXHIBIT 7.5

INNOVATION *IN ACTION: 2*

THE IRISH EXPERIENCE IN TOURISM AND HOSPITALITY

In most organisations innovation is regarded as the key to company success. Rising customer expectations, the speed of change and the globalisation of markets have created a new type of marketing environment in tourism and hospitality.

However, while there has been considerable focus on the need for innovation in manufacturing organisations, attention toward tourism and hospitality has been slower building. Science and technology, and research and development have become key terms in industrial activity in the late 1990s, yet many hotel and tourism organisations feel that they can continue to compete in the market with a standardised product which is delivered and distributed in the sàme way as a decade ago. Terms such as science and development are not often associated with organisations in the hospitality industry and, to date, there has been little evidence of any type of structured approach to innovation.

The Tourism Task Force Report in 1992, and the later report by the Tourism Innovation Centre of Shannon Development, criticised the understanding and implementation of innovation in Irish tourism. Both reports described it as narrow, not based on clear market development needs, not customer focused and confused with normal essential refurbishment of the product.

What is Innovation?

At its most basic, innovation is often misunderstood. Early definitions associated it directly with invention or discovery; being the first to come up with an idea and put it into action. Since most successful contemporary innovations are copied from elsewhere, this earlier perspective is no longer the *only* valid thinking. For example, Jurys Doyle Group were the first to introduce the concept of the limited-service or budget hotel to Ireland, yet this concept had been extremely well developed in the US and elsewhere, for over a decade. More recently, innovation has become recognised as a haphazard, creative, loose activity, which must occur throughout an entire organisation, not just in a research department. In services such as tourism and hospitality, it is also generally accepted that innovation tends to occur through a series of small, scattered changes, called *incremental innovation* instead of the major breakthroughs, called *radical innovation,* as described in other industries.

Innovation is also misunderstood because it is exclusively associated with new product development. A simplistic distinction may be made between *product* and *process* innovations.

Product and Process Innovations

Product innovations occur to the physical product and its component parts. Indeed, we have witnessed a huge surge in new tourism and hospitality *products* such as golf courses, marinas, hotels, attractions etc. The airline industry, too, has been proactive, focusing on areas such as products for children — Gulf Air's *Fun Zone* concept, Air France's *Planete Bleu* package and Delta's *Fantastic Flyer* programme.

Process innovations refer to changes in the way the company is run and the systems of management and planning. In many instances they may be less obvious to the customer than product innovations or not obvious at all. For example, new types of equipment may be used aimed at producing the same products or services as before; innovations in cleaning procedures in hotels can result in time and labour saving. Or it may be robotics which drive innovations such as those, for example, in the production of airline meals or sandwiches. Other critical innovations can be identified in areas such as training and rewarding employees, creative use of marketing channels, such as producing CD-ROMs of a destination, and new ways of branding a destination.

Innovation in Tourism and Hospitality

The term *innovation* makes most people think first about technology, and in listing some of the major innovations of the last few years, computer-related devices and the Internet would be top of many lists. Yet some of the more successful innovations in tourism and hospitality are subtler. Innovation in the very concept of the hotel may be witnessed in the emergence of the *boutique* hotel, such as the Morrison Hotel in Dublin. Other innovations in this product come from the hotel's strong association with the designer John Rocha, resulting in many innovations in the image and design of the hotel. The use of internationally renowned designers can be witnessed elsewhere, such as in the Versace Hotel in Australia.

Innovative design has moved to another level in the hotels operated by the Kimpton Group in the US; rock-and-roll themes and ancient sailing vessels have featured strongly, as well as more practical innovations such as Eco-Rooms.

Other innovations based in linking a product with a personality or theme can be seen in one of Dublin's newest hotels — Chief O'Neills, described earlier.

Such *theming* of a hotel has allowed for clever innovations elsewhere. For example, in Perugia, Italy, chocolate has been chosen as a means of lending originality to a hotel where guest areas and rooms are designed along chocolate-associated themes.

Companies such as Disney pride themselves on their commitment to constant innovation in all areas, from the range of products on offer, to less visible innovations such as those in queuing management. Such a constant commitment to innovation may also be seen in Richard Branson's Virgin Company. Here we can see many products and services, which have become market leaders in travel and tourism, including Virgin Atlantic, Virgin Express, Virgin Holidays and The Hotel Collection. However, the true innovative potential of the Company may be seen in their diversification into businesses such as Virgin Vie (cosmetics), Virgin Brides, Virgin Clothing and now Virgin Direct (PEP financial services), where the innovation lies in the accessibility and simplicity of the product and runs through to the organisational culture.

In short, successful innovation can take many forms, may be structured or unstructured and may be born of invention or adapted imitation. The true goal of innovation in tourism and hospitality organisations is to offer superior benefits to the customer. This is best done through a comprehensive market orientation.

Source: Exhibit contributed by Mary O'Rawe, Lecturer in Management, Faculty of Tourism and Food, Dublin Institute of Technology.

SERVICE MANAGEMENT ISSUES

Earlier in this book, we discussed the concept of the augmented services marketing mix. Some academics have argued that the product mix requires specific attention to the inclusion of three additional elements: *people, processes* and *physical evidence*. Of these, the management of people, both customers and company staff is probably the most critical in the delivery of overall customer satisfaction.

PEOPLE AND CUSTOMER CARE

The term *customer care* has become something of a buzzword in today's business vocabulary. Customer care means *the total identification and satisfaction of the customer at all stages in the delivery of a service*. Some aspects of the service delivery are more important to the customer, and have a disproportionate impact on how they perceive a service. For example, for many busy business executives, the checkout procedures in a hotel are extremely important. Those rushing for a plane, or a meeting, will not be too impressed to be delayed because of an archaic checkout system or untrained staff. For the leisure tourist, the checkout might not be so critical, but the welcome they get on arrival in a bed and breakfast might be. Jan Carlson, the head of Scandinavian Airlines, coined the phrase *moments of truth* to describe the critical elements in the service encounter between customer and company staff. Companies need to identify and manage these moments of truth. The identification of what customers expect from the service delivery forms the basis on which service quality can be measured.

SERVICE QUALITY

Volumes have been written about the concept of service quality.

Bateson et al (1981) has defined service quality as follows:

'Quality is generally conceptualised as an attitude, the customer's comprehensive evaluation of a service offering. Quality is built up from a series of evaluated experiences…more importantly quality is viewed as an attribute in a consumer's choice processes.'

This definition is noteworthy in that, contrary to earlier company-centred perspectives on what constituted quality, he sees it firmly as a concept that is based around the customer. Embracing this perspective, recent literature on service quality sees it as being a concept that is rooted in the set of expectations a customer has about a service and whether they are being met. Despite this, many companies persist in seeing quality in very narrow terms. In the tourism sector many of the international quality marks for hotels and tourism boards measure a set of standards that remain focused on the company performing to a set list of criteria. Rather than adopt this approach, firms should set about identifying the expectations that the customer has about their service.

Quality Determinants

Parasuraman et al (1985) propose that customers evaluate service quality along five broad categories: *tangibles, empathy, assurance, responsiveness, assurance* and *reliability.*

Tangibles

Those dimensions of the service offering that can be seen, heard, touched, felt or smelt are often used as a basis of determining quality by customers. Consider a hotel: consumers will make quick evaluations based on the exterior, the appearance of the staff, the appearance of the lobby, the location of the hotel etc. Often tourism providers concentrate on this dimension of quality, to the virtual exclusion of the others. This is a mistake; especially as the overall quality of the physical product today has improved dramatically and offers less opportunity to differentiate.

Empathy

Means the extent to which the staff can put themselves *in the customer's shoes.* The ability to sense customer anxieties and needs is highly valued. Much dissatisfaction, on the part of customers, derives from a perception that staff do not appreciate the customer's needs. Even if the service provider does not possess superior skills or facilities, customers often compensate for this, if sincere effort to resolve a problem is made.

Assurance

Customers need to feel a sense of trust and confidence that their expectations of service will be met. This can happen by companies constantly looking to reassure the customer, both during the service encounter and in advance. Many tour operators send out confirmation letters and resort information to visitors in advance of their arrival as a way of building confidence in their ability. Assurance is strengthened greatly by a favourable prior experience. A strong brand identity also serves to enhance assurance.

Reliability

Customer evaluation of service quality is strongly linked to the degree that they feel the service that was promised has actually been delivered. If a conference organiser finds that meeting rooms have not been laid out as agreed in previous conversations, then their confidence in a hotel will be dented severely. On consumer affairs television programmes there are regular complaints about the extent to which customers feel that they have been misled about what to expect on holiday — tourism companies should reflect on how their communication, most notably the brochure, is being received by the prospective customer. Above all criteria, this one is the most important contributor to service quality evaluation. Companies therefore need to *do as they say they are going to do.*

Considering each of the above criteria, companies need to fully understand the expectations customers have with regard to each one. Equally importantly, there is the need to see how consumers perceive the service they are receiving. Where a difference exists between the service expected and the perception of the service being received, it is called a *quality gap*.

Taking the criteria of responsiveness as an example, a guest arriving at a hotel might expect to wait no more than five minutes to be checked in (expectation), but might feel that they have been waiting for ten (perception). The perception is actually more important than the reality in this instance, and hotels and other tourism companies need to ensure that their measurements accurately assess the customer perspective on service delivery.

Service Quality Gaps

In assessing the gap that can occur Parasuraman et al (1985) have identified five categories of gap that can occur. Figure 7.7 below illustrates the gaps that exist.

Gap 1: The difference between what consumers expect of a service and what management perceives consumers to expect.

Gap 2: The difference between what management perceives, consumers expect and the quality specifications set for service delivery.

Gap 3: The difference between the quality specifications set for service delivery and the actual quality of that service delivery.

Gap 4: The difference between the actual quality of service delivery and the quality of that service delivery as described in the firm's external communications.

Gap 5: The most important, namely, the difference between the customers' expectation of service and their perception of the service actually delivered, is at the centre of the model. To close this first gap, management need to close the remaining four gaps which are explained below.

FIGURE 7.7 — SERVICE QUALITY GAPS

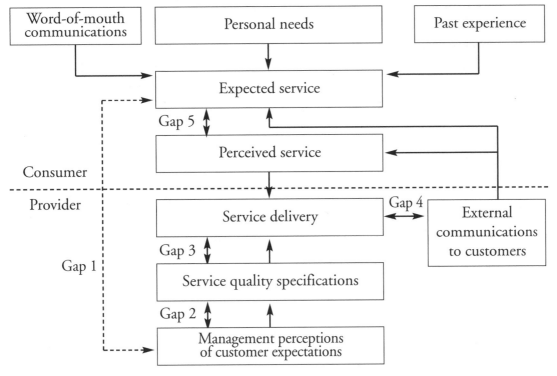

EXHIBIT 7.6

SERVICE QUALITY *IN ACTION*

RURAL TOURISM

What is Rural Tourism?

The rural tourism product is a complicated one and difficult to define. In some countries, any area that is not an urban one is deemed to be rural, with all tourism activities taking place in these areas being designated as rural tourism. This is a very broad definition of rural tourism. For example, is the siting of a 400-bedroom hotel in a coastal area an example of rural tourism? At the other end of the spectrum, many people associate rural tourism only with those tourism pursuits that are linked with farming and the agricultural economy. This is certainly a part of rural tourism and is known as *agri-tourism*. It includes visitor farms and farmhouse guesthouses.

In Ireland, rural tourism is understood to be a broader based phenomenon and includes such agriculturally based attractions, but also includes community-oriented projects in tourism, usually arranged on a geographic basis. There are over twenty-five such community co-operatives in existence in Ireland, with

---

most marketed under the umbrella brand of Irish Country Holidays. A typical rural tourism co-operative will include such ventures as small hotels, bed and breakfasts, heritage centres, visitor attractions and local tour guides. Because of the typically small-scale nature of such enterprises, rural tourism co-operatives have a high degree of difficulty in managing the quality of the product. Consequently there is a need to develop a professional approach to ensuring quality in the rural tourism sector.

Service quality is of supreme importance, incorporating both service and product delivery. Identification of the service and product provision is essential in compiling the full picture and enabling a comprehensive service quality audit of a rural tourism destination to be implemented. Service quality has been explored by a great number of individuals and many different theories and frameworks have been developed; such frameworks are customer focused and tend to identify gaps between the perception of service quality and what is actually experienced.

Research shows that essential success factors in providing sustainable and viable rural tourism are a strong sense of community, uniqueness, a clear vision and an awareness of quality (Henaghan, 1997). However, it is not the lack of awareness of quality issues that causes substandard service, but the improper operation of quality systems (Augustyn, 1998).

The quality of rural accommodation and the variety of services provided has been identified as being important levers in the successful development of rural tourism throughout many countries in Europe. Training and preparation of the rural tourism product provider is required, in order that maximum economic and social advantage can be achieved (Greffe, 1994). Figure 7.8 below illustrates a number of factors that are required, in order to ensure the successful delivery of service quality in a rural holiday.

FIGURE 7.8 — FACTORS FOR SUCCESSFUL SERVICE DELIVERY OF RURAL TOURISM

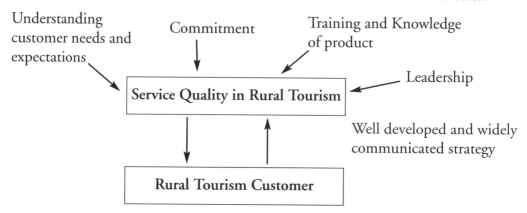

Throughout Europe, Canada and the United States, initiatives, organised both nationally and through community groups, have tackled issues relating to service quality through training. Among the surveys carried out into rural tourism quality is one conducted by Teagasc, the Irish agricultural advisory and training institute, in 1997. The research was carried out among visitors to rural areas in Ireland and looked at levels of visitors' satisfaction as well as the main attractions of the area visited. This survey helped to create an awareness of gaps in visitors' expectations and perceptions (Connolly and Heneghan, 1998–9).

In 1994, through the European Union funding scheme for rural areas, called LEADER, a pilot committee was involved in the implementation of quality plans by rural tourism groups in Greece and South Pembrokeshire (UK). A year later, a checklist for the marketing of rural tourism was identified by LEADER. Rural tourism is particularly complex in its tourism offering. Much of the tourist expectations rely on intangibles such as, the interaction with the host community, the culture of the area and the ambience of the location.

Source: Exhibit contributed by:
> Barbara A. Hunter, Postgraduate Researcher, Faculty of Tourism and Food, Dublin Institute of Technology
> Catherine Gorman, Lecturer in Tourism Marketing, Faculty of Tourism and Food, Dublin Institute of Technology

CHAPTER SUMMARY

The tourism product is a complex offering, including core, tangible and augmented elements. Managers of tourism companies need to fully understand how each of these elements interact with each other. To manage the product more effectively, the challenges posed by the various stages of the Product Life-Cycle need to be recognised, as does the need to meet the challenges of developing a comprehensive brand identity, whether for a tourism product or a destination. In developing new products, companies should follow a logical step-by-step approach. Finally, all product management and development needs to have an objective of ensuring the best possible quality. Quality is a somewhat subjective concept, but it does have a number of consistent determinants that need to be simultaneously managed.

KEY WORDS AND PHRASES

Marketing Myopia	Service Quality Gaps
Tangible and Core Product	Augmented Product
Product Life-Cycle	Brand Equity
Service Quality	Quality Determinants
Branding	Service Characteristics
Innovation	

QUESTIONS FOR REVIEW

1. Examine the Continuum of Tangibility model. Where on the continuum would you classify the following:
   * a museum
   * a guided tour
   * a cruise-ship, a cruising holiday
   * a tourism information centre
2. Consider the West Cork Fuschia Brand. Suggest other sectors that could possibly utilise the West Cork brand.
3. Identify possible problems an organisation such as Fuchsia Brands Ltd might face in using a single brand to promote various different products.
4. Can quality be measured? If so, on what basis should tourism products' quality be assessed?

QUESTIONS FOR DISCUSSION

1. Examine two tourism companies or organisations of your choice. Analyse the core, tangible and augmented elements of their *products*.
2. Identify tourism products at each stage of the product life-cycle. Can you detect any difference in the approach to marketing each?

REFERENCES AND FURTHER READING

Augustyn, M. and Ho, S.K., 'Service Quality and Tourism', *Journal of Travel Research*, vol. 37, No. 4, pp. 71–5: 1998.

Bateson, J., Lovelock, C. and Eiglier, P., *Services Marketing: New insights from Consumers and Managers*, Marketing Science Institute: Cambridge 1981.

Booz, Allen and Hamilton, *New Product Management for the 1980s*, Booz, Allen and Hamilton Management Company Consultancy: New York 1982.

Connolly, L. and Heneghan, M., 'Rural Tourism Survey', *Farm and Food*, Winter 1998/99, Teagasc: 1998.

Greffe, X., 'Is Rural Tourism a Lever for Economic and Social Development?', *Journal of Sustainable Tourism*, vol. 2, Nos. 1–2: 1994.

Levitt, T., 'Marketing Myopia', *Harvard Business Review*, July/August 1960, reprinted in *Marketing Imagination*, Chapter 8, Free Press: New York 1986.

Lumsden, L., *Tourism Marketing*, Thomson Business Press: London 1997.

Magee, F., *Interview on Morning Ireland*, June: 1998.

Parasuraman, A., Zeithmal, V. and Berry, L., 'A Conceptual Model of Service Quality and its Implications for Further Research', *Journal of Marketing*, Fall, p. 44: 1985.

Postma, A. and Jenkins, A.K., 'Improving the Tourist Experience: Quality Management Applied to Tourist Destinations', in Murphy, P., ed., *Quality Management in Urban Tourism*, John Wiley & Sons: New York 1997.

USEFUL WEB SITES

www.powerscourt.ie	Powercourt Estate
www.westcorkleader.ie	West Cork Tourism
www.ceol.ie	Ceol Music Centre
www.bah.com	Booz-Allen-Hamilton: Innovation Concepts
www.choicehotels.com	Choice Hotels Brands

CHAPTER 8

Pricing Products and Services

INTRODUCTION

At first glance price may seem to be the least complicated and perhaps the least interesting element of the marketing mix, not having the tangibility of the product, the glamour of advertising or the technological focus of distributions systems. Yet marketers rate pricing and price competition as their number one problem, why? Price is the only marketing mix element that produces revenue. All others represent cost. Pricing is the least understood of the marketing variables and frequently ignored or paid little attention and instead the focus is placed on the more *glamorous* side of marketing such as promotions. This is a mistake. If the product or service is not correctly priced the repercussions will be felt throughout the business. Incorrect pricing can lead to the demise of the entire business.

Attention paid to pricing methods and strategies will reap enormous rewards for the diligent marketer. Pricing is controllable in an unregulated environment. Price changes are often a quick fix made without proper analysis. The most common mistakes include pricing that is too cost-oriented, prices that are not revised to reflect market changes, pricing that does not vary enough for different products and services and market segments. A pricing mistake can lead to a business failure, even when all other elements of the business are sound.

CHAPTER OBJECTIVES

After studying this chapter you should be able to:

- Understand the role and perception of price
- Distinguish between the buyer's and seller's perspective of price
- Understand price elasticity of demand in tourism and hospitality services
- Be able to discuss the factors that influence pricing decisions
- To appreciate the general approaches to pricing used in tourism and hospitality businesses
- To distinguish a product's or service's pricing strategy
- Comprehend how *yield management* functions
- Appreciate the influence the Internet has on pricing

WHAT IS PRICING?

Price is the term used to describe what customers actually pay in exchange for the benefits accruing from a product or service. If the product or service has been carefully thought out with the customer's needs in mind, then there is a good chance that customers will be willing to pay the price being charged. The price placed on the product is critical: set too high a price and the customer will reject the offering; too low a price and the customer is suspicious that the product is too good to be true and there is a *flaw* in it. What constitutes a high price or a low price in tourism and hospitality depends on the buyer. Price is related to the buyer's perception of value, their perception of the entire marketing package and of the competitors' offering. Thus, it is important to the marketer to understand the meaning of price from the customer's point of view, and to price products in accordance with *the value the customer places on the benefits offered.*

BOX 8.1 — HOW MUCH IS SOMETHING REALLY WORTH?

Tickets with a face value of £35 for a major show at the Point Depot in Dublin can be advertised by touts at £100 each, often before the show even opens. Some segments of the market place a higher value on being amongst the first to see a new show rather than waiting until after the show had opened and tickets could be bought for £35 directly from the box office.

THE ROLE AND PERCEPTION OF PRICE

Price is the value that is placed on something. What is someone prepared to give in order to gain something else? Usually price is measured in money, as it is a convenient medium of exchange which allows prices to be set. Price is any common currency of value to both buyer and seller.

Price does not necessarily mean the same thing to different people, just because it is usually expressed in a number. You have to look beyond the price, at what it represents to both the buyer and the seller, if you want to grasp its significance in any transaction. Buyer and seller may well have different perspectives on what price means.

The most important factor is the consumer perception of price. If consumers choose not to buy, because the offering is perceived to be of lesser value than the asking price, then bookings or visits will decline. If price is low in relation to value offered, then demand will be difficult to manage and revenue loss substantial. Maintaining a balance between the two is the main task facing the marketer.

The key to understanding pricing in the service sector, it is argued, is to understand consumer perceptions of the price-quality dimensions. This is not easy as each particular market segment attributes different values to service offerings.

FIGURE 8.1 — ASHFORD CASTLE USES NON-PRICE FACTORS IN ITS ADVERTISING

In assessing price, the customer is looking specifically at the expected benefits of the product or service, and these include: functional, quality, operational, financial and personal benefits.

FUNCTIONAL

These benefits relate to the design of the product or service and its ability to fulfil its desired function. For example, Dublin promotes itself as a *cultural capital* of Europe. The tourist will judge the cost of getting to Dublin and cost (price) of staying there in relation to the range and variety of cultural attractions that the city has to offer.

QUALITY

The customer may expect price to reflect the quality level of the product or service. Thus, a customer may be prepared to pay more for room service in a hotel, better quality coaches or more comfortable seats on an airline. Quality perceptions may focus on tangible aspects of the product such as the design of the hotel, or intangible aspects such as quality of service, reputation or image. In the tourism and hospitality industry the emphasis is being placed on quality service as the distinguishing aspect of the business and consumers accept that these organisations charge more for their services.

OPERATIONAL

Price may be judged in organisational markets in relation to the product's ability to influence the production process. Even in consumer markets the operational issues may be considered. Consumers pay more for *ready cooked* meals in supermarkets because they reduce the preparation time. Airlines are experimenting with technology to reduce the procedures to check-in. Will this mean that these airlines can charge a higher price for this convenience?

FINANCIAL

Certain consumer products are sold on the basis of their money-saving potential. Self-catering and camping holidays are frequently sold this way. While the price for a family to camp in France for a week in high season can cost £1,500 to £2,000, the advertising highlights the saving of money in the long term (bring your own food, no extra charges for games and sports, etc.).

PERSONAL

Personal benefits is a difficult category to gauge, as it attempts to measure price against intangible, individual and psychological benefits such as status, comfort and self-image. Some high-involvement tourism and hospitality products, such as expensive holidays and luxurious hotels, use high pricing deliberately as a means of amplifying the up-market, sophisticated, exclusive images portrayed in their packaging, distribution and advertising strategies, thus increasing the status enhancement and feelgood factor of the purchase.

The problem is, of course, that different buyers put different value on different benefits. This requires markets to be segmented into groups with similar needs and wants so that appropriately tailored marketing mixes (including price) can be developed. So far, it has been assumed that price perceptions and judgements of value are constant in the mind of the potential buyer. They are, however, variable according to circumstances. For example, a family deciding on its annual holiday would probably be somewhat price sensitive and get quotes on a number of different packages/destinations before making a decision. A sudden business meeting, however, would have the business person paying premium price to get to that destination. In any emergency or *distress* purchase, the value placed on immediate problem solution, justifies paying a premium price. Another factor influencing price perceptions is scarcity. Where supply is severely limited and demand is high, prices can take on a life of their own and begin to spiral. One has only to try to book accommodation in Cork City during the Jazz Festival to feel the effects of scarce resources.

Lumsdon (1997) quotes a major study in Canada, which suggests that there is a strong link between price, quality and degree of competitiveness of a destination or a country. The study concludes that there are other factors in the marketing mix (such as image and accessibility) more important than price in determining a holiday destination, but that price becomes more important in peoples' minds when they are actually on holiday. Some of the key findings include:

- Price and quality perceptions are closely linked
- Value is more important than price
- Many product attributes are more important than price in selecting a destination
- The cost of getting to a destination does influence the overall price of the trip and visitors do distinguish between the overall price of the trip and the price of individual goods and services
- Prices take on increasing importance as visitors decide what they will do or buy on a trip
- Certain nationalities have different priorities regarding price and quality: Canadians are more price sensitive, while Japanese and Germans are very demanding on quality
- Visitor perceptions of quality and prices are influenced by past travel to a destination
- More affluent and older travellers are less price sensitive and place greater emphasis on quality
- Quality services appear to be a key to repeat visitation and to attracting potential visitors

THE SELLER'S PERSPECTIVE

Price is a distinctive element of the marketing mix for the seller, because it is the only one that generates revenue. All other elements represent outgoing costs. Price is important because it provides the basis of both recovering those costs and creating profit.

Profit = Total Revenue – Total Cost

Where total revenue is the quantity sold multiplied by the unit price, and total cost represents the costs of producing, distributing and selling the product.

In the tourism and hospitality industries, competitive pressure forces businesses to keep margins tight. To increase profits in such areas, therefore, the organisation may have to find a way of either reducing the costs involved or justifying higher prices. Service industries have been focusing on a number of strategies to reduce costs, in particular labour costs. To reduce labour costs, strategies include the use of technology, e.g. banks now make extensive use of automated teller machines (ATMs) to reduce queues and save labour. Hospitality industries look toward technology to make the repetitive tasks, such as cleaning of rooms and the preparation of certain foods, faster and quicker. If cost savings occur, they may be passed on to the consumer, thus giving the business a stronger foothold in the market.

The seller must always take care to think about price from the perspective of the customer. While costs set the lower limits of prices, the market and demand set the upper limits. Both the consumer and channel buyers, such as tour operators, balance the product's price against the benefits it provides. The seller must understand the relationship between price and demand.

PRICE-DEMAND RELATIONSHIP

Economic theory of supply and demand points to the inverse relationship between price charged and quantity ordered. Each price a company can charge will lead to a different level of demand. The demand curve illustrates the relationship between price charged and the resulting demand. It shows the number of units the market will buy in a given period at different prices that might be charged. In the normal case, demand and price are inversely related: the higher the price, the lower the demand. Hospitality and tourism organisations will see the immediate effects of a rise in price with a corresponding loss of customers. When prices are increased, the business may lose a percentage of its price-sensitive customers. Thus, in constructing a supply and demand curve, it is recognised that for any given tourism offering an equilibrium price can be reached where price is acceptable to both customer and supplier. This is illustrated in Figure 8.2.

FIGURE 8.2 — DEMAND CURVE

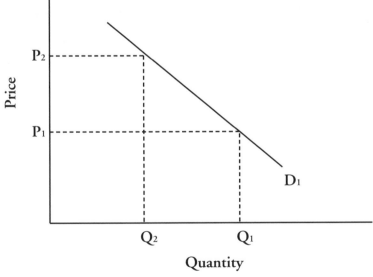

Most demand curves slope downwards in either a straight or a curved line. But, for prestige goods and services, the demand curve sometimes slopes upward. For example, a luxury hotel may find that by raising its price it will sell more rooms rather than fewer: consumers do not perceive it as a luxury hotel at the lower price.

Most marketing managers in tourism and hospitality understand the basics of a demand curve, but few are able to measure their demand curves. The type of market determines the type of demand curve. In a monopoly, the demand curve shows the total market demand resulting from different prices. But if the company faces competition, its demand at different prices will depend on whether the competitors' prices remain constant or change with the company's own price. Estimating demand curves requires forecasting demand at different prices. For example, a study by the Economist Intelligence Unit (EIU) in 1990 estimated the demand curve for holiday travel in Europe. Their findings suggested a twenty per cent reduction in the price of visiting a holiday destination increased demand by thirty-five per cent. A ten per cent reduction in price increases demand by twenty-three per cent, while a five per cent decrease in price results in a fifteen per cent increase in demand.

Reports such as these are useful to the marketer, however, in normal business situations other factors affect demand along with price. These factors include competition, the economy, advertising and sales effort. If a heritage centre cut its price and then advertised, it would be hard to tell what portion of business came from advertising and what was a result of the price cut. Price is difficult to isolate from other factors.

PRICE ELASTICITY OF DEMAND

Marketers in tourism and hospitality need to understand the concept of price elasticity — how demand will change with a change in price. If a small change in price leads to a large drop in demand, then demand is elastic. If demand hardly varies with a small change in price, then demand is inelastic. The less elastic the demand the more it pays for the seller to raise price.

What determines the price elasticity of demand? Buyers are less sensitive when:

- *The product is unique.* One of the core concepts of marketing is not to produce a product exactly like one on the market unless you can produce it cheaper. Instead, the marketing philosophy advocates the development of products and services that are unique and have a strong demand. The more *unique* the product the higher the price that can be charged. Creating the perception that your offering is different from those of your competitors is crucial; it also avoids price competition. In this way, the business lets the customer know it is providing more benefits and offering a value that is superior to that of competitors — one that will attract a higher price or more customers at the same price. Shane Gray from Scuba Dive West operates the only deep-sea-diving centre in the West of Ireland; thus the product is unique and Scuba Dive West will continue to dominate and encounter inelastic demand until a competitor moves in.
- *The product is high in quality, prestige or exclusiveness.* Consumers tend to equate price with quality, prestige and exclusiveness. A high price can bring prestige to a

product or service, because it limits availability. Restaurants where the average bill is over £80 per person would lose many of their present customers if they lowered their prices. In cases where price is perceived to relate to quality or where price creates prestige, a positive association between price and demand may exist with some market segments. For example, a restaurant had an excess of champagne in stock and could not sell it even though they reduced the price to a minimum. However, by increasing the price all the champagne sold in a few weeks!

- *When substitute products are hard to find. When buyers find it difficult to get alternative or services.* Many travellers will simply book into a hotel group that they are familiar with when visiting a new destination. There may be many individual hotels of better quality and cheaper, but the visitor simply does not know they exist. These hotels are not part of the visitors' *awareness set* and are therefore not chosen. Hotel restaurants often charge more for meals based on the substitute awareness set. The hotel guest that arrives late will use the hotel's restaurant even though there may be better value elsewhere. The meal in the hotel may be more expensive, but the guest is saved the trouble of locating a restaurant and travelling to it.

If demand is elastic rather than inelastic, sellers will generally consider lowering their prices. A lower price will produce more total revenue. This practice makes sense when the extra costs of producing and selling more products do not exceed the extra revenue.

TABLE 8.1 — FACTORS INFLUENCING PRICE SENSITIVITY

Influencing Factors	The Effect in Detail
The unique value effect	The better differentiated the product, the lower the price sensitivity.
The substitute awareness effect	The greater the number of substitutes available, the greater the price sensitivity.
The difficult comparison effect	The more difficult it is to make a direct comparison between different products, the lower the price sensitivity.
The total expenditure effect	The smaller the proportion of total spend this product represents, the lower the price sensitivity.
The end benefit effect	The greater and more valued the end benefit of the product, the lower the price sensitivity.

TABLE 8.1 — FACTORS INFLUENCING PRICE SENSITIVITY *contd.*

Influencing Factors	The Effect in Detail
The shared cost effect	A buyer bearing only part of the cost of a product will be less price sensitive.
The price-quality effect	The higher the quality and the prestige image of the product, the lower the price sensitivity.

Source: Adapted from *Principles of Marketing*, Blessington and Pettit, 1997

FACTORS TO BE CONSIDERED WHEN SETTING PRICES

A company's pricing decisions are affected by both internal company factors and external environmental factors (*see* Figure 8.3).

FIGURE 8.3 — FACTORS AFFECTING PRICE DECISIONS

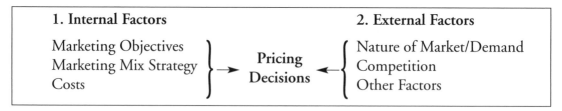

1. INTERNAL FACTORS AFFECTING PRICING DECISIONS

Marketing Objectives

Pricing objectives must be consistent with a company's overall marketing objectives. Pricing objectives must be realistic in terms of the company's position in the market-place and the product target market and positioning strategy. For example, Four Seasons Hotel would not set a pricing objective that would make it a low-cost leader in the accommodation market. Four Seasons is a luxury Dublin hotel, positioned to command a high price with a target market that expects to pay more for a hotel.

Not many tourism and hospitality businesses develop explicit, written marketing objectives. Instead, these objectives tend to be held as implicitly understood by management. Objectives, whether implicit or explicit, tend to fall into one of the three broad classes: profit objectives, sales objectives or competitive position objectives.

Profit Objectives

Profit maximisation and target return on investment are two major types of profit objectives. Profit maximisation means the firm attempts to earn the largest profit possible. To do this, the firm estimates what demand and costs will be at different prices and choose the price that will produce the maximum profit, cash-flow or return on investment. In all cases, the firm wants current financial results rather than long-term performance. Marketers in tourism and hospitality have to make decisions under uncertainty, and rarely attain true profit maximisation. To do so would require detailed information about customer demand and costs that is unlikely to be available.

Marketers are more likely to set a target return on net sales, where targeted profit is a specific percentage of every sale. For example, a food and beverage manager may wish a return of ten per cent on all food sales in the restaurants.

Sales Objectives

Many organisations state their pricing objectives in sales-related terms. The firm's objective will be to address sales volume in terms of turnover or units sold. When industry sales are flat or the economy is in recession, the best a company can hope for may be to keep sales volume flat instead of decreasing. Kotler (1999) refers to this as the *survival objective*. In other cases, larger volume can help a firm achieve economies of scale that lower the cost per unit sold. This policy is practised by tour operators and large hoteliers who can benefit from economies of scale and reduction in labour costs.

Market share may be the objective of some companies and prices can be kept to a minimum in order to gain market share. Budget Travel and Ryanair are two Irish companies that practice this policy.

Competitive Position Objectives

Some firms set pricing objectives in relation to the actions of competitors. Their goals may be to meet the competitor's price. Many firms attempt to match the exact pricing of competitors. This pattern is very common in the attractions, accommodation and catering sectors of tourism. Bed and breakfast operations are very heavily influenced by the prices charged by competitors. It is only the very unique bed and breakfast operations that can charge a premium price, and they must incorporate 'added value' into their product.

Marketing Mix Strategy

Price is only one of the marketing mix tools that a company uses to achieve its marketing objectives. Price decisions must be co-ordinated with product design, distribution and promotion decisions to form a consistent and effective marketing programme. Decisions made for other marketing mix variables may affect pricing decisions. Some companies make their pricing decision first, and then base the other marketing mix decisions on the prices they want to charge. Here, price is the crucial positioning factor that defines the product's market, competition and design. Such decisions in tourism and hospitality marketing do not refer to being the *lowest price*.

Frequently, products are positioned as the most expensive e.g. a new golf course being planned for Lahinch in Co. Clare has announced an annual fee of £50,000. The *price* immediately excludes the majority of Irish people and targets the wealthy American and European golfer and business person. The course will have to compete with the most exclusive courses in the world and the design will be expected to be flawless.

Other companies do not emphasise price and use other marketing mix tools to create a non-price position. Often, the best strategy is not to charge the lowest price, but rather to differentiate the marketing offer to make it worth a higher price. For example, tourist attractions will emphasise locations, the experience of the visit, educational elements and fun and enjoyment as benefits instead of price.

Thus, the marketer must consider the total marketing mix when setting prices. If the product or service is positioned on non-price factors, then decisions about quality, promotion and distribution will strongly affect price. If price is crucial to positioning, then price will strongly affect decisions made about the other marketing mix elements.

Costs

At the most basic level, a company has to cover its costs before it can make a profit. However, the process is really not that simple. First, the company must be able to identify its costs, then it must allocate these costs among the products and services it produces. Cost cannot be always shared out equally. One customer group, or one product or service, may bear more of the costs than another.

Traditional Types of Cost

Fixed costs are costs that do not vary with production or level of sales. For example, a heritage centre must pay each month's bills for mortgage repayments, heat and salaries.

Variable costs vary directly with the level of production. Variable costs can include heating, labour and cost of raw materials.

Total costs are the sum of fixed and variable for any given level of production. Marketers want to charge a price that will cover total costs. If it costs the company more than competitors to produce and sell its product, the company will have to charge a higher price or make less profit, putting it at a disadvantage.

Companies are changing their cost structures in order to set prices more competitively. This often means changing the entire approach to new-product development, so that costs are cut during the design stages. Sometimes, new technology is used to reduce production costs. Banks use ATMs to reduce staff costs, restaurants use the carvery to reduce the cost of serving each customer. The point to note is that costs that marketers have assumed as fixed can actually be cut through creative design and re-engineering the service process. Hotels have introduced the technology to allow guests to check themselves out from their hotel bedrooms, and airline reservations can be made directly on the Internet.

Costs have to be evaluated carefully to determine whether they are justified by added value to the customer. Sometimes unnecessary costs can be found in inefficient labour, inefficient distribution or inefficient marketing practices. These costs must be identified and rectified for the company to survive.

2. External Factors Affecting Pricing Decisions

External factors that affect pricing decisions include the nature of the market and demand, competition and other external factors.

The Market and Demand

Whereas costs set the lower limit of prices, the market and demand set the upper limits (Kotler). The consumer balances the price of a product or service against the benefits of owning it. Thus, the marketer must understand the relationship between price and demand for the product or service (*see* Figure 8.2, Demand Curve).

Pricing in Different Types of Markets

The seller's pricing can vary with different types of markets. Economists recognise different types of markets that present a different pricing challenge. Under pure competition, the market consists of many buyers and sellers trading in a uniform commodity such as coffee or financial securities. No single buyer or seller has much effect on the current market price. In a purely competitive market, market research, product development, pricing and promotion play little or no role. Thus, the seller in these markets does not spend much time on marketing strategy.

Under monopolistic competition, the market consists of many buyers and sellers who trade over a range of prices rather than a single market price. A range of prices occurs because sellers can differentiate their offers to buyers. The physical product or service can be varied in quality, features or style. Under oligopolistic competition, the market consists of a few sellers who are highly sensitive to each other's pricing and marketing strategies. In pure monopoly, the market consists of one seller. The seller can be a government monopoly (An Post) or a regulated monopoly (Eircom) or a private non-regulated monopoly (Microsoft).

Competitors' Prices and Offers

The level and intensity of competition and the pricing decisions that other organisations make in the market will influence any producer's own pricing. Once a company is aware of its competitors' prices and their offers, it can use this information as a starting point for deciding its own pricing. For example, if a customer perceives the Jurys Hotel in Cork is similar to the Ryan Hotel, then Jurys must set its prices close to those of Ryan or lose that customer. Jurys uses price to position its offer relative to its competitor's offer.

Other External Factors

When setting prices, the company must also consider other factors in the external environment. Economic conditions such as inflation, boom or recession and interest rates affect pricing. The boom in the Irish economy combined with low interest rates has influenced the increase in hotel occupancies and average rates. Economic conditions affect both the costs of production and consumer perceptions of the product's price and value. The Gulf War in 1991 caused international travel to come to a standstill, as travellers would not risk flying as a result of terrorist threats. Travel between America and Europe was very limited and, as a result, hotel and airline occupancies were badly effected. After the war was over, many hotel chains and airlines used price to stimulate demand.

All areas of the environment can affect pricing. Meeting new government regulations can cause costs to increase. Many food outlets in Ireland find it is no longer profitable to operate if they are to implement the new hygiene regulations. If pro-environmental groups succeed in getting pesticides banned, food prices may increase. Marketers must know the laws regarding price and make sure that their pricing policies are legal.

General Pricing Approaches

There are three broad approaches to pricing as indicated in Figure 8.4 below:

FIGURE 8.4 — APPROACHES TO PRICING

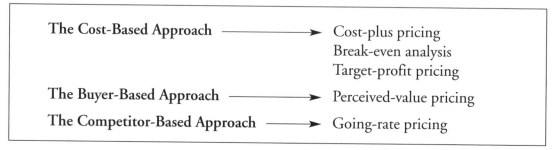

Cost-Based Pricing

This is one of the simplest pricing methods and usually involves adding a standard mark-up to the cost of the product or service. This method has been popular in restaurants and in pricing wines in particular. A bottle of wine may cost £9 and sell for £18, a 100 per cent mark-up on cost. The gross profit is £9. Cost as a percentage of selling price is a commonly used pricing technique used in Ireland. The manager targets certain food costs and then prices the menu items accordingly. Most managers, who use the cost as a percentage of selling price to price their menus, use this technique to develop their target price. They adjust the individual prices for menu items based on factors such as what the market will bear, psychological pricing and competitors' pricing. Mark-up pricing remains popular because of ease of use, sellers are more certain about costs than demand and because this method is so popular, prices are similar and price competition is minimised.

Some companies use a mix of full cost and marginal pricing based on the level of fixed overheads and the degree of fluctuation of demand. This approach takes into account a number of factors, especially the ability of different market segments to pay higher prices, the degree of seasonality and the need to offer a contribution to high fixed costs. Marginal-cost pricing directs attention to the costs that rise as the number of customers increases, rather than the fixed costs. Thus, the pricing approach does not reflect the total unit cost of provision (fixed plus variable, or directly attributable, costs). It takes into account only the additional costs in providing the extra use of facilities or service offering. For example, a coach operator in the low season might have days when part of the fleet is barely used. The full cost of running a fifty-seater coach for one day is £240; the marginal cost is £175. If seats are each priced at £8 each, assuming a loading of thirty passengers, the operator will just manage to break even at £250. However, at that price in winter, it might appear a little expensive to marginal passengers so the manager will price to achieve a return on the direct costs. Assuming a loading of thirty, seats can be priced at £5.80 to cover direct costs (£174) and therefore be more attractive to the market. While the price does not attempt to cover full costs, it will allow operating costs to be met and possibly a contribution to overheads or fixed costs. This type of pricing is common in tourism (Lumsdon, 1997). It relates to the characteristic of services known as *time perishability*; this means that the service, such as hotel rooms, covers in a restaurant or seats on a plane or train, cannot be stored. Pricing to cover marginal costs of operation, plus a contribution to overheads, is appropriate at times when demand is low.

TABLE 8.2 — HERITAGE CENTRE PRICING POLICY

	Year 1	Year 2	Year 3
Direct costs per visitor	£1·50	£1·50	£1·50
(staff, on-site demonstration, etc.)			
Fixed costs (buildings, displays, etc.)	£400,000	£400,000	£400,000
Estimated number of visitors	100,000	80,000	70,000
Cost per visitor			
Direct costs (heating, cleaning)	£1·50	£1·50	£1·50
Fixed costs per visitor	£4·00	£5·00	£5·71
Full costs per visitor	£5·50	£6·50	£7·21
Price per person	£5·50	£6·50	£7·20

Source: Adapted from Lumsdon, 1997

Break-Even Analysis and Target-Profit Pricing

The firm tries to determine the price at which it will break even or make the target profit it is seeking. A break-even chart shows the total cost and total revenue expected at different sales volume levels. Figure 8.5 shows a break-even chart for the manufacture of a product. In this example the fixed costs are £300,000 regardless of sales volume; variable cost per unit is £10. Variable costs are added to fixed costs to form total costs, which rise with volume. The total revenue curve starts at zero and rises with each unit sold. The total revenue and the total cost curves cross at 30,000 units. This is the break-even point. At £20 per unit, the company must sell at least 30,000 units to break-even: that is for total revenue to cover total costs. Break-even volume can be calculated using the following formula:

$$\text{Break-even volume} = \frac{\text{fixed cost}}{\text{price-variable cost}} = \frac{£300,000}{(£20 - £10)} = 30,000$$

If the company wants to target a profit, it must sell more than 30,000 units at £20 each. Profit is total revenue minus total cost.

FIGURE 8.5 — BREAK-EVEN CHART FOR DETERMINING TARGET PRICE

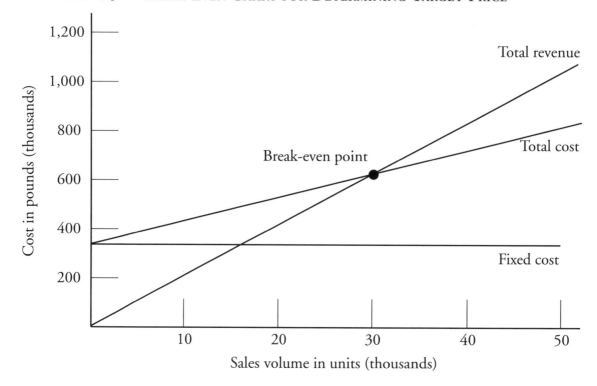

Buyer-Based Pricing

Value-Based Pricing. An increasing number of companies are basing their prices on the product's or service's perceived value. Value-based pricing uses the buyer's perceptions of value, not the seller's costs, as the key to pricing. Value-based pricing means that the marketer cannot design a product or service and marketing programme and then set the price. Price must be considered along with the other marketing mix variables, before the marketing programme is set.

Figure 8.6 compares cost-based pricing with value-based pricing. Cost-based pricing is product driven. The company designs what it considers to be a good product, totals the cost of making the product and sets a price that covers costs plus a target profit. Marketing must then convince buyers that the product's value at that price justifies its purchase. If the price turns out to be too high, the company must settle for lower mark-ups or lower sales, both resulting in disappointing profits.

Value-based pricing reverses this process. The company sets its target price based on customers' perceptions of the product value. The targeted value and price then drive decisions about product design and what costs can be incurred. As a result, pricing begins with analysing consumer needs and value perceptions and a price is set to match consumers' perceived value.

FIGURE 8.6 — COST-BASED VERSUS VALUE-BASED PRICING

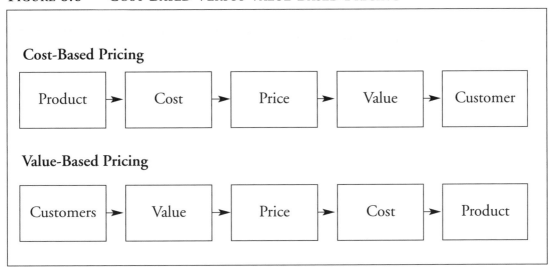

Source: Adapted from: Nagle, T.T. and Holden, R.K., *The Strategy and Tactics of Pricing*

Competitor-Based Pricing

Consumers will base their judgements of a product or service's value on the price that competitors charge for similar products and services. The main form of competitor pricing in tourism and hospitality is going-rate pricing. Sealed-bid pricing is used in the provision of certain services such as contract catering.

Going-Rate Pricing

The firm bases its price largely on competitors' prices, with less attention paid to its own costs or to demand. The business might charge the same, more or less, than its chief competitors. Often smaller firms follow the leader and change prices when the market leader changes prices. Going-rate pricing is popular. When demand elasticity is hard to measure, businesses often follow this method. It also prevents price wars.

Sealed-Bid Pricing.

Using sealed-bid pricing the business must bid for jobs. A firm bases its price on how it thinks competitors will price rather than on its own costs or on demand. The firm wants to win the contract and winning requires pricing less than other firms.

EXHIBIT 8.1

PRICING *IN ACTION*

USING THE INTERNET

In 1997, California based WorldRes introduced its global Internet-based reservation system. At the end of the year, industry sources claimed that WorldRes's hotel customer base on its *Places to Stay* web site was 3,000. At that time, this was one of the biggest customer bases for on-line reservation services on the Net. WorldRes's target market is independent hotels who cannot afford a Global Distribution System listing, (*see* Chapter 9) but want to increase their international exposure via the Net. However, several consortia and hotel chains are also using WorldRes as an easy way to provide web access to member properties.

In addition to making reservations, the Internet is providing new innovative schemes to help hotels and airlines fill empty rooms and airline seats. One of these methods is by the use of auction sites. Though auction sites have yet to prove particularly successful in Europe, they are creating massive amounts of excitement in America. One of the most popular web sites is *eBay*. The concept is simple, individuals and companies with something to sell put their wares on the eBay site. Visitors bid competitively against a deadline and the highest wins the item. Thanks to the power of today's technology, eBay processes more than one million auctions a day. A variation on this concept is *Priceline*, which auctions hotel rooms to the highest bidder on a daily basis. As the tourism product is *time perishable*, and can not be stored, Priceline has proved to be an efficient way of selling surplus capacity.

Pricing Strategies

A company does not set a single price, but rather a pricing structure that covers different items in its line. This pricing structure changes over time as products move through their life-cycles. The company adjusts product and service prices to reflect changes in costs and demand, and to account for variations in buyers and situations. As the competitive environment changes, the company considers when to initiate price changes and when to respond to them. Pricing decisions in tourism and hospitality are subject to an incredibly complex array of environmental and competitive forces. Key issues for the marketer are new product pricing strategies, product-mix pricing strategies, price-adjustment strategies and strategies for initiating and responding to price changes.

Source: Adapted from *Pricing and Yield Management*, published by Bord Fáilte; and 'For You, The Price is Right', by David Hewson, *The Sunday Times*, June 1999

New Product Pricing Strategies

Pricing strategies usually change as the product passes through its life-cycle. In the introduction stage the company faces the problem of deciding the position of the product in the market. It must decide where to position the product versus competing products in terms of quality and price. Kotler et al (1999) described four possible positioning strategies, see Figure 8.7.

FIGURE 8.7 — FOUR PRICE POSITIONING STRATEGIES

		High Price	Low Price
Quality	High	Premium Strategy	Good Value Strategy
	Low	Overcharging Strategy	Economy Strategy

Source: Kotler et al, *Principles of Marketing*, Prentice Hall, 1999

Premium pricing strategy focuses on producing a high quality product or service and charging the highest price. The Morrison Hotel, known as the *Designer Hotel* thanks to the help of John Rocca, commands room rates of £155 rising to £350 for a suite and £750 for the penthouse. At the other extreme is the economy pricing strategy producing a lower quality product but charging a low price; hostels are often an example of this strategy. The good value strategy represents a way to compete with the premium price. It offers high quality at low prices and includes many of the new budget-style hotels that offer a range of leisure facilities at prices less than bed and breakfast prices. Finally, the overcharging strategy occurs when the product is overpriced in relation to its quality. This strategy is to be avoided.

When introducing new products, companies can choose between two strategies:

Market Skimming

This involves the company skimming revenues layer by layer from the market. As initial sales slow down and as competitors threaten to introduce similar products and services, the company lowers the prices to draw the next price-sensitive layer of customers. Tourism destinations frequently follow this pattern of pricing. Initially, the destination can be exclusive and expensive but as it passes through its life-cycle, it becomes less fashionable and cannot command premium prices and starts to attract more price-sensitive visitors. An example in Europe is the French Riviera.

Market-Penetration Pricing

Rather than setting a high initial price to skim off revenues, some companies use market-penetration pricing. They set a low initial price in order to penetrate the market quickly, to rapidly attract a large number of buyers and gain market share. The high sales volume results in falling costs, allowing the company to cut its prices even further. First Choice Holidays used this pricing strategy to enter the Irish Market.

Other Product Pricing Strategies

Product-Bundle Pricing

Using product-bundle pricing, sellers often combine several of their products and services and offer the *bundle* at a reduced price. Thus, theatres and sports teams sell season tickets at less than the cost of single tickets; and hotels sell specially priced packages that include room, meals and entertainment. Price bundling can promote the sales of products or services that consumers might not otherwise buy. Tourists can be encouraged to visit new or less popular destinations as a result of price bundling.

Price Adjustment Strategies

Tourism and hospitality businesses usually adjust their basic prices to account for various customer differences and changing situations. Discount and allowance pricing takes many forms, as shown below:

- *Cash discount* is a price reduction to buyers who pay their bills promptly
- *Quality discount* is a price reduction to buyers who buy in large volumes such as tour operators and travel agents
- *Seasonal discount* is a price reduction to buyers who purchase out of season. The Quality Hotel in Clonakilty in Co. Cork has a tariff of £60 per night; however, in

low season it offers weekend packages, consisting of two nights bed and one dinner, for just £89.

- *Trade discount* is a reduction of the list price given by the pr intermediary for performing certain tasks or selling a certain ar frequently offer travel agents ten per cent discount.

Segmented Pricing

Companies will often adjust their basic prices to allow for differences in customers, services and locations. In segmented pricing, the company sells a product or service at two or more prices, even though the difference in prices is not based on differences in cost. Segmented pricing can take several forms:

- *Customer segment pricing* involves charging different prices for the same product or service. Museums and heritage centres will charge lower prices for students.
- *Product-form pricing* involves charging different prices for different versions of the product. A food item may be priced differently between the restaurant menu and the room service menu.

With *location pricing*, different locations are priced differently, even though the cost of offering each location is the same. Hotels vary their room rate depending on whether the rooms have a view or not. Theatres also vary their seat prices.

With *time pricing*, prices vary by the season, the month, the day and even the hour. Tourist attractions, accommodation providers and resorts give seasonal discounts. Yield management systems have attempted to perfect systems to adjust pricing to changing levels of demand.

Yield Management

Yield management is an approach to maximising profits by carefully monitoring and managing pricing and product availability. Tourism and hospitality operate in a highly competitive environment with high fixed costs, fixed capacity and fluctuating demand. The marketer must attempt to synchronise supply and demand. Yield management systems attempt to achieve this by the use of computer systems and detailed forecasting. Yield management is a pricing strategy that attempts to match the supply of the product and service with the ever-changing level of demand. It is based on segmented pricing and attempts to manipulate demand.

Yield management works best under certain conditions: for example, if the product is perishable, its demand patterns fluctuate from season to season so that the timing of the sale is important. The product and services tend to have high fixed costs and relatively low marginal costs for selling additional capacity. Finally, advance purchase or reservation of the product or service can occur.

Yield management allows the market to be segmented and identification of distinct groups, which behave differently, are relevant to the companies' marketing activities. Yield management allows the systematic offering of different prices to different segments of the market in response to changes in demand. It allows detailed forecasting on the basis of past turnover records combined with future events. A tourism and hospitality business can rationally and accurately anticipate the size of different market segments and the prices each will pay. It also allows the limiting and shifting of availability according to demand. Finally, yield management is both a reservation and sales process where management decisions about pricing and availability are implemented. Opportunities exist to negotiate and *up-sell* to a more expensive product or service, or *cross-sell* to an alternative product or service.

Different tourism and hospitality operations will implement yield management at different levels. Low levels will involve no real yield management techniques; for example, a bed and breakfast may charge a single price for its rooms all year round. Medium levels involve some intuitive use of the concepts. Managers may compare turnover with previous years and set seasonal prices accordingly. High levels of yield management involve the systematic use of information for all pricing decisions, past records are used, forecasts of future trends are examined and the experience of management is incorporated, but no special software is incorporated into the reservations system. Finally, very high levels of yield management involve the use of computerised systems and specialised software. Staff have to be fully trained in the use of the equipment and their ability to *up-sell.*

Psychological Pricing

Price says something about the product, and many consumers use price to judge quality. In using psychological pricing, sellers consider the psychology of prices and not simply the economics. When consumers can judge the quality of a product or service by examining it or by calling on past experience with it, they use price less to judge quality. When consumers can not judge quality because they lack the information or skill, price becomes an important quality signal. Package holidays are frequently judged by consumers, based on price and thus the saying 'you get what you paid for'.

Value Pricing

Marketers in tourism and hospitality are using *value pricing* more and more frequently in the 1990s. It involves offering the right combination of quality and good service at a fair price. In many cases, this has involved the introduction of less expensive versions of established, branded products and services. Jurys Hotel Group introduced 'Jurys Inns' offering simple accommodation, limited food and beverage outlets in central locations at much less cost than their traditional hotels.

Geographical Pricing

A company must decide how to price its products to customers located in different parts of the country or the world. Should a catering company risk losing the business of more distant customers by charging them higher prices to cover the cost of transporting the food and staff? Or, should the company charge all customers the same price regardless of location? There are no set rules and the company must decide its own pricing policies in such matters.

EXHIBIT 8.2

PRICING STRATEGIES *IN ACTION*

PRICING IS AN ART AS WELL AS A SCIENCE

Setting prices is one of the most difficult tasks for the marketer. Too high a price discourages potential customers, too low a price and the company loses potential revenue. Cian O'Carroll is a tourism and property consultant who specialises in heritage tourism, he has had many years of practical experience setting prices at Bunratty Folk Park in Co. Clare and offers the following advice on setting prices at tourism attractions:

- The product must offer the customer value for money
- The price charge must be related to the duration of the experience and the quality of the presentation
- Competitors prices must be reviewed and compared with the company's own proposed prices
- Prices will vary according to the key market segments being attracted to the site; tour operators, travel agents, school groups, senior citizens, families and groups. Separate prices should be considered for each of these segments.
- Tour operators will be the toughest segment from a pricing perspective

In addition, pricing strategies should be reviewed on an annual basis. Small adjustments of five pence, ten pence and fifty pence can make a big difference to the profits of the business at the end of the year. It is important that the managers of attractions understand what price levels the market can bear. Often, this information can be obtained from market research. However, Mr O'Carroll advocates testing the new price changes before implementation.

Customers visiting attractions often hesitate at the admission office. They arrive, view the pricing structure and decide to enter or leave. It is important not to lose potential customers at this point. Do not let the potential customer go away, instead offer them a limited view or *menu* of the attraction so as to encourage entry. Gift shops as well as food and beverage outlets should be

---

positioned at the exit; they can be a good source of revenue. Research by Tourism Development International indicated that visitors spend more money in the *ancillary services* such as the gift shop than at the entrance gate.

Tourist attractions in general are not profit-making. However, a number of strategies can be followed to reduce the cost of setting up and running a successful attraction. Some of the initial capital can be sourced from government grants; the attraction should look for favourable tax situations such as setting itself up as a non-profit organisation. Finally, many attractions in Ireland are being successfully operated and managed with the aid of FAS workers. Unless an attraction has a market of over 20,000 visitors per year it will not be viable. The concept must work well but this takes time, for example, Bunratty Castle and Folk Park evolved over thirty years. Sometimes projects are successful overseas but they must be adjusted for the Irish market. Just because an attraction or heritage centre deals with an Irish theme this does not guarantee success, as was seen with the demise of Celt World in Waterford.

Source: Cian O'Carroll, Tourism and Property Consultant, Limerick, has contributed this article. Mr O'Carroll can be reached at 061-326022

CHAPTER SUMMARY

Getting the price *right* is one of the greatest challenges facing the marketer. Ultimately, the customer will decide if the product and service is correctly priced. In assessing price, the customer is looking for benefits. These may be functional, quality, financial or personal benefits. The problem is that different buyers put different value on different benefits, so the marketer must know the target market extremely well before making pricing decisions. It is crucial to understand the price elasticity of demand for the product or service being sold, which is how demand will change with a change in price. When making pricing decisions, a number of key factors will influence the final price and these include both internal and external factors. Internal factors include marketing objectives, marketing mix strategy and costs; and external factors involve the nature of market and demand, competition and other factors in the business environment.

The three main approaches to pricing include: cost-based pricing, buyer-based pricing and competitive-based pricing. Service industries, such as tourism and hospitality, are moving away from cost-based pricing toward buyer-based pricing. Companies do not set a single price, but rather a pricing structure that covers different products and services. This pricing structure changes over time as products move through their life-cycles. Strategies for new products include: premium pricing strategy, good value strategy, economy strategy and overcharging strategy. Companies generally choose market-skimming or market-penetration pricing. Other popular strategies with tourism and hospitality operations are price bundling, segmented pricing, psychological pricing, geographical pricing and value pricing.

Yield management is the approach to maximising profits by carefully monitoring and managing pricing and product availability. It achieves this by use of computer systems and detailed forecasting. The system allows the offering of different prices to different segments of the market in response to change in demand. With the advent of the Internet, pricing has become much more dynamic.

KEY WORDS AND PHRASES

Price	Demand
Price Elasticity	Break-Even Analysis
Cost-Based Pricing	Value-Based Pricing
Competitor Pricing	Product-Bundle Pricing
Yield Management	Psychological Pricing
Value Pricing	Geographical Pricing

QUESTIONS FOR REVIEW

1. Conduct a random sample, street survey to test the sensitivity to price for travel routes between Ireland and England. Discuss the importance of price differences between ferry prices and air prices on these routes.
2. Research the pricing policy for a tourist hotel in your area. Explain the relationship between price and market opportunities for the hotel.

QUESTIONS FOR DISCUSSION

1. Discuss the factors that influence the prices set in a hotel.
2. Under what conditions is meeting the competitor's price an unsuitable policy for a travel agency.
3. Explain the use of Yield Management in a tourism or hospitality operation.
4. Why is price bundling a popular strategy in tourism and hospitality?
5. Discuss the pricing strategies available for the introduction of a new product to the market.

REFERENCES AND FURTHER READING

Bord Fáilte, 'Pricing and Yield Management', in the series *Marketing for Success*, Bord Fáilte: Dublin 1998.

Bord Fáilte, *Marketing Plan for Irish Tourism 1999*, Bord Fáilte Marketing Planning Department: Dublin 1999.

Kotler, P., Armstrong, G., Saunders, J. and Wong, V., *Principles of Marketing*, 2nd European edn.: Prentice Hall Europe 1999.

Laws, E., *Tourism Marketing: Service and Quality Management Perspective*, Stanley Thornes: Cheltenham 1991.

Lumsdon, L., *Tourism Marketing*, Thomson Business Press: London 1997.

Nagle, T. and Holden, R., *The Strategy and Tactics of Pricing*, 2nd edn.: Prentice Hall 1995.

USEFUL WEB SITES

www.priceline.com	Pricing of hotels, airline and car hire on the Internet
www.ashford-castle.ie	Ashford Castle, Co. Mayo
www.ireland.travel.ie	Bord Fáilte's web site
www.ebay.com	Auction site
www.ebay.ie	Irish auction site
www.lastminute.com	Last minute
www.DeckChair.com	Deck Chair (Sir Geldof's site)

CHAPTER 9

Distribution in Tourism and Hospitality

INTRODUCTION

One of the most important decisions facing today's marketing manager is the development of an efficient distribution system. Distribution systems provide a steady flow of customers. A well-managed distribution system can make the difference between a market share leader and a company struggling for survival. Many tourism and hospitality companies are making greater use of marketing channels available to them. For example, Ritz-Carlton receive a significant share of business from travel agents because of aggressively developing this channel. In Ireland, Jurys Doyle Hotel Group concentrate on travel agents as a key channel, other businesses have developed the Internet as a key means of distribution (and promotion) such as Killary Adventure Centre in Co. Mayo, which received over fifty per cent of its bookings via the Internet in 1999.

CHAPTER OBJECTIVES

After studying this chapter you should be able to:

- Understand distribution in tourism and hospitality
- Understand why marketing intermediaries are used
- The function of a distribution system
- Comprehend the main tourism and hospitality intermediaries
- Understand the development of electronic distribution systems
- Explain how *Gulliver* works
- Discuss the Internet as a distribution system

DISTRIBUTION IN TOURISM AND HOSPITALITY

In today's competitive environment it is not enough to count on a central reservation system and your own sales force. Tourism and hospitality businesses must develop increasingly complex distribution networks. As Kotler forecasted, 'the concept of marketing channels is not limited to the distribution of physical goods. Producers of services also face the problem of making their output available and accessible to target populations.' When marketing physical products, the emphasis is placed on logistics and transport. In tourism and hospitality, it lies with the flow of promotional material and information about destinations and the various products on offer. Therefore, given the nature of service marketing, i.e. the underlying principles of intangibility, perishability, and simultaneous production and consumption, the distribution channels which have grown up to serve tourism markets differ to those found in other sectors (Lumsdon, 1997).

Competition, a global market-place, electronic distribution techniques and the Internet as well as a perishable product have increased the importance of distribution and the speed at which it occurs. Innovative ways of approaching new and existing markets are being developed. The role of technology is very dominant and very few tourism and hospitality businesses have not felt its influence. Globalisation has meant that many businesses must choose foreign partners to help them market or distribute their products. Aer Lingus is becoming part of the gigantic *Oneworld* global alliance of airlines that includes British Airways and American Airlines. Accommodation providers all feel the need to be part of a larger organisation that has marketing expertise and thus we see the growth in networks and consortia such as *Leading Hotels of the World*, Logis de France, Manor House Hotels and Hidden Ireland. Many of the larger groups provide central reservations systems and thus add value to the services they offer.

CHANNELS OF DISTRIBUTION

'A distribution system is any organised and serviced system, created or utilised to provide convenient points of sale and/or access to consumers, away from location of production or consumption, and paid out of marketing budgets.'

(Middleton, 1989)

Channels are carefully planned by producers and serviced regularly by them with sales visits, literature, computer links, etc. Each channel becomes a pipeline through which flows a targeted volume of sales over a period of time. The purpose of the distribution system is to give potential travellers the information they need to make a travel choice, and to allow them to make the necessary reservations once they have decided on their choice.

WHY ARE MARKETING INTERMEDIARIES USED?

The use of intermediaries such as travel agents, tour operators, and tourist information offices depends on their ability to make tourism and hospitality services available to target markets. It is unrealistic to imagine that a hotelier in Ireland could personally deal with every transaction and booking that comes from overseas. The purpose of a channel of distribution is to get sufficient information to the right people, at the right time, in the right place to allow a purchase decision to be made. It can provide a mechanism where the consumer can make a reservation and pay for the required product or service. Traditionally, the bed and breakfast operation worked in this way, however, in recent years even bed and breakfasts are using intermediaries such as tourist offices, travel agents and some even have their own web sites!

Box 9.1 — Distribution of a Rural Tourism Business

Carmel Murray operates a successful Bed and Breakfast on the scenic sky road outside Clifden in Co. Galway. In recent times Carmel has encountered competition from new Bed and Breakfast operations located on the sky road also. Tourists end up checking into these newer Bed and Breakfasts before they reach Carmel's house. As a result of this threat, Carmel decided to try and reach her customers at the booking stage. At this time the town of Clifden was setting up a web site and Carmel saw the opportunity of forming a link with this site. The business now receives ten to fifteen per cent of its reservations through the Internet. Carmel finds it much more cost effective than traditional forms of promotion and distribution.

Intermediaries can have extensive contacts, experience, specialisation and expertise in the tourism trade. As a result they can offer more than a firm can achieve on its own.

DIRECT AND INDIRECT DISTRIBUTION SYSTEMS

A distribution system can be direct or indirect. A *direct system* is one where the supplier or destination communicates directly with the customer (*see* Figure 9.1). Direct systems, such as direct bookings, toll-free (1-800) numbers and automated ticketing machines, offer the supplier many advantages. The system is simple in that buyers and sellers have direct communication. It is profitable in that all the revenue paid by the customer goes to the supplier, and it offers good control as no one else can *direct* the customer elsewhere.

An *indirect system* involves one or more intermediaries between the supplier and customer, such as travel agent, tour operator, incentive travel firm, tourist information office, meeting and convention planners or business travel houses. The role of the travel intermediaries can be a very important factor in deciding the success of a tourism or hospitality business in certain markets, while in others they have a limited role. Domestic holidays tend to be arranged directly by the customer. The customer is more likely to book directly with accommodation providers at the destination and will then proceed to arrange their own transport requirements to and from this location. International travel will usually include the use of a travel agent or similar organisation such as a business travel house. Tour operators are very influential with popular urban destinations such as Dublin, Galway, Killarney and Cork.

FIGURE 9.1 — DISTRIBUTION SYSTEMS IN TOURISM AND HOSPITALITY

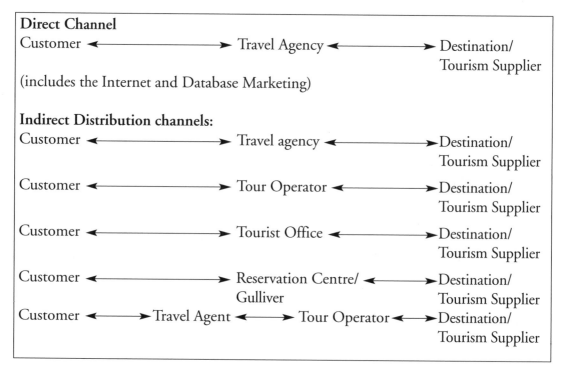

As can be seen from the above diagram there is no single dominant channel. A tourism or hospitality organisation must decide which channels to use and when. Thus, for the marketing manager the crucial decision is which channel(s) to choose in order to achieve their marketing objectives. There are a number of factors outlined by Lumsdon (1997) which affect channel selection.

1. THE NATURE OF THE MARKET

It is essential for marketers to understand how the market(s) in any given country chooses to buy a holiday, book a destination and chooses accommodation or catering. In southern Europe, the travel agent is used much more frequently in booking holidays than in northern Europe. Thus, if one is targeting Italy or Spain, then one would be advised to consider the use of the travel agent as a form of distribution. Bord Fáilte publish a series of market guides, called *Know Your Market* for all the main markets for Irish tourism and are worth consulting in regard to distribution systems. Each of the main countries have their own guides: Britain, US, France, Germany, etc., and they contain lists of the key travel agents and tour operators in each of these markets. Bord Fáilte hold annual workshops and bring key tour operators to Ireland to meet with the industry.

2. RESOURCE COMMITMENT

One of the major problems for lesser known destinations, or small tourism and hospitality operations, is that they are unable to afford the distribution costs of supplying brochures and paying a commission to market intermediaries in order to develop effective distribution channels. Such operations will have to seek other ways of reaching the customer, they may rely on tourist information offices, use database or Internet marketing or become involved in an alliance with a tour operator in the generating market.

3. COST

The cost of distribution has escalated in recent years. Yet it is essential that the tourist intending to come to Ireland can get the right information at the right time and book in a fast and efficient manner. Otherwise, if there is delay or inefficiencies, the tourist can quickly choose another destination. Efficient distribution can be costly. Companies are increasingly seeking to restructure their operations to reduce costs and are examining newer, more cost-effective ways of distribution. This process has been encouraged by new developments in technology and the development of Internet marketing, as well as the greater use of global distribution systems.

4. COMPETITOR ACTIVITY

Newer distribution channels are being developed all the time. At the same time competition between tourism and hospitality suppliers has never been so great. Each supplier is vying for their target market and using distribution channels as a means of gaining competitive advantage. Some tourism and hospitality suppliers have bought into distribution channels or formed alliances with them in order to secure market share.

EXHIBIT 9.1

INTERNET MARKETING *IN ACTION*

HOW TRAVEL AGENTS USE THE INTERNET

Travel and computers have long been linked. Among the earliest international networks were systems developed for airlines, which in turn made them available to travel agents, their principle source of business. Because of its dependency on technology, the travel industry has also been at the forefront of developing technology.

At first, the retail travel trade was apprehensive about the rise of the Internet, and five years ago there was much speculation about how quickly travel agents would become extinct. It has not happened and instead travel agents have warmed to the Internet as a tool — it helps them to do more business.

Travel agencies now encourage clients to use the Internet because that can free their own staff to do what they do best, deal with complicated itineraries. If clients can get basic information such as schedules and destination information for themselves, then the agent can concentrate on the added-value side of the business, the expertise the corporate clients want. Not only are travel agents encouraging the use of the Internet, but they are assisting clients to develop intranet travel applications such as *eTravel* (*see* Exhibit 9.2).
Find out more at sites such as:

www.amadeus.net	Global distribution system for airline availability
www.travelweb.com	Hotels all around the world
www.travelocity.com	Destination information
www.aerlingus.ie	Aer Lingus site
www.britishairways.com	British Airways site with itinerary pricing
www.travigator.com	Links to thousands of travel sites
www.epicurious.com	Travel and food on-line

Source: Adapted from the *Irish Times* and written by Joan Scales, Travel Manager

DEGREES OF INTENSITY OF DISTRIBUTION

A distribution strategy will take into account the degree of intensity planned:

- *Intensive Distribution.* This strategy aims to provide a wide coverage in most generating markets. For example, a larger international hotel chain like Accor would aim for total coverage in all the main markets to Ireland i.e. Britain, Mainland Europe and US. They will use an array of distribution channels, including both direct and indirect which may differ from country to country.

- *Selective Distribution.* This strategy will focus on distribution operations that are designed for selective markets. Use is made of specialist tour operators or use of direct marketing activities. Activity holidays or long haul exotic holidays are distributed this way. The five-star Merrion Hotel in Dublin uses *Leading Hotels of the World* both as a form of promotion and as a means of distribution. In general, hotels belonging to this group can receive up to twenty per cent of their bookings through the group's central reservation system.

- *Exclusive Distribution.* This is seldom encountered in tourism and hospitality, but some destinations and suppliers, such as exclusive island retreats or luxurious hotel resorts, are promoted in the same way as works of art. The buyer is invited to join an exclusive set of customers. In this respect, the very appeal is social status generated by association with other select guests.

Once a company or organisation establishes a channel strategy, the relationship between the supplier and distributor should focus on establishing an effective campaign suited to each particular market. Different methods of distribution may be used to reach different target markets, with distribution activities being scheduled throughout the year. The role of the intermediary is crucial to the distribution process, but there is a shifting emphasis toward direct communication. One of the most interesting developments in distribution has been the emergence of *disintermediation* in the sector, that is the lessening of importance of conventional intermediaries, as suppliers find ways to sell directly to consumers. The prime example in Ireland has been Ryanair who have deliberately encouraged consumers to book directly with them and avoid using a travel agent. Gerard Dunne (1999) has completed interesting research on how tourists book Dublin as a tourist destination and identified that four per cent of accommodation bookings and two per cent of travel bookings use the Internet to book directly (*see* Exhibit 9.4).

THE FUNCTIONS OF A DISTRIBUTION SYSTEM

A distribution system can offer the following:

- Point-of-sale and convenient customer access
- Distribution of tourist information
- Display and merchandising opportunities
- Advice and purchase assistance (itinerary planning)
- Issue of tickets and travel documents
- Receiving and transmitting sales revenue to principals
- Feedback and marketing intelligence for suppliers

COSTS OF DISTRIBUTION

The alternative channels of distribution have been illustrated and range from direct distribution to longer channels of supply. There is no one dominant channel and therefore costs also vary greatly. The costs of any distribution can include some of the following:

- Costs of installing reservations systems, computers, staff training
- Brochure production, distribution, and maintaining supplies at the point-of-sale
- Costs of sales promotion incentives aimed at motivating travel agents and other points of sales such as staff in local tourist offices
- Costs of support visits to distribution intermediaries
- Costs of workshops, training and familiarisation trips whereby travel agents, travel advisors and writers visit destinations to become *familiar* with the product and what it has to offer

ORGANISATION OF DISTRIBUTION CHANNELS

Historically, distribution channels have been a loose collection of independent companies, each showing little concern for the overall channel performance. These conventional systems have lacked strong leadership and have been troubled by damaging conflict and poor performance (Kotler et al, 1996). Channel conflict occurs when channel members act alone in their own short-term best interest. They frequently disagree on the roles each one should play and who should do what for which rewards. As a result of this, distribution channels are shifting from loose collections of independent companies to unified systems.

A *conventional marketing system* consists of one or more independent producers, wholesalers and retailers. Each is a separate business seeking to maximise its own profits, even at the expense of profits for the system as a whole.

A *vertical marketing system* (VMS) consists of producers, tour operators, and retail agents acting as a unified system. VMSs were developed to control channel behaviour and manage channel conflict and its economies through size, bargaining power and elimination of duplication of services. Franchising is an example of a VMS. It is a method of doing business by which a franchisee is granted the right to engage in offering, selling or distributing goods or services under a marketing format that is designed by the franchisor. The franchisor permits the franchisee to use its trademark, name and advertising. The most well-known examples of franchising in Irish catering are McDonald's and Supermacs.

TOURISM AND HOSPITALITY INTERMEDIARIES

Travel Agents

The retail travel agent is primarily in business to advise and sell a range of holidays and other tourism offerings to potential and existing customers. The travel agent is expected to supply information, offer travel advice, sell ancillary services, collect payment and administer the holiday and travel booking. Travel agents book more than ninety-five per cent of cruises, ninety per cent of airline tickets, fifty per cent of car rentals and twenty-five per cent of hotel rooms. Travel agents are changing the way they make accommodation reservations, from phone to electronic distribution (*see* Exhibit 9.2). Hospitality organisations that wish to work with travel agents must become listed in one of the major airline reservation systems. In Europe, the main systems are called Amadeus and Galileo and are referred to as Global Distribution Systems (GDS). In addition, hospitality organisations must be listed in the main guides, send information to key travel agents and keep agents up to date on promotions, packages and special events. Dedicated publications that target travel agents include: *Travel Weekly, Travel Trade* and *Travel Agent.*

Tour Operator

The tour operator brings together the essential elements of a holiday, such as transport, ground handling, accommodation and many other additional features of a destination. The tour operator acts as a catalyst of demand; they interpret the market needs and develop packages that will satisfy these needs. Tour operators buy in bulk and look for low rates, as they must give the consumer a package that is better value than what they could arrange on their own. Tour operators carry out market segmentation, targeting and positioning. Budget Travel is a typical tour operator that segmented the outbound travel market from Ireland and targeted the price-sensitive traveller. Budget Travel positions itself on price and sells few ancillary services.

Business Travel Houses

Major travel companies such as American Express and Wagonlit, as well as a number of smaller companies such as Ayscough or Business Routes, specialise in providing corporate travel. The business travel house operates in a different market as it specialises in business not leisure travel. These houses tend to have a limited base of customers, and each account can be worth between one and five million pounds in turnover per annum. Each account will have its own travel regulations and procedures and the business house usually has a very close working relationship with its clients.

EXHIBIT 9.2

CORPORATE TRAVEL AND THE INTERNET *IN ACTION*

ETRAVEL ARRIVES IN IRELAND

A new travel-planning system called *eTravel* has been introduced to Ireland by Tony Roche Travel and Core Technology. It uses Internet technology customised for a particular business to allow travellers to make their own arrangements for airline seats, hotel accommodation and car hire. The main benefit of eTravel (www.etravel.ie) is that company policy on travel and personnel profiles are loaded into the system and rigidly enforced. The travel manager controls overall policy, but the detail of planning and booking travel devolves to the users.

Behind eTravel is the Worldspan Global Distribution System (GDS), a huge database loaded with schedule and availability information for airlines, hotels and car-hire companies. Also loaded into the system are *consolidated fares*, the excess capacity of airlines other than national carriers, which offer extremely good value for business and economy travel.

Access to this information is live or in *real time* in computer jargon, and bookings made on the screen are automatically sent to a travel agent for tickets to be issued. A major drawback of using the Internet for corporate travel, until now, was the difficulty of knowing which staff members had booked and of obtaining accurate information. As a company resource, eTravel logs and files all corporate bookings and offers the travel manager marketing information system (MIS) data in whatever format is required.

If a company has negotiated special rates with airlines, hotels and car-hire companies, these can be loaded into the system and will appear as the only option for staff to book. Initially, setting up and customising takes time, how much time depends on the company. Unlike many older travel systems, eTravel uses a web browser interface rather than proprietary client software. This is in keeping with the overall idea of devolving travel planning to the consumer — the person who will be travelling. The price for this flexibility is £60 per year, per user, with some room for negotiation based on the amount actually spent on travel.

ELECTRONIC DISTRIBUTION SYSTEMS

A computerised reservation system (CRS) is an electronic database which enables a tourism organisation to manage inventory effectively and distribute it electronically to remote and external partners (Buhalis, 1996). There has been a surge in the provision of information and direct booking using enhanced communications systems, known as on-line systems.

The origins of hotel electronic distribution lie in the computerised reservation systems developed by the airlines in the 1960s. American Airlines was the first to realise the benefits of expanding its computer systems to include on-line terminals with direct reservation capabilities located in travel agencies (Go, 1992). American Airlines first began marketing their CRS extensively in this way immediately following the deregulation of the airline industry in 1982. Their CRS, named Sabre, has assisted American Airlines in capturing a large market share and has been an integral key to the competitive advantage the company has secured in late 1980s. Competition forced other airlines to develop their own systems or to merge with other firms that already possessed the technology. The reservation systems are on-line, so all information provided is current. CRS have also diversified into many other reservation functions such as car rentals, hotel reservations, train reservations and other tourism and hospitality sectors. Table 9.1 below details the ownership structure of the major CRS systems.

TABLE 9.1 — OWNERSHIP STRUCTURE OF THE MAJOR CRS SYSTEMS

Name	Owners
Sabre	American Airlines
System One	Continental Airlines
Worldspan	Delta, Northwest, TWA, Abacus
Amadeus	Air France, Iberia, Lufthansa
Galileo	United Airlines, British Airways, Swissair, KLM, Alitalia, Olympic, Aer Lingus, Australian Airlines
Fantasia	Quantas Airways, Ansett Airlines, Air New Zealand
Abacus	Cathay Pacific, Singapore Airlines, Malaysian Airlines, China Airlines, Royal Brunei Airlines, Dragon Airlines, Silk Air, Worldspan, Infini, Philippines Airlines

Source: Adopted from Seaton and Bennett, 1996

EXHIBIT 9.3

DISTRIBUTION *IN ACTION*

THE EVOLUTION OF HOTEL ELECTRONIC DISTRIBUTION SYSTEMS

The use of information technology to assist in marketing and distributing has become a ubiquitous feature of the hospitality and tourism industry. While the degree of sophistication may vary, its diffusion is almost complete in many sectors of the industry (such as in airlines and travel agencies), but hotels have adopted it much less comprehensively and with less enthusiasm. Marketers no longer question whether hotels should distribute electronically — it has become a competitive necessity, particularly for exposure outside the domestic market. The question now is which (or which combination) of the existing and emerging channels to use to effectively reach the hotel's target market?

From Airline Reservation System to Global Distribution Systems

The origins of hotel electronic distribution lie in the computerised reservation systems developed by the airlines in the 1960s. Originally conceived as internal control systems, they later developed into the offices of high volume travel agencies, giving agents the ability to find information and to make bookings directly on the system. For the airlines, operating a computerised reservation system was expensive, and they quickly realised that their systems could sell other complementary travel products such as car rental and hotel accommodation.

Keen to earn additional income to offset their high capital costs, the system providers gradually increased the range of products and services to include: cruises, tours, railway/bus/ferry tickets, theatre and sport tickets, travel insurance and foreign currency. This in effect gave agents access to a *one-stop shop* for all their information and reservation needs. This broadening of the product/service base was one of the factors which prompted the computerised systems being renamed *Global Distribution Systems* (GDS).

Hotel Central Reservation Systems

The growth in travel that prompted the airlines to develop computerised information systems put similar pressures on hotels. Many of the US hotel chains noted that the best way to serve the customer, and at the same time, provide a valuable service to their members, would be to centralise this function into Central Reservation Offices (CRO). These operated in a similar manner to the airline reservation office. Bookings were further simplified by the introduction of toll-free telephone services (known as *toll-free numbers*) in the 1960s, which allowed customers to find information about and book any unit in a hotel chain by telephoning a single, free number.

Gradually the CRS and GDS began to connect. Travel agents were able to book rooms directly with hotels and receive a response without human intervention. Today, travel agents can *see* directly into the CRS, using GDS as a form of electronic gateway to access the hotels' system. Developing these connections is expensive and is feasible for only the large, international hotel groups as they can spread the development costs among their members. They have sufficient booking volumes to bring the cost per transaction down to an acceptable level. However, the benefits of CRS use are equally as compelling for the small and medium sized hotel group as they are for independent properties. Smaller chains are using several different strategies to make themselves available electronically. These include joining marketing consortia, such as *Leading Hotels of the World*, which provide a wide range of marketing and promotion services to their members. These consortia use cost-effective access to electronic distribution as their key selling point. Another option is to outsource the reservations to a third party such as Utell Reservation System. Making an independent property available electronically is more difficult; some of the alternatives being explored by hotels include Destination Management Systems and attempting to reach the customer directly over the Internet.

Source: This exhibit has been contributed by Peter O'Connor, Institut de Management Hotelier International, Paris

GULLIVER

Gulliver InfoRes is the main electronic distribution service company in Ireland. It is based in Killorglin, Co. Kerry and is owned by FEXCO, an international financial services company, together with Bord Fáilte and the Northern Ireland Tourist Board. The system was designed in 1990. In 1996, Bord Fáilte and the Northern Ireland Tourist Board decided to sell a majority stake in Gulliver to FEXCO following recommendations from consultant's advice that the system would be best run as a stand-alone commercial operation. The new company, Gulliver InfoRes, intends to develop this network into the world's leading destination management system.

Gulliver is a comprehensive database of tourism and hospitality facilities in Ireland. The system links all major tourist information offices with the international call centre in Killorglin, Co Kerry. It also provides the information for the official Bord Fáilte web site (www.ireland.travel.ie). Its promotional literature claims it is a *one-stop shop* opportunity to promote and distribute tourism products and services, as well as the ability to conduct business transactions via the electronic market-place.

The call centre is the new headquarters of the system and operates seven days a week. It has forty travel advisers, taking an average of 1,500 calls a day and caters for eight languages. The projected volume of calls for 1999 is estimated at one million from potential tourists. In addition to the travel advisors, there are fifteen staff on the helpline who tend to the needs of the accommodation providers and tourism industry products.

The aim is to promote the Gulliver service worldwide. Gulliver InfoRes has introduced a universal Freephone number (00 800 668 668 66) in a number of countries, which enables prospective tourists to book their accommodation before coming to Ireland. The number is operational in Ireland, UK, Germany, France, Norway, Sweden, Canada and US. This service is being introduced to other countries worldwide. Bookings are made by credit card and a ten per cent deposit is taken. The customer then pays the accommodation provider the balance of ninety per cent on departure. Gulliver is advertised in Bord Fáilte promotions, Northern Ireland Tourist Board promotions, newspapers, in-flight magazines and trade promotions.

How Gulliver Works

Accommodation providers can link to Gulliver via fax or personal computers (PCs). With the *Faxlink Service*, the accommodation provider can manage a room allocation automatically. Gulliver supplies special pre-printed forms which are barcoded specifically for each premise. Faxlink allows the supplier to update their room allocation and receive confirmation of bookings immediately. The hardware supporting Gulliver is constantly being updated; rapid technological change means that equipment becomes out of date very quickly. One new development is the *Extranet Service* over the

Worldwide Web. This will be a private web site on the Internet, with access restricted to the following users: serviced accommodation providers, self-catering accommodation providers, tourist information providers and marketing organisations. The supplier extranet is promised to be simple to use, reliable, flexible and secure. It will become the communications link between Gulliver and its large membership, replacing the existing Minitel systems.

Finally, Gulliver's computer database also contains a comprehensive and up-to-date listing of all tourist attractions, events, and valuable practical information for the visitor. This information ranges from cultural interests and top regional attractions to concerts, sporting events, conference facilities and transport timetables. For the product and service provider, Gulliver Tourist Information provides an opportunity for advertising, marketing and distribution through Ireland via the tourist information offices, and worldwide through the Bord Fáilte web site. The information held can be updated any time by calling the Gulliver help desk.

Gulliver was initially plagued with technological difficulties and many tourism and hospitality providers rejected the concept of electronic distribution as being too cumbersome and time consuming. As technology develops, huge potential exists for an efficient and effective electronic distribution system that will support the efforts of Bord Fáilte and the industry as everyone pulls together to achieve the goal of marketing Ireland as a tourist destination.

THE INTERNET AS A DISTRIBUTION SYSTEM

The Internet describes a global network of computers that are connected as an open market, known as the Worldwide Web. It has been defined as an 'Internet-wide distribution system that operates on computer networks; a global information retrieval system with information stored at locations called web servers throughout the world'. (McGoey, 1998).

The Internet allows tourism and hospitality suppliers access to potential markets at a much lower cost than using other distribution channels. The system is seen as a new medium for conducting worldwide business transactions, together with a range of marketing activities such as market research, advertising, public relations, distribution, information provision and facilitation of general trading. The latest reports on the Internet as a marketing and distribution tool are encouraging, and all operators agree that the potential for the future is gigantic. Some commentators claim it is going to revolutionise marketing in future years. Kotler claims 'computers will soon be in eighty per cent of American homes. Ireland has 400,000 users in 1999 and increased to almost 600,000 by March 2000. Smart companies are jumping on the Internet bandwagon, using it as a research tool, a communications tool and a selling tool. Marketing will never be the same again. The main benefit of the Internet lies in cost advantage. It is providing a cost-efficient sales and marketing, communication and distribution forum. It also allows the distribution of products and services globally.'

Marketing activity on the Internet includes:

- hotel and airline reservations
- destination marketing
- guidebooks
- booking of package holidays
- information and advice

Some writers feel that technology may even threaten the tourism industry as we know it today. Ody (1998) proclaimed that the *virtual city* is being developed and will be a '3-D digitised database of information that at a point-and-click of a computer mouse, the visitor will be empowered to explore the topography, history, heritage, business, communication, culture and architecture of a city within a virtual format'. The development of the virtual city has created a future opportunity to market the city to an ever-information-hungry global market and give both *competitive advantage* and necessary *added value* to competing destinations.

Exhibit 9.4

DISTRIBUTION *IN ACTION*

THE EFFECTS OF DISINTERMEDIATION ON DUBLIN

One of the most interesting developments in the area of tourism distribution channels in recent years has been the emergence of *disintermediation* in the sector, that is the lessening in importance of conventional intermediaries as suppliers find ways to sell directly to consumers, i.e. a direct distribution described earlier.

One of the main reasons for this trend has been the willingness of suppliers to use technology such as the Internet to sell directly to consumers, thus eliminating intermediaries and, in the process, offering value in terms of lower costs. In contrast to traditional tourism marketing, the Internet gives the customer the means to access information customised to his/her needs. A web site is not something people read, it's something people do (Sterne, 1995). The interactive capabilities of the medium and its global tentacles, coupled with the innovative opportunity for customers to experience (in multimedia) a tourism product or to purchase travel from home, provides a platform for the development of customer relationships in a new dynamic way. Airlines, in particular, have been quick to grasp this new trend with many airlines reporting increases in sales on-line (Hodson, 1998). The accommodation sector which

---

was initially slow to use on-line reservations, is now embracing it at a very fast rate.

The growth in such bookings is likely to continue, with increasing numbers of people having access to the Internet in the future. Skelly (1999) estimates the amount of commerce conducted on the Internet will be worth some $400 billion within the next three years.

The trend of disintermediation is further fuelled by the growing demand for independent travel. An increasing number of people no longer need the security of booking through a travel agency or tour operator, instead they are quite confident making reservations themselves directly with suppliers. This is particularly the case with low-risk or familiar purchases.

Another factor is, of course, the savings that a direct booking yields both in terms of time and money, bringing added value to tourists in these two important ways.

Implications for Organisations that Market Destinations

If destinations can be seen as traded commodities, then a system of distribution channels must also exist. However, destination marketing organisations such as city/regional or national tourism bodies usually tend to deal with the promotion of the product and not the distribution of it. Pollock (1996) suggests that the role of destination marketing organisations 'is to match buyers with sellers, demand with supply, and producers with consumers by positioning and promoting a place, the geographical equivalent of a destination *brand*. Thus, most of these organisations have traditionally been seen as promotion-based entities who do not themselves actually supply the various elements that make up the destination product, i.e. travel, accommodation, activities, attractions, etc. Because the destination product is so diverse, consisting of these varied elements, it is sometimes difficult to think of its distribution in whole terms. This is why the distribution function is often overlooked or ignored when analysing destination marketing organisations.

In order to examine the existence of disintermediation in a real-life context, a survey of visitors to Dublin city furnished data highlighting the channels most used by tourists when making bookings. Dublin represents a typical destination product with a strong and well-established marketing body in Dublin Tourism.

Findings

The key objective of the study was to try to ascertain the methods employed by respondents when booking both their travel to Dublin and their accommodation in Dublin. A list of options was offered and the results can be seen in Table 9.2. The findings show only twenty-one per cent of respondents booked their accommodation through a travel agency, with just a further seven per cent using a tour operator. On the other hand, thirty-three per cent booked directly with the accommodation provider, with a further four per cent using the Internet to make the booking.

Not surprisingly, a higher number of people used travel agencies to book their transport to Dublin (forty-six per cent); however, quite a significant number also used the direct route (thirty-five per cent).

TABLE 9.2 — PERCENTAGE DISTRIBUTION OF RESPONDENTS BY CHANNEL TYPE

Accommodation	%	Travel	%
Directly with accommodation	33	Travel agent	46
Travel agent	21	Directly with transport company	35
Staying with friends or relatives	8	Tour operator	7
Tour operator	7	Part of an organised tour	7
Part of an organised group	7	Through the Internet	2
Directly with local tourist office	6	Other	2
Through the Internet	4	Did not book	1
Did not book	10	Other	4

For the purpose of this research, the nationalities of the respondents were categorised into five main groups with their representation as follows — United Kingdom forty-seven per cent, Mainland Europe twenty-three per cent, North America twenty-one per cent, Northern Ireland two per cent and Other seven per cent. The purpose of doing this was to cross-reference the data so as to highlight any differences in booking behaviour on the basis of these geographical groupings.

TABLE 9.3 — DIRECT AND INDIRECT CHANNEL USAGE BY NATIONALITY CATEGORIES

	Accommodation Booked Direct (as %)	Travel Booked Direct (as %)
UK	36	42
North America	30	18
Mainland Europe	32	38
Northern Ireland	50	25

TABLE 9.3 — DIRECT AND INDIRECT CHANNEL USAGE BY NATIONALITY CATEGORIES *contd.*

	Accommodation Booked with Tour Operator/Travel Agent (as %)	Travel Booked with Tour Operator/Travel Agent (as %)
UK	24	44
North America	37	67
Mainland Europe	27	47
Northern Ireland	25	25
Other	28	50

When the figures are broken down into visitor nationality categories (Table 9.3), it can be seen that the UK tourists were the most likely to use the direct channel option at thirty-six per cent. Interestingly, mainland Europeans and North Americans were not too far behind at thirty-two per cent and thirty per cent respectively. The relatively high figure for North Americans is particularly interesting, considering the higher perceived risk involved in a direct booking to Dublin for American and Canadian visitors who would be traditionally high users of travel agents. In fact, just thirty-seven per cent said they used a travel agent or tour operator. The number of mainland Europeans using a travel agent or tour operator was even smaller at twenty-seven per cent. This again is quite interesting considering the linguistic, cultural, and in some cases geographical barriers involved in a trip to Dublin.

The number of visitors booking travel to Dublin directly with the transport provider was quite significant in the case of the UK (forty-two per cent) and mainland Europe (thirty-eight per cent) but quite low in the case of North America (eighteen per cent). This seemed to indicate that North American visitors were much more likely to use a travel agent or tour operator to book their travel (sixty-seven per cent) rather than their accommodation (thirty-seven per cent).

The findings also show the percentage of respondents who used the Internet to book directly. Although the figures may seem relatively small (four per cent for accommodation and two per cent for travel), they are nonetheless significant in that they would not have even existed a few years ago.

The findings also highlight the number of visitors (six per cent) who used the local tourist office (Dublin Tourism) to make their accommodation reservations. This figure again seems relatively low and may need further analysis in terms of querying the appropriateness of providing such a service in the current climate of disintermediation.

The channels through which visitors to a destination purchase their holiday or components thereof is of vital importance to destination marketing organisations. The need for these bodies to be aware of the reservation-making behaviour of its visitors is crucial for a number of reasons. Firstly, destination marketing organisations usually perform some kind of advisory role for tourism suppliers in the destination area. It is imperative, therefore, that they be aware of important developments in the industry such as disintermediation, so as to perform this role effectively. Secondly, many destination marketing organisations often perform an intermediary role themselves by offering reservation services to visitors. This means that any changes in the booking behaviour of its visitors will have a direct impact on them. In the case of Dublin city, the phenomenon of disintermediation seems to be borne out in the survey findings in which a very significant number of visitors booked accommodation and travel directly with the product providers.

This is a fact that needs to be acknowledged by both Dublin Tourism and the tourism suppliers in the city. It also begs further analysis. The findings don't show the exact circumstances of the direct bookings. For example, which medium was used (telephone, fax, e-mail, mail, guidebook, etc.) when making the booking. Such information will be very useful for destination marketing organisations, both by helping them to perform their own reservation-making services more efficiently (if they provide such a service) and by advising the tourism providers in their destination area more effectively.

Source: This Exhibit was contributed by Gerard Dunne, Lecturer in Marketing at the Faculty of Tourism and Food, Dublin Institute of Technology

In addition to the phenomenon of disintermediation outlined above, the concept of *reintermediation* is now also being discussed. Reintermediation refers to the process by which intermediaries, both new and existing, are establishing themselves in cyberspace. A good example of this is in the GDS system, Sabre, the highly successful Travelocity Internet site.

CHAPTER SUMMARY

One of the most complex and difficult decisions facing the tourism and hospitality marketer is the development of an efficient distribution system. The purpose of a channel of distribution is to get sufficient information to the right people at the right time to allow a purchase decision to be made; and to provide a mechanism where the consumer can make a reservation and pay for the required product and service. Thus, various forms of intermediaries are used to distribute. The system can be direct or indirect. The selection of channel members is influenced by the nature of the market, resources available, cost and competitor activity. The most popular types of intermediaries in the tourism and hospitality industry are travel agents, tour operators, business travel houses and of course electronic distribution systems such as computer reservation systems (CRS) and global distribution systems (GDS). Gulliver is Ireland's electronic distribution system. A key trend is the greater use of the Internet as a means of distribution by suppliers in the tourism and hospitality industry as well as corporate travel managers and travel agents.

KEY WORDS AND PHRASES

Distribution System	Intermediaries
Direct System	Indirect System
Distribution Channel	Travel Agents
Tour Operators	Business Travel Houses
Electronic Distribution Systems	Gulliver

QUESTIONS FOR REVIEW

1. Why do tourism and hospitality operations need distribution systems?
2. Define the term a *channel of distribution.*
3. What are the major differences between a distribution channel for a business making a tangible product such as shoes and a business producing hospitality and tourism products?
4. What is the difference between a direct and an indirect system. Give examples of how a hotel might use both systems.
5. What are the functions of a distribution system?
6. Explain the difference between a travel agent and a tour operator?

QUESTIONS FOR DISCUSSION

1. Discuss how you think technology will change distribution channels in the hospitality and tourism industries. Carry out library research on recent journal articles to help you decide.
2. Interview a manager from a local hotel or interpretative centre and find out how many forms of distribution that business uses.

REFERENCES AND FURTHER READING

Dunne, G., 'The Effects of Disintermediation of Destination Marketing Organisations', *TTRA Conference Proceedings*, September: Dublin 1999.
Go, F., 'The role of computerised reservation systems in the hospitality industry', *Tourism Management:* 1992.

Kotler, P., Bowen, J. and Makens, J., *Marketing for Tourism and Hospitality*, Prentice Hall: New Jersey 1996.

Lumsdon, L., *Tourism Marketing*, Thomson Business Press: London 1997.

McGoey, I., *Marketing on the Internet*, Oak Tree Press: Dublin 1998.

O'Connor, P. and Frew, A.J., 'The Evolution of Hotel Electronic Distribution', *EuroCHRIE Conference Proceedings*, Oslo 1998.

Pollock, A., 'An integrated marketing management information system for destinations', The Strategy Group, UK: 1996.

Skelly, B., 'E Commerce: show me the money', *Irish Computer* 23(i), p. 26–29: 1999.

Stern, J., *World Wide Web Marketing: Integrating the interest into your marketing strategy*, John Wiley & Sons: New York 1995.

USEFUL WEB SITES

www.amadeus.net	Global distribution system for airline availability
www.travelweb.com	Hotels all around the world
www.travelocity.com	Destination information
www.aerlingus.ie	Aer Lingus site
www.britishairways.com	British Airways site with itinerary pricing
www.traveldirect.com	Travel Direct
www.travigator.com	Links to thousands of travel sites
www.epicurious.com	Travel and food on-line
www.expedia.com	Microsoft Travel and Tourism Site
www.lonelyplanet.com	Lonely Planet Site

CHAPTER 10

Marketing Communications Mix: 1

INTRODUCTION

Communicating with customers is vital to attract new visitors and to act as a reminder to past visitors. Large tourism and hospitality organisations, especially national tourism boards and multinational hotel and travel companies have substantial advertising and promotion budgets which need to be carefully managed. Even the smallest company has to plan their communication strategy carefully, even if this extends to no more than brochure design. As we shall see in the following two chapters, advertising is only one of a huge, and increasing, number of ways of communicating with a target audience. These various means such as advertising, public relations and direct marketing, need to fit together in order to achieve marketing objectives.

CHAPTER OBJECTIVES

Following this chapter, students should be able to:

- Describe the communication process, and the nature of the marketing communications mix
- Describe the nature of advertising in the tourism and hospitality industry and the role that it plays as part of the wider range of communication activities
- Understand the process of organising a tourism and hospitality advertising campaign from the setting of objectives to the evaluation of advertising activity
- Describe the various types of advertising media in Ireland that can be used by the tourism sector
- Describe the role, and nature, of public relations in the communication mix for tourism and hospitality organisations

MARKETING COMMUNICATIONS TODAY

On a daily basis we are bombarded with information and news from a huge variety of sources. These sources include news reports on television and radio, stock market information on the Internet, in-store promotional material, outdoor signs and personal conversations with friends. Many of these information sources are from commercial organisations seeking to influence consumer attitudes and purchasing; and the variety of means for such organisations to reach consumers is increasing at an enormous rate. As well as brand-new ways such as the Internet and e-mail, traditional ways of communicating with consumers, such as television and radio, are also changing rapidly.

There has been an explosion in the number and variety of media available to us. Local radio stations have achieved high listenership levels in the areas they serve. State-run media organisations such as RTE and BBC have seen their share of the audience being whittled away in the face of new competition. New national commercial radio and television stations have emerged such as Today FM and TV3. Cable television is rapidly offering people vastly increased numbers of viewing options. The advent of digital television is going to further change the media landscape and hundreds of channels will soon be available. Of even greater importance, these digital networks offer the potential for two-way, or interactive, communications. Consumers in the new millennium will be able to comment directly on programmes as they happen, choose their own camera angles for viewing and order products and services. This new era of interactive communications is an exciting one for marketers, as it offers the opportunity of tailoring communications to very small market segments, including the opportunity of personal two-way communication. The changes being predicted will be felt particularly in the tourism and hospitality sectors.

Until recently magazines and specialist guidebooks accounted for much of the advertising spending by Irish tourism marketers. However, huge changes in the way tourism organisations advertise are being predicted in the next decade. With the existing communication channels many more opportunities to target are opening up — local radio, new national television and radio station as well as new newspapers all offer tourism marketers choice in where to advertise. New media such as digital and inter-active television, Internet and multimedia offer exciting means to reach potential customers at low cost, even on a global basis.

MARKETING AND MARKETING COMMUNICATIONS

Let us first address an area of confusion. The terms *promotion mix* and *communications mix* are often used interchangeably in marketing literature, leading to some confusion. Both terms refer to exactly the same thing. The term communication mix is more popular today, as it better reflects a consumer-oriented perspective — namely we wish to communicate with consumers.

Marketing communications may be defined as *the process by which a marketer builds and communicates a set of elements to a defined target group with the intention of securing a specific response.*

Each element of the mix needs to interact in the right way with the other elements. The availability of a product will have a bearing on the price that can be charged, and will influence the perception of the product's quality. The quality of the product will influence the price that is charged. Marketing communications has a bearing on all other elements.

The marketing communications process does not entail solely communicating with the end consumer. The target for the communication can be quite varied. A tourism company would have to communicate with, among others:

- their own employees to keep them informed and motivated — this is part of the process known as *internal marketing*
- government agencies such as departments of tourism
- financial institutions to secure funding for new projects
- tour operators to keep them informed of new services and product lines
- the media and other opinion leaders to maintain a favourable company image

Finally, the company needs to communicate with the wider public to create and maintain a favourable *corporate image*.

COMPONENTS OF THE MARKETING COMMUNICATIONS MIX

The marketing communications mix *consists of a number of elements that can be used individually or in combination with each other to achieve a defined set of communication objectives.*

The major elements which comprise the marketing communications mix are:

- Advertising
- Public Relations
- Sales Promotion
- Direct Marketing
- Personal Selling

This chapter will deal with Advertising and Public Relations, with the other elements examined in the following chapter.

However, at this stage it is helpful to define each and provide a quick overview of their role in the overall communication mix.

Advertising is paid, non-personal communication in a mass medium (television, press, cinema, outdoor, Internet) used to communicate with a target audience.

Public Relations includes all activities designed to enhance and maintain favourable communication by companies and their brands with a variety of publics. These publics can include the Government, the financial institutions, the media and the general public.

Sales Promotion usually complements the organisation's advertising, personal selling efforts and publicity and includes those activities designed to encourage user-purchase at point-of-sale and dealer effectiveness, e.g. in-store displays, demonstrations and exhibitions. It is typically used as a short-term, rather than strategic, tool.

Direct Marketing is a two-way system of marketing, which uses one or more advertising media to communicate directly with consumers and/or obtain direct response from them.

Personal Selling is the process by which a salesperson communicates on a one-to-one basis with a potential buyer. The process can be conducted face-to-face or by telephone or videoconference etc.

Each element of the mix can be used on its own, though this is rarely the case. Usually one element is complemented by the use of at least one other element.

The process by which companies seek to co-ordinate several elements is called *integrated marketing communications.* The Bord Fáilte/NITB Tourism Brand Ireland campaign is often cited as a good example of integrated marketing communications. Print advertisements were reflective of the television commercials. Direct mail and brochures were designed in similar vein, as was the Internet site. Stands at overseas tourism fairs were also carefully co-ordinated with the overall campaign. The same colour designs, or *colourways*, were used throughout, with green and purple the dominant colours.

FIGURE 10.1 — EXAMPLE FROM TV ADVERTISEMENT

It is important that each element of the communications mix should integrate with the other elements of the mix, in order that a coherent message is communicated to the target market.

THE COMMUNICATION PROCESS

As stated earlier, today's market-place is a crowded one with consumers faced with a bewildering array of messages competing for their attention. The *noise* created by these messages is amplified as they are carried on a continually expanding number of media, both traditional and new. Marketers need a deep understanding of how the process of communication works if they are to break through the clutter that exists. The communication process is illustrated in Figure 10.2 below.

FIGURE 10.2 — THE COMMUNICATION PROCESS

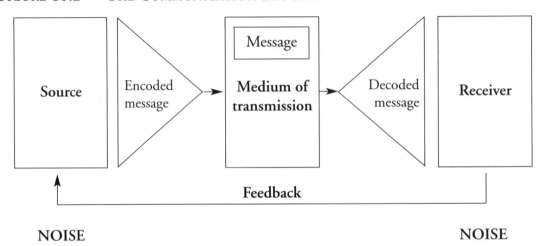

The *source*, or sender, of the message is the organisation or individual who wishes to communicate with a target market, called the *receiver* or *audience*.

The *message* is what the source wants to communicate and to be understood.

In order to convey a message, we need to encode it into a form that makes the correct impression. The encoding may take the form of words, pictures or both.

The message will require some form of *medium* to carry it. The medium, or media in plural form, can take a variety of forms including traditional (television, posters, radio), new (Internet, Minitel, touch screens) or non-traditional (beer mats, T-shirts, sandwich boards, bank automatic teller machines (ATMs), shopping trolleys).

The receiver has to *decode* the message. Essentially this refers to the way that the message is interpreted by the receiver. A tourism resort may use a glamorous model in an advertisement with the intention of communicating an up-market image. However, the receiver may interpret the model's presence negatively and feel that the resort is too exclusive for them.

This problem of decoding is made more problematic by the presence of *noise* in the communication channel. Noise is *the presence of any stimulus that is competing for the attention of the receiver, and which inhibits or prevents the full or partial interpretation of a message.*

The most obvious example of noise is competing advertising. A directory of country house hotels, for example, may feature dozens of such properties. This makes it extremely difficult for any individual country house hotel to have their advertisement noticed, let alone remembered. A company's image is also likely to affect how a message is interpreted. If we have had a favourable experience with a particular tour operator in the past, we are more likely to accept a new message from such a company. Certain media have also a higher likelihood of noise occurring. Advertisements aired during breakfast television are examples. In the morning there are numerous distractions that will affect our ability to concentrate on a message. By way of contrast, cinema advertising has fewer diversions to cause misinterpretation of the message.

HOW DOES MARKETING COMMUNICATION WORK?

Having examined the principles governing the process of communication, we now turn our attention to how communication works in a marketing context. A simplistic view consists of what is termed the *black-box effect*, namely that any communication of a message (advertising, direct mail, personal sale etc.) is processed in the consumer's mind (the black box) to result in a certain outcome (sales). This is depicted in Figure 10.3 below.

FIGURE 10.3 — THE BLACK BOX EFFECT

Naturally, the above model has come to be regarded as much too elementary to illustrate the complex nature of the effects caused by a communication. A more elaborate model of the way that communication works is what is known as the AIDA model, shown in Figure 10.4 below.

FIGURE 10.4 — THE AIDA MODEL

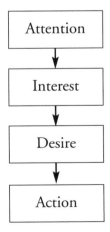

The AIDA model was originally proposed to explain how personal selling worked, but it soon became adopted to explain how marketing communication worked in general. The communication process takes the audience through a series of sequential steps, with each logically following on from each other. This sequential characteristic of the AIDA model, and other communication models, is called a *hierarchy of effect*. The receiver is taken through progressive steps (hierarchy) culminating in some form of action (effect).

The first stage in the communication hierarchy, according to the model, is to gain the *attention* of the audience. If a company cannot gain attention then, no matter how wonderful an advertisement is, it will not be effective.

The second stage is to secure the receiver's *interest* in the message. Many people who attend to a message will not necessarily be interested in it. Someone who owns their own holiday home in Ireland may not be very interested in advertisements for overseas destinations.

The third stage in the AIDA process is to create a *desire* for the product. The construction of the message is critical in this respect. The consumer needs to feel that the product solves problems that they identify.

The fourth and final stage in the process, *action*, may mean purchasing a product (a sale), but in a tourism context, it might also refer to the customer, having viewed a television commercial for a destination, then making a telephone call requesting a brochure be sent to them.

A second, and more recent, form of hierarchy of effects model is called DAGMAR. This is an acronym for *Designing Advertising Goals for Measured Advertising Results*. Although its developer Russell Colley proposed it for the advertising sector, its application is to the broader marketing communication mix. Figure 10.5 depicts the model associated with the DAGMAR approach.

FIGURE 10.5 — THE **DAGMAR** MODEL

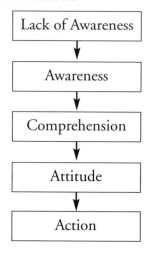

The above model is similar to the AIDA model, but there are a number of important differences. Firstly, the DAGMAR process identifies a pre-awareness stage. This is useful, as we shall see in our examination of the advertising campaign, as it focuses our attention on the fact that there is usually a much greater number of people unaware of our message than are aware. Increasing the awareness level is often a major challenge of many advertising campaigns.

Only after awareness is generated can the task of improving comprehension begin. Comprehension refers to the way that the message is understood. This will be affected by the physical attributes of the product featured in the communication, but equally important, the emotional and brand-building components of the message. The way in which the message is understood is often referred to as *consumer out-take* in the advertising industry. The attitude component of the process refers to the extent to which a consumer is persuaded to purchase the product, or to the extent that their existing views are supported by the message.

The final stage, *action*, is similar to the AIDA model, referring to a potential trial of a new product, sending away for more information, or taking some other action demanded by the sender of the message. Colley's model did, however, specify more clearly than earlier ones, the objectives for action that could be subsequently measured, to assess the effectiveness of the communication campaign.

Both of the hierarchy of effects models described above are not without their critics. The most commonly mentioned flaw in such models is the fact that they assume the receiver is a passive recipient of the message.

In fact, communication is a more complex phenomenon with *two-way flows* of information between sender and recipient. This is becoming ever more the case with the advent of interactive technologies such as the Internet. In addition a *two-stage effect* is also evident, where a recipient of a message in turn communicates to a third-party about the message. This happens, for example, when we discuss advertisements we have seen with friends.

Having discussed the overall communication process, the remainder of this chapter is devoted to discussing two elements of the communication mix that have a particularly important role in generating awareness and in altering images of the company; advertising and public relations.

ADVERTISING DEFINED

Advertising may be defined as:

'…paid communication by an identified sponsor through a non-personal medium.'

(Buttle, 1986)

The above definition recognises that advertising is a form of communication. Accordingly, the management of an advertising campaign needs to be consistent with the communication process with senders, receivers, a message and a means of carrying the message — a communication channel. The definition also distinguishes advertising from other forms of communication where the sender is not immediately identifiable such as public relations and sponsorship. Finally, the definition emphasises advertising's non-personal nature, as distinct from other communication mix elements such as direct marketing.

Other definitions include:

'…The word advertising means drawing attention to something, or notifying somebody of something. You can advertise by word of mouth, quite informally and locally, and without incurring great expense. But if you want to inform a large number of people about something, you might need to advertise in the more familiar sense of the word, by public announcement.'

(Dyer, 1982)

'Advertising is the use of mass communications media to influence existing or potential consumers' attitudes or behaviours toward a product or service.'

(Bord Fáilte, *A Guide to Effective Consumer Marketing for Tourism Enterprises*)

The stages in designing an advertising campaign are shown in Figure 10.6 below.

FIGURE 10.6 — STEPS IN DESIGNING AN ADVERTISING CAMPAIGN

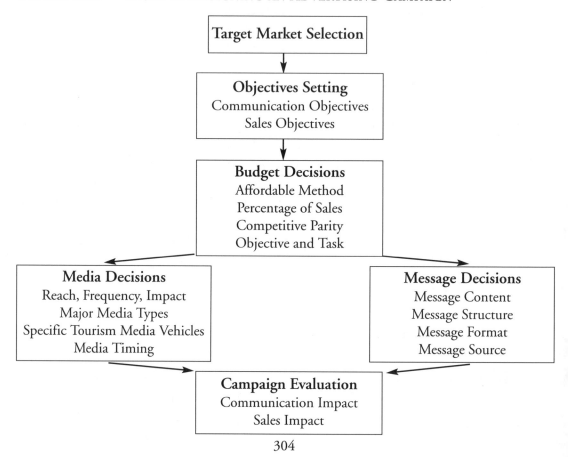

We now examine each of these stages in turn.

Target Market Selection

A starting point in any media strategy must be a clear understanding of the actual target market. The process of identifying and selecting target markets was discussed earlier in this book. Unless we know exactly whom we are trying to reach then much of the advertising budget will be wasted. If we can identify our market in demographic terms then the process of media selection is relatively easy. For Irish media, a huge wealth of demographic data is available to advertisers through three sources. Radio data can be obtained from JNLR (Joint National Listenership Research), magazines and newspapers through JNRR (Joint National Readership Research) and television data from TAM (Television Audience Measurement).

Objective Setting

There is considerable difficulty in determining the extent to which advertising can contribute to a particular level of sales and visitor numbers. Many other variables are at work, such as the weather, exchange rates, the economic state of source markets etc. Consequently, there has been a focus on assessing the broader communication impact of advertising. This view sees advertising as having a range of potential objectives, centred on the AIDA model discussed earlier:

- attracting *Attention*
- creating *Interest*
- fostering *Desire*
- inspiring *Action*

Communication and Sales Objectives

For an example of how the AIDA model might apply to the tourism sector, consider the case of a company that has a number of self-catering cottages in different locations. Some possible *broad objectives* the company might have for advertising include:

- To generate greater profits for the company by attracting new people to try the cottages
- To improve the competitive position or corporate image by emphasising the quality of the cottages in advertising messages

Some possible *specific and quantifiable objectives* may be:

- To raise sales from £20,000 per annum to £25,000 per annum
- To raise the level of awareness of the cottages from ten per cent to fifteen per cent of the market
- To generate 300 enquiries as a result of the advertisement

Some possible *qualitative subobjectives*:

- To convey information and remind past customers of the quality of service
- To create desire among potential visitors
- To improve the image of a specific group of cottages
- To help justify a high price

The final stage, *action*, need not only refer to the achievement of a sale. Few tours, for example, are booked solely on the basis of seeing an advertisement in a magazine. More commonly, the advertisement acts as a spur to readers to contact the tour operator using a telephone number or e-mail indicated in the advertisement. The *call to action* to the consumer is often to request a brochure, with a telephone operator dispatching a brochure direct to the consumer. In their most recent television advertising campaign, Bord Fáilte's use of short ten-second commercials was aimed at getting the viewer to respond by sending for further information in the form of a brochure. As the ultimate booking will still usually be made through a travel agent, the retail trade has come to regard this advertising as complementary, rather than competing.

Budget Decisions

Tourism marketers typically set a budget in one of four ways, as seen below:

Percentage of Sales Method

The most common method is to set advertising at some percentage of current or antici-pated sales. Tourism enterprises in Ireland have typically spent about two per cent of their sales budget on advertising.

Competitive Parity Method

Another approach is to spend the same percentage as competitors in the industry. While this is a very common approach it does not leave room for much flexibility of response to changing conditions.

Affordable Method

Another common method is to base spending on what the company thinks it can afford. If it is exceeding its budgeted profit, then marketing management are allowed to spend more on advertising and promotion. Again there is no logic in this approach. Changes are not related to the profit opportunities that can be exploited by advertising.

Objective and Task Method

Here the company spends according to the response required and the nature of the situation. At the start of a business operation there is a need to spend heavily to build awareness and trial, even though this may affect profitability at a crucial stage in the business. Subsequently, as the product becomes better known, the amount required for advertising may be reduced. This is the ideal way to set budgets.

The following example gives an indication of how an advertising budget might work in practice for a fifty-bedroom hotel.

Overall advertising spend established at 0.75 per cent of a £2·2 million turnover = £16,500

The three main objectives are:

- Maximising business from existing customers
  method: direct mail
  budget: £5,000
- Improving firm's reputation and profile
  method: by weekly advertisement in local paid newspaper
  budget: 52 × £100 = £5,200
- Reaching all residents of this area
  method: by monthly tactical advertisements in the local freesheets
  budget: 12 × £400 = £4,800

This leaves a figure of £1,560 for contingencies to which may be added any funds promised by principles for joint promotions.

Once the budget is established, then it is sensible to establish a plan that anticipates which products are to be featured, at what times of the year, and by which medium.

Message Decisions

Once the decision has been made about whom is being targeted and what the objectives are, the next task is to produce a message to achieve the objective. This is the creative part of the advertising process. There are no magic formulae to create advertising that will be remembered and motivate the prospect. This is particularly the case in the tourism and hospitality sectors.

In developing creative advertisements the intangibility of the tourism and hospitality product poses real difficulties. While we can show a beautiful landscape in a newspaper feature article, how do you illustrate a stay in the Donegal Gaeltacht, and convincingly communicate the warmth of welcome received during such a holiday?

An initial problem in advertising the tourism product is that it must be presented in a way that will attract attention. Typically, the potential tourist will be faced with dozens of advertisements vying for their attention in magazines and newspapers. Secondly, the advertisement must be motivating, clear and credible. Four aspects of the message should be considered: *content, structure, format* and *source*.

Message Content

Content refers to *the appeal the advertisement will employ to motivate the customer.* There are two broad types of appeal as explained below.

Rational Appeals: focus on the functional benefits that the product delivers. In a tourism context a hotel may seek to persuade the customer that it offers the best value or location. A rural tourism organisation may promote its area's tranquillity and range of passive leisure activities. The press advertisement shown in Figure 10.7 is an example of the use of such a rational appeal.

FIGURE 10.7 — PRESS ADVERTISEMENT SHOWING USE OF RATIONAL APPEAL

The advertiser, Irish Country Holidays, is emphasising price to encourage readers to contact their central reservations' number to make further enquiries. The *action* that the advertisement seeks to elicit is to encourage the reader to request further information.

Emotional Appeals: in contrast to rational ones, seek to evoke positive feelings about a brand to motivate purchase. Much of the recent Bord Fáilte campaigns have used emotional appeals. The commercials were designed to generate a strong interest in Ireland, and a sense that a holiday here would be a combination of personally unique experiences.

Message Structure

The order in which the selling points are presented in an advertisement can also influence its persuasive power. Usually, it is felt that the most positive points should be made at the beginning of an advertisement, rather than last or in the middle. It is also the case that comparative advertising can work but mainly for lesser-known destinations with a lower profile than the market leader.

Message Format

Format includes the following:

- *Copy:* refers to the words, either written or spoken, in the advertisement
- *Artwork:* consists of the illustrations that are used
- *Layout:* is the physical arrangement of headlines, subheadlines, copy, illustrations and brand identification

The creativity with which the elements are put together has a major impact on the effectiveness of the advertisement. In any press advertising the headline is particularly important, because gaining the attention of the reader is critical to success.

Message Source

The source in the advertisement may be the company itself, the brand name or the actor who endorses the product. Research shows that the effectiveness of a source depends upon its credibility and attractiveness.

Credibility means the degree to which the source is perceived as being an expert with respect to the product and is unbiased in the claims being made for it.

During the mid-1990s the British food and drink celebrity Keith Floyd featured in Bord Fáilte television advertisements in the UK. These sought to make Ireland appear a more fun and lively place to holiday, as well as addressing perceived weaknesses in the image of Ireland's food and drink offerings. As another example, in the run-up to Ireland's hosting of the start of the 1997 Tour de France, Irish cycling legend Stephen Roche featured in advertising in France, promoting Ireland as a cycling holiday.

Attractiveness is the second factor affecting the source's effectiveness and is the receiver's perception of the prestige of the source, the degree to which the source is similar to the receiver, and his or her physical or personal attractiveness.

One way tourism and hospitality marketers seek to enhance message credibility and attractiveness is through the use of advertorials.

Advertorials are articles that are part editorial and part advertising. Through their style and layout, they convey the impression they have been written in an impartial way by the editorial staff at the publication in which they feature. In the course of the article, the paying company is mentioned in favourable terms. This approach is felt to lead to higher acceptance of the message. Often such advertorials are placed in conjunction with a regular advertisement.

Media Decisions

The actual choice of media chosen also has a powerful impact on consumer perceptions. Media is the collective term for a medium which can be defined as any means of carrying a message. Newspapers, magazines and guidebooks are among the most popular media used by tourism marketers. Choosing the media to carry a message can sometimes be as important as the actual message itself. *The medium is the message* is a well-known phrase to those in the advertising industry. Advertising in a prestigious commercial guidebook such as the *Johanson Hotel Guide* or the *Hotel Travel Index* can say more for an enterprise than advertising in a regional newspaper. Many prestigious hotels choose to advertise on the back page of the *Irish Times* to confer a degree of exclusivity on themselves.

A key decision in putting together a media plan is to strike a balance between ensuring that enough people are exposed to your advertisement, and making sure that there are enough exposures at an individual level to stimulate a response.

Reach, Frequency and Impact

Reach (Coverage): refers to the number of people who are exposed to an advertisement during a specified period. For example, if you placed a single advertisement in the *Irish Independent* this would be a coverage level of twenty-four per cent of all adults (equating to the daily readership level).

Frequency: is the number of times that an average person is exposed to the message. As a hypothetical example, an advertisement placed on two consecutive nights in the *Irish Independent* might deliver a frequency of 1·2. This means that the advertisement was seen on average 1·2 times. This reflects the fact that some people will have the opportunity to see the advertisement once only, whereas some will be able to see it twice. It is important to note that the average frequency of 1·2 refers only to those who have been exposed to the advertisement at least once. It does not mean that on average across the whole population the average frequency is 1·2.

Impact (Weighting): Where an individual is exposed once to an advertisement this is called an impact. Advertisers must also consider the impact of the campaign as a whole. The impact of a campaign across the whole audience is a function of reach and frequency and is often measured in Gross Rating Points (GRPs).

Television Rating (TVR) is the most commonly used term when buying television media. A campaign's impact is determined as follows;

$$\text{GRPs} = \text{Reach (r)} \times \text{Frequency (f)}$$

For the *Irish Independent* example above, this would lead to an impact level of:

$$24 \times 1 \cdot 2 = 27 \text{ points}$$

If a campaign has an impact level of 300 points this means that 300 impacts per 100 of the target audience were made.

Some advertising agencies have developed a way of incorporating both reach and frequency into media schedule assessment.

Suppose a hotel places an advertisement six times in a national newspaper.

1+ cover = the percentage of the target market who are exposed to an advertisement at least once. If 1+ cover is twenty-five per cent, this means that a quarter of the *target audience* will see an advertisement at least once.

4+ cover = the percentage of the target market who are exposed to an advertisement at least four times. If 4+ cover for the advertisement is ten per cent, for example, this means that a tenth of the target audience will see the advertisement at least four times. Naturally, this percentage will be less than the 1+ cover.

To increase effectiveness of advertising a number of repetitions are required. Most customers, especially in tourism, will not make a response having seen only one advertisement. On the other hand it is possible to overexpose an audience to an advertisement. This is known as *wearout* and may indeed prove counter-productive, if the respondent becomes annoyed at too many exposures. This reinforces the need to invest a higher degree of attention to the design of advertisements, in order that they have a durability to be used in successive campaigns.

Major Media Types

In evaluating various media, the following questions should be considered.

Publications: (newspapers, directories and magazines)

- How many copies are produced and distributed?
- Of these, how many are distributed in the catchment area?
- Will the publication have a high *pass-on* quality?
- Are they wanted or unwanted, i.e. paid for or *freesheets*?
- How frequently are they published and how long is their effective life?
- Is colour advertising available?
- What is the reproduction method and quality like?
- Can the position of the advertisement be changed?
- What is the image of the publication: up-market, youthful, controversial etc.?

Television or Radio

- How many listeners or viewers can one expect on average?
- Is it possible to choose the days and times and relate them to a relevant programme?
- What proportion of listeners or viewers live within the catchment area?
- Are customers likely to be attracted from a wider area than would otherwise use your services?

Teletext or Internet

- How easy is it for the viewer to access your site?
- How many viewers can be expected to see the advertisement?
- How quickly and at what cost can the site details be amended?
- Where exactly is the advertisement to appear?
- What links has your site to other relevant sites that are of interest to the market?

Table 10.1 outlines the major advantages and disadvantages of the major media types.

TABLE 10.1 — MEDIA ADVANTAGES AND DISADVANTAGES

Media	Advantages	Disadvantages
Newspapers	Wide reach possible Can be targeted geographically Topicality is possible Can be placed in specific feature sections Detailed copy possible	Can be prone to clutter with competing offers, especially some holiday supplements Cost of advertising in overseas newspapers is high High rates for occasional advertisers
Magazines	Good at targeting specific interest groups High demographic and geographic selectivity Credibility and prestige High quality reproduction Long life and *pass along*	Long purchase lead times Some waste circulation Usually no guarantee of position Clutter Is costly for small enterprises to use overseas magazines
Television	Combines, sight, sound and motion Appealing to the senses High attention High reach (coverage)	High absolute cost High clutter Fleeting exposure Less audience selectivity Increasingly fragmented audiences
Radio	Mass use High demographic and geographic selectivity Relatively low cost Good for local profile	Audio presentation only Lower attention than TV generally A passive medium Fleeting exposure

TABLE 10.1 — MEDIA ADVANTAGES AND DISADVANTAGES *contd.*

Media	Advantages	Disadvantages
Guidebooks	High audience attention Good targeting potential International exposure relatively cheaply Good for direct response	Competitive clutter Lead times are high Circulation is variable
Internet	Global coverage at low cost per impact Visual medium High attention Direct response including commercial transactions possible	Huge clutter problem Accessing site may be very difficult Cost of developing and maintaining quality site is high Narrow range of target markets
Teletext (Aertel, Ceefax, Oracle etc.)	Very good at targeting, especially for domestic markets Good direct response media Can be amended rapidly Low cost	Competitive clutter Not very widely used yet Restricted visual capacity
Outdoor	Good at targeting visiting tourists in specific locations High impact High repeat exposure	High relative production costs Planning restrictions No audience selectivity Creative limitations

Many commentators see the traditional advertising media coming under increasing threat from the new media, where the user is offered greater control and choice through interactivity. Already the Internet is proving to be a powerful tool for some tourism marketers. Tourism is one area where the potential for electronic commerce is very strong. As consumers become more confident in using the Internet and reassured about the security of transactions, then we shall see the rapid growth in the use of the Internet for booking and paying for holidays, as well as continuing to provide information to consumers.

Specific Tourism Media Vehicles

Television, newspapers and the Internet are all examples of media types. Media vehicles are *the specific channels that will be used within each media type*. Therefore, the *Irish Independent*, *Irish Times* and *Sunday Business Post* are examples of newspaper vehicles. TV3, Ulster Television and Network 2 are examples of television vehicles.

There are a large variety of specialist media vehicles, especially magazines, that tourism marketers can use to target tourists. Some target specific special interest groups such as anglers and walkers; there are also several holiday- and destination-type magazines. Table 10.2 gives illustrative prices for major magazines.

TABLE 10.2 — TOURISM MEDIA VEHICLES

Magazine	Approx. Rate for Full Page Colour Advertisement	Frequency of Publication	Circulation
American Express Hotels and Restaurants Guide to Ireland	£2,000	Every 2 Years(June)	20,000
Anglers Guide to Ireland (in association with Bord Fáilte)	£2,000	Annual (November)	70,000
Be Our Guest (Irish Hotels Federation)	£3,475	Annually	260,000
Celtic Journey (Irish Ferries Continental)	£3,100	Annually (April)	50,000
Discover Ireland Spring/Summer (Bord Fáilte)	£3,750	Annually (January)	300,000

TABLE 10.2 — TOURISM MEDIA VEHICLES *contd.*

Magazine	Approx. Rate for Full Page Colour Advertisement	Frequency of Publication	Circulation
Fáilte Welcome (Irish Ferries UK routes)	£3,600	Annually	150,000
Ireland of The Welcomes	£3,000	Bimonthly	100,000
Aertel	£180 one-off (4 weeks)		
Visitor	£5,400	Annual	250,000

In addition to the above, most national newspapers run periodic special supplements on tourism breaks that attract a large and interested audience. Tourism marketers targeting domestic markets will also need to assess the effectiveness of other general media.

TABLE 10.3 — AN EXAMPLE OF TYPICAL COSTS FOR MAJOR MEDIA SOURCES

Media	Typical Cost of Advertising
RTE Television	£40–£4,000 per 30-second advertisement
Local Radio	£15–£100 per 30-second advertisement
Outdoor Advertising	£400 per month per billboard
Newspaper — *Irish Times*	£37·50 per square column centimetre
Magazine — *RTE Guide*	£3,900 per full page colour

Media Timing

Given their limited budgets, tourism marketers have to consider carefully the timing of their campaign. Even if budgets were larger, the seasonal nature of the tourism market means that, at certain times of the year, the search process among customers for information about holidays is more intense. In the case of outbound summer tourism, the winter months are key times for promoting to prospective customers. Every January, thousands of customers flock to the Holidayworld Experience tourism exhibitions held in Dublin, Belfast, Cork and Shannon. Marketers need to ensure that their brochures and advertisements are prepared for this key time of the year. For the domestic tourist market, there is less constraint on timings of advertising. During spring and autumn there is an emphasis in trying to build volume through tactical advertising, as discussed earlier. However, even in the summer season, especially one that is somewhat depressed through poor weather, it is not surprising to see last-minute hotel offers in the national press and on Aertel.

As a more general trend, whereas it was traditional for the majority to book their holidays in January or February, many people now wait to do so until a short time before departure. This is forcing more tourism marketers to evaluate both the timing of advertising and the appropriate channel. Tactical *late sales* advertisements and special price deals, whether placed by operator or travel agent, have strong *calls to book* the holiday then and there. Freephone hotlines, credit card facilities and seven day, twenty-four-hour service are a major feature of such advertisements. Certain media, especially newspapers and Aertel lend themselves well to capitalising on these later booking trends. We are likely to see a strong increase in the use of such tactical advertising in the future.

Campaign Evaluation

Advertising is itself a product and, like any other product, its effectiveness must be continually evaluated. Some of the most significant factors that impact on advertising effectiveness are:

- The idea chosen and the medium in which it is to be promoted
- The number of people to whom it is promoted and the frequency of repetition
- Competition from others at the time of the campaign
- The timing of the campaign in relation to the buying pattern

Communication and Sales Impact

It is important that in designing advertisements enough time is spent in ensuring the quality of the creative aspect. This can sometimes be a particular problem for co-operative types of advertisements where several companies are jointly funding an advertisement. It is also sometimes a concern in the advertising campaigns of national tourist boards who have similar problems in trying to reflect the agendas of many interest groups and types of product providers.

The Spanish Tourist Board have been widely acclaimed for their *Passion for Life* campaign, which sought to give an alternative image to the traditional view of Spain as a sun-only destination. It featured a series of images emphasising the rich history of Spain, and the architecture and variety of its landscapes. In Ireland, the joint Bord Fáilte/Northern Ireland Tourist Board advertising campaign for Tourism Brand Ireland included the production of television advertisements specially designed for the German, British, French and US markets. The advertisements were first shown in late 1996 and featured spectacular aerial photography of Ireland's coastline, and a variety of scenes which sought to emphasise the uniquely emotional experience a holiday in Ireland offered. To promote advertising excellence in Ireland, the Jacob's television awards are held annually. Television and radio advertisements are included and awards are made to those responsible for the best creative work each year. Experts then comment about their good and bad points at the presentation ceremonies.

The AIDA framework is a simple, yet effective, means of assessing whether objectives have been met. Larger organisations have the resources to employ specialist market research companies, such as Millward Brown, to evaluate the communications effect of their campaigns. Detailed studies conducted every month, called *tracking studies*, enable the long-term effect of advertising to change attitudes to be measured. Smaller tourism companies should continue to monitor how well each media type and vehicle is working for them, through simple questionnaires.

Joint Advertising

The small scale of most Irish tourism enterprises means a high reliance on forms of joint advertising activity. This joint activity even extends to national promotional campaigns. Recently there has been involvement in non-tourism companies such as Murphy's Brewery, in producing television commercials for Bord Fáilte. The major rebranding exercise by Bord Fáilte in 1996, is a novel variation on the type of joint promotion often required in tourism.

Often, joint advertising campaigns are mounted between tour operators and hotels especially if an overseas market is being targeted for the first time.

There has increasingly been recognition of the need to support and part subsidise advertising. As part of the 1994–9 Operational Programme for Tourism, the Irish Government provided the following assistance.

TABLE 10.4 — MAXIMUM AID RATES FOR THE MARKETING SUBPROGRAMME (PRIVATE SECTOR)

	New Markets %	Access/Product/ Niche/High Yield as %
Off-peak	20	50
Shoulder	50	30
Peak	50	20

Advertising Agencies

For larger tourism organisations it is likely that an advertising agency will be used to develop and implement the advertising campaign. In Ireland there are approximately sixty agencies employing over 500 people. The Institute for Advertising Practitioners in Ireland is the body that represents the interests of the Irish Advertising Industry.

A typical advertising agency has three main departments. The Account Department is led by an account director who is responsible to the client for the work of the agency. This involves constant liaison between the other departments in the agency and the client, as well as trying to secure new business through presentations, or *pitches*, to prospective clients. The Creative Department is responsible for the advertisement conception, planning and production. In the creative department different individuals will specialise in specialist areas, such as copywriters who are responsible for the verbal or written part of the advertisement. The Media Department is responsible for drawing up the media schedule and ensuring that the client gets the maximum number of impacts for the allotted budget.

The main source of income for advertising agencies comes from charging clients a commission on the media space that they book on their behalf. As they act on behalf of many clients, they are able to negotiate high discount levels on behalf of individual clients, especially those who have a long-standing substantial relationship with the agency. Typically the advertising commission charged is fifteen per cent of the cost of space. As an example, if a client wants to have £8,500 of radio airspace then they will be charged £10,000 by the advertising agency — the £1,500 extra representing their fifteen per cent commission. Advertising agencies also bill the clients separately for the cost of creative work done in producing the advertisement, although pitches for new business are often not charged for, even when asked for by the client.

Advertising Industry in Ireland

The advertising industry in Ireland has expanded rapidly in recent years, partly as a result of the improved economic fortunes and also because there is now a much expanded range of media options available, as discussed earlier.

Table 10.5 details the major media types in terms of expenditure. While the national press has seen its share of the media expenditure cake decline a little, it remains firmly ahead of television, accounting for nearly forty per cent of advertising revenue.

TABLE 10.5 — ESTIMATES OF ADVERTISING EXPENDITURE IN IRELAND DURING 1998

IR£ million	1998 Total	%	1997 Total	%	1998 v 1997 %
National Press *	158·9	40·7	154·0	39·4	+ 3·2
Regional Press	39·4	10·0	31·1	7·9	+ 26·7
Consumer Magazines **	10·1	2·6	12·7	3·3	− 20·5
TV	113·9	29·2	101·9	26·1	+ 11·8
Radio National/Dublin and Cork	34·3	8·7	29·1	7·4	+ 17·9
Outdoor	34·4	7·7	24·5	6·3	+ 24·1
Cinema	3·7	0·9	3·1	0·8	+ 19·4
Total	390·9	100·0	356·4	100·0	+ 9·7

Source: IAPI
* Calculated at ratecard
** Only cover certain major magazines

PUBLIC RELATIONS

Public Relations includes all activities designed to enhance and maintain favourable communication by companies and their brands with a variety of publics. These publics can include the Government, the financial institutions, the media and the general public.

Publics are groups or individuals who exercise varying degrees of influence over an organisation. This influence can vary over time. Consider the following examples:

- Local communities can have a direct effect on a hotel's building expansion plans, through their objections to the planning authorities
- The Government can affect the tourism and hospitality industry through numerous laws
- Stockbrokers can have an immediate effect on the share price and confidence in a publicly quoted company if they issue negative commentaries on its financial performance
- Journalists can change the general public's opinion of a company, with a newspaper article that paints it in a negative light

The major publics that an organisation has to deal with are:

- Customers
- Employees and their relations

- Trade unions
- Opinion leaders
- Media organisations
- Financial institutions including stockbrokers
- Government and its agencies
- Suppliers

THE OBJECTIVES OF PUBLIC RELATIONS

Public relations is similar to other elements of the communication mix in that we can set a series of defined objectives against which public relations activity can be judged. Like advertising, it is particularly useful in meeting strategic objectives of building awareness and changing or reinforcing brand or company image. In the tourism and hospitality area, public relations is also used tactically, as is the case when a new restaurant opens or a new destination brand is being launched. The major functions of public relations are *lobbying, corporate identity, internal communications, crisis management* and *generating publicity*: these are examined below.

Lobbying

The representations that the company makes to those legislators who pass laws having an impact on marketing activity. Representatives of the tourism industry were active, unsuccessfully in the end, in lobbying Government and EU agencies to retain the Duty Free shopping at Ireland's airports.

Corporate Identity

This refers to the overall image of the company or organisation. The person responsible for public relations will have to undertake the following tasks:

- Designing the corporate logo
- Ensuring the appropriate use of the logo in all communication
- Designing a manual specifying the use of the corporate identity
- Overseeing changes in corporate identity

Internal Communications

Companies need to keep their employees informed of their objectives and plans. This is part of the process known as *internal marketing*, where the employees are regarded as a target group in their own right. This often involves the production of a newsletter and other publications. Bord Fáilte's public relations department produces a monthly newsletter, called *LINK*, to keep the tourism industry informed of latest developments. It is distributed to over 10,000 recipients.

Crisis Management

When things start to go horribly wrong, the public relations department are usually in the front line trying to keep the media and others informed. When an incident occurs, such as food poisoning in a hotel's restaurant, the prompt and full disclosure of information to journalists is critical. Companies need to have contingency plans in place for just such occurrences and the public relations department.

Generating Publicity

Publicity can be termed the free coverage of a company by the media. It could involve a favourable comment from a radio personality about the hospitality they received while visiting a certain area, or a whole article in a newspaper about a hotel opening. Editors are continually looking for stories to feature in their papers and programmes. If a tourism company can be featured in such editorial material, it is more likely to be perceived as credible than if it were in the form of paid-for advertising. The obtaining of publicity in the media is particularly important for Irish tourism organisations, as they typically do not have large budgets for advertising. The media to be targeted can include magazines targeting the tourism industry (trade journals) as well as those targeting the tourist. The next section covers the process of publicity generation in more detail.

OBTAINING MEDIA COVERAGE

In order to secure editorial coverage the tourism organisation needs to recognise that there are a huge number of competing stories vying for an editor or journalist's attention. Those working in the media are typically working to tight deadlines, require genuinely interesting news stories, and are protective of their reputation for impartiality. Each of these factors needs to be respected by a tourism or hospitality organisation.

Creating News Stories

Tourism and hospitality companies need to continually look for opportunities to create newsworthy events. Opening ceremonies are an obvious opportunity to generate media interest. Planet Hollywood's Dublin opening was the subject of huge media hype, largely because its co-founder, Sylvester Stallone, made an appearance. Anniversaries, presentations, guest celebrities and charity events are all potential means of securing favourable coverage.

Familiarisation Trips

A key means of securing coverage, particularly from overseas media, is the familiarisation trip, or *fam trip*. Journalists are often invited by tourism organisations to visit an area for themselves, on an all-expenses-paid basis, in order to generate news stories. Such trips need careful organisation and planning to ensure that the journalists have an enjoyable experience and that their particular interests are catered for. The Kingfisher

Cycle Trail covers counties Donegal, Leitrim, Cavan, Fermanagh and Tyrone. The management arranged for several UK and French journalists writing for specialist cycling magazines to try out the trail. This generated a lot of quality publicity. Exhibit 10.1 outlines the major marketing activities undertaken.

EXHIBIT 10.1

MARKETING COMMUNICATION *IN ACTION*

KINGFISHER CYCLE TRAIL

The Kingfisher Cycle Trail is a cross-border cycling trail across the counties of Donegal, Leitrim and Fermanagh. Based in the Fermanagh and Leitrim Lakelands, the Kingfisher Cycle Trail loops around lakes and islands, along rivers and streams, through forest and country parks, up to scenic viewpoints, down village streets, circling historic monuments and attractive landmarks.

There has been a phenomenal growth in activity holidays, with cycling seen as one of the less strenuous and easier types of activity holiday. In the domestic market it has grown somewhat more slowly.

Marketing Manager of the trail is Pat Collum. The concept was based on the Shannon-Erne Waterway and was according to Collum designed to 'produce a *terra firma* version of that. It relies heavily on the roads in the area, which has one of the highest percentages of road network anywhere in Europe.' Coupled with the environment it seemed like the perfect location. The most southern point is Carrick-on-Shannon, which is on the main N4 road; and the most northerly point is Belleek in County Fermanagh. In between these points are 260 miles of mapped and signposted cycling, with ninety-nine per cent off main roads.

It circles Lough Erne, with Doon outside Fermanagh offering beautiful views over Fermanagh's numerous lakes. There is also a new scenic loop which goes along the Atlantic coast. The Kingfisher project is designed to act as a model to foster cross-border and cross-community co-operation. Its main funding routes are from the Programme of Peace and Reconciliation (PPR) and the Inter-Reg programmes. The challenge is to get the area established as a region for leisure tourism and there is scope in the area, which can sustain a lot of development. Eniskillen and Knock airports are very important routes, with the latter airport only forty minutes away from the start of the trail.

Typical packages for a three-night break including accommodation, based on bed and breakfast, luggage transferred between points, quality bike hire and all maps plus a full introduction to the trail, costs around £100. May, June and September/October are the best times to visit. Thirty to thirty-five miles per day is the most common tour schedule, but you can stop and start as you please.

The key markets of the trail that Pat Collum identifies are:

- Twenty to thirty-five-year olds, singles, who will make most of their arrangements themselves
- Over fifty-five-year olds, who book via the travel trade route, encouraging them to buy from a tour operator

The average cyclist stays four days at an average spend of £30 per day.

The Kingfisher Trail has a modest media budget of Stg£25,000 per annum. A wide variety of magazines are used, partly to build awareness of the Trail.

Advertising in specialist magazines is used, such as *Bicycling* in the UK, along with other specialist racing magazines. *Leisure Cycling*, *Cycle Plus* and *Bicycle* magazine have all had features on cycling in Northern Ireland.

Rather than ignore the problems of the Troubles, Pat Collum says, 'We try to accentuate the positive developments that have taken place in the last three years. We are only in the awareness stage, we've got to get the message out that there is a new product there.'

By the year 2000, Pat Collum felt that he could obtain the same results by halving the budget. Advertisements are designed to get the awareness and interest, the action is to get more information through the phone number that is included in the advertisements.

One particular headline in *Bicycle* magazine read, 'No bombs: just bags'. Pat Collum has an interesting perspective on such coverage. 'On initial impressions, I thought it was quite negative, but when you read through it you see that this guy felt quite safe cycling here.'

Familiarisation trips.
'We have a small amount of money set aside for trips. Mostly journalists rather than the trade. The trade are generally brought in through the tourist trade. The effectiveness of the campaign is assessed through the number of phone calls and the number of e-mails that are received.' Freelance journalists are courted as their articles can find their way into several magazines.

In terms of public relations, Pat feels that it had a particular importance when the trail was being launched in 1998. Following the initial flurry of activity, time constraints and the need for trade support have led to a focus on more direct forms of selling and promotion. 'We have two years really left to get the trail up and running and make it self-sufficient, and the only way we can do this now is dealing directly with the trade and the public.'

The Kingfisher Trail group is part of Eurovelo, a European cycling co-operative movement to link together routes all over Europe. It is also part of Sustrends UK, the sustainable transport group. Mailshots to their 38,000 members have been made. Further down the road, the trail is looking at combined holidays with other countries such as Scotland. The Internet is also predicted to be a very cost-effective way of targeting cyclists.

Source: Personal interview with Pat Collum

Funding Familiarisation Trips

Because familiarisation trips are so expensive, they are usually funded on a co-operative basis between tourism authorities, commercial concerns and destination companies. In 1999, Bord Fáilte and the Northern Ireland Tourist Board (NITB) invited several hundred journalists on familiarisation visits.

Bord Fáilte and the NITB organise itineraries for visiting media. The itineraries are usually of two to six days duration and are based on:

- the journalists' own research interests (cycling, heritage etc.)
- the marketing priorities of the tourist boards (niche products, regional spread etc.)
- the preferences of the access carriers who have transported their media visitors free of charge, e.g. fly-drive, escorted coach tours, short breaks and other special interest subjects and packages in line with the national preferences of the partners concerned

Itineraries are arranged to allow journalists to generate more than one good story a day during their visit.

Press Release

This is the main tool used by a tourism organisation to secure publicity. It is important that it obeys the basic AIDA principles of communication discussed earlier. Press releases should specifically have the following:

- *Notification:* Whether in fax or letter format, each press release should be clearly identified as a press release at the top of the page. If the company does not want the press release printed until a specific time, as in the case of a new appointment, then a *press embargo* time should be clearly indicated.
- *Headline:* The headline should attract the attention of the journalist and offer a clear insight into the subject matter.
- *Leading Paragraph:* This should answer the journalists' key questions, namely; who, what, where, why and when, and include the name of the tourism organisation. A

simple test of effectiveness is to consider whether this paragraph could be used on its own by a paper, radio station etc. If it could, then it is an effective leading paragraph.

- *Style:* The press release should be that of a news report and written in the third person in a factual fashion. Ideally the style of the publisher or broadcaster should be used.
- *Story:* A press release is next to useless if it does not have a story to report. As discussed later, there must be a newsworthy element to the material, and appeal to the audience of the publication.
- *Quotes:* Including a quote is a good way to enliven a press release and editors tend to feel that it adds human interest to a story.
- *Length:* Ideally a press release should be no more than one A4 page in length, double-spaced to allow for journalists to edit it.
- *Photography:* Including photographs will greatly enhance the chance of a press release being covered. Professional photographs which are clearly labelled are likely to get coverage, particularly if they are of a novel nature.
- *Contacts:* Every press release should contain names and contact details of the public relations person. A surprising number of press releases omit this basic rule and lose out on the chance for a follow-up interview which would ensure a great deal of coverage.

THE ROLE OF PUBLIC RELATIONS IN THE MARKETING COMMUNICATIONS MIX

As stated earlier, publicity carries the advantage of high credibility. In the tourism area, many people are strongly influenced in their destination, accommodation and transport choices by the holiday programmes they see on television, and the reviews they read in the lifestyles sections of the weekend papers. Securing such coverage is a huge boost to any tourism company.

Such media coverage is highly cost-effective too. Consider a ten-minute television feature on a new tourist attraction. To have similar length advertising slots on national television in Ireland would cost £100,000!

There are potential drawbacks with public relations. Unlike paid-for advertising, there is no real control over the message. Indeed, there is no guarantee that any coverage will be obtained. While local media and trade journals do cover a lot of tourism stories, it is more difficult to get national media to cover stories. Space constraints, the desire not to appear too local in focus, and the tendency to be attracted to controversy, are all factors accounting for the low coverage of many tourism stories in the media.

GENERATING NEWS STORIES

If a creative approach is used, there are numerous means of generating stories that can attract the attention of local, and national, media. Among the most commonly used angles are:

- Staff achieving a national distinction such as a culinary award; this is a story that papers may find of interest
- Staged news: organising events may be good at attracting publicity, but the press are becoming more sceptical of events that have an obviously commercial motive behind them
- Radio: one way of increasing publicity is to act as a willing commentator on a range of issues relating to the tourism and hospitality sector. This can lead to a constant stream of requests for interview, with consequent benefits for one's business.

EXHIBIT 10.2

PUBLIC RELATIONS *IN ACTION*

PARK HOTEL KENMARE

The Park Hotel of Kenmare (forty-nine rooms, five-star rating), is renowned for quality of service and prestigious surroundings. What makes the hotel different? Owner/Manager Francis Brennan describes the uniqueness of the Park Hotel in terms of being a traditional *olde* hotel, giving the very best treatment to the customer. It all comes down to knowing your market and knowing it well. 'It is better to do what you do well than to aspire to be something that you're not.'

'The typical customer is over fifty-five years and brings a good book', says Francis Brennan. This, in a nutshell, tells us that the Park Hotel has a particular appeal to a particular sector. 'The customer comes for good food, good accommodation and personal attention.' Francis and his staff have investigated additional facilities that they might invest in to have a broader appeal, but research indicates that existing custom might be alienated. If it isn't broke, why fix it?

The Park's customer base comes overwhelmingly from overseas and North American visitors in particular. They would like to broaden the mix of overseas visitors and are making progress in this area. Repeat business is very strong, running at forty per cent. In total, sixty per cent of customers are there because of a recommendation. The Park Hotel advertises very little. Individual bookings predominate, but hotel representation has worked well for the Park Hotel. Being a member of *Small Luxury Hotels, Relais and Chateaux* and *Ireland's Blue Book* helps enormously because there are no sales or marketing staff apart from Francis himself.

What? No advertising, no sales staff, what a recipe for disaster! Not really; the main and predominating marketing activity involves public relations in its broadest sense. Francis Brennan has attended all the major trade and consumer events in his time. There has been many a failure and some successes and

---

contacts made in the broadest sense. The trouble is you just don't know which ones are going to deliver. A chance contact in Hamburg in 1983 led to a booking in 1989, and over £100,000 of business since. Francis keeps in contact with journalists he has met all over the world, as well as at home. He takes a very proactive stance. He is aware that providing some tailored news that is different sets him apart. For example, he organised centenary picnics in Dunloe. He has networked hard at home and abroad on the basis that a certain proportion of contacts will pay off with business leads.

He has the advantage of many a famous celebrity visitor, and when they have gone a nice letter to an erstwhile columnist can deliver spectacular results. Each story is treated as an exclusive. There is no point blanketing the best news and this helps to build a rapport with the best contacts.

You will if you are in the publicity game, get bad coverage. The advice is do not react; if it was something beyond your control do not respond. Leave it, move on. The time will come to put that coverage right, and sometimes that will even be with the author of the offending item.

Each year targets are set and a few new experiments undertaken. The potential for publicity is huge. Recently the Park Hotel featured in the prestigious Condé Nast magazine's *Gold List* and was featured on RTE's *McKenna's Ireland*.

Source: Bord Fáilte Marketing for Success Series. Reproduced by permission.

CHAPTER SUMMARY

In drawing up a marketing communications mix, marketers should firstly be aware of the communication process, and specifically the hierarchy of effects that occur. Their messages need to be carefully encoded, as they are in competition for the attention of the customer with thousands of rival messages. Advertising decisions need to consider objectives, message and media components. There are a wide variety of media types available to the tourism and hospitality marketer today. Given the small budgets available to many Irish firms, public relations offers strong potential to meet many communications objectives.

KEY WORDS AND PHRASES

Communication Process

Hierarchy of Effects

AIDA

Advertising Campaign

Media Types and Vehicles

Public Relations

Familiarisation Trips

Communications Mix

DAGMAR Model

Media Timing

Advertising Agencies

QUESTIONS FOR REVIEW

1. Describe the communication process, using examples from the tourism and hospitality sector.
2. Discuss the advantages and disadvantages of any *three* media types.
3. Outline the stages involved in designing an advertising campaign.
4. Distinguish between the following: *reach, frequency* and *impact.*
5. There are several *publics* that tourism and hospitality marketers need to communicate with. Discuss.

QUESTIONS FOR DISCUSSION

1. Gather examples of tourism and hospitality advertising: comment on the message content, structure, format and source.
2. Research a recent crisis that affected any tourism or hospitality company. Comment on the press coverage and how the company used public relations to deal with the situation.
3. Gather examples from newspapers and magazines of advertorials and discuss the merits of this form of communication.

USEFUL WEB SITES

www.cahners.com	Used by the large Irish hotel chains, Cahners are the largest publishers of International hotel guides such as *OAG Business Travel Planner* and *Hotel and Travel Index International*
www.adworld.ie	Comprehensive coverage of Irish marketing and advertising industry
www.millward-brown.co.uk	Site of Millward Brown, specialists in advertising research
www.iapi.ie	Irish Advertising Practitioners Institute
www.prii.ie	Public Relations Institute of Ireland
www.medialive.ie	Irish Media Informatin
www.marketing.ie	Marketing Magazine

CHAPTER 11

Marketing Communications Mix: 2

INTRODUCTION

While advertising remains a dominant form of marketing communication, the increased range of new media types, and the spiralling costs of advertising, have led to an increased interest in more cost-effective and focused means of communication. New technological developments are leading to an explosion in the use of direct marketing, and the possibilities it offers of leading to a long-term, and profitable, relationship with the customer. Sales promotions, whether consumer or trade, remain a valued technique of achieving tactical objectives. While personal selling is expensive, it is critical for most Irish tourism and hospitality enterprises, given their limited marketing budgets and their reliance on tourism intermediaries to sell-on their product. The Internet promises to revolutionise marketing communications, because of its global reach, its relative ease of access and cost, and the opportunity it offers to enable bookings and other transactions to be made on-line.

CHAPTER OBJECTIVES

Following this chapter, students should be able to:

- Understand the role of direct marketing as part of the marketing communications mix
- Distinguish between trade and consumer tourism and hospitality sales promotions
- Recognise the importance of relationship building in the personal selling process
- Recognise the importance of the Internet as a marketing communications tool in tourism and hospitality marketing

In addition to Advertising and Public Relations, covered in Chapter 10, the major marketing communication tools are Direct Marketing, Sales Promotion, Internet, Personal Selling and Relationship Marketing.

1. DIRECT MARKETING

DEFINITIONS

Direct Marketing can be described as an interactive system of marketing, which uses one or more advertising media to effect a measurable response and/or transaction at any location.

FROM MASS COMMUNICATION TO ONE-TO-ONE COMMUNICATION

The era of mass communication to a mass market is rapidly declining. Companies and customers are becoming accustomed, through new technology, to a bewildering array of product and media choices. The cost of mass advertising has also contributed to a desire to find more cost-effective ways of precisely targeting communications. The ability to target more precisely is the most important characteristic of direct marketing. Effective direct marketing requires application of a concept known as *database marketing.*

Database Marketing is the process of systematically collecting, in electronic or optical form, data about past, current and/or potential customers, maintaining the integrity of the data by continually monitoring customer purchases and/or by inquiring about changing status and using the data to formulate marketing.

DIRECT MARKETING'S INCREASING IMPORTANCE

Several factors can be cited as contributing to the rapid growth of direct marketing techniques.

Cost

With the increasing costs of media such as television and press, and the inevitability of a high wastage factor, marketers have been encouraged to seek communications methods that are more precisely targeted and less wasteful.

Precise Targeting

As marketing and, in particular, market research techniques have improved, it has become increasingly possible to segment markets along different lines. Direct marketing offers the opportunity to develop a line of communication with these identified market segments and to tailor the message in ways that would not be possible using a conventional media approach. Indeed, some commentators have argued that potentially the emergence of *segments of one* has happened.

New Technology

The dramatic improvements in both computers and other areas of information technology have realised the potential of direct marketing. The processing of information, and the profiling of prospective customers, is made much easier with the widespread use of technology. Database packages are relatively inexpensive, allowing quite small enterprises to practice direct marketing. Also, desktop publishing packages enable companies to produce high quality print material for their campaigns. The emergence of the Internet, and its e-mail facility, means that extremely low-cost campaigns can be mounted. Thousands of e-mail communications can be sent for the price of a local call.

Changing Lifestyles

Today's hectic lifestyle means that consumers are looking for ways to save time and increase the convenience of shopping. Mail-order catalogues, telephone marketing, telephone shopping and banking are all increasing in importance.

OBJECTIVES OF DIRECT MARKETING

Generating Repeat Purchase

Once the name and address of a purchaser has been captured, they can be contacted on a continuing basis to achieve further sales of the same product. This is particularly appropriate where the purchase is of a high-cost item such as a car or a holiday. As it is much more cost-effective to convince a past customer to return, than it is to secure first-time business, tourism and hospitality organisations have a huge opportunity for increased business. This can only be achieved if they have a commitment to retaining as much customer information as possible.

Focusing on Specific Market Segments

Direct marketing enables the identification and targeting of small groups and indeed individuals. By giving them specific information of relevance to them, there is a greater likelihood that the AIDA communication process, as discussed in the previous chapter, can be followed. A brochure for a golf resort hotel, sent to a list of recreational golfers, is more likely to be noticed, and generate more interest and action, than would be the case if it were sent to a more general list of electors.

Relationship Marketing

Direct marketing is one of the main techniques of *relationship marketing*. The creation and maintenance of a bond between a company and its customers is the key to securing their loyalty and recommendation to others. Companies need to see this relationship marketing as being a long-term process that involves real commitment on their part. It is not a quick-fix gimmick to increase sales in a tactical way. We are seeing a move away from the more expensive *acquisition* to the much cheaper *retention* of customers through the use of direct advertising. Later in this chapter we take a more detailed look at relationship marketing.

ADVANTAGES OF DIRECT MARKETING TECHNIQUES

Targeting

As stated earlier, some forms of direct marketing, especially those relating to direct mail, can be very precisely targeted. With direct mail (promotional material sent through the post to selected individuals or companies) it is possible to reach a target market, or a segment of a market, with a minimum of overlap. The products that are particularly suitable for direct mail advertising have a well-defined target market, are novel in concept, are interesting to write about, and have a high profit margin.

Interactivity

Direct marketing has built-in response mechanisms that encourage a flow of information from the prospective consumer back to the manufacturer. With e-mail communication this response is practically instantaneous.

Flexibility

A direct-mail advertising campaign can be established relatively quickly, which gives you the flexibility to respond to changing market conditions. This is more difficult to achieve with mass media advertising. Depending on the direct-marketing medium you use, a high degree of flexibility is offered. A wide variety of attention getting items, such as CDs, can be sent through the post. E-mail messages can also be used creatively, by attaching pictures or video clips of visitor attractions.

Strategy Advantages

Companies find it difficult to monitor their competitors' direct marketing activity. Unlike conventional advertising, the activity is not visible to the general public. By the time the competitor receives the communication, so have customers, and it may be too late to retaliate effectively.

Measurability

Direct marketing activity can be easily measured. Companies can easily relate the cost of mounting a campaign to the response rate they achieve and the extra revenue this generates, in both the short and long term. Since all direct marketing campaigns have a response mechanism built in, the performance of the campaign can be speedily determined. Direct marketing has a unique ability to offer cheap international communications, especially through the use of the telephone and e-mail.

PROBLEMS WITH DIRECT MARKETING

Accuracy of Lists

A direct marketing campaign is only as good as the list you use for direct-mail advertising or outbound telemarketing. If the names, addresses or telephone numbers are not correct or current, of if some names on the list have been mistakenly included, your offer won't reach its intended audience. This is very often a problem. Hotel companies sending out their latest conference brochure to companies in surrounding industrial estates may find that a high percentage of the mailing is wasted, as many companies may have moved premises. Approximately one person in fifty moves address each year, making the electoral register an unreliable list to use.

Public Criticism

Unwanted direct-mail communication is termed *junk mail.* The direct marketing industry has suffered from negative publicity centred around the annoyance felt by many people about the flood of catalogues, letters and brochures they receive. The advent of e-mail as a direct marketing tool has not been without criticism either. *Spam-mailing* is the term used to describe the mailing of unwanted e-mail messages, often to thousands of recipients. The direct marketing industry is trying to address these criticisms — the problem will only be rectified if companies adopt a more professional approach and use accurate mailing lists and communicate with people who are receptive to the communication.

Lack of Content Support

Advertising in the print or the electronic media is interspersed with entertainment or information, which can help set a mood or put the advertising into context. Advertorials, described in the previous chapter, are particularly effective in this regard. In contrast, some forms of direct marketing (such as direct mail, billboard advertising) stand alone without the support of any editorial or programming material.

Clutter

With greater use of direct mail and other direct marketing techniques, an individual mailing has to compete with every other piece of mail the target audience receives that day.

PLANNING A DIRECT MARKETING CAMPAIGN

Database Construction

A database is a list of names that a company has of potential, and existing, customers. These lists are sometimes rented from specialised agencies. The lists that are available have become more numerous and sophisticated, enabling companies to be ever more precise in their targeting. The Irish Direct Marketing Association has more than 300 members, many of whom are specialist providers of lists. Among the largest list providers are the postal services. In Northern Ireland, the Royal Mail provide a service that companies can use to send mailings to identified groups. An Post have developed several different products for database construction. Of particular interest to tourism and hospitality marketers, is the Irish Consumer Marketing Database (ICMD), where lists of names and addresses of people with specific tourism and leisure interests are available. For example, the company can provide marketers with the names and addresses of 17,000 Irish people interested in golf, something that a hotel or golf resort would find very useful. For hotels and conference centres who want to target businesses there are specialist lists of key executives, including meeting planners available. The workings of the ICBM are described later in this chapter.

Among the best known of the other direct marketing lists are those available from Kompass as well as Business and Finance. Telephone company Eircom's CD of all their telephone directories on one disk has also proved very popular for direct marketing campaigns. Finally, Bord Fáilte and NITB both have available extensive lists of names and addresses of people who have inquired for information about holidaying in Ireland. These lists can be categorised according to interests in specific activities, attractions, regions etc.

Objective Setting

Direct marketing campaigns can be directed at past users of a service, or new users, or some combination of both.

Targeting Past Users

Many direct marketing campaigns aim to increase business through targeting past users. The return from targeting past users should be higher than trying to attract potential users, called *prospects*. Past users will be familiar with the product and will require less information to make a choice. The challenge with such customers will often be to ensure that they are continually made aware of new services and given a reason to visit again. Many companies derive a lot of business through such reminder campaigns. The key task for a company targeting these customers is to ensure that the information they hold on them is up to date and comprehensive. A hotel with a new golf course will find it difficult to use its database effectively if they have not gathered information on their past customers' leisure interests. Today there are many specialist sales and marketing software packages available to make the task of effective database compilation easier.

Targeting New Customers

Prospective customers, called *sales prospects*, can be targeted in a number of ways.

Consider the example of a hotel wishing to target companies to hold business meetings in their premises. As well as their own database, the hotel could use a variety of external databases are available, such as:

- Commercial business directories such as Eircom Telephone, Kompass and Thoms
- Chambers of Commerce
- Overseas business directories
- Trade press

For those targeting the leisure market a number of other sources are available. A company promoting a cycle trail could use any of the following:

- Cycling clubs, domestic and overseas
- Professional list compilation companies and companies who have access to a bank of lists from various sources. These are called *list brokers.*
- Bord Fáilte and Northern Ireland Tourist Board

USING EXTERNAL DATABASES

There are a huge number and variety of companies providing lists. For tourism marketers in Ireland, the Irish Direct Marketing Association can provide assistance in identifying the most appropriate company to use.

For overseas direct marketing campaigns a tourism company can also call on the services of Bord Fáilte and the Northern Ireland Tourist Board. Over one million enquiries are received annually at the various international tourist offices. From these enquiry lists, specialised lists can be produced of special interest groups such as golfers, walkers and cyclists etc. Companies wishing to target overseas markets can also use local list providers or brokers in the country they wish to target.

EXHIBIT 11.1

> #### DIRECT MARKETING *IN ACTION: 1*
> #### IRISH CONSUMER MARKETING DATABASE
> PMI, Precision Marketing Information, is a joint venture between An Post, Ireland's national postal service and Equifax (Europe), the European division of Equifax Inc., based in Atlanta, Georgia. The company provides a wide range of demographic, census and lifestyle information on Irish consumers including:
>
> - *Demographics:* Type of Residence, Length of Residence, Household Composition, Employment, Sector Occupation
> - *Lifestyle:* Education, Hobbies and Leisure, Cars/Motoring, Sports, Newspaper Readership, Musical Preference and PC Users

The company also collects data on the holidays and travel interests of those on its database.

This information is compiled on a platform known as the Irish Consumer Marketing Database (ICMD), which uses the information collected from 2·6 million individuals in over one million households throughout the country. This data was collected from a detailed postal questionnaire delivered to every household in the country. It is the first database to provide comprehensive consumer information covering the whole of the Irish Republic and uses the most advanced software specially developed to handle Irish names and addresses.

Having identified the target audience, individuals can be further qualified through the use of analysis and profiling techniques. PMI's analytical techniques enable the ICMD to recognise the distinguishing characteristics of a company's existing customer database, in order to find similar consumers in the Irish market. PMI has developed software which allows customers and prospects to be identified by the *thoroughfares* (i.e. streets/roads/towns/lands) where they live. At present PMI has identified a list of over 85,000 different thoroughfares throughout Ireland. This enables it to conduct detailed profiling analysis.

Profiling is the process by which a picture of the characteristics of those on a list is drawn up.

From any given list, its composition in terms of demographic and lifestyle characteristics can easily be determined through the use of sophisticated computer software. The PMI software enables profiling of databases in order to analyse the penetration of customers on a thoroughfare, and provide a prospect list of neighbours whose characteristics have the closest resemblance to those of their existing customers. This might be useful for a hotel trying to promote short breaks. If the hotel can provide a list of past Irish guests' names and addresses, PMI can provide mailing addresses of people that their software indicates closely resemble the hotel's guests.

Having supplied records based on demographic and lifestyle selections, PMI can profile that data and provide extra mail-responsive names and addresses using the thoroughfare analysis process.

Source: Reproduced with permission from An Post

USING LISTS EFFECTIVELY

Lists can be very general, such as anyone who attended a tourism fair; or they can be very specific, such as a list of Germans who are interested in angling in Ireland and have a preference for hotel accommodation. The more precise the specification, the higher the cost of the list will be. This is because the response rate will typically be higher if the target group is tightly defined. Typically, lists are priced on a per thousand names basis. As lists are expensive to collate they are a valuable commodity and are rented rather than sold to companies. List brokers often include names and addresses of their own employees to check that the list is being used in the way intended.

TABLE 11.1 — TYPICAL PRICES FOR MAJOR LISTS USED BY TOURISM MARKETERS

List	Approximate Cost Per 1,000 Names
Acorn: UK list of UK households according to residential neighbourhoods	£80
An Post-ICMD (Database with details of 2·6 million Irish consumers)	
Business targeted lists	£180
Consumer targeted lists	£135

Source: Marketing for Success: Direct Marketing, Bord Fáilte

The major types of direct marketing channels are outlined below in Table 11.2.

TABLE 11.2 — DIRECT MARKETING CHANNELS

Channel Type	Definition
Direct mail	Anything conveyed from one address to another by post. It can include distributing sales letters, brochures, sample products etc.
Telemarketing	Using the telephone to elicit an immediate response from customers. *Outbound telemarketing* occurs where the company initiates a sales call. This is known as cold calling. Most telemarketing today is *inbound telemarketing*, where the telephone is used to respond to calls that have been generated by a number of factors — complaints, order processing and as a result of seeing an advertisement.
Direct response advertising	Advertising, typically on television or in press/magazines, which includes some means of immediate response from consumers, usually in the form of a coupon or freephone telephone number.

Of the three methods described above, direct mail remains the most popular in the tourism sector. Telephone companies offer a variety of services to companies wishing to conduct telemarketing. For example, to promote more use of the telephone for inbound marketing purposes, Eircom offer services such as Freephone 1800, CallSave 1850 and LoCall 1890. There are also a range of special tariffs for companies to conduct outbound telemarketing campaigns. Telemarketing has grown enormously in usage, with new technologies permitting the establishment of a large number of call centres in Ireland. Some of the leading tourism players have established their European call centres in Ireland, including Best Western Hotels, Radisson Hotels, American Airlines and Hertz.

Direct response (DR) advertising is set to enjoy a boom with the advent of digital television, when dozens of channels can be made available for specialised shopping services. DR advertising is very commonplace in the tourism sector, where the objective of many advertising campaigns is to encourage people to make a further and more detailed enquiry. Tourism Brand Ireland television commercials conclude with the prominent display of a freephone number to call to get further information and brochures about Ireland.

Exhibit 11.2 illustrates the practical issues involved in establishing a database system for a small tourism operator.

Exhibit 11.2

Direct Marketing *in Action: 2*

Galway Bay Health Farm

The Galway Bay Health Farm is a family-run business providing specialised accommodation including a healthy regimen and activities. Being providers of a specialised service, they could not rely on the casual trade so common to the bed and breakfast sector. The owners, with professional advice, put together a marketing plan that included the creation of a customer database. They had always gathered detailed information about customers but, because it had been stored on paper, retrieving the data and analysing it had never been practicable. A database professional using the development package Access 2.0 developed the customer database. Using a relational database product allows the designer to insulate the user from the database itself, using Forms for data entry and Queries and Reports for data output.

FIGURE 11.1 — ACCESS DATABASE APPLICATION MODEL

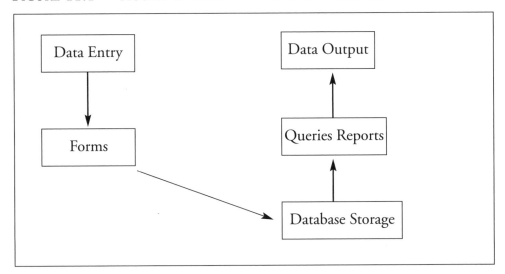

The final database system allows the users to record information for all customers, including the entry of past customer data from the paper files. Items recorded are shown below:

- Customer details
- Enquiries
- Actual visits
- Activities during visits
- Customer feedback

FIGURE 11.2 — A TYPICAL FORM FOR ENTERING CUSTOMER DETAILS

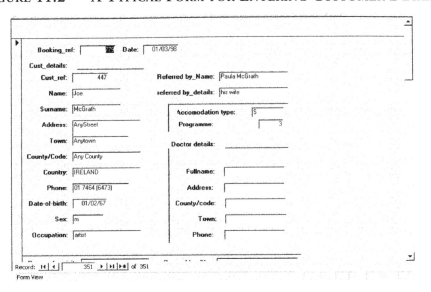

The system provides as outputs:

- easy retrieval of customer data
- reports and analyses enabling customer profiling

The database has already generated considerable benefits to the business.

Day-to-day operations are assisted by the provision of information about current activities. Examples are:

- bookings for the next month
- revenue figures, categorised by product type
- targeted mailshots regularly sent to selected groups of customers

More importantly, over the longer term the database provides information about the type of customer and what services they require. For example:

- the origin of visitors
- how they heard about the business
- the types of services and activities most used
- repeat customers

FIGURE 11.3 — REPORT IDENTIFYING REPEAT CUSTOMERS

Repeat Customers count

Customer		Number of Visits
Name	Dave	5
Surname	Kimmage	
Name	John	4
Surname	McGrath	
Name	Brian	4
Surname	Casey	
Name	Sinead	3
Surname	Spillane	
Name	Marian	3
Surname	McGoldrick	

This type of marketing information provides a platform on which marketing plans and the overall business plan can be developed.

Source: Exhibit contributed by: Phelim Murnion, Lecturer in Management Information Systems, GMIT

OBJECTIVE SETTING FOR DIRECT MARKETING CAMPAIGNS

The objectives set for any direct marketing campaign should reflect the need to move the target market through the communication *hierarchy of effects* described in the previous chapter. Typically, direct marketing has been used as a means of prompting a specific form of action, namely to build sales. Its broader role is now being recognised. Direct marketing plays a key role in fostering a deeper relationship with the customer — *relationship marketing*. Information gathered during direct marketing campaigns can be a useful source of potential contacts for a subsequent sales call. This is known as a *sales lead*. In tourism businesses a key objective of many direct campaigns is to prompt the customer to make a more detailed enquiry. This could take the form of a follow-up call, or a request for a more detailed brochure.

In 1996, a major study into the use of direct marketing in Ireland was commissioned by the Irish Direct Marketing Institute, (IDMA, 1996). The survey was conducted by Lansdowne Market Research among a representative sample of 801 adults to find out how they felt about purchasing products via direct mail, direct response advertising and telemarketing. Secondary research and a separate study among industry members, was conducted to try and predict the growth levels in direct marketing.

Detailed below are the projected levels of expenditure on direct marketing, deriving from the report.

TABLE 11.3 — THE FUTURE VALUE OF DIRECT MARKETING EXPENDITURE IN IRELAND IN £M

	1995	1996	1997	1998	1999	2000
Total Display Advertising	271	294	316	338	362	386
Direct Response Advertising	29	32	34	37	40	43
Total Direct Mail	69	77	84	92	101	110
Total Telemarketing	10	11	12	13	14	16
Total Direct Marketing	108	119	131	143	156	169
Advertising and Direct Marketing	351	381	412	444	478	511

Source: *The Coming Boom in Direct Marketing*, IDMA, 1996

From the survey of the general public, there were some interesting findings about attitudes to direct mail. In the survey, there was an examination of attitudes to using direct mail and telemarketing as a means of selling in a variety of product areas, including travel services and restaurants. Perhaps unsurprisingly, people were more open to the idea of receiving direct mail communication than telephone calls. This was particularly evident in the financial service area. Tables 11.4 and 11.5 below, show a high degree of willingness on the part of many Irish people to use direct marketing in the tourism and hospitality sector.

TABLE 11.4 — PERCENTAGE OF PEOPLE WHO WOULD BE HAPPY/NOT HAPPY TO BE CONTACTED *BY PHONE* ABOUT VARIOUS SERVICES

Service	Happy to receive info. by phone (%)	Unhappy to receive info. by phone (%)	Don't know (%)
Entertainment	21	75	4
Restaurants and takeaways	20	75	5
Travel services	20	76	4
Financial services	12	83	5
Household furniture	10	84	6
Clothes	11	83	6
Cars	11	83	7
Jobs and appointments	36	59	5

Source: The Coming Boom in Direct Marketing, IDMA, 1996

TABLE 11.5 — PERCENTAGE OF PEOPLE WHO WOULD BE HAPPY/NOT HAPPY TO BE CONTACTED *BY POST* ABOUT VARIOUS SERVICES

Service	Happy to receive info. by post (%)	Unhappy to receive info. by post (%)	Don't know (%)
Entertainment	53	39	7
Restaurants and takeaways	49	43	8
Travel services	56	38	6
Financial services	48	45	7
Household furniture	46	46	8
Clothes	46	45	8
Cars	42	49	9
Jobs and appointments	57	34	9

Source: The Coming Boom in Direct Marketing, IDMA, 1996

2. SALES PROMOTION

In recent years, sales promotion has become a particularly dynamic area within the overall context of marketing communications. It is commonly referred to as *below-the-line* marketing.

DEFINITIONS

Because sales promotion encompasses a wide variety of techniques it is difficult to define. The British Institute of Sales Promotion defines it as indicated below:

> 'Sales Promotion is a range of tactical marketing techniques designed with a strategic marketing framework to add value to a product or service in order to achieve specific sales and marketing objectives.'

Lumsdon (1997)describes sales promotion in tourism as indicated below:

> 'Sales Promotion is a set of associated techniques which when combined, offer customers or intermediaries a set of associated techniques which when combined, offer customers or intermediaries enhanced incentives to buy or to remain loyal to a particular brand.'

OBJECTIVES OF SALES PROMOTION

- *Sales promotion objectives must be defined clearly.* It is vital to define precisely what is expected of the campaign and over what duration it will run.
- *Sales promotion objectives must be amenable to measurement.* Some numerical value must be attached to the objective. This will enable a proper evaluation once the campaign has begun. By monitoring the results, it will be possible to determine whether the objectives have been met or exceeded, over what timescale the results have been achieved, and the cost-effectiveness of the expenditure.
- *Sales promotion objectives must be achievable.* It is important that targets are felt to be realistic within the constraints of the budget available and the organization's structure.
- *Sales promotion objectives must be budgeted realistically.* It is important that the organization is aware of the likely cost impact of the achievement of the objective.

Growth in sales promotion has resulted from a number of factors:

Short-Term Results Perspective

Marketers are under increasing pressure to deliver quick results. Unlike an advertising or public relations campaign, which may take years to have an effect on visitor numbers, tactical sales promotions can bring almost immediate results.

Accountability and Measurability

The effectiveness of sales promotion is easier to measure than advertising. Records of bookings resulting from a price promotion or attendance at a trade show can be determined, and the true cost-benefit of the activity can be calculated.

Breaking Through the Clutter

With so many destinations and tourism attractions vying for the attention of the consumer, a creative sales promotion can give a company a competitive edge in the market-place.

TYPES OF SALES PROMOTION

We can distinguish two types of sales promotion, namely, trade promotion and consumer promotion.

Trade Promotion

Trade promotions are targeted at tourism intermediaries, with the objective being to ensure that these intermediaries have an incentive to sell the company's services. This is known as a *push strategy*.

Consumer Promotion

In consumer promotion the objective is to communicate directly with consumers and achieve a direct response from them. This is known as a *pull strategy*, with the demand for the service being pulled through the system by consumers demanding it from intermediaries.

TABLE 11.6 — EXAMPLES OF THE MAJOR SALES PROMOTION TECHNIQUES

Sales Promotion Technique	Trade or Consumer?	Description	Example
Trial offers with coupons	Consumer	Consumers collect coupons allowing them to get tourism products at heavily discounted prices.	Ryanair discount fares offer with coupons from *Sunday Tribune*.

TABLE 11.6 — EXAMPLES OF THE MAJOR SALES PROMOTION TECHNIQUES *contd.*

Sales Promotion Technique	Trade or Consumer?	Description	Example
Competitions	Consumer or Trade	Competitions are often good at generating low-cost publicity, especially if run in collaboration with a media source such as a newspaper.	Ryanair 'Win two nights in Paris' competition in *Magill* magazine. Contestants typically have to answer a *tie-break* question. Panorama holidays trade-only competition aimed at travel agents.
Money Off — price promotion	Consumer or Trade	Special fares for limited time periods offered to stimulate sales in quiet periods.	Ryanair seat sales. Travel agents special deals.
Free gift: known as a premium	Consumer mainly	Generates interest especially if the item is perceived to be valuable.	Free Furbie characters at McDonald's restaurants.
Merchandising	Consumer and Trade	From small items such as pens, T-shirts to more expensive golf umbrellas.	Given to travel agency staff and customers at tourism fairs and exhibitions.

TABLE 11.6 — EXAMPLES OF THE MAJOR SALES PROMOTION TECHNIQUES *contd.*

Sales Promotion Technique	Trade or Consumer?	Description	Example
Point-of-Sale material	Trade	As the name suggests, material designed to secure a sale at the point-of-sale.	Displays of brochures, special window displays in travel agents, *specials* notice for menus etc.
Loyalty schemes	Trade and Consumer	With each purchase the consumer or intermediary collects points toward free gifts, extra product etc.	Aer Lingus Tab scheme, Holiday Inn Priority Club.

TOURISM EXHIBITIONS

The exhibition, whether trade only, consumer, or both, is a form of sales promotion that is worthy of particular discussion. It offers the strong advantage of face-to-face interaction and can be a cost-effective means of reaching customers. Rather than travel long distances to meet customers or intermediaries, the exhibition offers the opportunity to conduct a lot of business very quickly and effectively.

Exhibitions have become extremely important in the world of tourism marketing. There are a large number of categories of exhibition, detailed in Table 11.7 below.

TABLE 11.7 — TYPES OF TOURISM EXHIBITIONS

Exhibition	Focus	Description
Ireland tour operator workshops	Trade	These are held annually, and offer the opportunity to meet, in a single location, with a large number of overseas tour operators typically over a two-day period. Bord Fáilte and NITB meet the cost of bringing the tour operators to Ireland.

TABLE 11.7 — TYPES OF TOURISM EXHIBITIONS *contd.*

Exhibition	Focus	Description
Overseas tour operator workshops	Trade	Tour operators and travel agents are brought together in a single location in America and Britain, in order for Irish tourism providers to sell to them directly.
Trade Fairs	Trade	These are organised by professional exhibition companies in most European countries. Some, such as the World Travel Market in London attract over 4,000 exhibitors. Other major international trade shows include ITB Berlin, FITUR in Madrid, BIT Milan. All these fairs are heavily dominated by different destinations, but an increasing trend has been the growth in fairs targeting specific interest groups, such as golf and cycling.
Consumer Holiday Fairs	Consumer	Consumer fairs are an excellent means of face-to-face contact with the general public. Represented at these fairs are the international tourist boards, local, county and regional stands, as well as accommodation and attractions. The Holidayworld Experience is the major consumer fair in Ireland, and is staged in Dublin, Belfast, Cork and Galway in late January/early February each year. The Dublin show is the largest, attracting over 600 separate exhibitors, and an attendance of almost 50,000 over four days.
Specialist Promotions	Consumer	To target specific groups special promotions are organised. For example, Bord Fáilte set up a tent at the European Open in the K Club in Kildare to promote golfing breaks in Ireland to the attendance. Similar promotions are held at overseas golf competitions, boating shows, cultural events etc.

TABLE 11.7 — TYPES OF TOURISM EXHIBITIONS *contd.*

Exhibition	Focus	Description
		Imaginais Irlande was a huge cultural and commercial event, promoting all things Irish, including holidays. It was held in a variety of locations in France to coincide with the arrival of the Tour de France in Ireland in 1998.
Consumer Days/Evenings	Consumer	These are special events in overseas markets, designed to target specialist markets. The day usually includes Irish entertainment, holiday competitions with desks provided for participating tourism companies.

3. INTERNET MARKETING

For tourists, getting information about foreign destinations has often been a tortuous task. It often meant endless visits to travel agents, telephone calls and piles of glossy brochures gathering dust. Choice was often limited and getting bargains was often a matter of chance. Making the booking itself meant further visits with chequebook in hand. The Internet promises to change this forever.

The Internet has rapidly become a critical part of people's lives. Its influence as a marketing tool is already large, and it promises immense impact on our lives. Multibillion-dollar corporations have sprung up on the back of the Internet phenomenon. Most existing tourism enterprises are recognising that the Internet is already a powerful way to communicate with customers. Perhaps more significantly in the long run, it is seen as being the shopping centre of the future.

Companies such as Amazon, in book retailing; and Travelocity, in the travel sector; already conduct billions of dollars of business through the medium of the Internet. This facility to make an actual purchase, called electronic commerce or *e-commerce,* is attracting huge investment, at both the company and national government level.

Structure of the Internet

The Internet is an electronic medium based on broadcasting and publishing that facilitates two-way communication. It emerged in the 1960s in the US Department of Defence, and developed through a number of stages to become an amalgamation of many networks generally available for commercial ventures, culminating in the development of the Worldwide Web (WWW or the 'web').

Essentially the communication is through computers on networks, so that individuals and organisations can communicate directly with one another regardless of where they are or when they wish to communicate (Berthon and Lane, 1998). Often, the terms Internet and Worldwide Web are used interchangeably, but in fact the web is only one part, albeit the most important one, of the larger Internet. The web is a part of the Internet that links resources around the world. It has been responsible for the explosion in usage of the Internet. As a communication tool the Internet offers almost boundless possibilities for tourism marketers. The Internet offers marketers the ability to offer full-colour catalogues known as web sites.

FIGURE 11.4 — THE STRUCTURE OF THE INTERNET

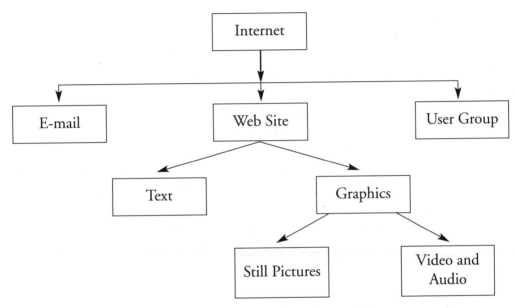

Source: Adapted from *The Structure of the Worldwide Web*, McGoey, 1995

These web sites can incorporate technologies such as on-line booking forms, virtual tours, video and audio effects plus interactive feedback effects. A web site is defined as a collection of web files on a particular subject that includes a beginning file called a *home page*. Figure 11.4 provides a simple overview of the Internet.

While the nature and extent of the Internet phenomenon has been studied at length, its exact role in the marketing communications mix is unclear; this is hardly surprising given the present speed of change. A *hierarchy of effects* model assumes that the buyer passes through a cognitive, affective and behavioural stage, in that order. Bearing this in mind there are three ways according to Briggs (1997) that people will use a web site, as outlined below:

Window shopping — they just visit the site and glance at the contents without absorbing them, quickly moving to another site.

Just looking, thank you — visitors browse through the site, clicking on different pages just as they might pick up and put down goods in a shop and then leave the store/site and go to the next.

Where do I pay? — visitors are more absorbed by the information which is presented to them and they have the opportunity to make an actual purchase.

The third stage is obviously the most lucrative, but it does require careful planning. Web sites can be used to move customers through successive phases of the buying process, first attracting Internet surfers, nurturing a group of interest surfers, converting a portion of these into interactive customers and ultimately keeping these customers for repeat business.

Different tourism organisations will have different marketing objectives for establishing a web presence. Sligo Tourism's site is used as a means of creating an identity for the county, providing information about events and acts primarily as an information resource.

Other sites, such as Jurys Doyle Hotel Group's site, allow *fast-track reservations* where prospective customers can make a booking *on-line* using their credit card. The web is in many ways a hybrid of other forms of the communication mix. It resembles direct selling in that it allows interactive dialogue with the customer. It has parallels with advertising in that it is a strong medium for generating awareness and illustrating the product. This feature is becoming even more sophisticated, with quality video and audio now becoming available. As the customer moves toward the final transaction, the web is also useful in helping the customer to make evaluations, and the ultimate purchase, through the aforementioned e-commerce technologies.

Exhibit 11.3

Internet Marketing *in Action*

Impact on Tourism

Tourism is regarded as the sector that stands to benefit most from the Internet. In 1997, air travel represented eighty-four per cent ($777 million) of the $911 million of all on-line travel revenues. The on-line consumer travel industry will be worth $16·6 billion by 2003, with air travel accounting for sixty per cent of the industry's revenue, according to Jupiter Communications. However, this will be far less than the on-line travel industry's full potential, due largely to the fact that travel companies, from airlines to hotels, have allowed their web sites to stagnate.

Although airline travel accounts for the biggest piece of this pie for now, Jupiter Research in a report called *On-Line Travel: Five-Year Outlook* predicts that air travel's share of the total on-line industry revenue will decrease from eighty-four per cent in 1999 to fifty-nine per cent by 2004. They predict that on-line booking of hotel reservations and car rentals will more than double.

While the United States is still at the leading edge of Internet usage, Europe is catching up quickly. During the summer of 1998, NPD Research surveyed 6,000 people in the UK about their use of the Internet for travel and tourism purposes. The researchers found that seventy per cent of web surfers visited a travel-related site. Of those that said they had visited a travel site, eighty per cent said they had visited airline sites. This is broadly in line with the experience in the US.

The NPD study found that the amount of people accessing travel-related web sites had doubled since a survey in 1996. The amount of people going to car rental, hotel, Expedia.com and ITN.com has tripled in eighteen months. Half of those polled said they had gone on-line to check travel rates and of those, nearly fifty per cent went on to buy tickets on-line. This is a good example of how the Internet can work at all levels of a *hierarchy of effects* model such as AIDA. The ease of checking airline rates on-line is a large factor in the surge of traffic to travel web sites over the last year.

Surprisingly, the survey found that only ten per cent of those surveyed said they would be extremely likely, or very likely, to avail themselves of a discount package in the next six months. The survey found that the average visitor to a travel-related site was wealthy, with an average salary of £40,000 and aged between twenty-four and fifty-four. Males are slightly more likely to visit airline sites than females.

The European on-line travel industry is expected to generate $1·7 billion in sales by 2002, up from $7·7 million in 1997, according to a report by Datamonitor. Currently, the most developed and lucrative sector of the on-line travel market is flight sales, however, on-line package holiday sales are expected to grow substantially in the future.

The advent of interactive TV over the next five years is also expected to be a major boost to on-line travel sales. The Datamonitor study also found that the cost of making a transactional booking on-line can be up to ten times less expensive than making such a booking through a call centre, an added incentive for would-be on-line consumers. Europe's Teletext culture, that of buying late-availability travel flights and packages as advertised on the service, is likely to make the transition to on-line purchasing easier for many European consumers, according to the report. The increasing sophistication of travel web sites, and the convenience of buying on-line, is also likely to entice consumers to purchase electronically.

As well as a huge predicted increase in travel and hotel booking, we are also seeing a big increase in the development of sites promoting particular destinations (Destination Marketing Systems). Among the best of these is the official Ireland tourism site run by Bord Fáilte. As the site is linked to the Gulliver reservations system, users can interrogate it for latest information on attractions and latest events. Tourism enterprises registered with Bord Fáilte can have a link, called a *hot link* to the site, and thereby benefit from exposure to its million plus visitors per annum. Its site was awarded the prestigious *ENTER '97 Gold Award* for the leading destination tourism site in the world, and was subsequently awarded a distinction by the *Financial Times* at their Annual Internet Awards.

Internet Not Hugely Important So Far in Ireland

The Internet is not hugely important so far in the Irish situation, according to John Casey, chief executive of The Marketing Institute. 'In the US they are investing significant money developing the Internet, but in Ireland marketing on the Internet is in its infancy. However, the potential of the Internet is massive. It has created a whole new kind of advertising.'

In Casey's opinion, the Internet has become the preferred medium to access entertainment and information for a new generation of people, whereas in previous generations this was found on television. 'The Internet poses two challenges, reaching a different target audience and re-examining the means to transmit messages. Unlike TV, flashy, eye-catching adverts may not capture the attention of Internet viewers.'

Stuart Fogarty, managing director of AFA Advertising, founder of Medianet and Club Internet, believes the industry cannot afford to ignore the Internet. 'The Internet is used by people in the evening, spending an average of forty-five minutes on-line. In other words they are on the Internet in the middle of TV prime time and they are not looking at other media. The Internet poses a threat and an opportunity to the [advertising] industry.'

By understanding the medium of the Internet and its differences from other forms of media, advertisers and marketers will know what products/services are best suited to on-line advertising.

Sources: Personal Interviews, Business and Finance website (www.businessandfinance.ie)

Exhibit 11.4 examines how the Internet has impacted on two Irish marketing groups — Sheen Falls and Bord Fáilte.

EXHIBIT 11.4

IRISH INTERNET SITES *IN ACTION*

SHEEN FALLS AND BORD FÁILTE

In 1996, Sheen Falls Hotel was one of the first Irish hotels to establish a web site. Carmel Flynn, sales and marketing manager, says, 'The site has made it possible to communicate messages to regular Internet users, particularly in the US, where you can access a high-earning bracket who use the Internet for research. The US market has responded very well, we have inquiries coming in all the time. We have linked our site effectively to special interest sites such as golf and travel sites, and all our brochures carry our web site and e-mail address.' As the web site is interactive, Flynn says it allows them to maintain personal contact with customers worldwide.

An important part of Sheen Fall Hotel's business is providing conference facilities for national and international clients. Their web site has been of particular value in promoting this line of business, providing visual images of their facilities with rates and details. 'Our web site is a means of providing immediate information for potential business clients. They can download the brochure or use the web site for presentations to managing directors when deciding on a location for conferences.'

The web site has radically reduced postage and printing costs for the hotel, particularly when sending literature to the US market. However, Flynn doesn't feel the web site will replace the need for a brochure, but it is an effective supplement. 'People still want a hard copy of the brochure and we still send out sales packages,' she says.

For the Irish market, e-mail is the most important on-line facility for Sheen Falls. 'We feature our e-mail address in all home advertising. When we respond to e-mail inquires, we include a link to our web site, encouraging people to use the web site.' Flynn says the correspondence through e-mail has developed remarkably in Ireland over the last twelve months and it has replaced telephone and faxes in many circumstances. She attributes this to an increase in the use of home computers.

John Rafferty, manager of marketing technology for Bord Fáilte has also found that the Internet has become a crucial method of correspondence. 'The Internet is our biggest source of inquires, exceeding fax, phone and walk-in inquires,' he said. Bord Fáilte re-launched its web site in September 1998 and planned to launch a series of additional sites for individual markets. 'These sites will be more specific and the information will be geared for the particular markets in question,' he said. Bord Fáilte are in the process of building a

Mapping and Route Planning Service with the Ordnance Survey. In 1999, Bord Fáilte also planned to launch an on-line reservation service.

According to Rafferty, the Internet serves as a means of creating an awareness about Ireland as a holiday destination among potential customers overseas. The site works in harmony with Bord Fáilte's call-centre service. The site gets 200 million hits per year and Rafferty hopes it will attract a million visitors next year. 'We are shifting our promotional mix to the Internet,' he says. 'The Internet is our dream come true, a global medium to promote Ireland as a holiday destination.'

Source: Reprinted courtesy of Bord Fáilte

4. PERSONAL SELLING

DEFINITION

Personal Selling can be defined as 'paid communication by an identified sponsor through a personal medium'. (Buttle, 1986)

The above definition recognises that the process of selling need not take place solely in a face-to-face situation; indeed selling over the telephone, telesales, has become a booming business. Personal selling is a critical part of the hospitality and tourism communication mix. Almost everyone in a tourism and hospitality organisation is involved in selling to some degree. While larger hotels and tourism organisations have professional sales staff, even in the smallest establishment the process of selling is taking place. Anyone who interacts with the customer has a potential to generate extra sales revenue.

TABLE 11.8 — THE VARYING DEGREES OF SALES RESPONSIBILITY IN TOURISM AND HOSPITALITY BUSINESSES

Major responsibility for selling	Sales and marketing director
	Sales manager
	Sales representative
	Hotel representative
	Travel agent
Moderate responsibility for selling	Food and beverage manager
	Banqueting manager
	Front office manager
	Reception staff
	Waiting staff
	Visitor centre receptionists
	Tour guide

TABLE 11.8 — THE VARYING DEGREES OF SALES RESPONSIBILITY IN TOURISM AND HOSPITALITY BUSINESSES *contd.*

Minor responsibility for selling	Chef
	Lift attendant
	Kitchen staff
	Chambermaid
	Porter

Source: Adapted from Buttle, 1986

THE SELLING PROCESS

The role of selling, as part of the communication mix, has been much misunderstood. Traditional models of selling saw it as being a process that was dominated by the need to persuade and get the sale at almost any cost. According to Berry (1999), the traditional model of selling looks something like that depicted in Figure 11.5 below.

FIGURE 11.5 — THE TRADITIONAL MODEL OF SELLING

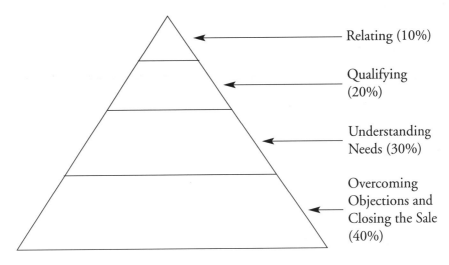

The traditional model of selling as depicted above was one where only a small percentage of the salesperson's time with a potential buyer was spent *relating* to them. With this approach to selling, establishing a relationship may consist of no more than a quick greeting and a cursory remark about the weather or sporting events.

Qualifying means ensuring that the potential customer, or *prospect*, is actually in a position to buy. They may not have responsibility to buy, they may be quite satisfied with their current customers or they may have no need for the product or service.

The next stage in the process requires the salesperson to establish the needs and requirements of the prospect. This calls for a high degree of listening skills on the part of the salesperson. The objective is to obtain a deep insight into the stated, and hidden, motives and attitudes of the customer.

The salesperson must then overcome *objections* on the part of the buyer. The prospect may feel that the product is too expensive, or does not meet their requirements. They may be anxious about the quality of the product or be distrustful of the company, or the sales representative. The salesperson needs to ensure that these objections are satisfactorily addressed. The final stage in the process is to *close the sale*. The salesperson is trained to observe the best moment to ask for the sale and to persuade the prospect to buy.

Traditionally, the majority of the salesperson's time was occupied with the process of closing the sale and understanding needs. More recently, there has been a different and new approach to selling (Berry, 1999).

FIGURE 11.6 — THE NEW MODEL OF SELLING

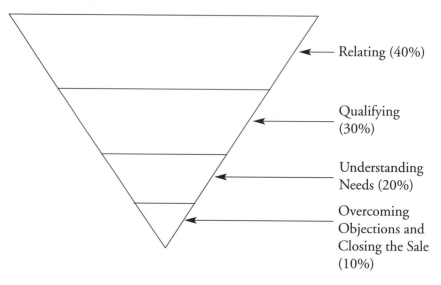

As can be seen above, the model is the reverse of the traditional model of selling. The model proposes that the salesperson spends a large percentage of his/her time with the prospect trying to establish a relationship and rapport with them. Selling is seen as a process of establishing two-way communication and trust, where the salesperson tries to build their reputation and credibility with the prospect. This is achieved only by a long-term attempt to know the prospect as a person first and a potential buyer secondly. It is argued, according to proponents of this model, that having the trust of the prospect, it takes much less time to understand their needs and to close the sale.

5. RELATIONSHIP MARKETING

DEFINITION

Relationship marketing can be defined as 'the exchange of relationships between the organisation and its customers'.

Retaining valuable customers is at the centre of the relationship marketing philosophy. For example, rather that merely taking a once-off booking, hotels need to see the long-term spending power of a potential guest. Similarly, golf courses cannot afford to lose loyal customers if, in the desire to increase revenue in the short term, they increase membership levels and lead to overcrowded greens.

CUSTOMER LIFETIME VALUE

The *lifetime value* of a customer to a company 'represents the spending potential of that customer over their lifetime'.

Take as an example a couple who stay in a luxury, self-catering lodge for a weekend at a cost of £200 pounds. If they are happy with the experience, and the owner can continue to satisfy their needs, they may return for a second visit that year. If they return for twenty years for two weekends their lifetime value is £8,000, (£200 × 2 weekends × 20 years). If the owner considers this lifetime value they will recognise the potential of each and every guest, and also the true financial consequences of each lost guest.

RELATIONSHIP INTENSITY

In *relationship marketing* the focus is on customer retention through higher levels of customer service, higher levels of customer contact, stressing of product benefits and effective internal relationships. Barnes (1995) depicts a continuum of relationships that we may have with commercial companies.

FIGURE 11.7 — RELATIONSHIP DEPTH OR INTENSITY

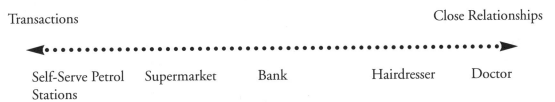

Transactions   Close Relationships

Self-Serve Petrol   Supermarket   Bank   Hairdresser   Doctor
Stations

At one end of the spectrum there are those relations of little depth; namely transaction-based relationships. The other end of the spectrum is typified by the close relationship that develops between a patient and their doctor. Most tourism and hospitality enterprises fall somewhere in the middle of this continuum. Trying to move further to the right should be a key objective of such businesses.

Modern technology offers the opportunity to develop and maintain relationships with customers, for example, through e-mail newsletters and correspondence. However, technology is a means to an end; relationship marketing requires a fundamental commitment on the part of the company to strive to get as close to the customer as possible and to maintain a continual contact, especially outside the periods when the customer can be expected to buy. For small enterprises, this may be as simple as sending a Christmas card to regular customers; larger companies, such as the international hotel chains have sophisticated database systems and loyalty cards to help them foster such customer relationships.

The benefits of the relationship marketing approach are many, not least of which is its cost-effectiveness. The cost of getting a new customer, the *acquisition cost*, is estimated to be five times that of encouraging a past customer to buy again, (Peters, 1987). This alone is justification for the fostering of deep relationships with customers. More and more companies are taking a radical look at their operations to ensure that they embrace the new marketing concept that relationship marketing represents.

Exhibit 11.5 below charts how one organisation has successfully pulled together all the elements of the marketing communications mix.

EXHIBIT 11.5

MARKETING COMMUNICATIONS *IN ACTION*
MARKETING SLIGO FORUM

Marketing Sligo Forum is the organisation responsible for promoting County Sligo internationally as a prime tourist destination. Established in 1997, it is a partnership of the local authority/public sector and the private sector throughout the county. The Forum was set up when County Sligo recognised its growth and development potential in the tourism sector.

A marketing officer, Collette O'Brien heads up the Forum, with an annual budget of £250,000. Prior to joining the Sligo initiative Collette set up and managed the Kent Tourism Business Advisory Service in Canterbury. Her assistant is Sile Haran, who has more than a decade of experience in the tourism sector. The Forum's Board is comprised of local tourism and public sector representatives and the chairman is Gerald Healy.

Key tasks for Collette O'Brien at the outset were to establish a brand identity for the county. The result was the *Sligo — Land of Heart's Desire* logo and positioning. This was a central part of the communications for Sligo in all print materials, including the first dedicated twelve-page county brochure. The logo, designed by Source Design Consultants, has graphics that include flora, a megalithic drawing and a shell. The three images are underlined by a flow of

---

land and water. The *Land of Heart's Desire* copyline comes from the writings of W.B. Yeats, Sligo's most famous historical figure.

SLIGO

land of heart's desire

Advertising

A wide variety of advertising media are used by Marketing Sligo Forum. Some magazines that target the travel trade were used such as *Northern Ireland Travel News*. Specialist magazines targeting specific interest groups included *Country Walking UK*.

Other publications used included:

- *Irish Independent* (Sligo Feature)
- *Sunday Tribune* (Destination Ireland)
- *Discover Ireland* (Spring/Summer 1999)
- *Belfast Telegraph*
- *Irish News*
- *Ireland of the Welcomes*

Radio advertising was used in a joint campaign with Donegal Tourism and the North West Regional Tourism Authority. The campaign began in October 1998 and lasted four weeks. Seven radio stations, both North and South, were used.

The advertisement for Sligo had three commercials of thirty seconds duration supported by a freefone number and an Aertel page for special offers. At the same time a concentrated print advertising campaign was undertaken to support the radio campaign.

Public Relations

A concentrated effort to heighten the profile of Sligo is conducted at local and national level. Monthly press releases and photographs are issued to local newspapers and radio stations. A press file is compiled which is used to support funding and marketing activities. Throughout the first year a number of public relations (PR) activities were undertaken with a TG4 documentary, Today FM and an *Irish Independent* editorial.

Equally important in PR terms is the need to communicate to the local community involved in tourism. They have a critical role in ensuring the success of tourism in the county. Central to the communication with this group is the quarterly *Tourism News* newsletter, which is sent to all the key representatives of the tourism sector and others in Sligo. It acts as a key means of informing people about the activities of the Forum and about new tourism services and attractions.

Familiarisation Visits

A large number of visiting groups are hosted throughout the year. Among the groups Marketing Sligo Tourism have hosted are:

- US Trade Mission.
- Antwerp Study Group (DIT)
- Geological Survey Ireland
- Benelux Tour Operators
- French Travel Agents

The familiarisation visits have been seen to have had a very positive effect, as can be seen from the comments of a group of Dutch tour operators, taken from the Forum newsletter.

'It proved to be a very successful visit and we are confident that some new business will definitely result from all our efforts.'

Direct Marketing

A database has been developed to co-ordinate a direct mail campaign. The Sligo Tourism web site (www.sligotourism.ie) has more than sixteen pages of information on County Sligo and allows e-mail enquiries. These enquiries enable the Forum to monitor responses and can be used for subsequent direct marketing activity. The breakdown of spending of the marketing budget is outlined in the Table below.

TABLE 11.9 — ANALYSIS OF THE MARKETING BUDGET SPEND

Marketing Activity	% of Total Budget
Tourism Brand Development	3·0
County Tourism Print Distribution	20·0
National Print Advertising	20·0
Direct Marketing — Internet, Direct Mail, CD-ROM	14·0
Radio Advertising Campaign	25·0
Domestic and Overseas Trade and Consumer Exhibitions	4·0
Tour Operator and Travel Trade Familiarisation Visits	1·5
Public Relations Campaign	7·5
Market Research and Monitoring	5·0
Total Annual Budget	£250,000

COMPARISON OF TOURISM MARKETING APPROACHES

This chapter, and the book, concludes with Table 11.10, illustrating the shift taking place today from mass marketing to database-driven marketing. In future, the realisation of *segments of one* is set to change the face of marketing forever.

TABLE 11.10 — COMPARISON OF TOURISM MARKETING APPROACHES

Mass Marketing	Database Marketing
Segmentation marketers measure the demographic and psychographic profiles of current customers or likely converts. They group together individuals with similar profiles giving them New Age names (such as *Attainers* and *New Builders*) and treat them as if they were identical.	Interactive marketers use actual behaviour to identify customers and prospects and statistical models to assess their value. Each customer can receive a customised offering.

TABLE 11.10 — COMPARISON OF TOURISM MARKETING APPROACHES *contd.*

Mass Marketing	Database Marketing
Advertising communications are designed for the mean, if not the lowest common denominator of the target group.	Advertising uses information on the individual customer. Computer-driven magazine bidding allows selective insertion of print advertising. In-line inject printing can add lines of copy to individual ads. Cable television promises to transmit commercials to specific homes. Private media reinforces customer loyalty.

Promotion

Focus on image advertising through television (a key source of agency profits) and magazines. Promotional offers are broadcast, using tools such as free-standing newspaper inserts, or mailed indiscriminately to homes defined by geo-demographics.	Direct marketing is integrated into the advertising program. Promotions are tailored to an individual's past behaviour, are based on the pay-out anticipated from promoting to that consumer, and are selectively delivered to that consumer.

Pricing

Promotional discrimination has to depend on customer self-selection.	Price discrimination exploits knowledge of the individual's price sensitivity and is delivered to that individual alone.

Sales Management

Customer data tends to reside with the travel agent and tour operator who use it at their discretion to achieve their own goals.	Sales management has access to customer files. It can implement targeting programs of prospect databases to improve sales force effectiveness.

TABLE 11.10 — COMPARISON OF TOURISM MARKETING APPROACHES *contd.*

Mass Marketing	Database Marketing
Distribution Channels The tourism supplier depends on intermediaries and direct selling from travel agents to reach customers. The customer tends to be owned by the intermediary or sales force.	The firm has a direct link to the customer. When it uses intermediaries, it can jointly manage leads and customer relationships. Other elements of the marketing mix (promotion, advertising) are timed to help move the customer toward purchase.
New Products Tourism product development is driven by the supplier's existing technology and production systems. Research and development is supply driven.	New tourism products and services are market driven on the basis of customer needs. Marketers may serve their loyal customer base by selling products on behalf of third parties.
Monitoring Market share, sales and profit are the indirect monitoring tools. Audience surveys measure a hoped-for level of awareness but not purchase behaviour. Reviews tend to be periodic, usually annual.	Traditional measures are supplemented by tracking purchase behaviour, measures of success in retaining customers and margin over cost of acquiring new customers. The value of the customer base is monitored with lifetime value calculations. Monitoring tends to be continuous, rather than

Source: Reprinted by permission, © 1998 Economics Research Associates

CHAPTER SUMMARY

The move toward one-to-one communication is having a huge impact on tourism and hospitality marketing. The direct marketing area is the most obvious one to benefit from the shift away from mass advertising, as new database technologies emerge, enabling sophisticated profiling of the tourist. Sales promotions, especially the tourism exhibition, remain important methods of effecting sales — they offer the opportunity for intense interaction with potential tourists and with the tourism and hospitality intermediaries. The Internet is set to have a profound impact on our lives, and is particularly suited for tourism marketing purposes, being one of the most important ways for companies to develop a relationship marketing concept.

KEY WORDS AND PHRASES

Direct Marketing

Database

Sales Promotion

Internet Marketing

Relationship Marketing

Personal Selling

QUESTIONS FOR REVIEW

1. Describe the three main types of direct marketing techniques.
2. Considering the communications mix, what advantages and disadvantages does direct marketing offer?
3. Distinguish between trade and consumer sales promotions.
4. Describe and discuss any two types of tourism exhibition.
5. Discuss the various responsibilities for selling that exist in any tourism or hospitality firm of your choice.

QUESTIONS FOR DISCUSSION

1. Conduct a search of the Internet for three tourism or hospitality firms. Compare and contrast their sites, in the context of the *hierarchy of effects* model of communication objectives.
2. Contact three tourism or hospitality firms who have participated in a consumer tourism exhibition. Detail their objectives for participation, the methods they used to evaluate participation and what changes they would make if they were to participate again.
3. What are the main criticisms levelled at direct marketing? Can you propose a way that these can be addressed?

REFERENCES AND FURTHER READING

Barnes, J., 'Establishing relationships — getting closer to the customer may be more difficult than you think', *Irish Marketing Review*, vol. 8, p. 112: 1995.

Berry, P., 'New Model of Selling', *HSMAI Meetings Seminar*, Herbert Park Hotel: Dublin 1999.

Bord Fáilte, *Calendar of Trade and Consumer Promotions*: Bord Fáilte.

Buttle, F., *Hospitality and Food Service Marketing*, Butterworth Heinemann 1986.

Lumsdon, L., *Tourism Marketing*, Thomson Press: London 1997.

Peters, T., *Thriving on Chaos*, p. 91 Macmillan: London 1987.

USEFUL WEB SITES

www.ireland.travel.ie	Official web site of the Irish Tourist Board
www.sligotourism.ie	Sligo Tourism's web site
www.jurys.com	Jurys Doyle Group — Ireland's largest hotel group
www.gmarketing.com	Examples of how to use the web more effectively
www.parkkenmare.com	Park Hotel Kenmare
www.idma.ie	Irish Direct Marketing Association
www.prii.ie	Public Relations Institute of Ireland
www.anpost.ie	An Post — details of the ICMD database

Index